Software Visualization

Programming as a Multimedia Experience

edited by
John Stasko, John Domingue, Marc H. Brown,
and Blaine A. Price

foreword by Jim Foley

The MIT Press
Cambridge, Massachusetts
London, England

This book was set in Times Roman and Helvetica by the editors and was printed and bound in the United States of America.

Library of Congress Cataloging-in-Publication Data

Software visualization: programming as a multimedia experience / edited by John Stasko . . . [et al.].
    p.   cm.
  Includes bibliographical references and index.
  ISBN 0-262-19395-7 (hc: alk. paper)
  1. Visual programming (Computer science). 2. Multimedia systems. I. Stasko, John.
QA76.65.S56   1997
005.1′01′1366—dc21   97-23612
                                                                                  CIP

To our parents

Contents

Foreword

Jim Foley

Visualization, the use of images to convey meaningful information, has a number of specialized foci that include:

- Scientific
- Information
- Geographic
- Business
- Statistical
- Process
- Software

All types of visualization share a common goal — transforming information into a meaningful, useful visual representation from which a human observer can gain understanding. In contemporary times, this transformation is commonly achieved via computer processing and the results are shown using computer graphics technology.

Similarly, all types of visualization share common foundations. All have a need for a vocabulary of graphic elements (words, if you will), ways in which to combine the graphic elements (a grammar) into meaningful visualizations (sentences, paragraphs). All must be informed by an understanding of human perception and cognition and the information-seeking tasks of those who use the visualizations. All must continually be asking how well a visualization meets the viewer's needs, hopefully inquiring in such a way as to not only understand that a particular visualization does or does not work, but to understand *why*, so that additional principles can evolve.

Of course, many visualization principles pre-date computer-generated presentations. After all, maps and organization charts and other diagrammatic representations of relationships have been in use for centuries if not millennia. Software Visualization is certainly the least mature of the various types of visualizations, having relatively fewer pre-computer precedents on which to draw. Yet software visualization catches the imagination of many a computer educator and practitioner, holding as it does the promise of helping students better understand algorithms, of helping programmers identify bugs, and generally enhancing learning and speeding development.

Certainly software visualization caught my attention, and I have eagerly followed its development, from the early animated flow charts through Baecker's classic *Sorting our Sorting* to the many contemporary systems described in this book.

My only disappointment with the field is that Software Visualization has not yet had a major impact on the way we teach algorithms and programming or the ways in which we debug our programs and systems. While I continue to believe in the promise and potential of SV, it is at the same time the case that SV has not yet had the impact that many have predicted and hoped for.

I am greatly encouraged about the future of this important field by the publication of this book, as it represents an important coming of age for the discipline of software visualization. The book integrates knowledge, suggests principles, provides perspective, and points the way to the future. I am particularly pleased with the inclusion of the last section, on empirical evaluations of software visualizations for teaching. Empirical evaluation, and the refinements and improvements it leads to, is for me the most critical remaining step in fulfilling the promises of software visualization. And, knowing that some of these evaluations took place at Georgia Tech's Graphics, Visualization and Usability Center during my directorship there adds an extra pleasure to seeing the book published.

As the field of Software Visualization continues to mature and develop and fulfill the promise so many of us see, I have no doubt that *Software Visualization: Programming as a Multimedia Experience* will be referenced as a classic. John Stasko, John Domingue, Marc Brown and Blaine Price will have the thanks and gratitude of many students, practitioners, researchers, and professors for bringing to us such a comprehensive work.

Preface

This book grew out of the workshop on Software Visualization (SV) at the ACM SIGCHI conference held in Boston in April 1994. The purpose of workshop was to provide the first international forum for software visualization researchers to meet and interact.

The workshop attendees addressed a variety of questions such as:
• What architectures are best for coping with large programs?
• What display techniques are available for SV?
• How can SV systems be evaluated?

Two overall themes emerged during the workshop. The first theme was that the majority of programmers today had "missed the Human-Computer Interaction (HCI) boat" and were working with needlessly impoverished environments — mainly due to the fact that programming environment designers did not provide appropriate visualization tools. The second theme was that, even though several vendors were represented at the workshop, there was a need to increase the awareness of SV among software developers and among computer science educators.

A challenge made during the workshop was to make SV disappear as a discipline so that it is considered just another part of mainstream software engineering. This book is part of our response to that challenge. Selected authors at the workshop as well as others were asked to contribute chapters to this book, to which we have also added chapters reviewing some of the seminal papers in the field. In addition to being a reference for practitioners, our aim is for this book to be accessible to a wide audience including software developers, researchers and students with an interest in HCI and programming environments, computer science educators and cognitive psychologists.

The first part of the book gives an overview of the area and describes the early history. The following two sections outline the mechanics of creating visualizations: what techniques can be used for displays and how they can be linked to an algorithm or code fragment. The next three sections describe software visualization in the context of some specialized domains as well as software engineering and education. The final section discusses the cognitive aspects of SV systems, in particular how they can be evaluated. It is our hope that this book will help in overcoming the previously stated challenge of embedding SV within both a standard software engineering life-cycle and appropriate commercial tools, thus enabling programmers to utilize innovative HCI techniques when understanding and debugging their programs. We believe that access to extensive SV tools and techniques, so that programming in effect becomes a multimedia experience, will not only make the day-to-day life of programmers that much easier, but will also enable them to tackle significantly more ambitious and interesting tasks.

We would like to express our thanks to Ron Baecker for his encouragement to undertake this task. Allen Cypher also graciously donated his style sheets from the book *Watch What I Do*, thus allowing us to follow the high precedent his book established.

John Stasko
John Domingue
Marc H. Brown
Blaine A. Price

Software Visualization

An Overview of Software Visualization

This first section of the book provides an overview of software visualization and situates the sections and chapters to follow. This section will be of interest to the reader who is new the the field and would like to catch up on the background. This section may also be of some interest to experienced researchers or practitioners who would like to read about the framework around which the book was organized.

Chapter 1 ("An Introduction to Software Visualization") defines terminology associated with this area of research. A variety of terms have been used to describe the area, so clear definitions are certainly needed. Next, the chapter presents a taxonomy within which software visualization research and systems can be classified and assessed. You will notice some similarity between the sections of this book and the main taxonomy categories. Section II on "Techniques" is related to the *Content* and *Form* categories. Section III on "Joining Pictures to Code" is derived from the *Method* category, while Sections IV, V, and VI are all attempts to address the *Scope* category by demonstrating systems in specific domains, including education and software engineering. Finally, Section VII represents the *Effectiveness* category. This chapter concludes with a discussion of where further work in the field is needed.

Chapter 2 ("The Early History of Software Visualization") examines the roots of software visualization research and provides a context for much of the work that followed. The chapter describes some of the motivating problems, many grounded in software engineering, and describes systems that exhibit early glimpses of software visualization. This chapter has examples of software visualization dating back to 1947 and provides an insight into the origins of many techniques still used today.

Chapter 3 ("A Taxonomy of Algorithm Animation Displays") presents a taxonomy of the display aspects of algorithm animation systems. The chapter characterizes the different visual techniques used by the systems in a large subarea of software visualization.

An Introduction to Software Visualization

**Blaine Price,
Ronald Baecker
and
Ian Small**

Visualization is a word that is often misunderstood, even by experienced English speakers. Because it contains the root word *visual* (which is from the Latin for *sight*), many people believe that visualization has something to do with making pictures. In the *Oxford English Dictionary* [Simpson 89] there are seven definitions of the word *visual;* the six most common definitions refer to images which people see with their eyes. The seventh definition suggests the formation of a *mental* image which is not necessarily related to something in one's visual field. It is from this later definition that *visualization* takes its meaning.

In this book we are concerned with the visualization of computer programs and algorithms, which we collectively refer to as *Software Visualization* (SV). A quick glance through the chapters of this book will show you that SV can take many forms, for there are a huge variety of sensory inputs that can cause you to form a mental picture of something. Even the simple indenting of control structures in programs, which most programmers take for granted, is a kind of visualization (albeit a weak kind by today's standards). Flow charting was an early form of visualization, and as you will find in the next chapter, the history of SV dates back to the days of von Neumann in the 1940's. You will come across a range of media and forms of expression in this book, all of which are designed to help you to form mental pictures of some aspects of software. In this

Introduction

vi su al(vîzh´oo-el) *adj.* [Middle English, from Late Latin *visualis,* from Latin *visus,* sight] (7 definitions)

vi'su al i za'tion (vîzh´oo-elîzâ´shun) n.—*the power or process of forming a mental picture or vision of something not actually present to the sight.*

chapter we will discuss some of the definitions from the SV literature in order to make some of the other chapters easier to understand. We will also discuss the relationship between SV and some related fields such as Visual Programming. Finally, we will present a framework for classifying and understanding SV systems which we have adapted to organize the sections of this book.

The most obvious definition to start with is a definition for SV itself. As you read through this book you may form your own personal definition of what SV means for your purposes, but to get you started, our definition appears in the margin opposite.

In the literature of SV you will often find the phrases *visual programming*, *program visualization*, and *algorithm animation* used interchangeably and in a misleading fashion. You may also see the phrase *programming by demonstration* or the older term, *programming by example*. All of these are forms of Software Visualization, but each visualizes a specific kind of information. In the framework that follows you will see how each of these kinds of information can be used, but for the moment, let us look at the fields to which these phrases refer.

The term *program visualization* (PV) was used in the late 1980's (especially in Myers's taxonomies [Myers 86] [Myers 88] [Myers 90]) to refer to what we call SV. We prefer to differentiate PV from other topics within SV because it connotes a connection with the program (lower level) as opposed to the algorithm (higher-level). Indeed, Myers's taxonomies refer to two orthogonal dimensions of code vs. data and static vs. dynamic which still form a basis for our division of the discipline. Systems that visualize program code or data (or combinations of the two) will tend to occupy some point along a static to animated (dynamic) dimension. Static code visualization might include some kind of prettyprinting or program map such as the SEE Program Visualizer (see Chapter 4 by Baecker and Marcus on Printing and Publishing C Programs or [Baecker 90a]), while an example of static data visualization might appear as a "boxes and arrows" diagram of a linked list data structure showing the contents. An example of an animated data visualization might show this same diagram with the arrows and contents changing dynamically as the program was running, while a simple animated code visualization could highlight lines of code as they are being executed.

Definitions and Taxonomies

Software Visualization *is the use of the crafts of typography, graphic design, animation, and cinematography with modern human-computer interaction and computer graphics technology to facilitate both the human understanding and effective use of computer software.*

Program Visualization *is the visualization of actual program code or data structures in either static or dynamic form.*

For higher-level descriptions of software (algorithms) there is also a dimension from the static to the animated. Flowcharts are a simple example of static algorithm visualizations, while the more interesting (at least from a teaching perspective) visualizations are those which use animation to communicate how the algorithm works. This dynamic algorithm visualization is often called *Algorithm Animation,* and some of the best examples may be found later in this book, such as the early film *Sorting Out Sorting* (SOS) of Baecker [Baecker 81] (see also Chapter 24), Brown's BALSA [Brown 88a] (see also Chapters 7 and 12) and Zeus [Brown 91] (see also Chapters 7 and 10), and Stasko's TANGO system [Stasko 90b] (see also Chapter 8). Figure 1 shows the relationship between the various types of SV and the related fields.

Algorithm Visualization *is the visualization of the higher-level abstractions which describe software.*

Algorithm Animation *is dynamic Algorithm Visualization.*

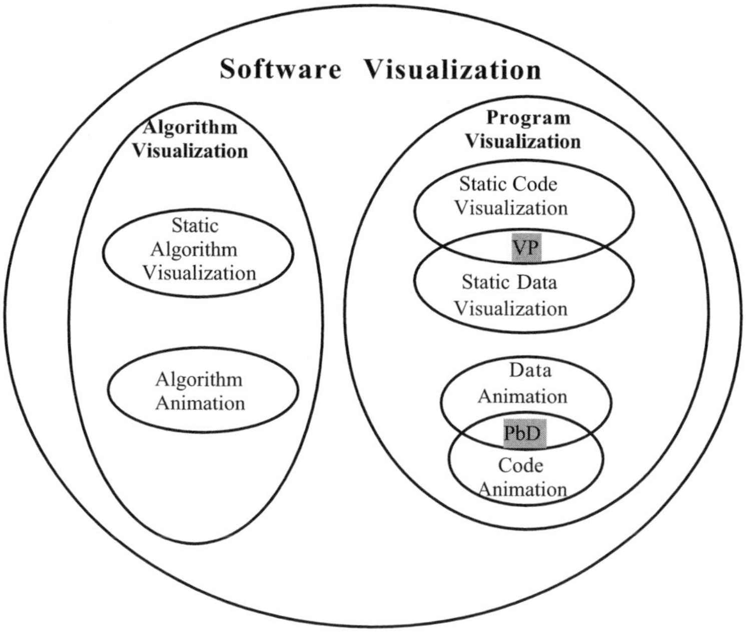

Figure 1. A Venn diagram showing the terms in the SV literature. The sizes are not relevant and the only intersections shown are those for Visual Programming (VP) and Programming by Demonstration (PbD). Note that VP and PbD are not subsets of PV, they merely have a partial overlap.

Visual Programming (VP) is a field in its own right and you will find a number of books on the subject [Shu 88] [Chang 90] [Glinert 90b] [Glinert 90a], including an annual IEEE Symposium dedicated to Visual Languages and the *Journal of Visual Languages and Computing* (Academic Press) which also covers SV topics. The main difference between VP and SV is the goal involved: VP seeks to make programs easier to *specify* by using a graphical (or "visual")

Visual programming *is the use of "visual" techniques to* specify *a program.*

notation while SV seeks to make programs and algorithms easier to *understand* using various techniques. Of course a visual specification may itself communicate information about a program since it is a kind of static code/data visualization, hence many VP systems do provide a kind of SV, but as this is not the primary function of the notation we do not address them in this book.

Programming by Demonstration *is the specification of programs using user demonstrated examples.*

An area related to VP that also resembles SV is *Programming by Demonstration* (PbD), sometimes called *Programming by Example* in earlier literature. The idea is that users may not need advanced programming skills to construct a program, but may be able to demonstrate an example and have the system infer a program. Thus, if users know how to perform a task on a computer, then that should be sufficient to create a program to perform the task. For example, they may show how some sample data is manipulated. This is usually accomplished using a graphical interface, which, as with VP, makes the result a kind of SV. Although we do not examine PbD systems in this book, Chapter 14 by Stasko discusses a PbD interface for the construction of software visualizations. Cypher's book [Cypher 93] provides an excellent survey of PbD systems.

Computation Visualization *is SV including such aspects as hardware performance.*

Stasko and Wehrli introduced the term Computation Visualization [Stasko 93c] to include visualization of aspects of hardware performance, sometimes called *Performance Visualization*. This kind of visualization is important in such things as load balancing or performance optimization on multiprocessor architectures, and although we do not focus on the area in this book, Chapter 23 by Heath, Malony, and Rover addresses some of the issues.

Programmer: *the person who wrote the program/algorithm being visualized.*

SV Software Developer: *the person who wrote the SV system being used.*

Visualizer/Animator: *the person who specifies the visualization.*

User/Viewer: *the person who views the resulting visualization, possibly navigating through it.*

In examining SV systems one comes across a number of people acting in different roles, some of whom take on multiple roles. There is usually a *programmer* who wrote the original program or algorithm which is being visualized. Programmers may not know that their programs are going to be visualized when they write them. A very important person (from the point of view of the authors of *this* book!) is the *SV Software Developer* who wrote the software which allows programs or algorithms to be visualized. Another important role is the *visualizer* or *animator* who takes the program or algorithm and the SV system and specifies how the visualization is to be connected or applied to the program. Finally, the person for whom the visualization has been written is the *user* or *viewer*, who may view the visualization statically, or

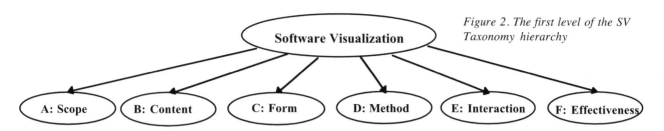

Figure 2. The first level of the SV Taxonomy hierarchy

interact and navigate through it. In the next section of this chapter we will examine the range of activities of the user more closely.

In this section we have covered basic definitions which we hope will assist you in understanding the taxonomy to be presented in this chapter. The next chapter gives a brief history of SV which may also be useful. If you are interested in other taxonomies, we suggest reading the early taxonomies of Myers [Myers 86] [Myers 88] [Myers 90] which provide a 2 x 3 grid for classifying systems, Stasko and Patterson's paper [Stasko 92c] which introduces four scaled dimensions (aspect, abstractness, animation, and automation), or the papers upon which this chapter is based [Price 92][Price 93].

In deriving the six top-level *categories* (see Figure 2) for this framework, we based our work on a commonly accepted model for software where each of the people mentioned above contributes to each of the categories in some way. The original *programmer* produces the code or algorithms ~~which~~ which may or may not be able to be visualized according to the *Scope* category. The *SV software developer* produces a system with certain capabilities which determine what aspects of a program can be shown, thus the second category: *Content*. The *visualizer* specifies the visualization resulting in the *Method* category. The output of the SV system takes some kind of *Form* and the *user* has some kind of *Interaction* with it. Finally, the whole visualization will have some degree of *Effectiveness* in helping the user understand the program or algorithm. We display these categories as a tree because they form the basis for our taxonomy, which, while extensive, is by no means "complete". We have identified a number of minor categories which make up each of the six major categories, and each of the minor categories may in turn have sub-categories which may in turn have sub-categories, and so on. Thus the entire taxonomy may be described by a multi-level *n*–ary tree. A good taxonomy must be expandable to permit new

A Framework for Classifying SV Systems

discoveries to be catalogued and more detailed study in specific areas, so we have designed the taxonomy structure to enable new categories and sub-categories to be added naturally without redesigning the entire tree.

Each category or sub-category that we use can be qualified for a particular SV system by a binary description (e.g. does the system support concurrent programs? yes/no), a range (e.g. to what degree does the system visualize data structures?), or a set of *attributes* (e.g. a subset of Pascal programs run under SunOS 4.2 on a Sun SparcStation running X11R5). For categories involving a range, one could assign a ranking of lowest, below average, average, above average, or highest. If you are interested in how we applied the entire taxonomy to 12 systems and how we ranked them on each, please refer to the original paper [Price 93].

All of these categories and sub-categories *together* describe an SV system and the relative rankings indicate the strengths of each system in each of the areas. Because we see each system as a hybrid of many properties, it is not possible to "pigeonhole" a system using this taxonomy (as, for example, is done in the taxonomy of living things where each creature has followed a distinct evolutionary path with a low degree of cross-mutation).

Figure 3. Scope Category Hierarchy

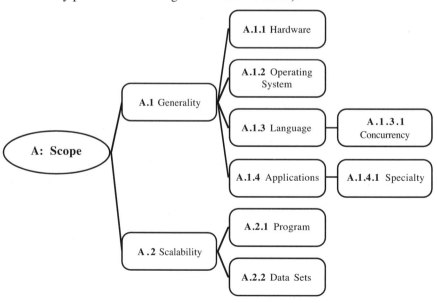

We see two major divisions of Scope information: *generality* and *scalability*. In Figure 3 we show a complete tree of all of the sub-categories, described below, that we believe characterize the scope of an SV system.

A generalized system can generate visualizations of arbitrary programs within a particular class while an example system displays a (possibly flexible) visualization of a particular algorithm, system, or set of existing programs. SOS is an example, since its presentation is fixed on videotape, while the remaining systems are generalized to some degree. A generalized system will usually have some restrictions governing its capabilities:

> A.1.1 *Hardware*: What hardware does it run on?
> A.1.2 *Operating System*: What operating system is required to run it?
> A.1.3 *Language*: What programming language must user programs be written in?
>> A.1.3.1 *Concurrency*: If the programming language is capable of concurrency, can the SV system visualize the concurrent aspects?
> A.1.4 *Applications*: What are the restrictions on the kinds of user programs that can be visualized?
>> A.1.4.1 *Specialty*: What kinds of programs is it particularly good at visualizing (as opposed to simply capable of visualizing)?

The *hardware* platforms used by many of the systems in the literature are split between Unix workstations and Macintoshes, probably due to the early availability of window-based graphics on these systems. Many of the systems in this book, TPM [Eisenstadt 88a] (see Chapter 15 by Eisenstadt and Brayshaw) and Pavane [Roman 92](see Chapter 13 by Roman) excepted, only work on traditional imperative languages, while the ANIM system [Bentley 91a] [Bentley 91b] [Bentley 92] is noteworthy for its ability to work in any language. In other languages, Lieberman and Fry [Lieberman 84a] [Lieberman 89] (see Chapter 19 by Lieberman and Fry) have produced interesting systems for visualizing Lisp while London and Duisberg [London 85] did pioneering work with Smalltalk. Although many languages support *concurrency*, Pavane is one of a few systems truly designed to produce visualizations of concurrent elements. Price has also built a prototype for a procedural language which shows process activity on a static representation of the module and procedure hierarchy as well as individual views showing the status of each process [Price 90] [Price 91]. The MRE system of Brayshaw [Brayshaw 93b] can visualize the logic language PARLOG, a parallel version of Prolog. For a detailed overview of Concurrent SV systems, see Kraemer and Stasko's [Kraemer 93] survey or Chapter 17 by Kraemer.

A: Scope

What range of programs can the SV system take as input for visualization?

A.1 Generality

Can the system handle a generalized range of programs or does it display a fixed set of examples?

Although most of the example systems are technically capable of producing visualizations of any *application* in the appropriate language, most have a particular *specialty* outside which the visualizations are not very informative. For example, SOS (see Chapter 24 by Baecker) specializes in exactly nine specific algorithms. BALSA (see Chapter 7 by Brown) demonstrates some excellent visualizations of array and graph algorithms while the University of Washington Program Illustrator (UWPI) [Henry 90] could only visualize simple data structures for a small set of graph searching and array sorting algorithms. The TPM system discussed by Eisenstadt and Brayshaw in Chapter 15 works only on Prolog programs and Chapter 16 by Domingue covers Knowledge Based Systems. De Pauw, Kimelman, and Vlissides present techniques for visualizing Object Oriented systems in Chapter 22. In Chapter 5, North discusses some techniques for visualizing graph models of software.

A.2 Scalability

To what degree does the system scale up to handle large examples?

Scalability includes a combination of:

A.2.1 *Program*: What is the largest program it can handle?

A.2.2 *Data Sets*: What is the largest input data set it can handle?

This characteristic refers to fundamental limitations of the system only; see category F: Effectiveness to determine how *well* it presents visualizations of large programs. Most of the systems are technically capable of visualizing large programs and data sets, but few have demonstrated examples. SOS visualizes large data sets, albeit fixed, while UWPI, as a prototype, would not be expected to work on large programs. Many of the chapters in Section V address the issue of scalability, especially Chapter 21 by Eick on maintaining large systems.

B: Content

What subset of information about the software is visualized by the SV system?

Two of the most important parts of this information are the *program*, by which we mean the program source code, and the *algorithm* or "high-level" description of the software. The differentiation between program and algorithm is subtle and can best be described from a user perspective: if the system is designed to educate the user about a general algorithm, it falls into the class of *algorithm visualization*. If, however, the system is teaching the user about one particular implementation of an algorithm, it is more likely *program visualization*. Signs that the line from algorithm visualization to program visualization has been crossed include displays of program code listings as opposed to higher-level abstract code diagrams, and labelled displays of the values of particular variables, as opposed to generic data displays. Some systems are sufficiently flexible to produce both types of visualization, depending on what the user desires and specifies. Note that many authors may refer to their system as "algorithm animation" when their visualization refers to program code or variables: this kind of system would be program, not algorithm, visualization in our taxonomy. The other two important parts of this category are *fidelity and completeness*, which characterize the accuracy of the visualization, and *data gathering time*, which describes the point at which information about the software is gathered. Figure 4 shows the complete tree for the sub-categories described below.

This category is further subdivided as follows:

> B.1.1 *Code*: To what degree does the system visualize the instructions in the program source code?
>> B.1.1.1 *Control Flow:* To what degree does the system visualize the flow of control in the program source code?
>
> B.1.2 *Data***:** To what degree does the system visualize the data structures in the program source code?
>> B.1.2.1 *Data Flow:* To what degree does the system visualize the flow of data in the program source code?

While the distinctions between *control flow* and *data flow* become blurred when considering languages or architectures that use a message-passing paradigm, these characteristics are still generally applicable. Examples of *code* visualization include pretty-printed source code, structured diagrams, and call trees. While the nature of the underlying code may be implicitly visualized by the way in which data evolves, this is not considered to be code visualization; a more concrete visualization of the code (either statically or in execution) is required. Program *data* visualization is characterized by drawings of compound data structures showing their contents in terms of simple data structures, while program data flow can be represented by data flow diagrams or live views of the call stack.

As with the program category, this can be further divided as:

> B.2.1 *Instructions:* To what degree does the system visualize the instructions in the algorithm?
>> B.2.1.1 *Control Flow*: To what degree does the system visualize the flow of control of the algorithm instructions?
>
> B.2.2 *Data:* To what degree does the system visualize the high level data structures in the algorithm?
>
> B.2.2.1 *Data Flow:* To what degree does the system visualize the flow of data in the algorithm?

B.1 Program

To what degree does the system visualize the actual implemented program?

B.2 Algorithm

To what degree does the system visualize the high level algorithm behind the software?

Figure 4. Content Category Hierarchy

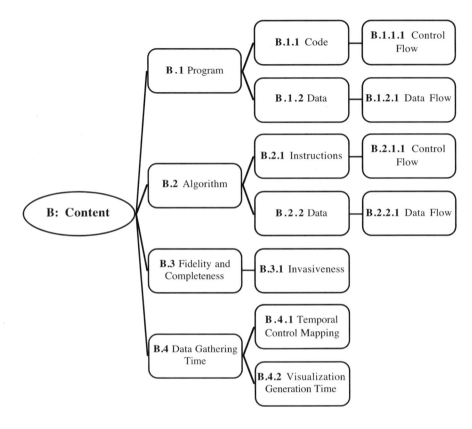

Systems like SOS, BALSA, Zeus, TANGO, UWPI, and Pavane are all firmly established on the algorithm side, although UWPI gets a lower ranking because its examples are not as closely hand-tuned as the others.

B.3 Fidelity and Completeness

Do the visual metaphors present the true and complete behaviour of the underlying virtual machine?

Systems designed for software engineering may pose stronger demands than do pedagogical systems, since the latter may wish to take liberties in order to provide simpler, easier-to-understand visual explanations. Automatic systems like UWPI may produce a misleading abstraction for a data structure while visualizers using a system like TANGO may only animate a particular part of an algorithm for expository purposes. The highest fidelity and completeness values tend to go to the systems that are tied closest to the program code while the hand-designed systems are difficult to rank because they depend so much on the individual visualizer.

B.3.1 *Invasiveness:* If the system can be used to visualize concurrent applications, does its use disrupt the execution sequence of the program?

Disruptive behaviour is not desirable in a visualization system for concurrent applications, as the effect of activating the visualization system may change the relative execution rates of processes, thereby producing a different result. The system of Flinn and Cowan [Flinn 90] used a bus monitor to avoid this, but most of the systems that handle concurrency that we have observed are invasive.

In general, systems which depend on data gathered solely at compile-time (such as SEE) are limited to visualizing the program code and its data structures. These systems cannot produce any visualization of the actual data values, since they do not have access to that (run-time) information. Visualizations of data gathered at compile-time are generally not animated, as there is no relevant temporal axis along which to change the visualization. Visualizations generated from data gathered at run-time can produce complex displays of the variable space used by the program, and often rely on animation for an intuitive mapping between the temporal aspects of the program in execution and the presentation of the visualization. This is the most common style in interactive visualization systems. Systems like UWPI gather data at both compile-time and run-time to provide their data displays.

This category can be subdivided into two other temporally-related sub-categories which apply if the visualization is based on data gathered at *run-time*:

B.4.1 *Temporal Control Mapping:* What is the mapping between "program time" and "visualization time"?

B.4.2 *Visualization Generation Time:* Is the visualization produced as a batch job (post-mortem) from data recorded during a previous run, or is it produced live as the program executes?

If the visualization is based on information gathered at a single point in time during the program's execution, and generates a static visualization, then its *temporal control mapping* is "static to static"; the system generates a *snapshot* (Incense does this to draw data structure diagrams). If the visualization generated is animated, the mapping is "static to dynamic"; we do not know of any examples of such systems. If the visualization gathers information over a span of time during program execution, and produces a single still visualization based on that information, the mapping is "dynamic to static": the visualization system is generating a *trace* (the `stills` program from ANIM does this). If the visualization uses information gathered over a period of time during the

B.4 Data Gathering Time

Is the data on which the visualization depends gathered at compile-time, at run-time, or both?

program's execution to generate an *animation* (this is the most common type), then the mapping is "dynamic to dynamic".

The *visualization generation time* affects how the user can interact with the visualization. The *post mortem* style of visualization (used by both ANIM and TPM) combines the advantage of the rich information available at run-time with the opportunity to lay it out in the most optimal way, since the entire range of display use (i.e. the "future") can be known in advance. This also has the disadvantage of the user being unable to interact with the visualization based on program output and thus have an immediate effect on the visualization. *Live* is the most popular method, although TPM has versions with both live and post-mortem modes. Live visualizations have the advantage of allowing the user to interactively specify the data set, perhaps using a graphical tool to specify data abstractions such as trees or graphs.

C: Form

What are the characteristics of the output of the system (the visualization)?

This category is concerned with how the fundamental characteristics of the system are directly related to what can be displayed, which we have divided into five broad areas: *medium, presentation style, granularity, multiple views,* and *program synchronization*. Figure 5 shows the complete hierarchy.

C.1 Medium

What is the primary target medium for the visualization system?

While systems which are designed for one medium can often run on another (e.g. SEE, which was designed for a paper medium, can easily produce visualizations on workstations which support Display PostScript), we only list the primary target medium. Common choices include paper, film or videotape, plain terminal, or graphical workstation. We expect virtual reality environments eventually to become a common target medium of SV systems. The most common medium for older systems is a black & white workstation monitor, but most systems today use color. SEE is an exception in that it only uses paper (although it could easily be implemented on a workstation monitor) [Small 89] while ANIM is capable of producing paper output using the `stills` program.

C.2 Presentation Style

What is the general appearance of the visualization?

Presentation style has no individual rankings because it simply serves to group the following sub-categories:

C.2.1 *Graphical Vocabulary:* What graphical elements are used in the visualization produced by the system?

C.2.1.1 *Color:* To what degree does the system make use of color in its visualizations?

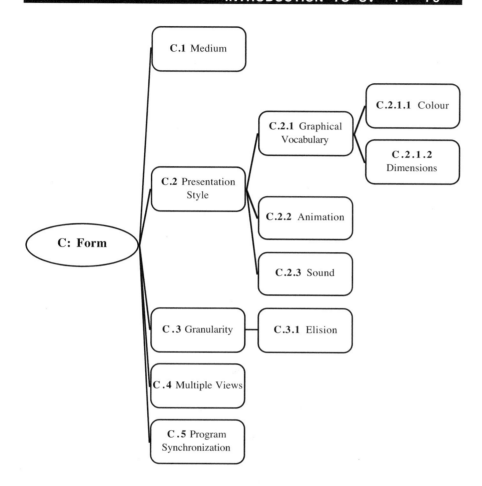

Figure 5. Form Category Hierarchy

C.2.1.2 *Dimensions:* To what degree are extra dimensions used in the
    visualization?
C.2.2 *Animation:* If the system gathers run-time data, to what degree does
    the resulting visualization use animation?
C.2.3 *Sound:* To what degree does the system make use of sound to convey
    information?

A system's *graphical vocabulary* provides some idea of the complexity of the
visual primitives which make up the system's displays. Bertin [Bertin 83]
describes the primary feature of a graphical vocabulary as being made up of the
marks used (which could be individual *point* objects, *lines*, or *enclosed shapes*)
which have a *position* in space. Each mark has six orthogonal retinal subtypes:

color, size, shape, gray level, orientation, and *texture.* All of these can be used to encode information and an SV system can be characterized by the size of its graphical vocabulary.

Color can be used to convey a great deal of information while imposing a low cognitive load but has been greatly under-utilized in SV systems. Brown and Hershberger [Brown 92] note five effective uses of color: to reveal an algorithm's state, to unite multiple views, to highlight areas of interest, to emphasize patterns, and to capture history. See Chapter 7 by Brown and Sedgewick for more details.

Traditional systems have used simple two-dimensional graphics, although more recent work has used projections of 3-D images onto a 2-D screen. Pavane does this and provides tools for rotating the image in 3-space (see Chapter 13 by Roman for examples). Some workstations now allow alternating polarized spectacles to be synchronized with the screen display to provide a binocular depth illusion. Some displays in ANIM have been constructed using this 3-D technique. The emerging virtual reality systems promise to provide an even better 3-D display and techniques such as Stasko's 3-D graph traversal [Stasko 93c] may become commonplace. Note that simply *using* a 3-D display to show information that is naturally three-dimensional is not the most effective use of the extra dimension; Brown and Najork's Zeus-3D system (see Chapter 9, and also [Brown 93]), Stasko's sorting animation in POLKA-3D [Stasko 93c], and Pavane are examples of the use of the extra dimension to encode non-dimensional information. The 3-D views in ANIM are simply a 3-D projection of naturally 3-D data.

The most obvious and frequent use of *animation* in program visualization systems is to capture and convey the temporal aspects of the software in execution. Does the system make use of animation in any other novel ways? Note that animation is not a binary characteristic; rudimentary erase-redraw techniques such as those found in UWPI are considered to be animation when compared with purely static visualizations such as SEE, but they compare poorly with the smooth animations found in TANGO or Pavane. Chapter 8 by Stasko discusses animation in detail.

The audio output capability of most computers in the early 1980's was limited to a single beep, but most modern workstations have digital *sound* capability.

Gaver and his colleagues [Gaver 91] [Mountford 90] have demonstrated how sound can be used to communicate complex information, but of the systems we are considering, only LogoMedia [DiGiano 92b] and Zeus have made effective use of it. Brown and Hershberger [Brown 92] (see also Chapter 10) have identified four distinct uses of sound in SV: to reinforce visual views, to convey patterns, to replace visual views (so that visual attention may be focused elsewhere), and to signal exceptions. Other work includes that of Francioni, Jackson, and Albright [Francioni 92], who have investigated the use of sound in parallel programs.

Chapter 6 by Jeffery provides more detail on some techniques for presenting visualization information.

Many systems can visualize fine-grained details in a manner similar to that of a debugger, but the ability to filter out fine-detail to get the big picture can be an advantage. The "table of contents" view in SEE or the course-grained view in TPM are examples of built-in coarse-grain visualization support. A sub-category of granularity is:

C.3.1 *Elision:* To what degree does the system provide facilities for eliding information?

An important feature for dealing with large amounts of information at one level of granularity is the ability to *elide* or temporarily hide sections that are not of immediate interest. Few systems currently provide this (SEE and TPM excepted).

Multiple views might include simultaneous coarse-grained and fine-grained views of data structures, or a graphical view of changing program data with a corresponding view of the executing source code. This is different from the *program synchronization* characteristic because it shows different synchronized views of the *same* program as opposed to a race between different programs. Zeus has the best facility for multiple views because it allows each view to be edited by direct manipulation with the result directly affecting the data. ANIM can also produce multiple views although they require some work on the part of the visualizer. SEE, TPM, and LogoMedia all provide multiple default views.

C.3 Granularity

To what degree does the system present coarse-granularity details?

C.4 Multiple Views

To what degree can the system provide multiple synchronized views of different parts of the software being visualized?

C.5 Program Synchronization

Can the system generate synchronized visualizations of multiple programs simultaneously?

This capability is useful for comparing the execution speeds of two programs (by running a race), for determining how one algorithm differs from another similar algorithm, and for investigating how a particular algorithm is flawed with respect to a correct algorithm. Note that modern windowing systems and operating systems will allow almost any window-based visualization system to be run in parallel. Running two versions of a system on two algorithms in different windows would not qualify under this category because there is no centralized control or synchronization between both running visualizations. For example, SOS, BALSA, Zeus, and ANIM provide this feature.

D: Method

How is the visualization specified?

This area describes the fundamental features of the SV system which the visualizer uses to create a visualization. We have divided this into two areas, one describing the *style* in which the visualizer specifies the visualization and one describing the way in which the visualization and the program source code are *connected*. Figure 6 shows the complete set of *method* categories and sub-categories.

D.1 Visualization Specification Style

What style of visualization specification is used?

Visualizations can be completely *hand-coded* (the user writes special purpose programs which visualize a particular algorithm or program) as with ANIM, or they can be built from a *library* or hierarchy of existing visualizations as with BALSA and Zeus. SOS is a *fixed* system since it cannot be changed from the original specification (the programmer, SV system builder, and visualizer were all the same person). Debugging tools (e.g. UWPI, SEE, TPM, and LENS [Mukherjea 94]) which are tied tightly to the program code all use some degree of *automation* to specify the visualization, thus making them appropriate tools for programmers. Most other systems use some degree of hand coding to produce visualizations, with BALSA/Zeus and TANGO providing a *library* from which to build them. Even tools which use a library can be refined further: TANGO provides specialized tools for describing smooth trajectories and the ALLADIN system [Heltulla 90] provides rich graphical editing tools, thus making a high level specification of the visualization easier. Automatic systems have the advantage of making the programmer, visualizer, and user into the same person. They also take much of the work out of the visualization step and are more likely to be used by a professional or novice programmer looking for debugging assistance [Eisenstadt 93b]. The sub-categories of visualization specification style include:

D.1.1 *Intelligence*: If the visualization is automatic, how advanced is the visualization software from an AI point of view?

D.1.2 *Tailorability*: To what degree can the user customize the visualization?

D.1.2.1 *Customization Language*: If the visualization is customizable, how can the visualization be specified?

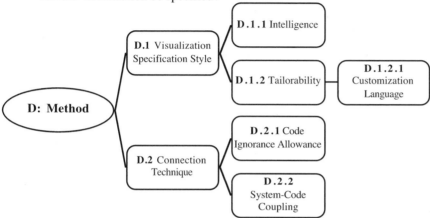

Figure 6. Method Category Hierarchy

Automatic visualizations using syntactic information to generate hierarchy diagrams, such as TPM, use a "low" degree of *intelligence* while systems that are able to recognize algorithms or high-level data structures and display abstractions of them would be classified as "higher" intelligence. UWPI uses a moderate degree of intelligence because it can display abstractions, even though it does not "understand" them. Few systems that we know of demonstrate even moderate intelligence.

In terms of *tailorability*, SOS is *fixed* and cannot be customized at all, while BALSA allows some interactive manipulation on the part of the user. The X11 version of TANGO only allows window resizing, scrolling, and zooming but the original also had an interactive editor for customization. LogoMedia allows the user to choose which parts of the program will be visualized and which sounds will be associated with them (as well as change them while executing), while Zeus allows representations of data to be changed live by direct manipulation with the corresponding data in the program and the other views changed automatically. Note that being able to visualize different data sets does not qualify as customizing the visualization; the layout or presentation of the visualization must be changeable by explicit user instruction.

The *customization language* describes the way in which the system can accept customization instructions from the user. Systems which support *interactive manipulation* of the visualization, such as Zeus, have their visualizations specified interactively through direct manipulation. Systems which require the user to program explicit visualization code, like ANIM, rely on *procedural visualizations*. Systems which allow the user to describe the desired visualization using high-level tools or declarations, such as Pavane (discussed in Chapter 13), support *declarative specification*. SEE uses simple command line flags to customize the printouts. Visualization systems can easily support more than one of these approaches for different aspects of the complete visualization specification.

D.2 Connection Technique

How is the connection made between the visualization and the actual software being visualized?

Systems like ANIM and BALSA require the visualizer to *instrument* their code by adding statements to print visualization commands at interesting events (see Chapter 12 by Brown). TANGO, with the Field Environment [Reiss 90a], and LogoMedia allow the visualizer to *annotate* a user program using a special editor so that the original source code remains unchanged (although the executable code differs from the unannotated version). It is also possible to have code *automatically annotated* by a pre-processor before it is compiled or interpreted, but all of these techniques are an *invasive* form of connection and may be dangerous from a software engineering point of view. Pavane, LogoMedia, and TPM provide an instrumented execution environment (interpreter or compiler) which allows the visualizer to attach non-invasive *probes* to data structures or code in a declarative manner so the structures can be monitored without affecting the source code at all. Another non-invasive technique is the use of a monitor which "listens" to the bus or another part of the hardware and shows a live report of commands, such as the work of Zimmermann et al. [Zimmermann 88]. Note that one system can use several connection techniques. Other sub-categories related to connection technique include:

> D.2.1 *Code Ignorance Allowance*: If the visualization system is not completely automatic, how much knowledge of the program code is required for a visualization to be produced?
>
> D.2.2 *System-Code Coupling*: How tightly is the visualization system coupled with the code?

As one might expect, all of the automatic systems have a high *code ignorance allowance* since they can produce visualizations without any code knowledge on the part of the visualizer, which is one of the main attractions of this approach.

Visualization systems which require modifications to the program source, however, require the user to "know" the program in order to produce a visualization of it. Systems which provide hooks or probes to which users can attach visualization code may require some knowledge of the program if the user wishes to make the best use of the potential probes available.

System-code coupling is a measure of how closely the SV system is tied to the program it is visualizing. Systems like BALSA are tightly coupled and require programs to be run and visualized within an environment while some post-mortem systems like ANIM do not require any coupling at all since the visualization system simply reads an output file produced by print statements in the program. Most systems are tightly coupled with the programs that they are visualizing (TANGO, SEE, and ANIM are exceptions).

We have found three major areas where interaction issues affect the fundamental design of SV systems: *style, navigation,* and *scripting facilities*. The complete hierarchy is illustrated in Figure 7. Gloor provides a detailed description of techniques in Chapter 11.

Examples include on-screen buttons, menus, command line statements, or scripted programs. A variety of techniques may be employed by a system depending on the action required. The most common style of interaction involves buttons and menus (as with most window-based programs).

This is especially important when considering very large programs or data sets. If the system and its navigation tools do not scale up then they will not be useful for professional programmers. Eisenstadt et al. [Eisenstadt 90b] suggest that navigability may be achieved by changes of resolution, scale, compression, selectivity, and abstraction. Few systems support large space navigation. Other navigation-related sub-categories include:

E.2.1 *Elision Control:* Can the user elide information or suppress detail from the display?

E.2.2 *Temporal Control:* To what degree does the system allow the user to control the temporal aspects of the execution of the program?

E.2.2.1 *Direction:* To what degree can the user reverse the temporal direction of the visualization?

E.2.2.2 *Speed:* To what degree can the user control the speed of execution?

E: Interaction

How does the user of the SV system interact with and control it?

E.1 Style

What method does the user employ to give instructions to the system?

E.2 Navigation

To what degree does the system support navigation through a visualization?

Figure 7. Interaction Category Hierarchy

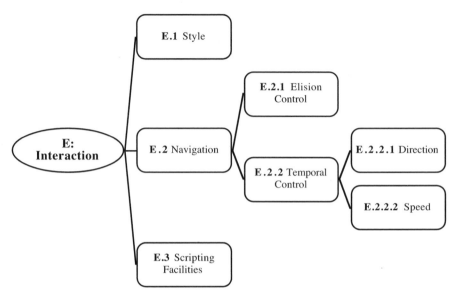

Elision control techniques are useful for information culling, the removal of excess information which is not relevant to the user's line of inquiry and which serves only to clutter the display. This also applies to audio visualizations, since temporal elision (speeding up sounds) can suppress audio detail. Elision is of primary use with large problems, for which the entire data set cannot be simultaneously displayed. Few systems provide elision control facilities (SEE and TPM are exceptions).

Temporal control techniques allow the user to change the mapping between execution time and real time. The most common technique is *speed* where the user can make the program stop and start as well as run faster or slower. Most of the systems at least allow the user to stop and start the visualized program while BALSA, Zeus, and UWPI all have an explicit speed control. Reversing the *direction* of time, so that the program runs backwards, is a rare feature as the table shows, but can be extremely useful when trying to understand an algorithm. Even the ability to "rewind to the beginning", such as that provided by TPM, is a useful kind of temporal direction control.

This facility is important when demonstrations are required and it is particularly useful in classroom situations where a demonstration can be run like a videotape or students can go through it at their own pace. Even though many of the systems are designed for novice and expert demonstrations few serious scripting support (BALSA and Zeus are exceptions).

This is a highly subjective measure and may be made up of many factors. As shown in Figure 8, we see four categories characterizing the effectiveness of a given SV system.

Once one knows what a system is intended to do, one can evaluate how effectively it achieves the intended goal. Most systems built to date are suited to novice classroom demonstration while a few are intended for expert algorithm demonstration or debugging. Few are actually suited to expert software engineering except those tied tightly to the source code.

This might also be expressed as: "How rapidly do the visual metaphors inspire understanding?" Systems tightly connected to source code, like SEE, don't do this very well, while others are difficult to distinguish because the quality of their output is highly dependent on individual examples. This is largely dependent on the tools provided by the SV software developer and the skill of the visualizer.

Most SV system developers perform little or no empirical evaluation even though a sound scientific evaluation could prove the effectiveness of their system. One of the reasons that few studies are performed is the poor state of the art in software psychology, where there are few reliable methods for comparing programming environments. Overall, the number of systems that have been evaluated empirically is low. One of the best documented empirical evaluation of an SV system is that for TANGO [Stasko 93a]; although BALSA, SEE, TPM, and LogoMedia have been subjected to some empirical study, much of it has been informal. A proper empirical study, in addition to convincing people of the efficacy of a system, can also serve to guide system improvements and help define new areas for SV research. Section VII addresses evaluation issues with Chapter 28 by Stasko and Lawrence and Chapter 29 by Mulholland. In Chapter 30, Petre, Blackwell, and Green discuss some of the cognitive issues surrounding SV.

E.3 Scripting Facilities

Does the system provide facilities for managing the recording and playing back of interactions with particular visualizations?

F: Effectiveness

How well does the system communicate information to the user?

F.1 Purpose

For what purpose is the system suited?

F.2 Appropriateness and Clarity

If automatic (default) visualizations are provided, how well do they communicate information about the software?

F.3 Empirical Evaluation

To what degree has the system been subjected to a good experimental evaluation?

Figure 8. Effectiveness Category Hierarchy

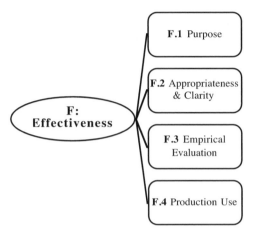

F.4 Production Use

Has the system been in production use for a significant period of time?

This category helps to indicate if people are actually using the system and to what extent. Production use includes publication, sale, and distribution, or consistent use by students in a course. Many of the systems are now publicly available over the Internet by anonymous ftp or even executed remotely via WWW pages with CGI scripts, while others must be purchased from software suppliers. This category probably now merits two sub-categories (although we do not display them in Figure 8):

F.4.1 *Education:* Has the system been used in teaching (primary, secondary, post-secondary)?

F.4.2 *Industry:* Has the system been used in industrial settings?

SOS, BALSA, Zeus, TANGO, Polka, and TPM have all been released publicly and used in schools and universities to varying extents. Chapters 24, 25, 26, and 27 describe developments and educational uses of animated algorithms at the University of Toronto, Brown University, the Open University, and MIT.

Chapters in Section V cover industrial use on large systems at major corporations such as AT&T (Chapter 21) and IBM. (Chapter 20), as well as the role of software visualization in software engineering (Chapter 18).

Further Work

Probably the largest impediment to the use of SV by professional programmers is the issue of *scope*. Most SV systems are still dealing primarily with toy programs; many issues of scalability remain to be solved. While small-scale prototypes are useful for exploring new research ideas, there are also valid research issues involved in scaling these ideas up to larger implementations.

The challenge now is to implement and test SV techniques on production scale systems. The work in Section V, especially the SeeSoft system described by Eick in Chapter 21 which deals with very large programs, is pushing back the frontiers of the Scope category. Furthermore, SV has tremendous potential to aid in the understanding of concurrent programs and we expect more fruitful developments in this area as multiprocessors become more common: Chapter 23 by Heath, Malony, and Rover shows one of the ways forward.

The *content* of an SV display can vary widely over the *program* to *algorithm* spectrum. When designing an SV system, it is important to note the system's intended goals and select the content accordingly. For example, systems designed for classroom teaching might intentionally show algorithm-level displays and avoid program-level displays in order to keep the students' minds off implementation details. Systems designed for expert or even novice interactive use might require the ability to move smoothly between algorithm-level and program-level displays depending on their needs. More work is needed to determine how SV systems can perform these kinds of transitions. Control and data flow are both important to software engineers, yet very little work has been done in showing effective transitions between these, especially in a run-time model. A dynamic-to-dynamic temporal control mapping seems to be the overwhelming choice among designers, yet dynamic-to-static mappings have the potential to convey information in a much more concise manner. The choice of content illustrated by the different systems in chapters in Sections V and VI provide a good indication of where SV system designers are currently focussing their attention.

Most of the work to date has only scratched the surface in terms of the *form* of software visualizations. We have the beginnings of a diverse graphical and auditory vocabulary for communication, but much of our knowledge in this field is informal. New systems have only just started to explore the use of color, sound, and multi-dimensional output as a communication medium as Brown's Chapters 7, 9 and 10 in Section II show. We expect a great deal more work to be done in this area, but it should be done in conjunction with *empirical evaluations* and proper psychological studies to determine which techniques are effective. New techniques and forms of presenting information are always being discovered, and SV system designers must remain open to new ways of presenting information, such as some of the novel suggestions in Chapter 6 by Jeffery.

The automatic layout of information is crucial if we are to expand the *scope* of systems as mentioned earlier. Research into the automatic choice of data displays has only just begun (e.g. [Mackinlay 86]) and much more needs to be done if there is to be a chance of addressing *scope* concerns. The ability to change levels of *granularity* is often overlooked in SV systems yet it has the potential to help overcome the boundaries of scale by providing a range of coarse- and fine-grained views. Providing *multiple views* of different elements in a visualization is well established and we expect interfaces for controlling multiple views to improve. The ability to compare programs with *synchronized* views provides a powerful teaching tool as well as a performance debugging resource for experts, but to date synchronized views have only been used on toy programs.

The *methods* for specifying software visualizations are quite crude and are a likely reason for the dearth of professional SV systems. If programmers are to use SV systems as program understanding and debugging aids, a great deal more automation must be provided, as the SeeSoft system by Eick (Chapter 21) shows. Otherwise, the effort required to get a visualization will exceed the perceived benefit. The simple automatic displays found in many systems are not enough: some of the power of automatic program understanding and data layout must be employed if the cognitive load on the programmer is to be significantly reduced. Requiring the programmer to understand the code in order to produce a visualization is not appropriate in such cases.

Software visualizations can be very large and complex, both spatially and temporally. *Interaction* with such visualizations requires facilities for advanced *navigation* through large programs and data spaces. We expect to see visualization prototypes which use virtual reality technology to advantage for navigating large, complex spaces. Scripting facilities have not been used extensively in SV systems but their worth has been demonstrated in many kinds of software interfaces, so we expect that production SV systems would include at least rudimentary scripting facilities.

Over one hundred fifty software visualization prototypes and systems have been built in the last twenty years, yet very few of these were systematically evaluated to ascertain their *effectiveness*. The number that have seen any kind of *production use*, particularly in the domain of tools for professional programmers, is particularly small and of these few have been evaluated: Chapters 28 and 29 both present evaluations of *student* use. The most disturbing observation is the lack of proper empirical evaluation of SV systems, for if the systems are not evaluated and shown to be effective, what is the point of building them?

If we can make progress with these issues, there are obvious benefits for the fields of software engineering and computer science education. Yet the potential goes beyond this to the entire domain of interactive systems, to the users as well as the programmers of interactive systems. Increasingly, the learning and use of complex systems is being facilitated by augmenting conventional textual and still graphic presentations with animation [Baecker 90c] [Baecker 91], video, and speech and non-speech audio [Mountford 90]. There is also promising work coming out of interfaces being developed for visually impaired programmers [Raman 94] [Raman 95]. In synthesizing all of this work, software visualization can be applied to the development of self-revealing technology that can aid in demystifying and explaining system behaviour to users across the novice to expert continuum.

Acknowledgements

The initial ideas for this paper were first presented in a conference paper [Price 92] and developed in the journal paper [Price 93] upon which this chapter is based. This work was funded by the UK SERC/ESRC/MRC Joint Council Initiative on Cognitive Science and Human Computer Interaction (Project 90/CS66), the Natural Sciences and Engineering Research Council of Canada, Apple Computer, Inc., the Information Technology Research Centre of Ontario, and the Institute for Robotics and Intelligent Systems of Canada.

The Early History of Software Visualization

Ronald Baecker
and
Blaine Price

This chapter presents the early history of software visualization. It positions the field as a branch of software engineering that strives to aid programmers in managing the complexity of modern software. Unfortunately, as systems such as Windows 95 contain over 10,000,000 lines of code, software visualization has a long way to go if it is to play a substantial role where the need is greatest.

A *program* is a precise description, expressed in a *computer programming language*, of a system, process, or problem solution. Large programs typically progress through a *life cycle* [Belady 76] which includes *debugging*. They are refined and often redesigned and reimplemented as part of an iterative, user-centred design approach [Baecker 95a] involving interactions with and feedback from users. Long-term use requires that *maintenance* be done throughout the program's lifetime. Maintenance often consumes 50% to 75% of the total costs incurred over that lifetime [Boehm 81, p. 533].

Managing Complex Software

Software creation and maintenance is difficult and costly because most real programs are complex and hard to understand. Reasons for this include:

• We increasingly demand more and more functionality in programs and in *systems* of programs, therefore often requiring millions of lines of code.

• The specifications of large programs continually evolve as they are used. Systems must frequently be modified to meet these changing specifications.

• Turnover in the software development and support community is great; development tools become obsolete; source code is even lost!

The result is that we have programs of greater and greater size that are incomprehensible, understood neither by their authors nor by their maintainers.

In *Computer Power and Human Reason,* Joseph Weizenbaum [Weizenbaum 76] asserts that this is a very dangerous phenomenon (p. 236):

> "Our society's growing reliance on computer systems that were initially intended to `help' people make analysis and decisions, but which have long since both surpassed the understanding of their users and become indispensable to them, is a very serious development. It has two important consequences. First, decisions are made with the aid of, and sometimes entirely by, computers whose programs no one any longer knows explicitly or understands. Hence no one can know the criteria or the rules on which such decisions are based. Second, the systems of rules and criteria that are embodied in such computer systems become immune to change, because, in the absence of a detailed understanding of the inner workings of a computer system, any substantial modification of it is very likely to render the whole system inoperative and possibly unrestorable. Such computer systems can therefore only grow. And their growth and the increasing reliance placed on them is then accompanied by an increasing legitimation of their `knowledge base.'"

Already our society's health is tightly coupled to computer programs that control vital functions such as the financial markets. For example, the design and linkage of computer-controlled financial systems has already contributed to wild fluctuations of the market [Sanger 87].

Software Engineering Approaches

The field of *software engineering* concerns itself with the technology and processes of software development, and thus it has approached the problems of software complexity and incomprehensibility in a number of ways.

The most widespread development has been the concern with the logical structure and expressive style of programs, resulting in modern software development techniques such as top-down design and stepwise refinement [Wirth 71], structured programming [Dahl 72], modularity [Parnas 72], and software tools [Kernighan 76].

A second advance has been the improvement in the clarity and expressive power of programming languages, as can be seen, for example, in Modula [Wirth 77] and Turing [Holt 89], and in the development of object-oriented approaches to software design and development [Booch 91] [Gamma 95].

There has also been progress in the organization and management of the team that produces the writing. This has given rise to concepts such as chief programmer teams [Baker 72], structured walkthroughs [Yourdon 79], and active design reviews [Parnas 85].

The fourth development has been enhanced technology that supports the writing and maintaining of programs. This includes high-performance workstations and integrated software development environments [Wasserman 81] [Dart 87].

Another important activity is CASE — computer-aided software engineering [Chikofsky 88]. Insights derived in the first four approaches are used to produce integrated environments in which programs can be created from specifications that are far terser and higher level than those required by conventional high-level languages.

A sixth more recent and related development is the attempt to build increasing amounts of knowledge and intelligence into software engineering tools and environments [Balzer 83] [Barstow 87].

Yet despite these advances, the current appearance of programs typically:

Enter Software Visualization

• Does not contribute positively and significantly toward making a program easier to understand
• Does not reflect the history of a program as it has progressed through the software development cycle
• Does not facilitate the transfer of strategies and insights achieved by software developers to the ultimate readers and maintainers of the program
• Does not make important program structure as visible as it could
• Does not deal, therefore, with the fundamental problem of software comprehensibility, that of software complexity.

This motivates the seventh software engineering approach [Price 93] — *software visualization*, which focuses on enhancing program *representation, presentation, and appearance*.

Visualization may be defined as "the power or process of forming a mental picture or vision of something not actually present to the sight" [Simpson 89]. Notice that this definition allows for the use of sensory modalities other than vision, e.g., hearing (see Chapter 10 by Brown and Hershberger), to assist in the formation of mental pictures or images.

Programmers have always employed pictures and diagrams informally as aids to conceiving, expressing, and communicating algorithms, as aids to illustrating *function*, *structure*, and *process*. If prepared thoughtfully, precisely, and imaginatively, typography, symbols, images, diagrams, and animation can present information more concisely and more effectively than the formal and natural languages typically used by the programmer.

In the remainder of this chapter, we shall sketch the early history of software visualization in terms of four major threads of activity:

• presentation of source code
• representations of data structures
• animation of program behaviour
• systems for software visualization.

A fifth important thread is the animation of concurrency (see Chapter 17 by Kraemer), but work in this area began relatively late.

Presentation of Source Code

An early attempt to improve program appearance was the development of a "presentation," or "reference" form of the programming language ALGOL 60 [Naur 63]. Another idea with a long history is *prettyprinting* [Baecker 90a, p. 18], the use of spacing, indentation, and layout to make source code easier to read in a structured language. *Prettyprinters* are programs that systematically indent the source code of a target program according to its syntactic structure. The earliest work was done on LISP, so that program readers would not drown in a sea of parentheses. Other early examples were NEATER2 [Conrow 70] for PL/I and Hueras and Ledgard's [Hueras 77] system for Pascal. The problems of prettyprinting Pascal elicited vigorous debate in early ACM SIGPLAN notices [Baecker 90a, p. 18].

More recent developments have used computerized typesetting and laser printing to improve the presentation of source code. The Vgrind utility of the Berkeley Unix system makes modest use of typographic encoding of keywords and user customizability of appearance. The Xerox Cedar user community has adopted a consistent publication style for softcopy and hardcopy listings of Cedar programs, making use of typeface, math notation, indentation, spatial separation, and headings [Teitelman 85]; see also [Baecker 90a, p. 20].

An ambitious recent attempt to enhance the presentation of source code is the work of Baecker and Marcus [Baecker 90a] (see Chapter 4 by Baecker and Marcus). Their SEE Program Visualizer automatically typesets a C program according to an elaborate style guide based on graphic design principles. They also propose a method for documenting sets of C programs in a "program book." Knuth's [Knuth 84] WEB system also seeks to enhance program publishing, combining program source text and documentation in a single publication using a sophisticated markup language.

The role of visual representations in understanding computer programs has a long history, beginning with Goldstein and von Neumann's demonstration of the usefulness of flowcharts [Goldstein 47]. Haibt developed a system that could draw them automatically from Fortran or assembly language programs [Haibt 59]; Knuth produced a similar system which integrated documentation with the source code and could automatically generate flowcharts [Knuth 63]. [Abrams 68] is a review of such early systems. Although later experiments cast doubt on the value of flowcharts as an aid to comprehension [Shneiderman 80], recent results are more encouraging [Scanlan 89]. The 1970's saw the first of many alternatives to flowcharting, the development of Nassi-Shneiderman diagrams [Nassi 73] to counter the unstructured nature of standard flowcharts.

Diagramming Control Flow and Data Structures

Baecker's prototype interactive debugger for the TX-2 computer produced static images of high-level language data structures and of the computer graphics display file [Baecker 68]. Articles by Stockham [Stockham 65] and by Evans and Darley [Evans 66] review the then current state-of-the-art in debugging technology which motivated this work. Myers's Incense system was a more ambitious system for the display of data structures [Myers 83]. Martin and McClure survey a variety of diagrammatic methods for the representation and display of program structure and behaviour [Martin 85].

More recently, there has been an explosion of interest in *visual programming*, the use of visual representations of programs as both an input and an output modality [Glinert 90a] [Glinert 90b].

Animating Program Behaviour

Licklider did early experiments on the use of computer graphics to view how the contents of the memory of a computer were changing as the computer was executing. A different approach was taken with Knowlton's [Knowlton 66a] [Knowlton 66b] influential films, which demonstrated L[6], Bell Lab's low-level list processing language. This work was the first to use animation techniques to portray program behaviour and the first to address the visualization of dynamically changing data structures.

Baecker, Hopgood, and Booth continued this work in pedagogical directions. Baecker outlined the potential of program animation and sketched many of the key research issues [Baecker 73]. Hopgood produced a series of short films illustrating hash coding and syntax analysis techniques [Hopgood 74]. Yarwood explored the concept of program illustration, and methods of embedding graphical representations of program state within program source text [Yarwood 74]. Booth produced a short film animating PQ-tree data structure algorithms [Booth 75]. Baecker reported on work in which he and his students were investigating the portrayal of data structure abstractions and algorithms [Baecker 75], eventually leading to the important film *Sorting Out Sorting* [Baecker 81]; see Chapter 24 by Baecker).

Software Visualization Systems

The availability in the 1980's of personal workstations with bit-mapped displays and graphical user interfaces allowed researchers to go beyond the prototypes and specific animations of the 70s and develop software visualization systems. One of the earliest attempts to build a debugging system to aid visualization was the work done in Lisp by Lieberman [Lieberman 84a].

The most important and well known system of the new era was BALSA [Brown 84b], followed by Balsa-II [Brown 88b], which allowed students to interact with high level dynamic visualizations of Pascal programs. BALSA (see Chapter 12 by Brown) evolved from a principled design, was used by hundreds of undergraduates and as a tool in algorithm design and analysis [Brown 85a] [Brown 88a]; see Chapter 7 by Brown and Sedgewick, and was influential in inspiring many of the systems described in this volume.

Further Reading

Two good sources where one can continue reading about the history of software visualization research and development are Brown [Brown 88a, Chapter 2], and [Price 93].

A Taxonomy of Algorithm Animation Displays

Marc H. Brown

Chapter

3

As discussed in Chapter 1, *algorithm visualization* is the visualization of the abstractions which describe software, and *algorithm animation* is dynamic algorithm visualization, using either a passive medium, such as videotapes or movies, or an interactive system. In essence, algorithm animation communicates how an algorithm works by graphically or aurally depicting its fundamental operations. Typically, algorithm animation systems also include displays of program code and program data, referred to as "program visualization" rather than "algorithm visualization" in Chapter 1.

Introduction

Because algorithm animation is an important part of software visualization, and a significant portion of this book discusses interactive algorithm animation systems and the displays prevalent in such systems, it is useful to examine the nature of algorithm animation displays in detail. The taxonomy presented in this chapter will be used in Chapter 12 to analyze those types of algorithm animation displays that can and cannot be created automatically from unmodified source code. We do not consider algorithm auralization, the topic of Chapter 10.

We characterize algorithm animation displays along three dimensions:

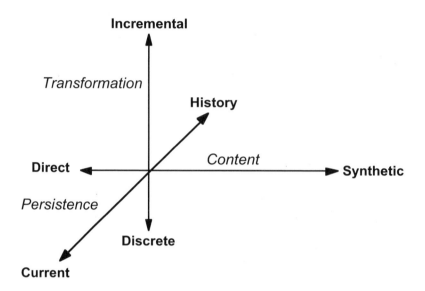

The *content* of the displays ranges from direct representations of a program's data or code to synthetic images of information not necessarily inside the program. The *persistence* dimension ranges from displays that show only the current state of information to those that show a complete history of each change in the information. The *transformation* dimension ranges from displays that show changes in the pictures discretely to those that show incremental and continuous changes.

Before elaborating on each of the axes, readers are encouraged to pause at this point to scan through the screen images appearing in this chapter. Figures 1 and 2 are from the BALSA algorithm animation system [Brown84b], Figures 3 and 4 are from BALSA-II [Brown 88a][Brown 88b]; and Figures 5 and 6 are from Gloor's *Animated Algorithms* project [Gloor 92][Gloor 93][Gloor 96].

First, we will look at the content axis. *Direct* displays are pictures that are isomorphic to one or more data structures in the program or to the program itself. At a given instant, the data structure(s) could be constructed from the display, and the display could be constructed from the data structure(s). No additional information is needed. For example, the Bins view in Figure 1 is a direct view of the array bin. The Sticks view in Figure 3 and the Dots view in Figure 4 are direct views of the array of numbers being sorted. The Code view in Figure 1 is a direct view of the static algorithm code itself, along with the dynamic program counter (shown as the highlighted line in the topmost procedure box) and the dynamic calling stack (displayed by the overlapping of the procedure boxes).

Synthetic displays, on the other hand, do not have a mapping to any program variables. They can show the operations causing changes in the data, or can be abstractions of the data. The Waste view in Figures 1 and 2 is a good example of a synthetic view: after each weight is inserted in the bin, the graphs are continued at the right edge to show how much space is wasted. The top graph shows the wasted space and the bottom graph shows the lower bound of this quantity. The concept of wasted space is not in the program.

Many displays are composites of direct and synthetic components. For example, the Compare-Exchange view in Figure 3 shows some values of the array; additional information showing the results of comparisons or exchanges is encoded as the color of the elements. A proper reading of the picture would enable the current contents of the array to be reconstructed, although this property is not invertible: the picture could not be reconstructed just by knowing the contents of the array at an instant of time. In addition to showing the algorithm's fundamental operations (i.e., comparisons and exchanges), the display illustrates the algorithm's flow of control (i.e., each iteration of the algorithm's main loop is displayed on a separate line).

The Partition-Tree view in Figure 4 also has both direct and synthetic aspects. It is a direct view of the array being processed in the sense that each node correspond to an element of the array, and an inorder traversal of the tree would reveal the elements of the array in proper order. (Of course, the user would have to zoom into the view, or make the window larger, in order for the contents of each node to be visible on the screen.) The view is synthetic because the tree

Content Axis

Figure 1. First-fit binpacking algorithm. The binpacking problem is to arrange a set of weights into the fewest number of bins possible, subject to the constraint that each bin has a capacity that may not be exceeded. The First-fit algorithm determines into which bin a new weight should be placed by examining the bins from left to right and stopping at the first bin with enough room. This algorithm does not guarantee optimal packing.

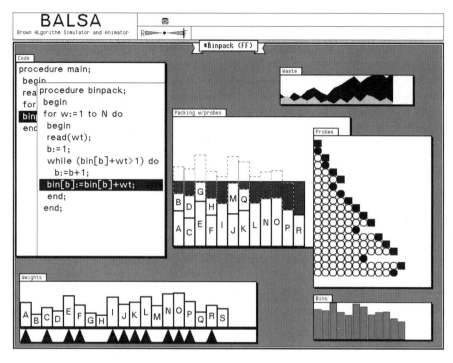

shape reveals far more than just the data in the program: it shows the way in which the algorithm has processed the data.

Persistence Axis

A second criterion for classifying displays is whether a display shows *current* information or illustrates a *history* of what has happened. In Figure 1, all views except for the Bins view show some history. The Weights view is a history of each weight inserted into a bin, the variable wt. A triangle is drawn beneath a weight when that weight causes a new bin to be started; thus, it is a history of a synthetic entity. In the Waste view, only the right edge shows the current waste; the part of the graph leading up to the right edge is a history of the waste as each weight is processed. The Probes view shows a history of each and every bin that was tested to see whether or not it could support the new weight. Even the Code view shows some history!

The Compare-Exchange view in Figure 3 can be thought of as illustrating the history of the comparisons and exchanges that have taken place in the algorithm. This view is a particularly effective way to show that Insertion sort is a quadratic algorithm: When the algorithm is given *N* items to sort, there will be *N* rows and

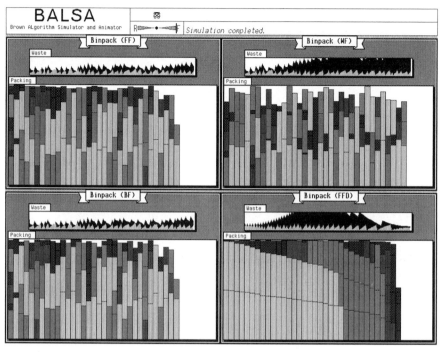

Figure 2. Four binpacking algorithms all operating on the same set of weights. The weights are evenly distributed between 0 and 50% of a bin's capacity. Note the regularity of the packing in the First-fit Decreasing algorithm in the lower right.

N^2 potential spots for a black or gray marker. On average, each row will be filled about half-way from the diagonal to the left edge, leading to $1+2+...+(N-1)/2 = (N^2-1)/4$ markers. In the worst case (running on data that is in decreasing order), half of the N^2 potential spots will be filled.

The third and final criterion by which we classify algorithm animation displays is based on the nature of the transitions from the old displays to the new ones. *Incremental* transformations show a smooth transition. For example, in the Packing w/probes view in Figure 1, the dotted box showing the attempt to put a new weight into each of the bins advances smoothly from one bin to the next, while also keeping a trace of itself. Chapter 8 discusses the path-transition paradigm for constructing program visualizations with smooth animation. *Discrete* transitions are just that: the old value is erased and the new value is drawn. All of the views in Figure 1, with the above mentioned exception, are discrete transitions.

Discrete transformations are perceived as incremental when the difference between the new and old pictures is "small enough" in relationship to the

Transformation Axis

Figure 3. Insertion sort in action. The Sticks *view on the left represents the array being sorted as a set of sticks whose heights correspond to their values, with a rectangle drawn beneath a stick when it is processed. The* Compare-Exchange *view on the right represents comparisons by gray circles and exchanges by black ones. A row is started each time an array element is processed.*

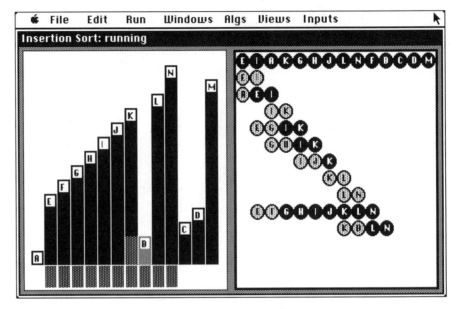

complexity of the data. Genuinely discrete transformations tend to be most useful on large sets of data. Incremental transitions are most effective when users are examining an algorithm running on a small set of data; in fact, incremental transformations tend to hinder the display of large data because they slow down the animation significantly and contain too much low-level detail. Unless a good animation package is available, incremental transitions are tedious and difficult to program.

Incremental transformations must address the issue of how much time they should consume. For example, changing a single pointer in, say, a tree, might cause a very large subtree to move a large distance (which might, in turn, necessitate repositioning all nodes in the tree). How fast should the subtree movement be? Should it be at the same speed as if it moved a small distance? Or should the total movement consume a constant amount of time, so that it moves quickly if it has a large distance to cover?.

Reusing Views

Another aspect of algorithm animation displays is *versatility*: Can a view be used in different situations, or is the view tailored for a particular situation?

Generic displays have the advantage that once implemented for one algorithm, they can be easily adapted to display other related algorithms A trivial example

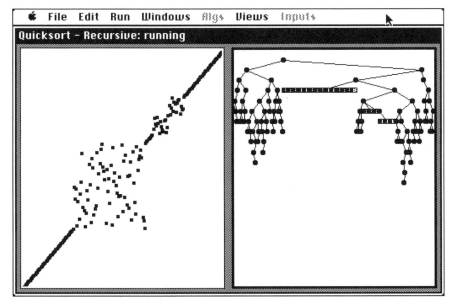

Figure 4. Quicksort in action. The Dots *view at the left displays a dot for each element of the array being sorted: the horizontal coordinate corresponds to its position in the array, and the vertical corresponds to its value. The* Dots *view makes obvious distinctive rectangular blocks of dots which correspond to subfiles waiting to be processed. The* Partition-Tree *view at the right displays each array element as a node in a tree, with the horizontal coordinate corresponding to its position in the array. Circular nodes are in their final sorted positions in the array; the contiguous square nodes represent the subfiles awaiting processing with their depths indicating in what order they will be processed.*

of a generic display is the Code view seen in Figure 1. This view can be used for any algorithm, and once the viewer has understood the meaning of the overlapping boxes and the significance of the highlighted lines in the partially overlapped boxes, the view is understandable for all algorithms. In Figure 4 the Dots view is generic to all sorting algorithms, whereas the Partition Tree view is meaningful only to Quicksort. Figure 5 shows generic views of four sorting algorithms.

For the user, there are two advantages of generic views. First, once the view is understood for one algorithm, it becomes part of the user's "visual vocabulary" and it helps the user to understand new algorithms. Second, the behavior of related algorithms can be compared more easily because of the common base. The disadvantage of generic views is that they often do not illustrate salient features of an algorithm.

Customized displays are coded from scratch for each algorithm (perhaps starting with an existing view, as appropriate). It takes considerable effort to animate algorithms this way because the algorithm has to be understood thoroughly before a meaningful representation can be found. Figure 6 shows customized displays of four sorting algorithms. Try to identify the sorting algorithms in that figure before reading the figure caption.

Figure 5. Four generic views of sorting algorithms. Note that with the exception of the "Step Size" field in the Shell Sort image at the lower left, it would be extremely difficult to differentiate the algorithms based on these static images.

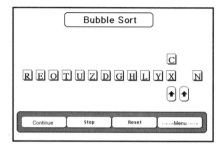

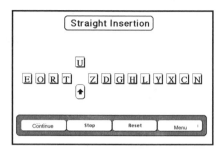

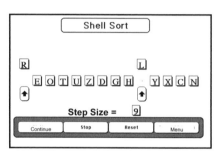

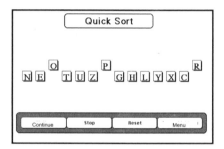

Figure 6. Customized views of four sorting algorithms. In clockwise order, starting in the upper-right, the algorithms are Bucket sort, Counting sort, Quicksort, and Radix sort.

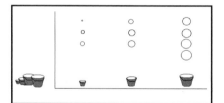

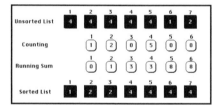

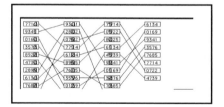

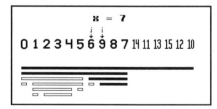

Gloor feels that it is worthwhile expending the additional effort for customized views because they communicate much more information about the intrinsic workings of a particular algorithm [Gloor 92].

Acknowledgments

This chapter is based on [Brown 88c], and used with permission. Figures 5 and 6 are from [Gloor 96], and are reprinted with permission.

Techniques: What to Draw?
How to Draw it?

One of the hardest tasks within the construction of a SV is the design of the display. Although, as with design in general, an element of inspiration is sometimes useful, basic principles and techniques have emerged. This section describes these techniques, which range in their granularity from specific types of display views to SV construction paradigms.

Chapter 4 ("Printing and Publishing C Programs") applies a book metaphor to displaying program source code. Inspired by Donald Knuth's assertion that programs should be considered as works of literature, it is argued that the human understanding of programs is greatly enhanced by the use of modern printing technologies such as multiple typefaces and variable linespacing. This is followed by a detailed description of how the metaphor was applied to the C programming language.

Five chapters in this section discuss specific display techniques. Graphs (node-link diagrams) are commonly used in SV displays and Chapter 5 ("Visualizing Graph Models of Software") gives an overview of automatic graph layout algorithms. The chapter also shows how a particular graph layout system, *dot*, has been used within a number of SV systems. Rather than concentrating on a single visualization technique, Chapter 6 ("A Menagerie of Program Visualization Techniques") characterizes a number of relatively simple, but effective, techniques into three classes. In addition the chapter outlines five underlying principles for the illustrated techniques.

Chapter 7 ("Fundamental Techniques for Algorithm Animation Displays") shows how systems such as BALSA and Zeus allow SV designers to construct color algorithm animations with tightly integrated multiple views. The chapter gives examples of how algorithm animations can be constructed by associating multiple *views* with a set of *events* generated by an algorithm.

A problem found in early SV systems was that users would sometimes miss updates as an interface 'jumped' from one state to the next. This problem can be alleviated by using smooth animation for state transitions. Chapter 8 ("Smooth Continuous Animation for Portraying Algorithms and Processes") describes the path-transition paradigm for constructing SVs with smooth animation and its embodiment in three tools Tango, Polka and Polka-RC.

Chapter 9 ("Algorithm Animation Using Interactive 3D Graphics") discusses how 3D graphics can be used in three ways: capturing time, uniting multiple views and expressing additonal information. The three uses are illustrated with a number of examples.

Sound is, in general, under-utilised in computer interfaces and this is true within SV. There are however some notable exceptions and one such is described in Chapter 10 ("Program Auralization"). Using examples of sorting and hashing algorithms among other examples, the chapter describes how audio has been used to reinforce and replace visuals cues, and to signal exceptional conditions.

Obviously, as well as ensuring that the components of an SV 'look right', the SV designer has to think about the usability of the system as a whole. Chapter 11 ("User Interface Issues for Algorithm Animation") discusses user interface issues focussing on the consistency of display objects and their motion, and on the consistency of the control interface. The issues involved are discussed in terms of 'the ten commandments of algorithm animation'.

Printing and Publishing C Programs

Ronald Baecker
and
Aaron Marcus

Program Appearance

Program appearance has changed little since the first high-level languages were developed in the 1960s. With a few exceptions, most notably APL, programs have been expressed and composed almost entirely out of alphanumeric symbols ("ASCII text"). They are typically presented in a single typeface, often without even the use of boldface or italic; in a single point size, with fixed-width characters, fixed wordspacing, and fixed linespacing; and without the benefit of symbols, rules, grids, gray scale, diagrammatic elements, and pictures.

Why is program appearance so impoverished? In part, this is an artifact of the composing and printing technologies of the early days of computing — keypunch, teletype, and line printer. These obsolete technologies have been superseded by the interactive raster display and the laser printer. Programs can now easily be represented using those elements heretofore omitted, such as multiple typefaces; variable weights, slants, point sizes, wordspacing, and linespacing; and rules, gray scale, and pictures.

Yet this should just be the beginning. In our professional and personal lives we employ symbolic systems such as circuits, maps, mathematics, and music that have sophisticated and well-developed notations, appropriate diagrammatic elements, and typesetting and graphic conventions. There are printing and publishing industries dedicated to facilitating effective communication in these disciplines. Why should we not do the same for computer science? Or, in the words of Donald Knuth [Knuth 84, p. 97]

"I believe that the time is ripe for significantly better documentation of programs, and that we can best achieve this by considering programs to be *works of literature*. Hence, my title: `Literate Programming.'

Let us change our traditional attitude to the construction of programs: Instead of imagining that our main task is to instruct a *computer* what to do, let us concentrate rather on explaining to *human beings* what we want a computer to do.

The practitioner of literate programming can be regarded as an essayist, whose main concern is with exposition and excellence of style... He or she strives for a program that is comprehensible because its concepts have been introduced in an order that is best for human understanding, using a mixture of formal and informal methods that nicely reinforce each other."

Research Claims

In this chapter we seek to demonstrate and explain (as does [Oman 97]) how communication about programs and comprehension of programs can be aided by paying attention to the visual schema embodying the programs and the visual appearance of programs. What appears here is a summary of a previously published book-length treatment of the same material, *Human Factors and Typography for More Readable Programs* [Baecker 90a].

We show that the presentation of program source text matters, and demonstrate, by existence proof, that it is possible to produce significantly better program presentation than that to which we are accustomed. Effective program presentation portrays program structure and helps us deal with its complexity, making good programs more understandable and bad programs more obvious.

Effective program presentation, visually enhanced source code, and improved legibility and readability can be achieved through the systematic application of graphic design principles [Marcus 92] [Marcus 95]. The design for the appearance of a language can and should be documented in a *graphic design manual* for that language. Our prototype graphic design manual for C appears in [Baecker 90a].

The fact that principles are applied to achieve a design does not imply that the result is uniquely determined. There are many plausible designs that may be derived from the principles. They must be evaluated by generating page after page of visual examples and by thoughtful scrutiny and testing of the strengths and weaknesses of each. Examples of these *systematic design variations* for the appearance of C appear in [Baecker 90a], and represent the first published "catalog" of possibilities for the appearance of program source text.

Effective program appearance may be automated. Most of the examples included in [Baecker 90a] have been produced by a *visual compiler* for the C language, which takes unmodified C source text as its input, and produces as its output high-quality typeset presentations on a laser printer. The SEE visual compiler is also heavily parameterized to allow the customization of text displays to suit individual taste.

The concepts developed in this research may be applied to other programming languages. With languages similar to C, like Pascal, the principles and specifications are easily extendible; with those more distant, such as Prolog, significant new work will be required.

Enhanced program presentation produces listings that facilitate the reading, comprehension, and effective use of computer programs. Baecker and Marcus [Baecker 90a] and Oman and Cook [Oman 90a] [Oman 90b] present both theory and experiments which lend credence to the following assertion: *Making the interface to a program's source code and documentation intelligible, communicative, and attractive will ultimately lead to significant productivity gains and cost savings.*

Our approach can be considered part of a broader effort to enhance the art of program writing, documentation, and illustration, Knuth's "literate programming" (see also [Ramsey 94]). We have considered the entire context in which code is presented and used, a context which includes the supporting texts and notations that make a program a living piece of written communication. We seek thereby to enhance programmers' abilities to construct, refine, store, retrieve, scan, read, and manipulate the texts and documents required to do their jobs.

To summarize, our goal is for computer science to learn and apply the lesson that the discipline of graphic design teaches so vividly: *Visual form matters. Effective representation and presentation aids thought, the management of complexity, problem solving, and articulate expression.*

We present as Figures 1 and 2 a short, self-contained illustration of fairly typical C code that accepts a phone number expressed as a sequence of digits and prints out a list of equivalents with all digits between two and nine replaced by corresponding letters from a phone dial, with the constraint that the words produced must each contain at least one vowel. Thus, given "765" as its input,

An Example of a C Program Designed and Typeset

Figure 1. Page 1 of the designed and typeset program. [Baecker 90a, p. 9].

*We explain our design's salient features with reference numbers, e.g., (**1**) and (**17**), that refer to the small numbers in circles appearing in the right margin of the corresponding program pages. The notes are organized in terms of a taxonomy of C constructs introduced in [Baecker 90a].*

The Presentation of Program Structure

*The program is output on loose-leaf 8.5" X 11" pages, each of which is separated into four regions, a header (**1**), a footnote area (**17**), a main text column for the code and most of the comments (**3, right**), and a marginalia comment column (**3, left**).*

*Each file appears as a separate "chapter" with the filename shown as a very large, bold title (**2**).*

Extra white space is used to provide adequate separation between the prologue *comments (see below) and the code (**5**), between function definitions and sequences of declarations (**10**), between individual function definitions, and between the header and the body of a function definition (**14**).*

*Cross-references relating uses of global variables to the location of their definitions are included as footnotes to the source text (**17**).*

The Spatial Composition of Comments

Each file may include, at or near its beginning, a prologue *comment describing the module's purpose (**4**).*

The prologue is displayed in a serif font over a light gray tone. Type size and gray value have been selected to insure legibility of two generations of photocopies. There is a margin around the text ample to ensure readability.

Comments that are located on the same lines as source code, which we call marginalia *comments, are displayed in a small-sized serif font in the marginalia column (**9, left**). These items are intended to be short, single-line phrases.*

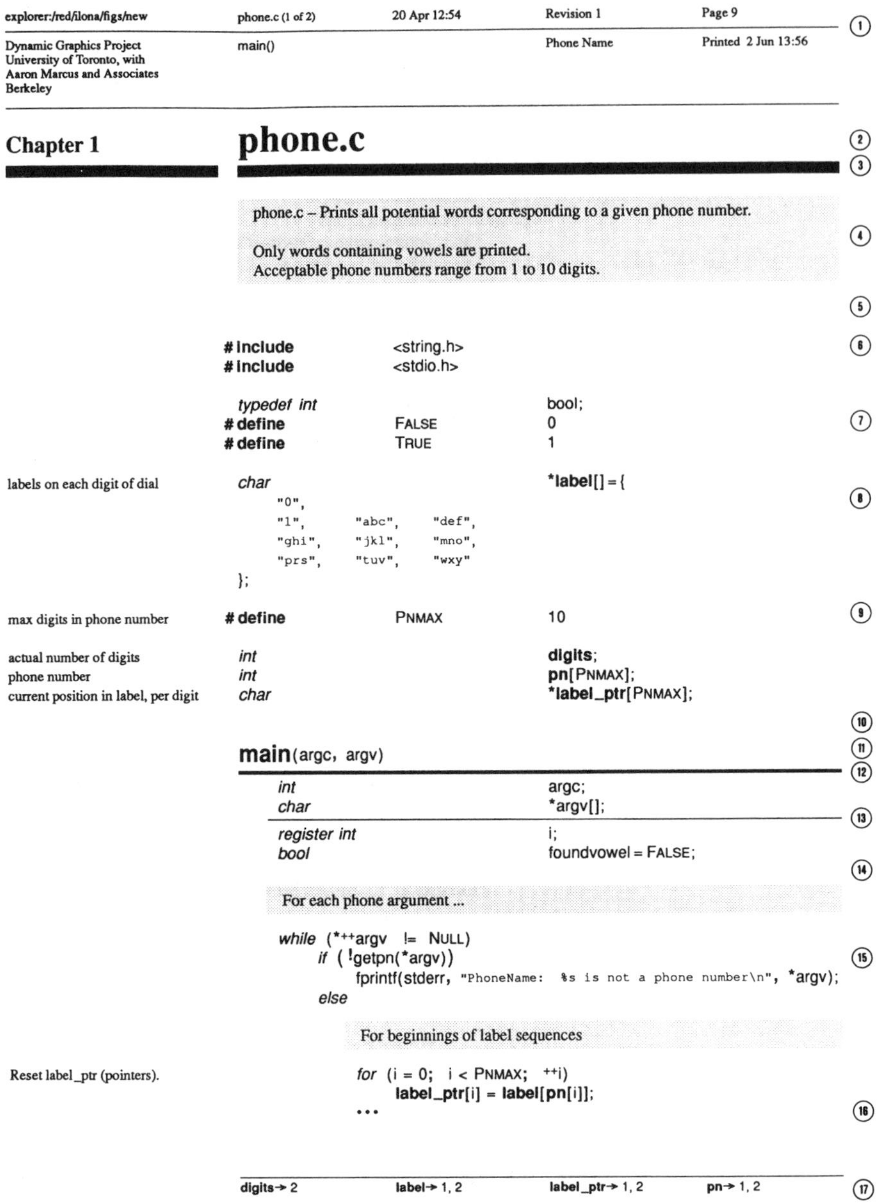

```
explorer:/red/ilona/figs/new   phone.c (1 of 2)   20 Apr 12:54   Revision 1    Page 9               (1)
Dynamic Graphics Project       main()                            Phone Name    Printed 2 Jun 13:56
University of Toronto, with
Aaron Marcus and Associates
Berkeley

Chapter 1                      phone.c                                                               (2)
                                                                                                     (3)
        phone.c – Prints all potential words corresponding to a given phone number.                 (4)
        Only words containing vowels are printed.
        Acceptable phone numbers range from 1 to 10 digits.
                                                                                                     (5)
                               # include       <string.h>                                            (6)
                               # include       <stdio.h>

                               typedef int                     bool;
                               # define        FALSE           0                                     (7)
                               # define        TRUE            1

labels on each digit of dial   char                            *label[] = {                          (8)
                                    "0",
                                    "1",     "abc",   "def",
                                    "ghi",   "jkl",   "mno",
                                    "prs",   "tuv",   "wxy"
                               };

max digits in phone number     # define        PNMAX           10                                    (9)

actual number of digits        int                             digits;
phone number                   int                             pn[PNMAX];
current position in label,     char                            *label_ptr[PNMAX];
per digit
                                                                                                     (10)
                               main(argc, argv)                                                      (11)
                                                                                                     (12)
                                   int                         argc;
                                   char                        *argv[];                              (13)
                                   register int                i;
                                   bool                        foundvowel = FALSE;                   (14)

                                   For each phone argument ...

                                   while (*++argv  != NULL)
                                       if ( !getpn(*argv))                                           (15)
                                           fprintf(stderr, "PhoneName:  %s is not a phone number\n", *argv);
                                       else

                                           For beginnings of label sequences

Reset label_ptr (pointers).                for (i = 0;  i < PNMAX;  ++i)
                                               label_ptr[i] = label[pn[i]];
                                           ...                                                       (16)

                               digits→ 2       label→ 1, 2       label_ptr→ 1, 2       pn→ 1, 2      (17)
```

the program produces the following as its output: poj, pok, pol, roj, rok, rol, soj, sok, and sol. Figures 1 and 2 show SEE's output, altered only in the addition of details in headers and footnotes that were not handled automatically by SEE.

Design Method

To develop this new software visualization technique, we followed traditional analysis and design procedures as follows:

Visible Language Taxonomy We first produced a visible language taxonomy for computer-based documents and publications (see also [Gerstner 78] [Ruder 73] [Chaparos 81]). This organization was intended to be a checklist to guide approaches to enhancing source code presentation.

C Taxonomy We simultaneously developed a taxonomy of C constructs, a systematic enumeration and classification of logical components of the language [AT&T 85] [Kernighan 78] [Harbison 84]. This was intended to be a companion checklist for ensuring completeness in the representation of C source text. We also added notions not in the formal language description, for example dealing with various categories of comments.

Review of Current Practice Next, we collected, organized, and reviewed typical mappings from C constructs to visible language constructs, examples abstracted from real C programs prepared by typical experienced C programmers. These "folk designs" often embody valuable design insights from non-designers, as opposed to the "professional designs" such as the conventions proposed in this chapter.

Design Principles We then developed a systematic set of principles that govern the design of mappings from C constructs to visible language constructs. These principles guide detailed visual research into the effective presentation of C source code.

A New Design We applied these principles and informally reviewed the merits of interim designs to develop a new set of conventions for the presentation of C programs. The design specifications have been illustrated by applying them to the concrete example presented above.

(Figure 1, continued)

The Presentation of Function Definitions

The introductory text of a function definition — the function name — is shown as a "headline," in a large sans-serif type (11). A heavy rule appears under the introductory text of a function definition (12). A light rule appears under the declaration of the formal parameters (13).

The Presentation of Declarations

Identifiers being declared are aligned to a single implied vertical line located at an appropriate horizontal tab position, 16 picas into the main code column (7).

Initializers are displayed at reasonable tab positions, with the programmer's carriage returns being respected as requests for "new lines" (8).

The Presentation of Preprocessor Commands

The "#" signifying a preprocessor command is extended to enhance its distinguishability from ordinary C source text (6).

Within macro definitions, macros and their values are presented at appropriate horizontal tab positions, 8 and 16 picas into the main code column (6).

The Visual Parsing of Statements

Systematic indentation and placement of key words based on the syntax of the program is employed (15).

Since curly braces are redundant with systematic indentation, they are removed in this example (15). Whether this happens or not is under control of the user.

In conventional program listings, it is impossible to tell without turning the page where a particular control construct (in this case, the for) continues on the following page. Our solution is an ellipsis, in line with the for, signifying that the first statement on the next page is at the same nesting level as the for (16).

Figure 2. Page 2 of the designed and typeset program [Baecker 90a, p. 11].

The Spatial Composition of Comments (continued)

Comments that are external *to function definitions are displayed in a serif font laid over a light gray tone (26).*

Comments that are internal *to function definitions are also displayed in a serif font laid over a light gray tone, appropriately indented to match the current statement's nesting (28).*

The Presentation of Function Definitions (continued)

The function type specifier, indicating the type of the value returned by the function, if any, appears on a line by itself above the function name (27).

The Visual Parsing of Statements (continued)

When nested statements cross a page boundary, the "nesting context" is displayed in the second column of the header (19), just above the code.

The Visual Parsing of Expressions

Parentheses and brackets are emboldened to call attention to grouped items. Nested parentheses are varied in size to aid parsing (25).

*Unary operators such as ++ and the unary ** are raised (turned into superscripts) to make them easier to distinguish from binary operators (30).*

The wordspacing between operators within an expression is varied to aid the reader. Operands are displayed closer to operators of high precedence than to operators of low precedence (29).

Typographic Encodings of Token Attributes

Most tokens are shown in a regular sans-serif font; reserved words are shown in italic sans-serif type (20).

Since the global variable in C is a fundamental mechanism through which functions communicate

| explorer:/red/ilona/figs/new | phone.c (2 of 2) | 20 Apr 12:54 | Revision 1 | Page 11 |
| Dynamic Graphics Project University of Toronto, with Aaron Marcus and Associates Berkeley | main() | | Phone Name | Printed 2 Jun 13:56 |

```
                          while...else...

                    For each combination of characters ...

        do
            for (i = 0;  i < digits;  ++i)
                if (strchr("aeiou", *label_ptr[i]) != NULL)
                    foundvowel = TRUE;
            if (foundvowel)
                for (i = 0;  i != digits;  i++)
                    printf("%c", *label_ptr[i]);
                printf("\n");
            foundvowel = FALSE;
        ↑while (incr());


        Encode phone number as a vector of digits, without punctuation.
        Returns number of digits in phone number, or FALSE to indicate failure.

    static bool
    getpn(str)
        char                        *str;
        int                         i = 0;
        while (*str != '\0')
            if (i >= PNMAX)
                return FALSE;

        Set pn to the digits ignoring spaces and dashes

            if (*str != ' ' && *str != '-')
                if ('0' <= *str && *str <= '9')
                    pn[i++] = *str - '0';
                else
                    return FALSE;
            ++str;
        return (digits = i) != 0;


        Advance a single label_ptr; return FALSE when done.

    static bool
    incr()
        register int                i;
        for (i = digits;  --i >= 0;)
            if (*++label_ptr[i] == '\0')
                label_ptr[i] = label[pn[i]];
            else
                return TRUE;
        return FALSE;


    digits ← 1        label ← 1        label_ptr ← 1        pn ← 1
```

Only print things with vowels!

not a number or empty

Set digits to length of phone no.

Design Refinement To facilitate our systematic approach to the design of program presentation, we constructed SEE, a visual C compiler, a program that maps an arbitrary C program into an effective typeset representation of that program. We produced numerous examples using this automated tool, which has in turn enabled us to modify and improve the graphic design of program appearance.

Design Testing The design was also tested informally and more formally in an experiment in an attempt to substantiate and quantify its value.

Design Formalization The final specifications (that is, a precise, complete mapping of all elements of C to selected appearance characteristics) were then embodied in a graphic design manual for the appearance of C programs.

Iterative Design We did not proceed through these steps in a linear fashion. Analysis of examples produced with the help of the visual compiler, feedback from members of the project team and other interested parties, and results from experiments were all used in an ongoing process of *iterative design* refinement and improvement.

Program Publishing Finally, we shifted our viewpoint away from code appearance and considered the larger issue of the function, structure, contents, and form of the *program book*, the embodiment of the concept of the program as a publication. (See also [Oman 90a] [Oman 90b] for a similar development of this concept.) Although we did not automate its production, we developed and included in [Baecker 90a] a mock-up of a prototype of a program book. We shall now, following Figures 1 and 2, turn our attention to this aspect of our work.

(Figure 2, continued)

indirectly, and thus also a major source of programming errors, we call attention to most uses of globals (but not function names, invocations, or manifest constants) by highlighting them in boldface (20).

Macro names, which by C convention are all upper case, are shown with the first letter normal size and the remainder of the word in "small caps" (22). String constants are shown in a small-sized fixed-width serif font (21).

The Typography of Program Punctuation

In this example the ";" appears in 10 point regular Helvetica type, and thus uses the same typographic parameters as does much of the program code. On the other hand, in order to enhance legibility and readability, the "," has been enlarged to 14 points, the "*" has been enlarged to 12 points, and the "!" has been set in boldface (24). Slight repositioning has also been carried out on individual punctuation marks.

The letterspacing between individual characters of multi-character operators such as the "!=", the "<=", and the "++" has been adjusted, to make the symbols more legible as a unit (23).

Symbol substitutions are employed where they can reduce the possibilities for error and thereby enhance readability. Since C's two uses of while can be confused under some circumstances, we add an upwards-pointing arrow to the while that is part of a do...while (25).

The Presentation of Program Environment

The header describes the context of the source code that appears on the page, including the location of the file from which the listing was made, the last time the file was updated, the page number within the listing, the time the listing was made, and, in the second column, the function name of the code that first appears at the top of the page (18).

Programs as Publications

Programs are publications, a form of literature. English prose can range in scope from a note scribbled on a pad to a historical treatise appearing in multiple volumes and representing a lifetime of work. Similarly, programs range from a two-line *shell* script created whenever needed to an edition of the collected works of a research group, for example, the UNIX operating system. The line printer listing, which represents the output of conventional program publishing technology, is woefully inadequate for documenting an encyclopedic collection of code such as the UNIX system, or even for such lesser program treatises as compilers, graphics subroutine packages, and database management systems.

The problem is that computer program source text consisting of code and accompanying comments does not itself have sufficient communicative depth. A program is a large document, an information narrative in which the components should be arranged in a logical, easy-to-find, easy-to-read, and easy-to-remember sequence. The reader should be able quickly to find a table of contents to the document, to determine its parts, to identify desired sections, and to find their locations quickly. Within the program source text, the overall structure and appearance of the page should furnish clues regarding the nature of the contents. The page headers and footnotes should also serve to reinforce the structure and sequencing of the document.

Other document elements that aid and orient the reader are needed. For example, a published program requires an *abstract*, a summary of the function, significance, and capabilities of the program. It should have several kinds of *overview* and *index* pages, all providing the reader with summaries of other facets of the program's function, structure, and processing. The program should also be augmented by a variety of kinds of documentation, some for its users and some for its programmers and maintainers.

Program Publications

More formally, we define a *program publication* as a document (either paper or electronic) consisting of program *text* and *metatext*. The text is the program proper, its source code and comments. The metatext is the body of supporting texts and illustrations that augment, describe, clarify, and explain the text.

A more elaborate concept of a program publication can be formulated in terms of the concepts of *primary text*, *secondary text*, and *tertiary text*:

• Primary text includes what typically appears in a program listing: the program's source code and comments.

• Secondary text is metatext that augments the primary text directly on the program listing pages. Examples of secondary text are headers, footnotes, and annotations. These typically are *metadata* describing the context in which the program is used, and short *commentaries* (some mechanically produced) pointing out salient features of the program.

• Tertiary text is metatext appearing on pages that supplement the program pages. Tertiary text is the source of additional information about the program, how it was built, and how it is to be used. Examples of tertiary text include the overview and index pages described above, as well as the longer descriptions and explanations of the program that typically are called documentation.

Program Views

More specifically, we have invented and systematized a set of *program view*s, presentations of program source text or representations computed from program source text or program execution that enrich the documentation of the source text and thereby aid the design, construction, debugging, maintenance, and understanding of the program's function, structure, and method of processing.

Each new method encapsulates essential aspects of the program's function, structure, or behavior and provides an answer to a question about the program that could reasonably be asked by an experienced programmer. Thus each technique adds richness that aids in communicating the meaning of a program to its readers and users and can help programmers in carrying out required tasks.

Baecker and Marcus propose and gives examples of twelve kinds of program views [Baecker 90a]:

• *Program source text* consists of source code, i.e., text expressed within the programming language, and comments, i.e., text written in English or some other natural language that is embedded within source code and for the most part ignored by processors of programs in that programming language.

• *Program page metadata* appear in the headers and footnotes of program pages and clarify the context in which code on a particular page is to be understood.

• *User documentation* is English prose created to help the user understand the purpose, functionality, and use of the program.

• *Program documentation* is English prose created to help the programmer understand the design and construction of the program.

• *Program introductions* are intended to help a reader of a program publication become oriented with respect to the entire series of documents. In books, such introductions are known as "front matter."

• *Program overviews* are concise textual or diagrammatic descriptions or summaries of the program's function, structure, or processing.

• *Program indices* are sorted lists of program elements organized in such a way as to facilitate reference and access to groups of "related" program elements.

• *Structured program excerpts* are presentations of fragments of program source text within the context of "surrounding" or "nearby" text, in which some text has been omitted (elided) in order that the most relevant information be displayed on the page in relative proximity to the program source fragments.

• *Program change descriptions* are presentations of program source text or fragments thereof showing how the program has changed through one or more recent revisions. This component is extremely important for large programs created by teams of people that require version management and control.

• *Program annotations* are superimpositions on pages of program source text of various metatext explaining and clarifying the program's authorship, history, function, structure, processing, problems, or other useful information. Given appropriate technology, these could include commentaries (possibly hand-written) by previous readers and/or maintainers of the software.

• *Program illustrations* are graphic presentations, e.g., charts or diagrams, that explain or clarify aspects of the program's function, structure, or processing.

• *Program animations* are dynamic program illustrations, i.e., "movies" depicting the program in execution.

To illustrate these concepts, we include as Figures 3, 4, and 5 miniature pages from our program publication prototype. The example is based on the famous Eliza program devised by Joe Weizenbaum [Weizenbaum 69]. The new implementation was written in C by Henry Spencer and modified by Alan J Rosenthal. The SEE program visualizer was used to produce listings of the source text of Eliza, which were modified only in terms of better pagination and the adding of nesting information and footnotes, features not handled automatically by SEE.

These listings were then been combined with metadata, commentaries, indices, overviews, user documentation, system documentation, and other program views to form the program book. Most of the program views began with relevant data about the sample program or its execution being produced automatically using existing or new UNIX tools and utilities. These were then processed using other tools and utilities into an appropriate TROFF or Postscript form suitable for printing. It would not be terribly difficult to automate these processes.

The examples we chose for the program book were meant to be illustrative rather than exhaustive. Numerous other kinds of documentation, such as lists of requirements and system specifications, could also have been included. The program book is organized as follows:

The book begins with introductions — tertiary text which may include, for example,
• a cover page [Baecker 90a] (p. 147, included as Fig. 3a),
• a title page (p. 149, included as 3b),
• a colophon,
• an abstract and program history page (p. 151, included as 3c),
• an authors and personalities page (p. 152, included as 3d), and
• a table of contents page (2 of 3 pages, pp. 153-154, included as 4a,b).

Chapter 1 is tertiary text that comprises the user documentation:
• a tutorial guide (first page, p. 158, included as 4c),
• a command summary, and
• a user manual.

**A Prototype Program
Publication**

Figure 3a-d. 4 miniatures of pages from a C program book. a) is the book's cover page, including the title, list of authors, and an illustration. b) is the book's title page, stating the title, authors, and publisher. c) is the abstract and program history page, providing both a summary of what the program does and a capsule history of its development. d) is the authors and personalities page, designed to acquaint readers with key individuals in the development and maintenance of the program.

Dynamic Graphics Project
University of Toronto
Toronto, Ontario, Canada

Aaron Marcus and Associates
Berkeley, California, USA

Eliza:
The Program

Henry Spencer
Alan Rosenthal
Ronald M. Baecker
Aaron Marcus
Ilona R. Posner
D. Hugh Redelmeier

(a)

---

explorer:/gmsn/flaps/sen/pb   fm   1 Jun 20:59   Revision 3.1   Page Ei / 149

Dynamic Graphics Project
University of Toronto, with
Aaron Marcus and Associates
Berkeley

Eliza: The Program   Printed 2 Jun 17:34

▮▮▮▮▮▮▮▮ **Eliza: The Program**

Subtitle	A Prototype Program Book of Henry Spencer's Implementation of Joseph Weizenbaum's Eliza Program, including a "Doctor" Script
Authors	Henry Spencer, Alan Rosenthal, Ronald M. Baecker, Aaron Marcus, Ilona R. Posner, and D. Hugh Redelmeier
Publisher	Dynamic Graphics Project Computer Systems Research Institute University of Toronto Toronto, Ontario, Canada

(b)

---

explorer:/gmsn/flaps/sen/pb   fm   7 Jul 10:12   Revision 3.1   Page Eiii / 151

Dynamic Graphics Project
University of Toronto, with
Aaron Marcus and Associates
Berkeley

Eliza: The Program   Abstract   Printed 7 Jul 12:49

Abstract

Eliza is a program that carries on a dialogue with a user and pretends to a very limited extent to understand English language input. Driven by the "Doctor" script, it tries to simulate a Rogerian therapist.

Eliza operates with a very simple keyword and pattern-matching scheme that sometimes enables it to appear to recognize significant phrases. It reuses these phrases in a dialogue, thus sometimes conveying the illusion of comprehension. Extensive or even modest use of Eliza should make apparent to even the most naive of users that one is not communicating with an intelligent entity but merely with a simple-minded and very limited automaton.

Program History

The original implementation of Eliza was done by Joseph Weizenbaum. (See Joseph Weizenbaum, "Eliza – A Computer Program for the Study of Natural Language Communication between Man and Machine," *Communications of the ACM*, Volume 9, Number 1, January 1966, pages 36 to 45.) Eliza had made a name for itself through the grapevine in the early 60's, and Weizenbaum eventually felt compelled to publish this CACM paper to explain just how simplistic it really was. He is reported to have been horrified by how readily people accept a simple imitation of intelligence as the real thing. The original was written in a Fortran-based list handling package. There have been Snobol implementations since then, and some in LISP as well.

Shapiro and Kwasny, at Indiana University, experimented with using radically different Eliza scripts as smart "help" commands. (See Stuart C. Shapiro and Stanley C. Kwasny, "Interactive Consulting via Natural Language," *Communications of the ACM*, Volume 18, Number 8, August 1975, pages 459 to 462. More details can be found in their technical report, Computer Science Technical Report #12, "Interactive Consulting via Natural Language," by Stuart C. Shapiro and Stanley C. Kwasny, Indiana University, Bloomington, June 1974.)

Interest in these notions motivated Henry Spencer to implement a new version of Eliza in C for a UNIX environment. This book presents the implementation and documentation of this version of Eliza, based on the original idea of Joseph Weizenbaum, and with further refinements of Spencer's code made by Alan J Rosenthal.

(c)

---

explorer:/gmsn/flaps/sen/pb   fm   7 Jul 10:12   Revision 3.1   Page Eiv / 152

Dynamic Graphics Project
University of Toronto, with
Aaron Marcus and Associates
Berkeley

Eliza: The Program   Authors and Personalities   Printed 7 Jul 12:49

Authors and Personalities

1   Ron Baecker directed the research that conceived of and produced this program book. Although he has been on sabbatical leave, he may be reached via baecker@dgp.toronto.edu, which will forward his mail electronically.

2   This book was designed by Aaron Marcus and Associates. Send suggestions for design improvements to Aaron Marcus and Associates, 1196 Euclid Avenue, Berkeley, California 94708-1640, or to marcus3@violet.berkeley.edu.

3   Henry Spencer, implementor of this Eliza version. You may reach Henry at (416) xxx-xxxx, or via mail to henry@zoo.toronto.edu.

4   If you have trouble with the Eliza program, call the person in charge of its maintenance, Alan J Rosenthal, at (416) xxx-xxxx, or mail to flaps@dgp.toronto.edu.

5   Joseph Weizenbaum, originator of Eliza and creator of the first implementation.

6, 7, 8, 9, 10   Need help in improving or replacing the "Doctor" script for Eliza? Call Hugh Redelmeier, Ilona Posner, or Cynthia Wong, other members of the project team, at (416) xxx-xxxx (but not before 11 a.m., please!!!), or Greg Galle or Sandra Ragan at (415) xxx-xxxx.

(d)

(a)

explorer:/gnem/flaps/xec/pb — toc — 1 Jun 19:18 — Revision 3.1 — Page Ev / 153
Dynamic Graphics Project, University of Toronto, with Aaron Marcus and Associates, Berkeley — toc — Printed 2 Jun 15:51

Table of Contents: Program Metatext

(a)

(b)

explorer:/gnem/flaps/xec/pb — doc — 1 Jun 19:54 — Revision 3.1 — Page Evi / 154
Dynamic Graphics Project, University of Toronto, with Aaron Marcus and Associates, Berkeley — doc — Printed 2 Jun 15:52

Table of Contents: Program Text

(b)

(c)

explorer:/gnem/flaps/xec/user — user — 31 May 16:59 — Revision 3.1 — Page E2 / 158
Dynamic Graphics Project, University of Toronto, with Aaron Marcus and Associates, Berkeley — Eliza: The Program — Chapter 1: User Documentation — Section 1.1: Tutorial Guide — Printed 2 Jun 15:53

Section 1.1 — Tutorial Guide

To use Eliza with its default "Doctor" script, just wait until it asks you about your problem, and type at it. Your input can be only one line, but Eliza generally will pay attention to only one sentence of each input anyway, so this isn't a hardship.

To get out of Eliza, just give it end-of-file (often expressed as control-D) or interrupt it (DEL, RUBOUT, or control-C depending on how your system is set up).

Eliza is easily confused, so don't expect miracles. In particular, this version is probably a bit simplistic compared to the one around which all the folklore has grown up.

No record of your inputs is being kept, so you can be frank with Eliza.

A Sample Dialogue with Eliza

In the following "classic" dialogue, the "Doctor" script makes Eliza look pretty good. Eliza's output is denoted with a ">", the user's input with a "<".

```
> How do you do. Please tell me your problem.
< Men are all alike.
> In what way?
< They're always bugging us about something or other.
> Can you think of a specific example?
< Well, my boyfriend made me come here.
> Your boyfriend made you come here?
< He says I'm depressed much of the time.
> I am sorry to hear you are depressed.
< It's true. I am unhappy.
> Do you think coming here will help you not to be unhappy?
< I need some help, that much seems certain.
> What would it mean to you if you got some help?
< Perhaps I could learn to get along with my mother.
> Tell me more about your family.
< My mother takes care of me.
> Who else in your family takes care of you?
< My father.
> Your father?
< You are like my father in some ways.
> What resemblance do you see?
< You are not very aggressive, but I think you don't want me to notice that.
> What makes you think I am not very aggressive?
< You don't argue with me.
> Why do you think I don't argue with you?
>
```

(c)

(d)

explorer:/gnem/flaps/xec/map — mapheader1.t — 5 Jul 12:44 — Revision 3.1 — Page E14 / 170
Dynamic Graphics Project, University of Toronto, with Aaron Marcus and Associates, Berkeley — Eliza: The Program — Chapter 2: Overviews — Section 2.1: Program Map — Printed 6 Jul 11:48

Section 2.1 — Program Map

(d)

Figure 4a-d. 4 miniatures of pages from a C program book. a) is one of the table of contents pages, describing the overall structure of the book including primary, secondary, and tertiary text. b) is one of 2 table of contents pages describing the program text, in which each file appears as a separate chapter. c) is one of the pages of user documentation, the beginning of a tutorial guide. d) is one of a set of program overviews, a program map consisting of condensations of all program source text pages. At normal size, one can see features of the program source text which are useful for orienting oneself within the text.

Figure 5a-d. 4 miniatures of pages from a C program book. a,b) are the first two pages of the program source text, typeset and printed according to the design guide described in this paper. c) is one of a set of indices into the source text, this one listing each called procedure and the name and location of every caller of that procedure. d) is the back cover of the program book, giving high-level information about the program which would be useful to those considering its acquisition.

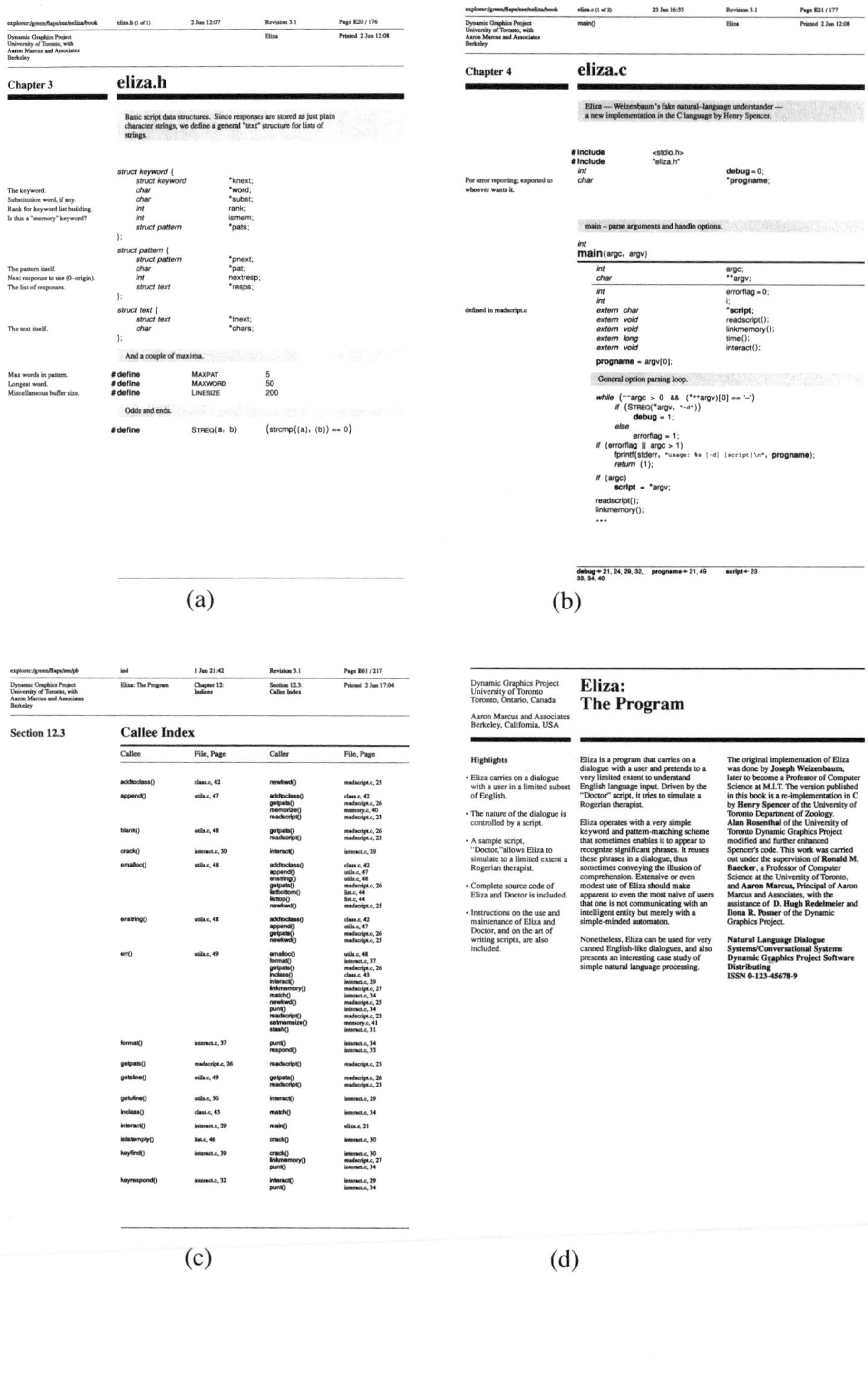

(a) Chapter 3 eliza.h

Basic script data structures. Since responses are stored as just plain character strings, we define a general "text" structure for lists of strings.

```
struct keyword {
    struct keyword   *knext;
    char             *word;     The keyword.
    char             *subst;    Substitution word, if any.
    int              rank;      Rank for keyword list building.
    int              ismem;     Is this a "memory" keyword?
    struct pattern   *pats;
};
struct pattern {
    struct pattern   *pnext;
    char             *pat;      The pattern itself.
    int              nextresp;  Next response to use (0-origin).
    struct text      *resps;    The list of responses.
};
struct text {
    struct text      *tnext;
    char             *chars;    The text itself.
};

And a couple of maxima.
#define  MAXPAT    5     Max words in pattern.
#define  MAXWORD   50    Longest word.
#define  LINESIZE  200   Miscellaneous buffer size.

Odds and ends.
#define  STREQ(a, b)  (strcmp((a), (b)) == 0)
```

(b) Chapter 4 eliza.c

Eliza — Weizenbaum's fake natural-language understander — a new implementation in the C language by Henry Spencer.

```
#include  <stdio.h>
#include  "eliza.h"
int       debug = 0;
char      *progname;     For error reporting; exported to whoever wants it.

main – parse arguments and handle options.

int
main(argc, argv)
    int    argc;
    char   **argv;

    int           errorflag = 0;
    int           i;
    extern char   *script;       defined in readscript.c
    extern void   readscript();
    extern void   linkmemory();
    extern long   time();
    extern void   interact();

    progname = argv[0];

    General option parsing loop.
    while (--argc > 0 && (*++argv)[0] == '-')
        if (STREQ(*argv, "-d"))
            debug = 1;
        else
            errorflag = 1;
    if (errorflag || argc > 1)
        fprintf(stderr, "usage: %s [-d] [script]\n", progname);
        return (1);
    if (argc)
        script = *argv;
    readscript();
    linkmemory();
    ...
```

(c) Section 12.3 Callee Index

Callee	File, Page	Caller	File, Page
addtoclass()	class.c, 42	newkwd()	readscript.c, 25
append()	utils.c, 47	addtoclass() getpats() memorize() readscript()	class.c, 42 readscript.c, 26 memory.c, 40 readscript.c, 23
blank()	utils.c, 48	getpats() readscript()	readscript.c, 26 readscript.c, 23
crack()	interact.c, 30	interact()	interact.c, 29
emalloc()	utils.c, 48	addtoclass() append() enstring() getpats() listbottom() listtop() newkwd()	class.c, 42 utils.c, 47 utils.c, 48 readscript.c, 26 list.c, 44 list.c, 44 readscript.c, 25
enstring()	utils.c, 48	addtoclass() append() getpats() newkwd()	class.c, 42 utils.c, 47 readscript.c, 26 readscript.c, 25
err()	utils.c, 49	emalloc() format() getpats() inclass() interact() linkmemory() match() newkwd() punt() readscript() setmemsize() stash()	utils.c, 48 interact.c, 37 readscript.c, 26 class.c, 43 interact.c, 29 readscript.c, 27 interact.c, 34 readscript.c, 25 interact.c, 34 readscript.c, 23 memory.c, 41 interact.c, 31
format()	interact.c, 37	punt() respond()	interact.c, 34 interact.c, 33
getpats()	readscript.c, 26	readscript()	readscript.c, 23
getsline()	utils.c, 49	getpats() readscript()	readscript.c, 26 readscript.c, 23
getuline()	utils.c, 50	interact()	interact.c, 29
inclass()	class.c, 43	match()	interact.c, 34
interact()	interact.c, 29	main()	eliza.c, 21
islistempty()	list.c, 46	crack()	interact.c, 30
keyfind()	interact.c, 39	crack() linkmemory() punt()	interact.c, 30 readscript.c, 27 interact.c, 34
keyrespond()	interact.c, 32	interact() punt()	interact.c, 29 interact.c, 34

(d) Eliza: The Program

Dynamic Graphics Project, University of Toronto, Toronto, Ontario, Canada
Aaron Marcus and Associates, Berkeley, California, USA

Highlights
- Eliza carries on a dialogue with a user in a limited subset of English.
- The nature of the dialogue is controlled by a script.
- A sample script, "Doctor," allows Eliza to simulate to a limited extent a Rogerian therapist.
- Complete source code of Eliza and Doctor is included.
- Instructions on the use and maintenance of Eliza and Doctor, and on the art of writing scripts, are also included.

Eliza is a program that carries on a dialogue with a user and pretends to a very limited extent to understand English language input. Driven by the "Doctor" script, it tries to simulate a Rogerian therapist.

Eliza operates with a very simple keyword and pattern-matching scheme that sometimes enables it to appear to recognize significant phrases. It reuses these phrases in a dialogue, thus sometimes conveying the illusion of comprehension. Extensive or even modest use of Eliza should make apparent to even the most naive of users that one is not communicating with an intelligent entity but merely with a simple-minded automaton.

Nonetheless, Eliza can be used for very canned English-like dialogues, and also presents an interesting case study of simple natural language processing.

The original implementation of Eliza was done by **Joseph Weizenbaum**, later to become a Professor of Computer Science at M.I.T. The version published in this book is a re-implementation in C by **Henry Spencer** of the University of Toronto Department of Zoology. **Alan Rosenthal** of the University of Toronto Dynamic Graphics Project modified and further enhanced Spencer's code. This work was carried out under the supervision of **Ronald M. Baecker**, a Professor of Computer Science at the University of Toronto, and **Aaron Marcus**, Principal of Aaron Marcus and Associates, with the assistance of **D. Hugh Redelmeier** and **Ilona R. Posner** of the Dynamic Graphics Project.

Natural Language Dialogue Systems/Conversational Systems
Dynamic Graphics Project Software Distributing
ISSN 0-123-45678-9

Chapter 2 contains program overviews, i.e., tertiary text such as
• a program map (p. 170, included as 4d),
• a call hierarchy,
• a function call history, and
• an execution profile.

Chapters 3 through 10 is the primary text — the program code and comments. Each program file is a separate chapter. Each program page (pp. 176-7 are included as 5a,b) has useful secondary text included in its headers and footnotes.

Chapter 11 contains the programmer documentation, i.e., tertiary text such a
• the installation guide and
• the maintenance guide.

Chapter 12 contains indices, e.g., tertiary text in the form of
• a cross-reference index,
• a caller index, and
• a callee index (one page, p. 217, is included as 5c).

The last miniature is the back cover page (p. 220, included as 5d).

Although our example is shown in paper, a program publication would clearly be more useful if it were an *electronic book*. Information should be interactively computed, generated, and presented (and perhaps then printed) upon demand, based on requests and specifications from the user [Small 89]. This will aid programmers in obtaining maximal insight from concurrently displayed representations of a program.

Significance and Accomplishments

In our research [Baecker 90a], we applied the tools of modern computer graphics technology and the visible language skills of graphic design, guided by the metaphors and precedents of literature, printing, and publishing, to suggest and demonstrate in prototype form that enduring programs should and can be made perceptually and cognitively more accessible and more usable. (See also [Oman 97], for a current review of approaches to achieving this goal.)

In carrying out this work, our goal was to make computer program source text more valuable for the programmer, that is:

• more *legible*, meaning that individual symbols comprising the program should be clearly discriminable and recognizable.

- more *readable* and *comprehensible*, meaning that we should be able to read a text with greater speed and deeper understanding.
- more *vivid*, meaning that the text should be able to stimulate our thoughts and our imagination.
- more *appealing*, so that we enjoy and appreciate the experience.
- more *memorable*, so that we are better able to recognize and recall what we have read.
- more *useful*, in terms of such common programmer tasks as scanning, navigating, manipulating, posing hypotheses and answering questions, debugging, and maintaining the program.

At first glance, it may have seemed that we are talking only about work on "prettyprinting". (see Chapter 2 by Baecker) Our work, however, goes significantly beyond conventional approaches to prettyprinting in several ways:

- The availability of rich typographic and pictorial representations with many more degrees of freedom changes the nature of the problem to one that is *qualitatively different* from that of prettyprinting on a line printer.
- We have identified basic graphic design principles for program visualization and developed a framework for applying them to programming languages.
- We have systematically carried out graphic design experimental variations in order to arrive at a carefully considered set of design guidelines and recommended conventions for program appearance.
- We have formalized these guidelines and specifications in a graphic design manual for C program appearance.
- We have developed a flexible experimental tool, the SEE *visual compiler*, which automates the production of enhanced C source text. SEE is highly parametric, thus allowing easy experimentation in trying out novel variations, and also suiting the great variety of style preferences that characterizes the community of programmers.
- Finally, we have enlarged the scope of the study of program printing from the narrow issue of formatting source code and comments to a far broader concern with programs as technical publications. This includes an investigation of methods for designing, typesetting, printing, and publishing integrated bodies of program text and metatext, and also the invention of new displays of essential program structure, called *program views*, designed to help programmers master software complexity. In the spirit of [Knuth 84], *Human Factors and*

Typography for More Readable Programs helps to establish programming as a literary form deserving a mature graphic appearance.

Acknowledgments

Many people, all acknowledged in detail on pp. xiii-xiv of [Baecker 90a], contributed to this research. We are especially grateful to Michael Arent, Ilona Posner, Hugh Redelmeier, and Alan J Rosenthal for their competent and dedicated work on this project, and to the US Defense Department's Advanced Research Projects Agency and to Canada's Natural Sciences and Engineering Research Council for financial support.

Visualizing Graph Models of Software

Chapter 5

Stephen North

Automatic graph layout is one of the most common and practical forms of software visualization. It is a key component in many common commercial programming environments. There are several reasons why graph drawing has succeeded in this domain.

• Graphs are suitable models for software. Large programs are extremely complex, consisting of many thousands of interrelated objects. Abstraction is a powerful technique for managing such complexity. Graphs are well-understood models in many domains for representing relationships between abstract objects. There is a strong theoretical foundation for approaching many problems formulated in terms of graph properties.

• Graphs models of software are available. Effective analysis and abstraction tools for extracting graph models from source code have been created for most common programming languages. Graphs can also be generated from dynamic execution logs and traces. So it is usually not too difficult to obtain graph models of software. This offers good prospects for automated visualization.

• Graph diagrams are informative. Visualization can be a powerful aid to understanding the global structure of graphs. As evidence, graph drawing has a long history of prior art in hand-made software engineering design diagrams. Relevant examples include diagrams of flow-charts, function calls, data flows and dependencies, type inheritance, finite state machines, Petri nets, software processes and work flow models, and database schemas. New visual formalisms

Introduction

based on graphs have also been proposed. Harel's StateCharts are an outstanding example [Harel 88].

• Effective visualization techniques have been invented. Research has yielded effective algorithms for some important families of graph layouts: hierarchies, orthogonal drawings and forced-based (spring) models[DiBattista 94], as described below. These techniques have been incorporated in practical systems[Rowe 87] [Paulish 90] [Himsolt 89] [North 94]. These domain-independent techniques may be applied in many settings.

Graph Drawing Techniques

In any setting, effective visualization should reveal patterns in underlying data but hide irrelevant details and avoid misleading display artifacts. This suggests that *making readable diagrams is the central problem* in graph-based software visualization. Clever GUI design cannot compensate for bad diagrams. Of course some layout styles are more appropriate than others for specific tasks, depending on the patterns or relationships being sought.

Difficulty arises because optimal graph layout is intractable for many reasonable definitions of "optimal." Properties pertinent to effective visualization, including minimizing edge crossings and bends in edges, minimizing total layout area, finding layouts with short edges or emphasizing symmetry are computationally infeasible. Even worse, these properties may conflict. So we need to prioritize aesthetic properties. Also, we may be forced to settle for heuristics instead of exact solutions.

The computer science theory community has made substantial progress in characterizing properties of a graph drawings and drawing algorithms. In practice, though, three particularly effective families of layout heuristics stand out:

• hierarchical layout of trees and DAGs (directed acyclic graphs)

• orthogonal layouts of planar and general graphs

• virtual physical (spring) models

Hierarchical layouts of directed acyclic graphs emphasize dependence between objects by ranking nodes, or assigning them to discrete levels, so that edges are aimed somewhat uniformly, *e.g.* from top to bottom. This makes it easy to find sources and sinks and to trace directed paths. Graphs containing cycles can also be drawn by reversing enough edges to break all cycles. (Though it seems attractive to try to minimize the number of reversed edges, we have found in practice it is better instead to preserve natural "source" nodes implied by the input file order.) Successive heuristic layout passes adjust node and edge placement to avoid crossings and keep edges short and straight (avoiding bends) [Sugiyama 81]. Some system draw edges as polylines; others including ours use smooth splines following the rationale that it is desirable to avoid unnecessary visual discontinuities.

Undirected graphs can be drawn by virtual physical modeling [Fruchterman 91] [Frick 95]. The origin of this technique can be traced to force-directed modeling for printed circuit layout pioneered in the 1960s [Fisk 67]. The idea is to interpret the input graph to be drawn as a physical system. Nodes may be treated as "ions" that repel, while edges impose an attractive force on their endpoints. When a suitable physical model is chosen, layouts can have the desirable property that geometric distance between two nodes tends toward their logical path distance in the graph. Unfortunately, optimizing placement of objects in complex N-body systems is computationally expensive. A practical approach is to make some simplifying assumptions (such as modeling nodes as points), and to employ heuristic solvers. Many solvers operate by setting some reasonable initial placement for nodes (random, or perhaps embedded in a tree determined by a straightforward graph search), then iteratively improve the solution by applying the simulated forces exerted on nodes until a local minimum is achieved. This approach has the benefit that it works on any graph (not just certain restricted class such as planar graphs). It often yields good layouts of sparse graphs. Unfortunately, it is also easy to find denser example graphs that yield incomprehensible layouts.

Orthogonal layouts have edge routes constrained to 90-degree bends, and are usually integer grid-aligned as well. These are well-studied and practical techniques have been discovered [Tamassia 90]. On the one hand there is ample precedent in manually-drawn diagrams in this style (for example, entity-relational data models and electrical circuit diagrams [Batini 84].) On the other hand it is not clear whether the 90-degree bend constraint contributes to effective visualization (particularly on raster displays where aliasing artifacts should be avoided) or whether it serves mainly to make the layout problem tractable. In any case, good results have been achieved on orthogonal drawing of planar, degree-constrained graphs, and substantial progress has also been made on drawing general graphs.

An Example Software Visualization System

We have several years' experience in applying the *dot* system to software visualization, working with dozens of AT&T software developers, and less closely with a wider audience at several hundred external sites. The system scales well and is robust and portable across most Unix and Microsoft Windows platforms. It has a convenient assortment of graphical symbols and an extendible graphical user interface that enables constructing higher-level visualization systems.

Our system consists of several programs:

• libgraph - a base library including file I/O for graph programming
• *dot* - a directed graph layout program [North 91] [North 93].
• neato - a spring embedder compatible with *dot* [North 92].
• *dotty*, a programmable graph viewer written in a graphical scripting language [Koutsofios 91].
• graph stream filters for preprocessing large graphs to be visualized. For example, *tred* applies a transitive reduction algorithm to remove edges in dense graphs; *sccmap* decomposes graphs into strongly connected components; *gpr* selects nodes or edges by predicate expression, and optionally contracts paths or subgraphs.

We have applied *dot* to several practical software visualization problems, as described below.

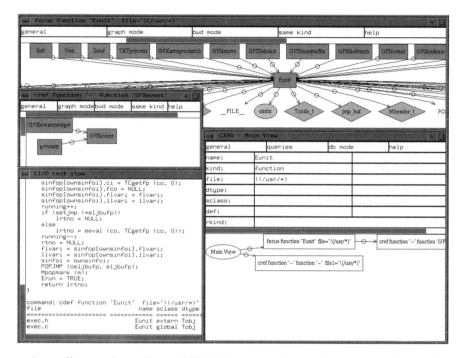

Figure 1. CIAO.

• According to its authors, "*CIAO* is a graph-based navigator that helps programmers query and browse structural connections embedded in different software and document repositories. *Ciao* supports repositories organized in an architecture style called Aero, which exploits the duality between a class of entity-relationship (ER) databases and directed attributed graphs (DAGs). Database queries and graph analysis operators in Aero are plug-compatible because they all take an ER database and produce yet another ER database by default. Various presentation filters generate graph views, source views, and relational views from any compatible ER database. The architecture promotes the construction of successively more complex operators using a notion of virtual database pipelines. *Ciao* has been instantiated for C and C++ program databases, and program difference databases. The latter allows programmers to explore program structure changes by browsing and expanding graphs that highlight changed, deleted, and added entities and relationships. The unifying ER model under *CIAO* also allows users to navigate different software repositories and make necessary connections. We have linked program difference databases and modification request (MR) databases so that users can investigate the connections between MRs and affected entities." [Chen 95]

Figure 2. LDBX.

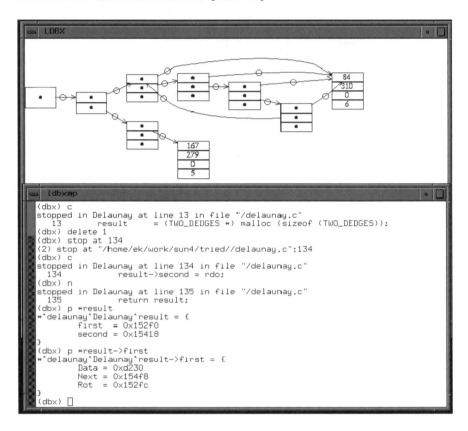

• *LDBX* is an interactive front end for the standard text-based debugger *dbx*. It provides a terminal window for ordinary text debugging commands, and a graphics window for data structure displays drawn as graphs. The user may select pointer fields to be traced as a means of controlling the size of the displayed graph.

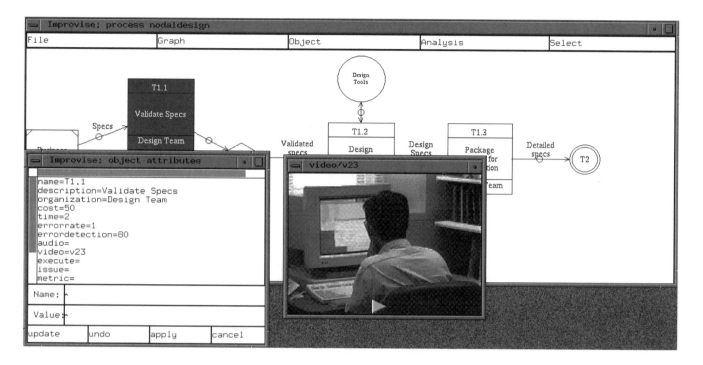

• *Improvise* is a software process modeling tool created by Barghouti, Koutsofios and Cohen. They state, "Improvise is a multimedia system for modeling, visualizing and documenting software and business processes. Improvise provides facilities for drawing multi-layered process flow diagrams and graphical information models, and annotating the nodes and edges of the diagrams with multimedia information and executable attachments. The layout of the diagrams is computed automatically to minimize edge crossings and to reflect dependency among process steps and data types. The set of node shapes used to create process flow diagrams and information models is customizable. Each node and edge in the diagram is treated as an object with a customizable set of attributes that can be assigned values interactively. The expected steady-state behavior of a process can be computed from these attributes. Improvise is an open system that can be easily connected to other tools, such as process simulation and performance analysis tools. It has already been integrated with the process support environment *Marvel* as part of the implementation of the Provence architecture." [Barghouti 95]

Figure 3. Improvise.

• *VPM*, (Visual Process Monitor) displays distributed programs as compound graphs. Processes and their resources are drawn as nodes with various shapes and colors. Hosts are represented as clusters. Trace data from system calls is captured by a shared library and written to a network socket set up by VPM. Graph displays in VPM are extremely dynamic. We cope with this by batching updates, but efficient incremental layout algorithms might aid more effective visualization of such dynamic systems.

These examples illustrate that effective graph drawing tools can provide an important foundation for novel software visualization systems. Figures 1-4 are snapshots of these systems.

Current Trends

Ongoing research in graph drawing algorithms and systems concerns several areas important to software visualization.

User Interfaces and Cognitive Issues What visual formalisms are appropriate to graph visualization? What interaction modes and features in browsers make it easier to navigate within and understand the structure of large, complicated graphs?

3D layout. What are good ways to draw graphs in 3D? Are 3D representations worth the increased layout and user interface complexity?

Undirected graphs. How can better, more understandable layouts be made efficiently? As mentioned, most virtual physical model solvers assume that nodes are drawn as points and edges as straight lines. This is not fully satisfactory in practice when nodes are drawn as shapes or icons, they can unintentionally touch each other and non-adjacent edges. Layouts with such defects are not only inferior to good hand-made drawings, they can even be misleading. Techniques such as "cluster busting" [Lyons 92] may solve these problems, but more implementation experience is needed.

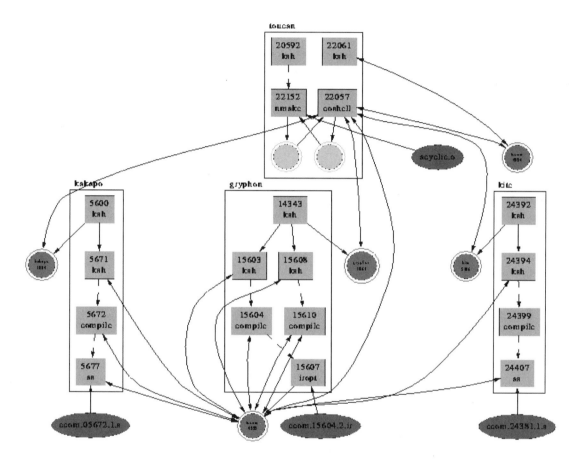

Figure 4. VPM.

Dynamic layout. How should drawings be adjusted incrementally when underlying graphs change? Can this be done efficiently when the rate of updates is high? Is dynamic layout a good way to browse extremely large graphs? If stability is interpreted as imposing weak constraints on node and edge placement, can user-driven hints and constraints be accommodated within a common algorithmic framework?

Hybrid representations and higher-order graphs. More sophisticated graph models that incorporate mixed directed and undirected edges, hyper-edges, and higher-order objects are employed in some software engineering and data models. How can these more complex structures be visualized? Some recent research suggests starting points [Sugiyama 91].

Tool and Task Integration. Visualization is one of many services that an effective software engineering system should provide. It should fit well into the global user interface architecture. Rather than build a graph visualization system "along side" of a programming system, there is an opportunity to combine it with other visualization tools that provide consistent access to underlying data or knowledge bases. Standards such as Microsoft OLE, CORBA, and OpenDoc address client-server interfaces and integrated multi-component documents, and thus seem pertinent to graph visualization services.

Acknowledgments

The author thanks David Belanger, director of AT&T's Network Service's Laboratory, and Ken Church, head of Information Analysis and Display Research, for supporting research in software and information visualization. The author also particularly thanks Naser Barghouti, Robin Chen, Emden Gansner, Eleftherios Koutsofios and Phong Vo for stimulating technical collaborations.

A Menagerie of Program Visualization Techniques

Chapter

6

Clinton L. Jeffery

Introduction

A good software visualization environment augments conventional textual techniques with graphics that present information to the user more effectively. In order for graphical techniques to yield better results than conventional techniques, they must present information that is relevant, filter and prioritize information presented, and employ a graphic design that is easily interpreted.

This chapter describes and characterizes the performance of a number of visualization techniques that are well-suited to exploratory situations in which the behavior(s) of interest are not necessarily known in advance. Many of the techniques described in this chapter were originally developed in the Icon programming language using the Alamo execution monitoring framework [Griswold 96] [Jeffery 94]. The emphasis is on techniques that are readily implemented and provide rapid animated feedback, rather than on the sorts of complex graphics that provide nice static images but are difficult to program and even more difficult to put in motion. The following section provides the rationale for this emphasis on simple, animated visualization techniques.

Motivation and Design Principles

The principles of graphic design form a basis for the evaluation and selection of all visualization techniques. It is not worth implementing elaborate graphics if the graphic design does not convey information clearly. Some of these principles may be self-evident, such as abstracting away irrelevant detail; other principles are not so obvious, but are learned by experience. Two of the best references on graphic design are by Tufte [Tufte 83], [Tufte 90]. One of the strongest constraints on graphic design imposed by visualization is the low resolution of current display devices compared with the resolution available in printed graphics. Even when displays become capable of typesetting resolution, the necessity for interactive selection of elements within the displayed graphics limits resolution in exploratory tools.

Visualization does impose additional constraints on graphic design; the different types of software visualization that have been identified have differing requirements. Several papers have characterized these differences or developed taxonomies that describe them [Myers 86], [Eisenstadt 90b], [Stasko 92c], [Price 93], [Roman 93].

Although software visualization plays by the same graphic design rules as other information presentation tasks, visualization of *dynamic* execution behavior such as run-time control flow or memory usage is different from visualization of a large, relatively static data set in several key ways. These differences motivate the techniques presented in the rest of the chapter. They may be summarized in the following basic principles:

Animation

The ability to depict temporal relationships by animating dynamic behavior is a crucial tool. Effective animations can be produced by changing object position, structure, shape, or appearance. There are trade-offs between visual sophistication and the associated computational cost.

Metaphors

A familiar or readily-inferred visual metaphor for the behavior being presented can lower the cognitive load imposed on the user and increase the rate of comprehension. Although some metaphors are drawn naturally from a specific application domain, others are drawn from nature or from nontechnical symbols found in daily life.

Interconnection

Understanding a complex piece of software entails an understanding of a variety of distinct behaviors and the relationships between them. For example, control flow, data structures, memory allocation behavior, and input/output all have distinct but interrelated patterns in program execution. Visualizations that consume most or all of the screen do not allow for simultaneous display of other forms of execution behavior.

Interaction

Visualizations are more effective when the user can steer them in appropriate directions. A graphic design used in visualization should allow for natural interactive controls, an issue not addressed by designs based in print media.

Dynamic scale

The scale imposed in the depiction of dense information on a computer screen is extreme, but in addition, the scales are highly dynamic. If the scale does not change dynamically, a visualization wastes space and loses detail over a large part of the execution being observed. On the other hand, changing scale too frequently is both computationally expensive and disorienting. Logarithmic scales are one answer to this problem, but they are not always appropriate and typically need to be tuned to the size of the execution being observed.

Classical graphic design techniques used in print media vary in their suitability for visualization. Scatterplots, for example, animate easily and allow high information density, but do not lend themselves particularly to interaction, unless the plotted points are drawn to a scale that is easily selectable. Histograms, bar charts, and pie charts allow relatively easy animation and interaction but show a relatively small amount of information.

Structure-oriented techniques utilize the mental models of the programmers who develop the code under study. Appropriate views of arrays, linked-lists, or trees may be adapted and reused to visualize broad classes of applications that employ similar structures. Several early SV systems employed structure-oriented techniques, such as Incense [Myers 83].

This section presents several alternative techniques for drawing trees. Traditional graphic designs for trees, such as the one shown in figure 1 based on an algorithm in [Moen 90] allocate most of the screen space to the structure of the

Figure 1. A traditional depiction of a tree structure.

Structure-oriented Techniques

tree and emphasize aesthetics over the amount of information to be presented at each node. Scalability to large trees is limited, and it is difficult and computationally expensive to maintain an aesthetic layout when the tree undergoes rapid changes.

The opposite extreme is exemplified by graphic designs such as the tree-map, a relative of the Venn diagram [Johns 91]. Tree-maps allocate minimal space to the structural information and maximal space to the nodes themselves. The first tree-map shown in figure 2 depicts a tree of depth 3. The root, outmost rectangle has five children laid out horizontally with a width proportional to their size. The next generation is laid out vertically; the first, third, and fifth of these children have two children as leaf nodes, while the second and fourth children have three and four leaf children respectively. For trees of greater depth, successive generations alternate between horizontal and vertical layout. The second tree-map (figure 3) depicts a large tree that corresponds to an entire filesystem with hundreds of files in many directories. For the depiction of very large trees, tree-maps have much better scalability than conventional techniques.

The tree-map algorithm allocates space for the nodes of the tree as a hierarchy of containers in which each parent node contains its children, similar to a Venn diagram. Within each parent, space for children is allocated proportional to each child's weight, which in turn is a sum of the child's descendants weights plus the child's own value. Given these criterion for allocating space, the primary remaining goal is to retain some legible semblance of the hierarchical structure. One solution is to alternate horizontal and vertical slicing so that each level within the tree is distinct. Like many conventional layouts, dynamic views using tree-maps are computationally expensive for trees with rapidly changing structure, since changes in one part of the tree affect the amount of space allocated to other parts of the tree.

Fundamentally, it will not always be possible to show all structural details with a nice appearance and smooth motion. These problems lead to compromise techniques that sacrifice details within the structure in order to provide smooth animation. Algae (figure 4) is a metaphor that displays general characteristics of a tree (height, width) and preserves most of the screen-space for detailed node information, at the expense of actual parent-child relationships. It allows easy incremental updates as the tree changes and is designed for animations in which

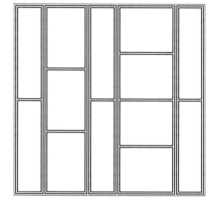

Figure 2. A tree-map.

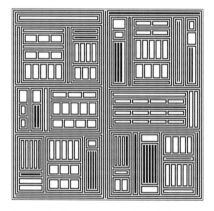

Figure 3. Tree-maps scale well for large structures.

parent-child relations can be conveyed temporally by highlighting related nodes as the tree-structure changes. It is designed to augment conventional layout techniques, not replace them; for example, algae might be used for animations, and full tree structure might be superimposed whenever the visualization is paused for detailed inspection.

Algae's geometry consists of a two-dimensional grid of cells; tree nodes are allocated cells starting from the upper left corner. A hexagonal grid is employed rather than a cartesian grid in order to reduce area discontinuities along diagonals. As a simple solution to the problem of tree animation, Algae's primary role is to serve as a template for applications that display quantities of information within tree nodes. A simple application might simply color-code tree nodes by their node type, while more sophisticated visualizations utilize each cell as its own, miniature visualization area.

One fundamental problem with many graphic designs is that they have no intuitive interpretation, and the user must be trained in order to understand them. Metaphors found in nature or in the real world avoid this by providing a graphic design that the user already understands. For example, the "desktop metaphor" utilized in many user interfaces reduces the amount of training and memorization required in order to operate personal computers. Both the term "tree" and the most common depictions of hierarchical structure rely on an analogy to nature; another example of utilizing a metaphor from nature is the cartographer's choice of colors to depict elevations on a map. The use of color to depict numeric values in a visualization is problematic, because the human eye does not perceive changes in hue as a linear progression through the visible spectrum. Rather than make up an ad-hoc sequence of colors that requires memorization, cartographers often use a progression that ostensibly corresponds to the colors found in the land and the foliage at various elevations, from snowy white mountaintops to brown mountains to yellow plains to green lowlands to deepening blue shades for underwater elevations. Although this mapping of numbers onto colors is far from ideal, for the visualization author it provides at least one color scale that many users will interpret without training due to their prior experience reading maps.

The tree-ring, shown in figure 5, provides an example of a nature-based metaphor with a strong temporal component in the form of a chronological sequence of

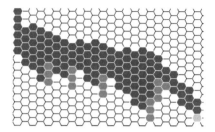

Figure 4. An algae view omits details but preserves overall characteristics in rapidly changing structures.

Metaphors Found in Nature and in the Real World

Figure 5. A tree-ring view shows the history of a program's memory usage.

circular bands. Thicker bands indicate more activity within a given time span. More recent activity naturally receives more screen-space due to larger radii. And extraordinary events can leave behind marks in the same way that a forest fire leaves a mark on a tree. For example, a tree-ring memory monoitor might use black rings to indicate garbage-collections; multiple black rings close together create a vivid image of thrashing problems in the memory management system.

Graphic designs based around circles such as the tree-ring discussed above have many intrinsic advantages. For large, symmetric information spaces, space utilization may be more efficient when plotting is done around a center point, illustrated by comparing the large classical tree shown earlier with the circular tree shown here. Circular trees (figure 6) laid out in a hyperbolic geometry can provide an especially attractive appearance [Lamping 94]. The mapping from hyperbolic space onto a 2D picture provides a natural fisheye view; circular views in general lend themselves to symmetric images with a natural center of attention suitable for fisheye techniques [Furnas 86].

When cartesian coordinates x and y are exchanged for polar coordinates r (radius) and t (theta, the angle), sequences plotted along the t axis wrap around naturally, allowing replacement of previously-drawn data by newer information in a style reminiscent of a radar-sweep.

The nova visualization shown in figure 7 on the left employs a simple radar-sweep metaphor to animate a large sequence of elements that have a primary numeric component [Griswold 94]. For each element, the primary component is depicted by ray length radiating from the center point. Secondary information may be depicted using color, linewidth, or linestyle. Successive elements are plotted at successive angles around the circle, and the view wraps around naturally, erasing old elements after 2 * Pi radians are consumed.

Radial Views

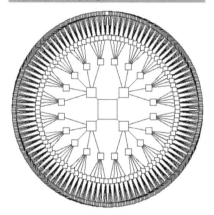

Figure 6. A circular tree uses space more effectively than a traditional layout.

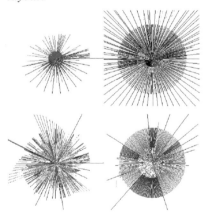

Figure 7. Nova views of individual memory allocations.

One application of nova has been the visualization of individual memory allocations, in which each segment's length indicates a number of bytes allocated, while color indicates the data type (structure, array, etc) allocated. This application of nova has been successful in drawing attention to anomalous behavior associated with performance bugs, such as the repeated copying shown by the spirals in the lower left figure. The upper and lower right images show before and after views of a program for which nova revealed that an inefficient use of list concatenation was taking place.

Another novel radial view is the kaleidoscope view shown in figure 8. The primary spiral axis allows more distinct values to be plotted in a square region than would be possible even in a long rectangular region plotted in 2-d cartesian coordinates. Kaleidoscope visualizations have been used to summarize the entire execution of a parallel program [Tick 91]. They work best when the extent of the primary axis is known in advance, so that the scale to be plotted can be determined.

Standard techniques for presenting information graphically have the advantage of familiarity, but may not lend themselves to the rapidly changing views that are needed in visualization of dynamic program behavior. The best visualization technique for a given domain of program behavior may entail an innovative graphic design in order to achieve visual clarity without an unacceptable penalty in runtime speed. When no one technique has the necessary characteristics, a combination of techniques may be used.

Figure 8. Spiral axes allow long sequences to remain intact in limited space.

Summary

Fundamental Techniques for Algorithm Animation Displays

Marc H. Brown
and
John Hershberger

Designing an enlightening software visualization is a tricky psychological and perceptual challenge. What information should be presented? How should it be arranged, in space and in time? What will help the viewer to notice patterns? And how can different perspectives be tied together?

Software visualization introduces problems that "classical" graphic designers do not face. Screens are smaller (especially when partitioned into multiple views) and have much lower resolution than paper. Screen views are dynamic; paper diagrams are not. Multiple views of software must be united and consistent, yet not interfere with each other; traditional graphic design is typically concerned with a single picture. Finally, displays must be robust enough to handle many different sets of data, not necessarily known in advance. This contrasts with static graphic designs, which can be tuned to a particular data set.

This chapter discusses the fundamental techniques for creating algorithm animations that have been reported in the literature. The first part of this chapter reviews the techniques developed by Brown and Sedgewick [Brown 85a] in the mid-1980s using the BALSA algorithm animation system in Brown University's "electronic classroom" (see Chapter 25). The second part describe techniques we developed that focus on color [Brown 92]; those techniques are based on five years working with the Zeus algorithm animation system [Brown 91]. The techniques described in this chapter have not been formally evaluated; see Section VII for information about evaluation of software visualization.

Although the techniques described in this chapter evolved in the context of BALSA and Zeus, they are nevertheless independent of those systems. They can be applied directly to other algorithm animation systems. They are also relevant to most other software visualization systems mentioned in this book.

This chapter contains screen dumps from six different algorithm animations developed using Zeus. Of course, static images, printed in black-and-white, cannot do justice to interactive color animations, but hopefully the extensive figure captions provide enough information about the algorithms for you to imagine their dynamics.

As we discuss a topic, we illustrate the issues by referring to all relevant figures. Because the remainder of this chapter refers extensively to the figures, we recommend that you scan the figures and captions before proceeding.

Basic Techniques

Multiple views

A monolithic view concentrates all the information about an algorithm into a single dynamic image. Monolithic views are successful for simple algorithms, such as quicksort in Figure 1a. However, a monolithic view of a complicated algorithm, or of multiple aspects of even a simple algorithm, must encode so much information that the user quickly runs into difficulty picking out the details of interest on the screen. It is generally more effective to use several different views to illustrate an algorithm.

For the most part, our animations use multiple views, each displaying only a few aspects of the algorithm. Each view is easy to comprehend in isolation, and the composition of several views is more informative than the sum of their individual contributions. The hashing animation in Figure 2b and the polygon decomposition animation in Figure 3a exemplify this approach.

Another benefit of using multiple views is that they are usually conceptually simpler and easier to implement. This encourages the animator to experiment with different views and abandon those that don't seem effective.

State cues

Animators can show changes in the state of an algorithm's data structures by changing their graphical representations on the screen. For example, in the quicksort partition trees of Figure 1b, a node is round while its associated subfile is being sorted, then changes to square when that subfile is finished.

State cues reflect an algorithm's dynamic behavior. In Figures 1b and 1c of the quicksort animation, horizontal boxes represent unsorted subfiles of elements. When a subfile is partitioned, the animation replaces its box by a tree node at the splitting element with two smaller boxes as children. Watching the boxes split and the tree develop gives a dynamic sense of the way the algorithm works.

Finally, state cues link different views together by representing specific objects the same way in every view. The examples in this chapter use color, rather than other graphical techniques, for this purpose.

Static history

A static view of an algorithm's history and data structures helps explain the algorithm much like a textbook example. Such a view lets users become familiar with the algorithm's dynamic behavior at their own speed. It also lets them focus on the crucial events where significant changes occur, without paying too much attention to repetitive events.

For example, the view at the top of the hashing animation in Figure 2c records the history (moving from left to right) of the dynamic hash tables in Figure 2b. The algorithm's significant events are table rehashings, and the animation makes them clearly visible as sharp discontinuities in the historical record.

Figure 3a also displays static histories. The Formula view (bottom right) shows the development of a Boolean formula over time as the algorithm adds parentheses and operators to it. The CSG Parse Tree view on the left displays the planar region corresponding to every subformula ever constructed during the algorithm's execution.

Continuous versus discrete transitions

The graphic representation of a change to a data structure can be either incremental or discrete. Incremental change is most helpful for small data sets. For example, when two dots exchange places in the sorting animation of Figure 1a, the exchange is easier to see as a smooth transition instead of an abrupt erase-and-repaint. For large enough amounts of data, small discrete changes look smooth, and "in-betweening" would not generate noticeably smoother motion. See Chapter 8 for more information.

Multiple algorithms

Running several algorithms simultaneously lets a user compare and contrast them readily. For example, Figures 1c, 3c, 4c, and 5b show multiple algorithms.

Algorithm animation systems vary widely in the support they provide for this technique. Figures 3 through 6 in Chapter 12 describe how "interesting events" were used in BALSA-II for synchronizing multiple algorithms. In Zeus, algorithms are run in separate threads; when an algorithm reaches an "interesting event" that changes the display, it waits until all other algorithms have also reached "interesting events." (The figures in this chapter predate this functionality in Zeus. Hence, the algorithm "races" in Figures 1c, 3c, and 4c were done manually by running multiple instances of the application simultaneously. In Figure 5b, the comparison of algorithms is implemented within the algorithm code, also without support from Zeus.)

Input data selection

The choice of input data strongly influences the message conveyed by an animation. Brown and Sedgewick found that small amounts of data work best for introducing a new algorithm, whereas large amounts of data help develop an intuitive understanding of an algorithm's behavior. Our work with Zeus confirms this conclusion and has added new observations on the importance of choosing input data for animations.

Amount of input data

Animations that complement an algorithm's textual description should be introduced on a small problem instance, preferably with textual annotation. This helps users relate the visual displays to their previous understanding. For example, in Figure 3a, we illustrate the algorithm on a seven-vertex polygon, complete with textual labels (A-G) on all the edges and on the corresponding nodes in the Parse Tree view. Because the example is small and well labeled, the user can easily understand the connections between the views.

Once the user makes these connections, larger and more interesting data sets can be introduced to use the dynamic capabilities of animation more fully (as in

Figure 3b). We omit the labels when displaying these large problem instances, since they would clutter the screen unnecessarily.

Pathological data

Choosing pathological data can push the algorithm to extreme behavior. For example, in the polygon-decomposition animation, we ran the algorithm using both perfectly convex polygons and tight spirals as input. Each input produced a characteristic parse tree (balanced or skewed). Armed with this understanding, users could easily pick out the unbalanced subtrees of the parse tree corresponding to the spirals of the input polygon when the algorithm was run on less contrived data, as in Figure 3b.

In the sweepline animation of Figure 4c, we chose a regular pattern of lines (tangents to a parabola) to understand how different implementations of the algorithm work. The regular arrangement reveals the algorithm's structure better than the more chaotic example of Figure 4b.

In fact, running the polygon-decomposition animation on regular data was instrumental in discovering a subtle bug in the algorithm's implementation, as mentioned in the caption for Figure 3c. A perfectly convex polygon as input should have generated a perfectly balanced tree, not merely a well-balanced tree. This bug had gone unnoticed in the non-pathological input polygons we had been using.

Cooked data

Figure 2 on multilevel adaptive hashing presents another example of choosing data for pedagogical purposes. The hashing algorithm of that animation is so effective that rehashings almost never occur in practice. To make the animation more interesting and instructive, we stacked the deck, so to speak, by filtering out some of the randomness in the input data. The "crippler" filter, whose control interface is shown in the Data box of Figure 2a, runs in a separate thread. It selects input data that hash into a fixed subset of each hash table, thereby ensuring enough collisions to force rehashings.

Color Techniques

Color has the potential to communicate a tremendous amount of information efficiently. This goal, however, is not easy to achieve. Graphics theorists, most notably Jacques Bertin [Bertin 81][Bertin 83] and Edward Tufte [Tufte 83][Tufte 90], offer excellent advice on the pragmatics and pitfalls of using color (and, in general, of displaying data graphically). We have tried to follow their principles, although the psychology of color in enhancing communication is beyond the scope of this chapter.

We use color in five distinct ways: encoding the state of data structures, highlighting activity, tying views together, emphasizing patterns, and making history visible.

The first two uses are common in many other algorithm animation systems. In fact, these fundamental uses of color date back to some of the earliest work in algorithm animation — movies such as Booth's *PQ Trees* [Booth 75] and Baecker's *Sorting Out Sorting* (see Chapter 24).

Encoding the state of data structures

In the parallel quicksort algorithm (see Figures 1a and 1b), the colors of dots and blocks indicate the partition of the elements among the sorting processors. In Figure 2b, a colored band around the hash table indicates the current hash function; the band changes color when a new hash function is chosen. In Figures 5a and 5b, bars are colored magenta and green to show when the algorithm is spinning and when it is blocking. In Figure 6b of the robot algorithm, green, pink, and gray indicate the suitability of different starting points for robot motion. In Figure 6c, pink and light blue distinguish the algorithm's two key data structures, which are otherwise similar in appearance.

As an indicator of an algorithm's state, color enhances and complements the graphical techniques described earlier. It gives an extra dimension for state display: Information is conveyed by both the shape and the color of objects. It allows denser presentation of information: Fewer pixels are needed to give an object a distinct color than to give it a distinct shape: hence, more objects can be displayed at one time. Color also displays global patterns very effectively. For example, perceiving global patterns when a monochromatic group of small triangles changes to a monochromatic mixture of circles and squares is much harder than seeing the patterns when a group of black dots changes to a mixture of red and blue dots.

Highlighting activity

Many animations temporarily paint a small region with a transparent, contrasting color to focus attention on the painted area. Because the highlight color is transparent, it does not interfere visually with the data elements on the screen, but simply draws the eye to them. For example, in Figure 3a, the active polygon edge C is highlighted in brown.

Highlighting is also used to display transient computations without permanently altering the on-screen state. In Figure 3b, the convex hull is an essential part of the algorithm, but it changes too rapidly to belong to the relatively stable state displayed in Geometry view of Figure 3a: it would be distracting if it were always visible. Instead, it is drawn as a temporary brown highlight in a specialized Geometry (CH) view that illustrates the role of the convex hull in the algorithm. Similarly, the robot paths of Figure 6 are drawn only in highlighting when the user clicks in the view, since they don't change the underlying data structures.

The mechanism we developed for highlighting involved color-table trickery. Because a highlight is only temporary. we must be able to remove it and quickly restore the parts of the scene it had overwritten. In the absence of double buffering, we accomplish this by assigning the highlight to one bit of the eight-bit color-table index. Painting or erasing a highlight means setting or clearing that bit. The colors in the table are carefully arranged so that this gives the effect of painting with transparent color. Because each view appears in its own window installed in the window manager, the views must cooperate and use the same color table to ensure that users see the correct colors in all views simultaneously.

Figure 4 shows the use of this same highlighting technique to move the sweepline without overwriting the line arrangement below it. If we just used XOR on a standard color table. as is often done for highlighting, we would not get the uniform highlight color we want. The sweepline would be black except where it crossed lines of the arrangement, where the color would be unpredictable. (It would be based on the XOR of the color of the line that is crossed.)

Uniting multiple views

Multiple views often show different aspects of the same data structure or different representations of logically related objects. In these cases, an application can create an integrated, more harmonious picture by painting corresponding features with the same colors in all the views. The polygon-decomposition animation in Figure 3 uses blue, red, and black to denote objects that respectively have been, are being, or have not yet been processed. The animation applies this idea uniformly. Combined with the visual prominence of the color red, this makes it easy to see the connection between the active edges of the polygon and the corresponding active sites in the Formula and Parse Tree views.

The hashing animation of Figures 2b and 2c associates keys with tables by painting them the same color. In the sweepline animation in Figure 4, the edges that cross the sweepline are painted red in all the views in which the sweepline is important (see especially Figure 4a). Similarly, vertices where the sweepline can advance are marked with black disks.

Figure 5a of the spin-blocking animation uses blue, magenta, green, red, and brown consistently in all three views. This consistency makes it each to learn the "visual vocabulary" of more complex views like the Back-to-Back Stem and the VBars Superimposed from the simpler VBars view.

Emphasizing patterns

In the polygon-decomposition animation of Figure 3b, each deep subtree in the right view grows downward at the same time that the highlighted vertex in the left view runs inward along one of the spirals. The subtree and spiral colors also change in concert. The kinetic connection between the two views underlines the linkage between spirals and deep parse-tree subtrees.

Making history visible

We often use a spectrum to show an algorithm's history. Tufte warns that humans do not perceive the rainbow color sequence as ordered. Nevertheless, a sequence of colors ordered by hue can be used to represent a linear time order, especially when the regions to be painted have some spatial monotonicity. Figures 4b and 6b illustrate this point. In both cases the time order of the colored regions is roughly the same as their spatial order. Hence the viewer does not need a sense of the global color order; it is enough to perceive differences between neighbors.

Summary

Creating effective visualizations of computer programs is an art, not a science. Although the techniques in this section have not been formally evaluated or verified, they are based on extensive experience and experimentation. The other chapters in this section present additional techniques for software visualization

Acknowledgments

This chapter is based on [Brown 92] and used with permission.

Figure 1: Quicksort *See Plate 1*

Figure 1a shows three views of a naive parallel implementation of quicksort. The algorithm first partitions the elements to be sorted into two subfiles. Then the partitioning thread recursively sorts one subfile while a new thread is forked to sort the other.

The Dots (Par) *view on the right displays a dot for each element in the array being sorted. The horizontal coordinate corresponds to its position in the array, and the vertical coordinate corresponds to its value. This is undoubtedly the most famous visualization of sorting algorithms. It was developed by Ron Baecker at the University of Toronto in his seminal 1981 film,* Sorting Out Sorting *(see Chapter 24). Here, the classic view is augmented by coloring each subfile of dots with a color corresponding to the thread sorting the subfile.*

The same color is used in the Partitions *view on the left, where a rectangle is drawn each time a thread is forked. The horizontal extent of the rectangle indicates the section of the array the thread is to process, and the vertical extent indicates the values of the elements in that section.*

The small window at the top of the screen displays the number of active threads. This is the visual component of an "audio view" that represents the same information by the pitch of a tone played through the workstation's speaker. See Chapter 10.

Figure 1b presents two binary -tree views of the partitioning process. In both trees, each node represents a position in the array being sorted, and each subtree represents a subfile of elements to be sorted recursively. The subfile is partitioned into two subfiles separated by the root of the subtree. In the lower tree, the colors of nodes and edges reflect the threads assigned to partition each subfile. In the upper tree, red and blue distinguish active from inactive subfiles. While a subfile is being sorted, its node and the edge to its parent are red. These change to blue when the subfile is finished In both trees, horizontal boxes represent unexamined subfiles.

Figure 1c compares three different quicksort implementations using the red/blue tree view. The top tree shows a sequential algorithm; exactly one root-to-leaf path is active at any time. The view on the right shows the naive parallel implementation; many threads are active at once. The left view shows a more sophisticated parallel algorithm. It sorts small subfiles by insertion sort (indicated by the unexpanded boxes) and forks a new thread only when the subfile to be sorted is large enough to justify the overhead of forking.

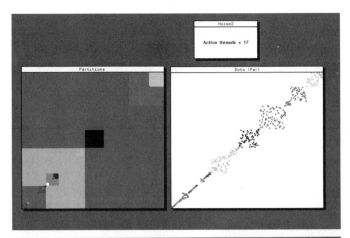

Figure 1a

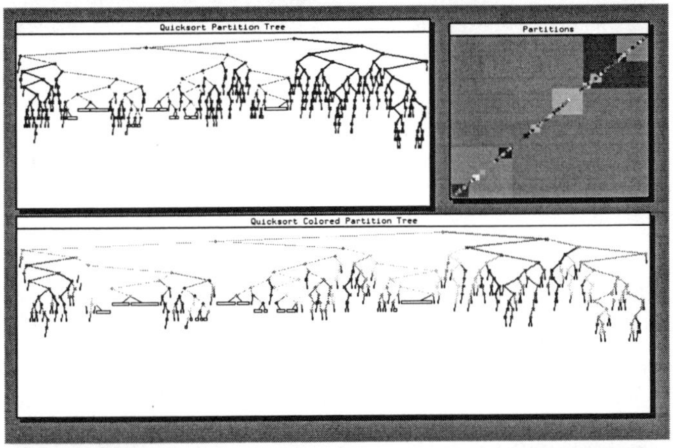

Figure 1b

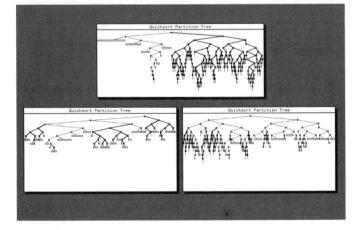

Figure 1c

Figure 2: Multilevel Adaptive Hashing

Figure 2a shows the Zeus control panel. It provides menus to select algorithms, views, and input data. The data menu can be customized to the application, as in this case; otherwise, the default menu is a browser for selecting an input file. Zeus provides a snapshot/restore capability for preserving settings between program runs. Finally, the control panel contains buttons for starting/stopping/stepping the algorithm, as well as a slider for controlling its execution speed.

Figure 2b illustrates a hashing scheme that uses multiple hash tables to store an on-line dictionary [Broder 90]. The tables are linked in a chain from left to right, so a collision in one table causes the colliding element to percolate into the next table. Each table has a percolation limit; the limit of the last table is zero. Whenever a new element collides in all tables, the algorithm rehashes any table that has exceeded its percolation limit, along with all its successors. ("Rehashing" means changing the hash function and reinserting all the table's elements.) This scheme provides constant-time lookup, provided that the hardware accesses the tables in parallel.

Elements in The Keys *view of the animation (bottom of the screen) are color-coded to indicate the tables they belong to in the* Hash Tables *view (top left). The color of the band surrounding each hash table corresponds to the hash function currently in use for that table. When an element is inserted, the animation highlights the location in each table to which it hashes.*

The two statistics views on the right show the number of percolations out of the table and the table load for each hash table. The third table has reached its percolation limit, so the third and fourth tables will be rehashed after the next all-tables collision.

The Sound Effects *view plays a table-specific tone each time an element is inserted into a hash table; it plays a "car crash" whenever an all-tables collision occurs (see Figure 5 in Chapter 10).*

Figure 2c shows the history of the hash tables over time. The four tables are stacked, and time runs form left to right. Keys are shown in their table's color code; the background color changes when the table is rehashed. In this example, the algorithm rehashed all the tables halfway through the execution: It emptied the tables and reinserted the elements one at a time. The tables were rehashed sequentially. Each table was loaded with as many noncolliding elements as possible, then the remaining elements were passed on to the next table.

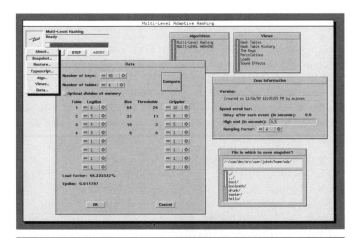

Figure 2a

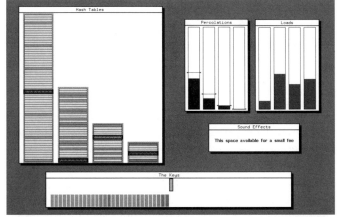

Figure 2b

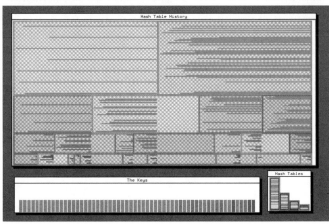

Figure 2c

Figure 3: Boolean Formulas for Simple Polygons

The interior of a simple polygon can be represented as a monotone Boolean combination of the half-planes determined by its edges. Recall that a simple polygon is a closed polygonal path free of self-intersections, and a monotone Boolean combination is a Boolean formula containing only unions ("+") and intersections (""). Negations are not allowed. Finding such a formula is a basic problem in constructive solid geometry (CSG).*

Figure 3 illustrates an algorithm that finds the formula for a given simple polygon [Dobkin 88]. The algorithm first splits the polygon at its leftmost and rightmost vertices to produce two polygonal chains, an upper chain and a lower chain. It then finds formulas for the two chains and intersects them. To find the Boolean formula for a polygonal chain, the algorithm splits the chain at a vertex on the chain's convex hull and combines the formulas that it finds recursively for the two subchains. If the two chains join at a vertex to form a convex angle, the formulas corresponding to the two chains are intersected; otherwise, the formulas are unioned.

The views in Figure 3a display the polygon itself, the Boolean formula and its development, and two versions of the parse tree corresponding to the formula. Color is used consistently in all views: Red represents the subpath of the polygon being processed, blue the parts already processed, and black the parts yet to be processed. Transparent brown highlighting focuses attention on the edge or vertex where the formula is being changed. In the CSG Parse Tree view, each node contains a representation of the (green) planar region that results from evaluating its subformula. The Parse Tree view is a compact version of the same tree that omits the CSG regions.

The parse tree is especially appropriate for large examples like the mazelike polygon in Figure 3b. This example emphasizes a strength of algorithm animation by revealing hitherto unnoticed algorithm features. The deep zigzag subtrees in the Parse Tree view correspond to the spirals of the polygon, a fact underlined by the dynamic visualization.

Figure 3c illustrates the helpfulness of graphical output in debugging. We expected the parse tree for the circle polygon to be balanced, like the one in the bottommost view. When the algorithm instead produced the parse tree in the upper view, which has leaves at four different depths, we investigated and soon turned up a subtle error in the algorithm's implementation.

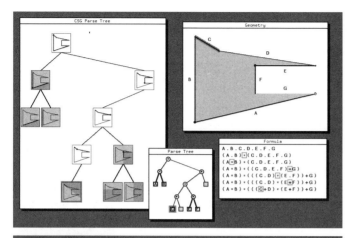

Figure 3a

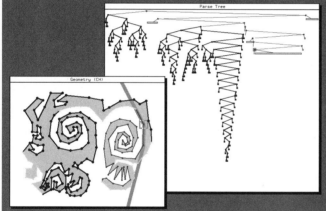

Figure 3b

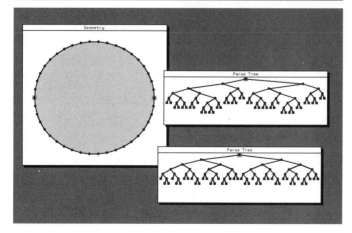

Figure 3c

Figure 4: Topological Sweepline

An ordinary sweepline is a vertical line that visits the $O(n^2)$ intersections in an arrangement of n lines in the plane by sweeping across the arrangement from left to right. Such a sweepline uses only $O(n)$ working storage, but because it sorts the intersections in x-order, it spends $O(n^2 \log n)$ time. In many cases, the sorting is unnecessary. It is enough just to visit all the intersections in any order. A topological sweepline [Edelsbrunner 86], shown in Figure 4, visits the intersections in optimal $O(n^2)$ time by sacrificing the straightness of the ordinary sweepline while retaining the $O(n)$ space bound.

Between visiting intersections, the topological sweepline crosses n edges of the arrangement—an upper and a lower edge from each convex face it crosses. The active edges—those crossed by the sweepline—are shown in red in the upper left view in Figure 4a. The light blue edges have already been swept; the thin black edges remain to be swept. The black dots show intersections that the sweepline could visit next (it could move from the two edges left of the intersection to the two edges right of it). The sweepline can arbitrarily choose which black dot to advance over next, or it can even advance over all of them in parallel. The Lower Horizon *and* Upper Horizon *views display the data structures that the algorithm uses to identify intersections that it can visit next.*

In Figure 4b, a color spectrum displays the history of the sweepline's movement. Each region of the arrangement is flagged with a triangle whose color tells when the sweepline passed the rightmost intersection on its boundary. Figure 4c juxtaposes two different algorithms, the left one sequential and the right one parallel. The sequential algorithm always advances the sweepline at the uppermost possible intersection, whereas the parallel algorithm advances over all possible intersections concurrently. This concurrent advance makes the sweepline look ragged. An auralization of these algorithms appears in Figure 4 of Chapter 10.

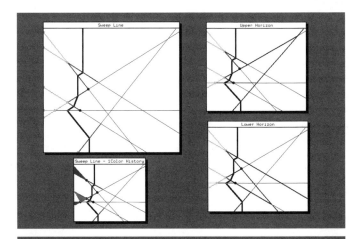

Figure 4a

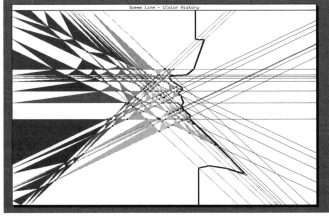

Figure 4b

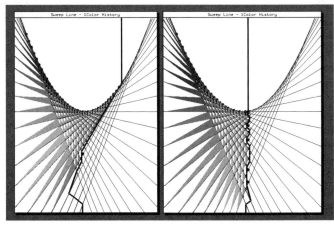

Figure 4c

Figure 5: To Spin or to Block?

When one thread of a multithreaded program needs a shared resource (like a file server or a semaphore), it must wait until the resource is available before it can proceed. While waiting, the thread can spin *(busy wait) or* block *(suspend itself). The former wastes processor time that other threads might use, while the latter incurs a fixed context-switch overhead.*

The better choice — to spin or to block — depends on the waiting time, which cannot be known in advance. The ratio of processor time spent to the time actually needed is potentially unbounded. But a program that spins for a while and then blocks can come within a small factor of the optimal off-line algorithm, which knows the waiting time in advance. Figure 5 is an animation the used as part of an empirical study of competitive spinning algorithms for a shared-memory multiprocessor [Karlin 91].

Figure 5a compares an on-line algorithm that considers only the previous three waiting times against the optimal algorithm. The three windows present different views of the same data. The actual waiting times are shown in blue, the remembered times in brown, algorithm spin time in green, and blocking time in magenta. In the VBars *view, the top row shows the waiting times, the middle row represents the optimal algorithm, and the bottom row represents the on -line algorithm being demonstrated.*

The VBars Superimposed *view superimposes these three rows for easier comparison. The* Back-to-Back Stem *view places the waiting times on the left and the on-line algorithm's spinning/blocking time on the right of a vertical line. The red vertical line below the bars shows the current threshold at which the algorithm stops spinning and decides to block.*

Figure 5b uses back-to-back stems to compare six different on-line algorithms with the optimal off-line algorithm. Each method's performance is shown graphically by the progress downward in its column. The Stats *view at the bottom of the screen shows the performance ratios numerically and graphically. We constructed this view using the FormsVBT multiview editor for user interfaces [Avrahami 89]. Figure 5c shows the graphical editor on the left. A thermometer gauge has been selected, which pops up a property form (right side of the editor) and highlights the textual description of the gauge in the text editor (bottom right).*

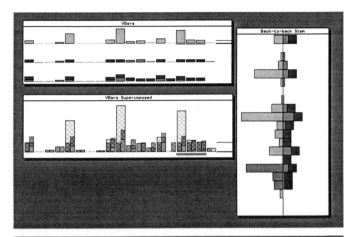

Figure 5a

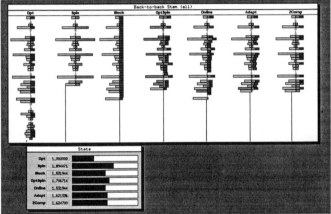

Figure 5b

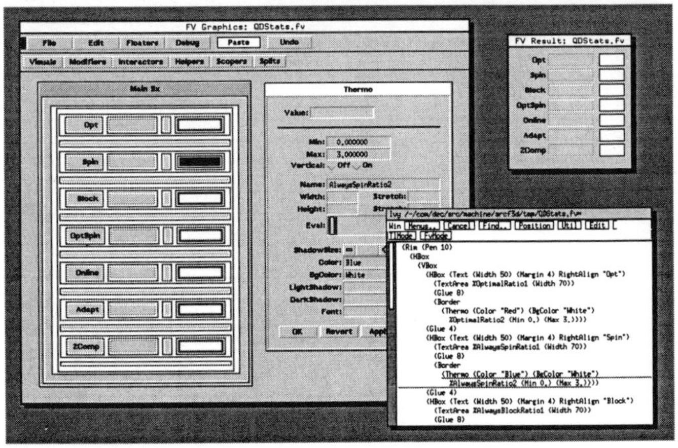

Figure 5c

Figure 6: Compliant Motion Planning

Compliant motion is a simple model of robot motion: Once the robot starts moving, it always heads in the same direction. When the robot hits an obstacle obliquely, it slides along the obstacle so as to make positive progress in its programmed direction. Figure 6 is an animation of an algorithm for determining the compliant motion path from a starting point to a specified goal point in a simple polygon [Friedman 89].

Figure 6a shows compliant-motion paths from two different starting points to a specified goal point, shown as a red dot. The algorithm in this animation computes the set (shown in green) of all points from which the robot can reach the goal in a single programmed movement.

For any point, the set of directions in which the robot can reach the goal forms a single angular range. To find these ranges, the algorithm first computes the set of points from which the robot can reach the goal by moving in a particular fixed direction. It then maintains the set while rotating the direction through 360 degrees.

The directions at which a point enters and leaves the set bound its angular range. When a point enters the set, it is added to a start subdivision; when it leaves, it is added to a stop subdivision, as shown in Figure 6b. Color encodes the directions at which points are added to the two subdivisions, and hence records the history of the algorithm. The pink region in the top right view is the current set of points — points already in the start subdivision, but not yet in the stop subdivision.

After the two subdivisions are completed, the user can specify an initial robot position with the mouse, as in Figure 6c. In response to the query, the algorithm locates the point in the two subdivisions (the results are shown in green), combines the results to get the range of feasible directions(the black angle in the upper-right view), and computes the robot's path (highlighted and emanating from the black angle).

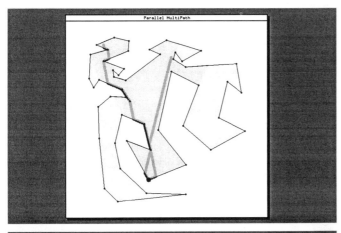

Figure 6a

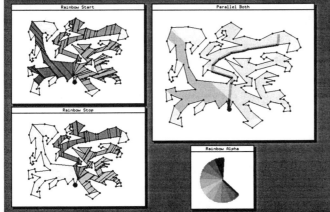

Figure 6b

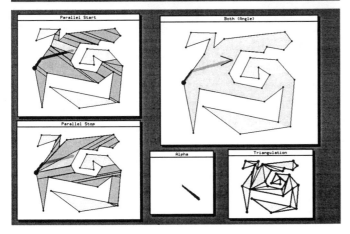

Figure 6c

Smooth, Continuous Animation for Portraying Algorithms and Processes

John Stasko

Many different types of software visualizations exist. Some show the data, large or small, manipulated by a program. Others depict attributes or artifacts of code, such as its last modification date. Yet others show the procedural steps of a process or algorithm. This last area is our focus in this chapter; we discuss animation techniques that can assist in portraying the steps of an algorithm or process.

Consider a visualization of data structures that involve pointer operations, as shown in Figure 1. If the code modifies a pointer and changes its referent, the arrow representing the pointer can be updated by erasing it and redrawing a new arrow pointing to the next reference.

What if the program performed many of these operations in succession and the updates occurred instantaneously one-after-another as described above? We believe that it would be difficult for viewers to track the series of updates that occurs. The visual updates simply would be too small and too immediate for viewers to perceive the changes and understand what occurred. In fact, we speculate that viewers would have to step through the changes in a very deliberate manner and carefully watch for the view updates, in order to understand the updates.

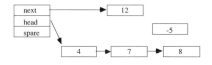

Figure 1. Sample visualization of a program manipulating pointer data structures.

Now, consider an alternative. Suppose that the pointer updates occurred in a gradual, continuous manner. That is, a pointer would not simply be erased from its old position and redrawn at its final destination. Rather, the arrow would be smoothly animated moving away from its prior referent and eventually pointing to its future referent. The end result would be the same as the immediate update---we would simply introduce a series of intermediate frames to act as a form of interpolation between the beginning and ending states.

One could argue that introducing a smooth animation like this misleads the viewer about what the program did. In the code, the variable representing the pointer was updated to a new value in one simple assignment. The new value did not gradually appear. We would argue, however, that the graphical technique of smoothly animating the pointer change benefits the viewer in such a way to overcome the false depiction. It would not be difficult to convey this fact to viewers also so that they would not be deceived.

Fundamentally, smooth continuous animations like this can help us portray the individual operations of a process or algorithm. Gradual updates allow people's visual systems to easily perceive and understand the changes. The updates also provide context and facilitate tracking of patterns and actions. Because smooth updates have durations, however, they are best suited for illustrating the fine-grained operations of a process working on a relatively small data set. If continuous animations are applied to large systems or data sets, they may simply take too long to occur and the viewer will become impatient.

Many other examples of using smooth animation, in addition to the pointers mentioned above, come to mind. For example, whenever two values are swapped in a sorting program, the graphical elements representing the values can smoothly exchange positions. In algorithms that perform complex rotation and restructuring operations on tree data structures, smooth animation of the operations can help viewers track the updates. If an algorithm "walks" a data structure, a graphical artifact can be introduced to smoothly moves around the strucuture's visual representation. In general, animation can be useful to help smooth the transition between discrete states of a complex algorithm or process.

In the software visualization community, the Animus simulation system was one of the first systems to show continuous updates [Duisberg 86a]. Animus utilized temporal constraints and could easily portray processes such as a spring flexing after being pulled.

In the remainder of this chapter, we describe our work on providing primitives to support continuous animations in software visualizations. First, we describe the Tango system and the path-transition paradigm it provides for building algorithm animations. Next, we describe the animation methodology of the Polka system, a descendant of Tango. Polka improves shortcomings in Tango's methodology and provides a more flexible, robust design environment. Finally, we conclude by describing a variant of Polka that supports real clock time durations and animations.

The Tango algorithm animation system and its X Windows-based follow-up XTango system's primary contribution to the software visualization community was its path-transition paradigm supplying primitives for building smooth continuous animations [Stasko 90b]. Tango's framework included three main components: identifying fundamental operations in the algorithm, building animations of those operations, and mapping the algorithm operations to their graphical representations. The primary goal in the design of the animation component was to provide a powerful graphical library that would still be easy to learn and use by non-experts. This section provides a brief overview of the animation component and the primitives used to build animations. For more details on the path-transition paradigm, see [Stasko 90a].

TANGO and the Path-Transition Paradigm

The animation component of Tango's framework contains images which are the graphical objects that undergo changes in location, size, and color throughout the frames of an animation and operations which control the sequence of these changes to simulate an action. Four abstract data types, the graphical *images* on the screen, the *locations* that images and other objects occupy, the *transitions* that the images make, and the *paths* that modify the images' transitions, are included in the formal model of the animation component.

As an example of the way that the image, location, path, and transition data types function, consider the following activity that might occur in an animation. Suppose that we have a rectangle and a line in the animation viewing area as depicted in Figure 2. We would like to design an animation that consists of the rectangle moving in a straight path over to the top of the line.

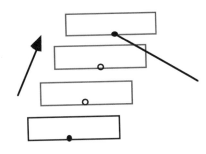

Figure 2. An example animation in which the rectangle moves up to the top of the line.

The rectangle and line objects are instances of the image data type. We will assume that some form of image creation operation put them in their current positions. Because we would like the rectangle to move to the top of the line, we need to acquire the current positions of the center of the rectangle's lower edge and the top endpoint of the line. These coordinate positions are examples of the location data type. We can utilize the two locations as endpoints in a path that consists of a sequence of interpolated offsets between the two endpoints; this track is an example of the path data type. The motion of the rectangle along the path provides an instance of the final data type, the transition.

Since animation design in the framework is based on defining paths and transitions, we call it the *path-transition paradigm*. A designer producing an algorithm animation in the path-transition paradigm creates, manipulates, and edits instances of the four abstract data types. The framework also includes a set of constituent operations for defining and modifying instances of the data types. Consequently, the framework exhibits a strong object-based appearance. Table 1 shows a complete list of the data type operations.

An image is a graphical object that undergoes changes in location, size, and color throughout the frames of an animation to simulate action. Two types of images exist in the framework: *primary* and *composite* images. Primary images are basic types of graphical objects such as lines, rectangles, circles, text, etc. We provide a general model for a primary image so that the framework is not restricted to a certain set of picture objects. Composite images are collections of primary images that have a geometric relationship to one another. They are defined by a list of primary images in a local coordinate system, and they allow us to repeatedly create instances of more complex pictures, thereby simplifying animation design. The *Locate* operation is a bounding box oriented method of accessing image parts and extremities. It receives an image and a parameter specifying one of the eight compass directions such as *SouthEast*, *West*, or the *Center* designation, and it returns a location corresponding to the designated part on the image's current position.

Image	Location	Path		Transition
Create	Create	Create	Rotate	Create
Locate	X	Load	Scale	Concatenate
	Y	Store	Example	Iterate
	Modify	Length	Motion	Compose
	Equal	Dx	Distance	Perform
		Dy	Concatenate	
		MakeType	Iterate	
		Null	Compose	
		Copy	AddHead	
		Color	AddTail	
		Extend	DeleteHead	
		Interpolate	DeleteTail	

Table 1. Operations on Tango data types.

A location is a position of interest within the animation coordinate system and is identified by an *(x,y)* coordinate pair. The ability to save and reference particular locations is an important tool for animation design. Frequently, locations are used to denote a particular variable in a program, whereas the variable's value is denoted by the image residing at the location. In our framework, animations are laid out in a real-valued infinite coordinate system so animations can be designed to function regardless of the animation window size. Primary operations on locations include *Create*, *Equal*, and *Modify*.

A path designates the magnitude of changes to image attributes from one frame to the next. Images can only be modified through paths; for example, images are moved along paths, images are colored along paths, and the visibility of images is changed along paths. A path is formally defined as a finite ordered sequence of real-valued *(x,y)* coordinate pairs, where each pair designates a relative offset from the previous position. The length of a path p, denoted $|p|$, is the number of coordinate pairs it includes.

A typical path designates a two-dimensional route in an abstract real coordinate system. A path is not restricted to modifying geometric *(x, y)* coordinate offsets, however. The same path can be interpreted to modify values of color, size, and so on. A path also contains a time interval component because each offset corresponds to a new animation frame. For example, moving an image along a path of length 20 creates a 20 frame animation. Designers can use the changes in path offsets to control the smoothness of an animation.

The use of paths to control two-dimensional animation is a natural and tested notion. An ancestor of our concept of the path data type is the *p-curve* structure of Baecker [Baecker 69b]. A p-curve consisted of a continuous trail of symbols placed along a two-dimensional route at short, uniform intervals.

Because the path is such an integral part of animation design in our framework, a large set of path inquiry and creation operations exist. Inquiry operations such as *Length*, *DeltaX*, and *DeltaY* return those respective values of a path. Three basic path types, *straight*, *clockwise*, and *counterclockwise*, are predefined to help designers create simple paths. The *Null* operation creates a path with a specific number of null (0.0,0.0) offsets. It is useful for creating a path of a particular length in which the individual offset values do not matter. The *Color* operation returns a one offset path that will change an image to a desired color when applied with the appropriate action. Additionally, paths can be padded, truncated, rotated, interpolated, iterated, composed, and concatenated via operations. Another set of path operations, *Example*, *Motion*, and *Distance*, receive two locations and create a path between them. The *Example* operation, for instance, receives three parameters---two locations that designate starting and ending points of a motion and an example path that specifies the style of the motion. The operation produces a path similar to the example path that moves between the provided "from" and "to" locations. This operation is particularly useful when a path pattern is desired but the coordinates of the path's endpoints are not known until run-time.

A transition provides an animation with action by utilizing a path parameter to modify the attributes of an image such as its position or appearance. Like images, transitions have an extensible definition that does not restrict the framework to a predefined set of types. Simple transitions are defined by a transition type, the image being altered, and a path argument modifier. Some examples of typical transition types include *move*, *resize*, *color*, *fill*, *raise*, lower, *delay*, and *alter visibility*. Different types of transitions use their path arguments in different ways. In a *move* transition, each path offset defines how an image should move before the next animation frame. *Visibility* transitions simply toggle an image's visibility for each path offset. *Fill* transitions use the

x component of a path offset by adding its value to an image's fill value that ranges from 0.0 (outline) to 1.0 (solid colored fill).

More complex forms of transitions can be created using the *Iteration*, *Concatenation*, and *Composition* transition operations. Composition is the most interesting, as it introduces a form of concurrent execution of transitions. When two transitions are composed, their respective actions in the first frame all occur simultaneously, as do their actions in subsequent frames. Therefore, composition provides a natural way to perform an animation in which more than one object changes. For example, to animate two rectangles exchanging positions, first we create two *move* transitions, each corresponding to one of the rectangles moving to the other's position. Then we compose the two transitions into a single, new transition that denotes their concurrent movements.

As a more sophisticated example, suppose we wish to define a transition that moves an image i along a path p_1 that has length 20. We also would like the image's visibility to toggle during the middle 10 movements in the path. Let us define the following notation to represent the transition operators:

$$t_1 \bullet t_2 \equiv \text{concatenate transitions } t_1 \text{ and } t_2$$

$$t^{num} \equiv \text{iterate the transition } t \text{ num times.}$$

$$t_1 \ominus t_2 \equiv \text{compose transitions } t_1 \text{ and } t_2.$$

By creating the paths

$$p_2 = \text{Null}(5), \quad p_3 = \text{Null}(1),$$

and the transitions

$$t_1 = \text{Create}(\text{delay}, i, p_2),$$

$$t_2 = \text{Create}(\text{visible}, i, p_3),$$

$$t_3 = \text{Create}(\text{move}, i, p_1),$$

the desired animation is described simply by the following formula:

$$(t_1 \bullet t_2^{10} \bullet t_1) \ominus t_3.$$

Once a transition has been defined, the *Perform* operation executes it. Intuitively, this operation works by modifying image attributes as specified by all the changes to occur for a particular animation frame. Once the complete list of modifications to attributes has been performed, the animation display is cleared and all the images are redrawn in their new configuration. By repeatedly processing the lists of changes, the frames of the animation are generated.

Designers create animations by assembling collections of the image, location, path, transition and association operations that accomplish desired animation actions. We call such collections *animation scenes*. For instance, in an animation of a sorting algorithm such as in Figure 3, the exchange of the positions of elements being sorted might correspond to an animation scene. We use the word "might" because there is no correct decomposition of an animation into scenes; the process is strictly subjective to the animation designer. The next section includes an example code fragment corresponding to an animation scene.

Figure 3. An animation of a sorting algorithm in which a number of animation frames have been superimposed to illustrate the smooth movements of the objects

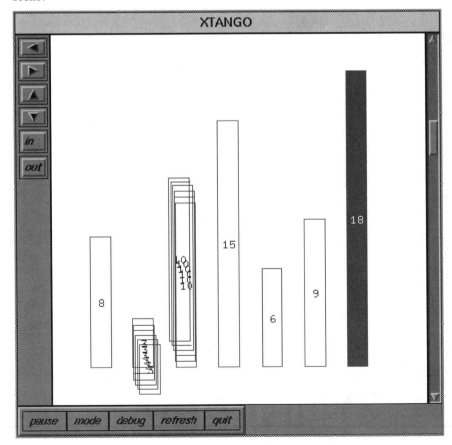

We have developed precise semantic specifications of all the data type objects, operations, and models in the algorithm animation framework. For reasons of brevity, we will not discuss the specifications here. Readers wishing to learn more about this aspect should see [Stasko 89] [Stasko 90a].

The Tango and XTango systems have proven to be very useful for building software visualizations. The path-transition paradigm and its primitives have been very easy to learn for programmers, and the paradigm is able to produce quite sophisticated animations. Certain types of animations, however, particularly those possible in visualizations of parallel programs, have been awkward to build with the path-transition paradigm.

To achieve any type of concurrent animation (one image performing multiple transitions concurrently, or two images performing concurrent transitions) with Tango, it is necessary to *Compose* two transitions into a new transition. For two or three transitions this is straightforward and not particularly a problem. When multiple transitions overlap repeatedly, this formalism quickly becomes awkward. Consider the diagram in Figure 4. It represents an animation in which a new transition commences before the previous transition completes. In Tango, we would have to compose all these transitions into one "super" transition, and we can only perform that transition and view the animation result at the very end.

POLKA

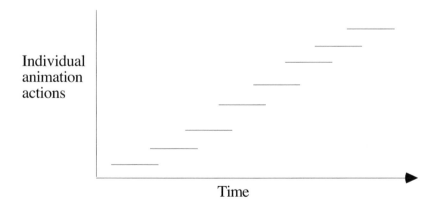

Figure 4. Timeline representation of an animation with cascading overlaps of actions (transitions).

Individual animation actions

Time

To address difficulties such as this and to further simplify animation design, we developed a derivative methodology of the path-transition paradigm. This new methodology is used in the Polka software visualization system [Stasko 93b].

Polka provides an object-oriented toolset of primitives for building software visualizations. Its fundamental difference from the path-transition paradigm is the addition of an explicit animation clock (frame count). Rather than having to compose two transitions to make them concurrent, individual *actions* (the Polka analog of a transition) are simply scheduled to begin at the same clock time. The scheduling of the two actions is done independently as well. Further, animations can now be generated a frame at a time, rather than having to perform a complete transition.

Let us look at the data types of Polka in more detail. Each animation being built must have an instance of an *Animator* object. Actually, animation designers must subclass Animator and utilize an instance of the derived class. The Animator is responsible for managing the visualization, and in particular, handling the receipt of messages (events) from the driver program being visualized and coordinating the dispersal of the events to *Views* of the software. A View corresponds to a window on the computer display. A Polka visualization can have one or more Views associated with it; Each can provide a unique visual perspective onto the software. Views utilize a floating point world coordinate system for flexibility just like the display window in Tango. As done for the Animator, Polka provides a View base class which must be derived by animation designers.

Views include one critical data member (slot), an integer variable named *time*. This variable corresponds to the clock time in the View and it is used to maintain the number of animation frames generated so far in the animation. It is initialized to zero, and is incremented through use and assignment via the View member function (method) *Animate*. For example, the command

```
time = Animate(time, 20);
```

generates 20 new animation frames beginning at the clock time held in the *time* variable. The call returns what the resultant frame number will be, so assigning that value to *time* maintains the desired running value.

Polka provides three data types that correspond closely to the four data types of the path-transition paradigm. *Locations* in Polka are exactly analogous to their equivalent in Tango. Graphical objects in Polka are called *AnimObjects* and they correspond closely to Tango's images. Actually, Polka provides an abstract base class called AnimObject and a number of subclasses such as Line,

Rectangle, Text, etc. Polka does provide a few new subclasses (Pie, Spline) beyond the image types of Tango, and Polka provides the formal notion of a Set of AnimObjects that can be referenced as an individual AnimObject.

Finally, Polka includes a third data type, *Action*, that corresponds roughly to a combination of the path and transition data types of Tango. An Action does include a path component (Animation still occurs relative to continuous paths as in Tango) along with a type (Motion, Resize, Color, etc.). An Action is bound to an AnimObject and scheduled to begin at a particular time through the use of the AnimObject member function *Program*.[1] The *Program* call on an AnimObject takes an Action and a time (frame number) as arguments. It returns the duration of the Action in frames.

To better understand this methodology, consider the following example. The XTango path-transition paradigm code below creates a rectangle and a circle. It then performs a concurrent animation of the rectangle moving to a new position as the circle's radius grows.

```
TANGO_IMAGE rect, circ;
TANGO_LOC center, toLoc;
TANGO_PATH path1, path2;
TANGO_TRANS trans1, trans2, doBoth;
double delta[5] = {0.1, 0.1, 0.1, 0.1, 0.1};

rect = TANGOimage_create(TANGO_IMAGE_TYPE_RECTANGLE,
          0.2, 0.2, 1,TANGO_COLOR_RED, 0.1, 0.3, 0.5);
circ = TANGOimage_create(TANGO_IMAGE_TYPE_CIRCLE,
          0.6, 0.8, 1, TANGO_COLOR_BLUE, 0.05, 0.0);
center = TANGOimage_loc(rect, TANGO_PART_TYPE_C);
toLoc = TANGOloc_create(0.2, 0.7);
path1 = TANGOpath_motion(center, toLoc,
          TANGO_PATH_TYPE_STRAIGHT);
path2 = TANGOpath_create(5, delta, delta);
trans1 = TANGOtrans_create(TANGO_TRANS_TYPE_MOVE, rect,
          path1);
trans2 = TANGOtrans_create(TANGO_TRANS_TYPE_RESIZE, circ,
          path2);
doBoth = TANGOtrans_compose(2, trans1, trans2);
TANGOtrans_perform(doBoth);
```

---

[1] *Program* was a poor name choice for this operation. *Schedule* would be much more meaningful.

Below is the Polka code that corresponds to the XTango code above. Note the use of the *Program* and *Animate* calls.

```
Rectangle *rect;
Circle *circ;
Loc *center, *toLoc;
Action *action1, *action2;
double delta[5] = {0.1, 0.1, 0.1, 0.1, 0.1};
int len1, len2;

rect = new Rectangle(view, 1, 0.2, 0.2, 0.1, 0.3, "red",
                       0.5);
circ = new Circle(view, 1, 0.6, 0.8, 0.05, "blue", 0.0);
center = rect->Where(PART_C);
toLoc = new Loc(0.2, 0.7);
action1 = new Action("MOVE", center, toLoc, STRAIGHT);
action2 = new Action("RESIZE", 5, delta, delta);
len1 = rect->Program(action1, time);
len2 = circ->Program(action2, time);
time = Animate(time, MAX(len1, len2));
```

The code for these two examples is quite similar, but it differs in important ways. The independent scheduling and alignment of Polka Actions simply provides more flexibility. Also, the time at which a Polka Action is scheduled can be farther in the future. Typically, this value is passed in as a parameter and the *Animate* call is moved out to an overseer control procedure.

Polka's animation methodology moves even further beyond that of Tango and XTango by providing a number of new capabilities not found in the path-transition paradigm. These include

• A subclass of View called a Static View. It is essentially a color bitmap, and does not have AnimObjects. It has very low overhead and is extremely fast.
• The ability for the viewer to interactively select coordinates and AnimObjects with the mouse pointer.
• The ability to programmatically map and unmap (show and hide) views.

• Callbacks in the animation code that are keyed to particular animation frames. That is, whenever a specified animation frame (time) is generated, a user routine can be called.

• The capability of an AnimObject to change its type (Line to Rectangle, for instance) at a specified frame.

• Callbacks registered on AnimObjects so that a particular user routine will be called whenever a viewer interactively selects the AnimObject with the mouse.

• The notion of Continuous Actions. These are animation Actions that commence at a specified frame and simply loop forever, or until the Action is explicitly terminated. This capability supports a state-based animation model as opposed to the more traditional event-based animation model.

• Simple attachment constraints that allow one AnimObject to be "connected" to another. If the primary AnimObject is subsequently moved, the connected AnimObject is automatically moved the same way also.

To learn more about Polka's animation methodology, see [Stasko 93b]. It has been used to build a number of interesting algorithm animations, both of serial and parallel algorithms. It also has been used to build animation libraries for particular concurrent programming systems and methods including distributed systems such as PVM [Topol 95b] and Conch [Topol 95a], shared memory threads programs [Zhao 95], and High Performance FORTRAN programs. Further, a three-dimensional variant of Polka has been develped for exploring how 3-D graphics can help illustrate program executions [Stasko 93c].

Animations created using Polka are frame-based, that is, each animation Action's duration consists of a particular number of discrete steps or animation frames. On a fast computer with a rapid graphics redisplay cycle, an animation will run much more quickly than on a slower machine. The number of frames generated would be the same; They would simply be drawn faster on the more poweful computer. To a certain degree, a speed control bar available in Polka can be used to adjust these speeds, but it affects all parts of the animation in an equal way.

POLKA-RC

We have developed a variation of Polka that supports the creation of animation actions whose initiations and durations are specified in precise clock times such as seconds and milliseconds. Polka-RC (Real Clock) is designed in the same general fashion as Polka, but it allows much more detail in animation design [Stasko 95a] [Stasko 95b]. Polka-RC includes primitives similar to those developed for adding animation to user interface toolkits [Hudson 93]. Below we'll highlight some of the key differences between this new system and the original Polka.

One fundamental change in Polka-RC is that the driver program or algorithm and its animation run in separate processes and communicate through a socket. This allows the redisplay loop of the animation never to be blocked because the driver program has control.

In terms of the constituent animation data types, Polka-RC's Animator, View, Location, and AnimObject data types function much as they do in Polka. The key difference is that Polka's Actions have been replaced by a combination of the *Traj* and (new) *Action* data types.

A Traj(ectory) is a curve used as the control path of modifications to an AnimObject. It has three components: The *displacement* specifies the total change or offset from the start to end of the Traj. The *motion type* describes the path curvature such as a straight path or a clockwise arc. The *pace* refers to the speed at which the curve is traversed. It is simply a function, and it has two predefined values, uniform or slow out/slow in. Two example Traj definitions are shown below.

```
Traj t1(STRAIGHT, -0.1, 0.3, uniform);
Traj t2(CLOCKWISE, loc1, loc2, slowinout);
```

An Action in Polka-RC is similar to an Action in Polka, but it provides a few new options for the animation designer. First, Actions in Polka-RC are either *continuous* or *discrete*. Discrete Action types include color, visibility change, raise and lower. Their update is instantaneous. Continuous Actions types include move, resize, fill, and so on. They have a duration. Both styles of Actions require an AnimObject, an Action type, and an initiation time argument. A continuous Action also utilizes Traj and duration arguments.

Timing parameters such as the initiation and duration arguments can be specified in seconds, milliseconds, or by using the special values *Now*, meaning the current time, or *ASAP*, meaning either the current time if no other Actions are pending, or the first time whenever all other pending Actions have completed. Below, we provide examples of both discrete and continuous Actions.

```
Action disc1("LOWER", line1, START_AT, Now());
Action disc2("VIS", line2,
    START_AFTER_START_OF, &disc1, Sec(2));
Action cont1("MOVE", circle1,
    Traj(CLOCKWISE, 0.3, -0.1, slowinout),
    START_AT, ASAP(),
    VELOCITY, 30);
Action cont2("RESIZE", circle2,
    Traj(STRAIGHT, loc1, loc2, uniform),
    START_AFTER_END_OF, &cont2, MSec(50),
    DURATION, Sec(1.5));
```

Once Actions have been defined in this manner, they are added to the list of pending Actions in an animation via the *Schedule* View operation. From that point on, Polka-RC insures that the Action commences and executes at the specified times. It adjusts the animation display according to how busy the machine is at that time. If the animation is able to acquire many cycles, many frames of an animation will be shown and it will appear to be very smooth. If the machine is loaded down with much computation, an animation may generate relatively few frames in order to meet its timing specifications. In either case, Polka-RC insures that the specified real time initiation and duration of the Action is followed as best it can.

The fundamental change from Polka is that no explicit *Animate* call is used to generate animation frames. Rather, Polka-RC is always ready to animate. Whenever it encounters Actions whose changes are scheduled to occur since the last update, Polka-RC updates the AnimObjects' appearances and position accordingly. In essence, Polka-RC provides the purest form of continuous animation of the three systems we have discussed in this chapter: Designers do not specify individual offsets as in Tango or Polka. They simply describe a curve and pace at which an animation should occur. For much more detail about the design and implementation of Polka-RC, see [Stasko 95a][Stasko 95b].

Conclusion

When illustrating the fine-grained steps of an algorithm or process, continuous animation can be a useful tool to help viewers follow the operations that are occurring. Animation helps viewers identify and track changes between states, thus helping them understand how the operations evolve over time. This chapter has described the evolution of three systems that provide libraries for building smooth, continuous animations of programs: Tango, Polka, and Polka-RC. Experiences in building animations with the systems helped guide the changes and refinements in the subsequent systems. Readers seeking more hands-on experience with these animation systems can acquire both the XTango and Polka systems via anonymous ftp. They are maintained at the machine `ftp.cc.gatech.edu` in the directory `pub/people/stasko` as the files `xtango.tar.Z` and `polka.tar.Z`.

Acknowledgments

Scott McCrickard collaborated in the development and implementation of the Polka-RC system. This research was supported by the National Science Foundation under contract CCR-9121607. Portions of this chapter are reprinted, with permission, from [Stasko 90b] Copyright 1990 IEEE.

Algorithm Animation Using Interactive 3D Graphics

Marc H. Brown
and
Marc A. Najork

Overview

Throughout the history of algorithm animation, advances in computer hardware have driven the evolution of algorithm animation systems.

The first general-purpose algorithm animation systems in the early 1980's used monochrome displays. Systems such as BALSA [Brown 84b] were constrained by a lack of computational power for real-time two-dimensional graphics. As computational power has increased, so has the sophistication of the graphics techniques used for animating algorithms.

In the mid-1980's, Animus [Duisberg 86a] showed the utility of smooth transformations of 2D images, especially for looking at small examples. TANGO [Stasko 90b] in the late 1980's provided an elegant framework for specifying 2D animations. Color was an integral part of Zeus [Brown 91]. The Zeus system also pioneered "algorithm auralization"—using non-speech sound to convey the workings of algorithms [Brown 92]. Not surprisingly, each new advance in technology has enabled an extra level of expressiveness to be added to the visualizations.

This chapter describes our use of interactive 3D graphics for algorithm animation. Interactive three-dimensional graphics provides another level of expressiveness to the animations, akin to the way that smooth transitions, color, and sound have increased the level of expressiveness in the past.

We are not proposing to use 3D for showing objects that are intrinsically three-dimensional, such as the convex hull of points in 3-space. We are also not advocating the use of 3D for enhancing the beauty of a picture that is easily shown in 2D. Rather, we are using 3D to increase the quality and quantity of information conveyed in a graphical display. Specifically, we have explored three distinct uses of 3D:

- *Expressing fundamental information about structures that are inherently two-dimensional.*

  Consider how one might display the values of an N-by-M, two-dimensional matrix of positive numbers. An obvious 3D display is to draw sticks at each cell of an N-by-M grid, where the height of each stick is proportional to the value of the corresponding element. Of course there are other techniques for displaying the matrix without using 3D graphics, such as displaying a number in each cell or modifying the color, shape, or size of each cell according to the value of the corresponding element of the matrix. However, showing sticks of varying heights seems to be an extremely effective technique, perhaps because it allows direct visual comparison of the elements.

- *Uniting multiple views of an object.*

  Finding a single view of an object that reveals all of its features can be difficult, if not impossible. Therefore, presenting multiple views of that object is a helpful visualization technique. However, it can be difficult for the user to understand the relationship between the multiple views. A carefully crafted 3D view can incorporate multiple 2D views into a single image, thereby helping the user to see how the views are related.

- *Capturing a history of a two-dimensional view.*

  Often, a visualization of a program's entire execution history can be just as helpful for understanding a program's behavior as an animation of the current state of the program. When running programs on small amounts of data, a history often gives the user a context of how the algorithm has progressed each time the state has changed. When running programs on large amounts of data, a history often exposes patterns that are not otherwise observable.

In any event, identifying and quantifying the advantages and drawbacks of visualization techniques is beyond the scope of this chapter.

This chapter presents six example animations that exemplify our three distinct uses of interactive 3D graphics. The first two examples, Shortest Path and Closest Pair, use 3D for showing additional information on a structure that is inherently two-dimensional. The next three examples, Heapsort, k-d Trees, and Balanced Trees, use 3D for uniting multiple views. The final example, Elementary Sorting, uses 3D for augmenting a view with a history of how it has changed over time.

The techniques used in the Closest Pair and Elementary Sorting examples are particularly noteworthy because they can be applied to many arbitrary 2D views. We shall return to this point when describing those two examples.

The images in this chapter are screen dumps of views we developed using the Zeus algorithm animation system [Brown 91]. In the Zeus framework, strategically important points of an algorithm are annotated with procedure calls that generate "interesting events." These events are reported to the Zeus event manager, which in turn forwards them to all interested views. Each view consists of two windows that are installed on the user's desktop. One window displays the actual 3D image and the other window contains a control panel (see the Balanced Trees example). The control panel allows the user to change generic rendering parameters (e.g., lighting), as well as view-specific parameters (e.g., in the case of Balanced Trees, the distance between the two trees). The rendered scene can be moved, rotated, and scaled through mouse controls. In addition, one can use the mouse to specify a momentum, which will cause the scene to rotate continuously.

It is important for readers to realize that the figures in this chapter cannot do justice to the animations: Not only is information lost when printing color images in black-and-white, but the reader is unable to manipulate the 3D scenes. Moreover, the scenes themselves are not static! They are constantly changing as the algorithm runs.

Example 1: Shortest Path

Single-source shortest-path algorithms are a family of algorithms which, given a directed graph with weighted edges, find the shortest path from a designated vertex, called the *source*, to all other vertices. The length of a path is defined to be the sum of the weights of the edges along the path.

All single-source shortest-path algorithms have certain common features: First, they assign a cost to each vertex, indicating the length of the shortest path found so far from the source to this vertex. Initially, the cost will be infinite. Then they repeatedly choose an edge e from vertex u to vertex v, test if it can lower the cost associated with v, that is, if $COST(v) > COST(u) + WEIGHT(e)$, and if so, indeed lower v's cost. Algorithms differ in their choice of which edge to examine next.

A 3D view of one such algorithm is shown in Fig. 1. The graph is drawn in the xy plane, with a green column above the node in the z dimension. The column represents the cost of each node. An edge from u to v with weight w leaves the column above u at height 0, and goes into the column above v at height w.

Figs. 1a and 1b show the initial state of the algorithm, from above (Fig. 1a) and from an oblique viewing perspective (Fig. 1b). Edges are drawn in gray; a shadow of the edges is projected into the xy plane and drawn in black, along with the vertices.

Whenever an edge e from u to v is examined, a highlighted, red copy of it is lifted to the top of u's green column, hence its tip will hover over v at height proportional to $COST(u) + WEIGHT(e)$. If v's column is taller, the edge can indeed lower v's cost, so v's column is shortened, otherwise, the highlighted edge disappears. The set of highlighted lifted edges forms the shortest-path tree when the algorithm terminates. Fig. 1c shows the algorithm about halfway complete; Fig. 1d shows the algorithm upon completion, with the initial edges not drawn.

This view uses the third dimension to provide state information (namely, cost of vertices and weight of edges) about an algorithm as it operates on a data structure that uses two dimensions for placing objects. The view uses animation effects to show the fundamental operations of the algorithm: lifting an edge represents addition, lowering a highlighted edge indicates the outcome of a comparison, shortening a column shows assignment.

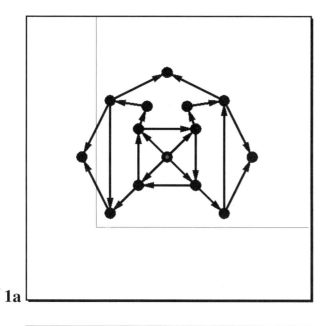

1a

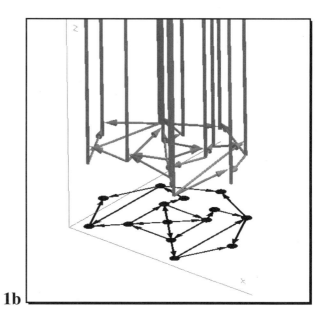

1b

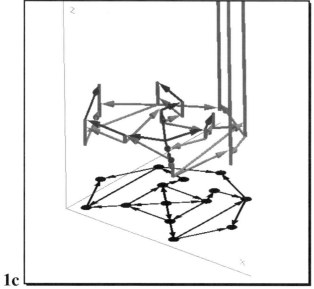

1c

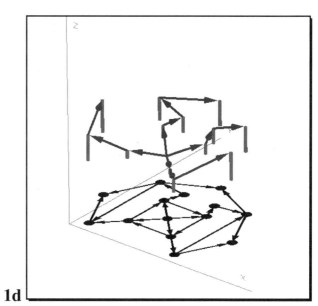

1d

Example 2: Closest Pair

The closest-pair problem is to find the two points in a collection of n points that are closest to each other. An algorithm that does a pairwise comparison of all points takes $O(n^2)$ time; however, a recursive, divide-and-conquer algorithm can improve this time bound to $O(n \log n)$.

The algorithm (for points in the plane) is as follows: First we divide the plane by a line parallel to the y-axis such that each half contains the same number of points. Next, we recursively find the closest pair of points in each half. And finally, we merge the two halves, checking if there is a new pair of points (saddling the dividing line) that are closer to each other than the closest pairs in each half. The crux of the algorithm is that we need to consider only those points in each half that are fairly close to the dividing line (in x) and fairly close to the other endpoint (in y).

The 3D view of this algorithm, shown in Fig. 2, draws each half-plane in the xy plane and uses the z axis to show the division process and the induced recursion structure. In each divide step, the half-plane is lifted, split in the middle, and the two halves are moved apart. In the merge step, the halves are moved back together, the eligible points are compared pairwise, and then the merged plane is lowered. The region of interest around the dividing line is highlighted. The globally best pair found so far is also highlighted.

In Fig. 2, the user has specified that the half-planes should not be moved apart, and that the half-planes should be displayed almost completely opaque. Fig. 2a shows the initial splitting, Fig. 2b shows the merge of the two half-planes split by the initial left half-plane, and Fig. 2c shows the algorithm deep in recursion as it is processing the initial right half-plane.

As in the Shortest Path example, the third dimension is used to display additional information (in this case, the recursion structure) about an algorithm that operates on two-dimensional data, and animation effects are used to show operations crucial to the algorithm.

The visualization technique used here is an example of a general-purpose way to integrate a visualization of a program's calling structure with the contents of its data structures. We believe that it can be applied to other views, although we have not explored this yet.

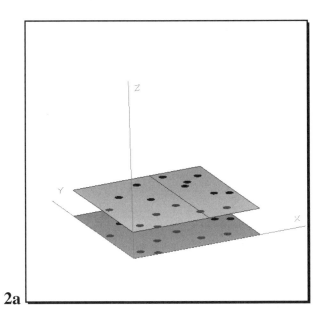

2a

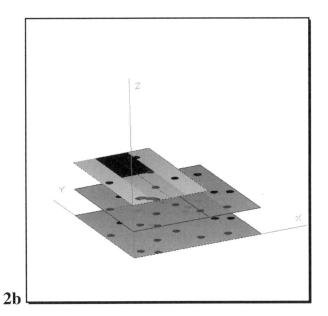

2b

2c

Example 3: Heapsort

Heapsort works in two phases. First, it arranges the elements being sorted into a *heap*, a complete binary tree in which the value of each node is larger than the values of each of its children. Second, it repeatedly removes the root (i.e., the largest value among the elements) from the heap, sets it aside, and reestablishes the heap property, doing so until the heap is empty.

Heaps can be implemented as arrays by placing the root node at position 1, and for each node at position i, placing its left child at position $2i$, and its right child at position $2i+1$.

The 3D view in Fig. 3 exposes both of these properties. When viewed from the front as in Fig. 3a, we see the heap configured as a traditional tree (drawn in the xy plane). Each node in the tree is an element of the array being sorted, and has depth (in the z dimension) proportional to its value. Thus, nodes at the top of the tree are longer (or deeper) than those near the leaves. When the tree is viewed from the side as in Fig. 3b, we see a classical sticks view of sorting algorithms (cf. Fig. 6a). Fig. 3c shows the same structure from an oblique viewing angle. Notice the relationship between the two representations. Fig. 3d shows the algorithm when it is almost completed.

The values of elements are also encoded by colors along the spectrum: large elements are displayed in red and small elements in blue. Color is not crucial in the sticks representation, because the value of a stick is encoded by its length, but it is quite helpful in the tree view.

Of course, it is possible to show the two perspectives—the tree and the array—as separate views, each in its own window, without using 3D graphics. However, the viewer must mentally integrate the different views in order to understand them as a whole. The 3D view alleviates this problem.

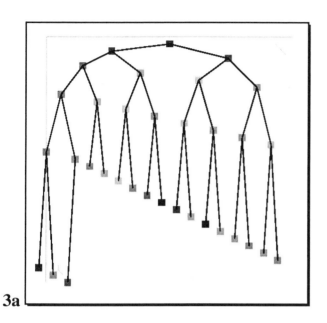

3a

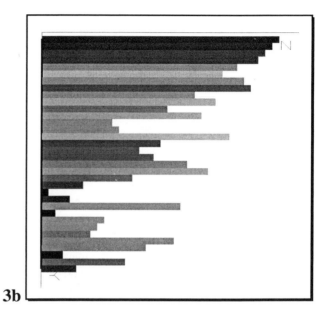

3b

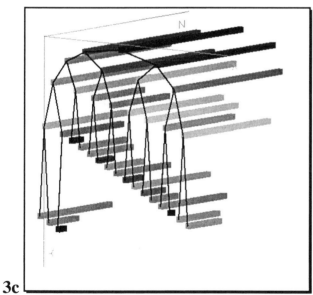

3c

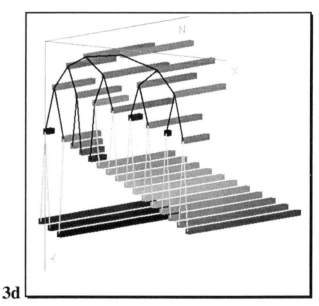

3d

Example 4: k-d Trees

k-d trees are a special kind of search tree, useful for answering range queries about a set of points in k-space. The algorithm for the two-dimensional case (i.e., $k = 2$) with points in the xy plane is as follows: The algorithm selects any point and draws a line through it parallel to the y axis. This line partitions the plane vertically into two half-planes. Another point is selected and is used to horizontally partition the half-plane in which it lies. In general, a point that falls in a region created by a horizontal partition will divide this region vertically, and vice versa.

This division process induces a binary tree structure: The first point becomes the root, and each point falling into the left half-plane is inserted into the left subtree, and each point falling into the right half-plane is inserted into the right subtree. For points that divide regions horizontally, the points in the upper half-plane are inserted into the left subtree whereas points in the lower half-plane are inserted into the right subtree. Thus, nodes at even levels in the tree divide the set of points into left and right half-regions, and nodes at odd levels divide a region into upper and lower half-regions.

There are two obvious views of this algorithm: a view of the partitioning of the plane, and a view of the binary tree that is induced. The 3D view shown in Fig. 4 merges and unites these two views.

The points in the plane are drawn as circles in the xy plane, and the partitionings caused by them are drawn as transparent walls extended in the z dimension. On top of each wall and above each point is a sphere, representing the corresponding node in the 2-d tree. Therefore, the height (as well as color) of each wall reflects the node's level in the tree. The tree edges are represented as lines connecting related nodes.

When viewed from the top and with the tree edges hidden, as in Figs. 4a, 4c, and 4e, we see the traditional view of the partitioning of the plane. Exposing the tree edges would show the 2-d tree in a representation that a graph-theorist would be comfortable with: as a connected, acyclic graph. However, when viewed from the side (and with the walls mostly translucent), as in Figs. 4b, 4d, and 4f, we see a tree more familiar to the computer scientist: each node is below its parent.

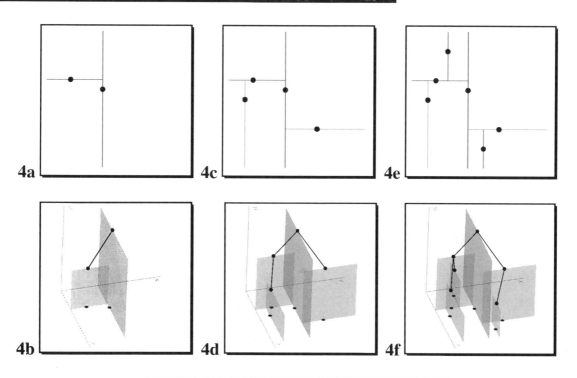

4a

4c

4e

4b

4d

4f

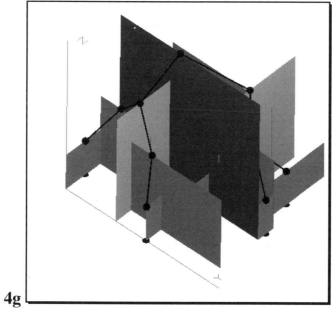

4g

Figs. 4a and 4b show the state of the algorithm after it has processed the first two points. Figs. 4c and 4d show the state after the algorithm has processed the third and fourth points, and Figs. 4e and 4f, after the algorithm has processed the fifth and sixth points. Finally, Fig. 4g shows the state of the algorithm after all points have been processed, with opaque partitioning walls. Notice how the 3D view merges the traditional plane-partitioning view and the induced 2-d tree view.

It is disconcerting to see edges of the tree overlapping. (Moreover, the left and right children are not necessarily drawn to the left and right of their parent!) Fortunately, when the tree is rotated in real-time about the z axis, it appears to have depth. The real-time animation provides the viewer with the visual clues needed to understand the overlaps.

Example 5: Balanced Trees

A 2-3-4 tree is a balanced search tree in which nodes can contain 1, 2, or 3 keys and can have 2, 3, or 4 children. Inserting keys into a node might eventually cause it to overflow, which results in the node being split into multiple nodes. Performing the split operation judiciously will keep the tree balanced. Unfortunately, 2-3-4 trees are cumbersome to implement, mainly due to their irregular structure. Therefore, it is common to implement 2-3-4 trees as Red-Black trees. These are ordinary binary search trees with an extra bit (the "color") attached to each node.

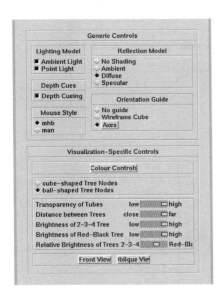

The 3D view shown in Figs. 5a, 5b, and 5c illustrates the mapping between a 2-3-4 tree and a Red-Black tree. The two trees are drawn with one in front of the other. More precisely, each tree is drawn in the xy plane, and the trees have different values of z. Each node in the 2-3-4 tree is associated with its corresponding nodes in the Red-Black tree by enclosing the nodes in both trees into a horizontal transparent envelope, and thus grouping them together.

This view, like the others, is somewhat hard to appreciate fully as a static image. Spinning the scene very slowly helps the viewer to see the mapping. The controls for manipulating this 3D view are shown on the side.

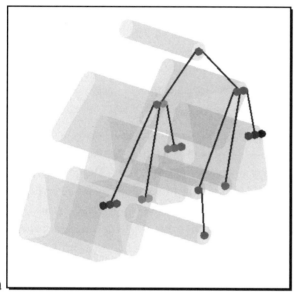

5a

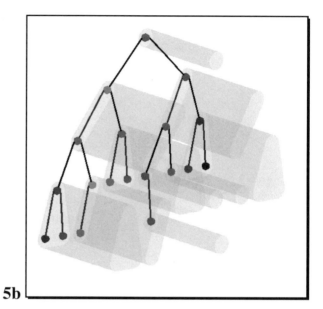

5b

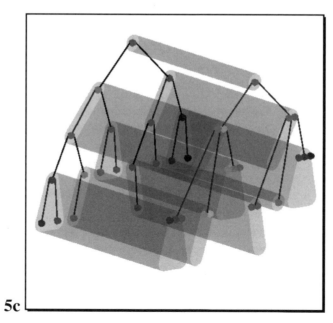

5c

Example 6:
Elementary Sorting

Perhaps the most famous algorithm animation is the "sticks" view of sorting algorithms such as Insertion Sort, shown in Fig. 6a. This view, introduced in Baecker's seminal 1981 film *Sorting Out Sorting*, shows the array of elements as a row of sticks. The height of each stick is proportional to the corresponding element in the array, so when the sort is completed, the sticks are arranged from short to tall, from left to right.

This view is superb for understanding the dynamics of many sorting algorithms, especially when the algorithm runs on small amounts of data. However, this view does not provide any history of the execution. We see the current state only. However, if we consider the sticks as being drawn in the xy plane, we can see an execution history by drawing the sticks at increasing values of z as the algorithm progresses. That is, we stack the new row of sticks in front of the old ones. This results in a 3D solid.

In order to emphasize the importance of the current row of sticks, we chose to flatten all previous sticks and to encode by color the value of the corresponding array element. In addition, we keep the current row fixed at $z = 0$, and move the stack of flattened sticks forward at each step. This results in a horizontal plane of "paint chips" giving a complete history of the algorithm. (Another way to think of the "chips" view is as the sticks stamping their color onto the chips plane, which is pulled forward as execution progresses.)

Fig. 6b shows the same scene as in Fig. 6a, but viewed from above. Fig. 6c shows the same scene again, but viewed from an oblique viewing perspective. Notice how we can see both the current contents of the array and the history of the algorithm's execution in the 3D view.

Fig. 6d uses the same view and viewing angle to display Shakersort. In the BALSA system, the chips view was a separate view of sorting algorithms, one among a dozen or so views. The chips view of Shakersort was instrumental in providing the insight that led to Janet Incerpi's Ph.D. thesis on the worst-case analysis of Shellsort (Brown University, 1985). The insight suggested by the picture of Shakersort is the "zipper" effect: in one left-to-right pass, many elements are moved one position to the left, only to be moved back to their previous position on the subsequent right-to-left pass.

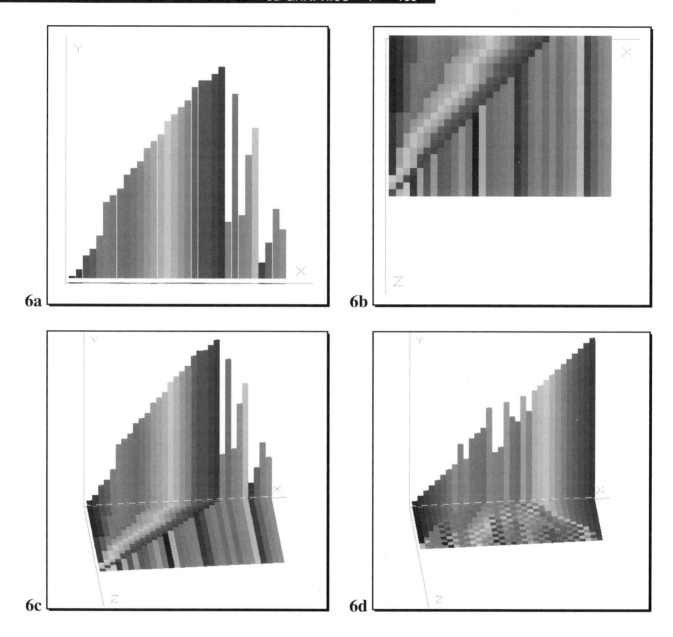

6a

6b

6c

6d

This digression is important because the 3D visualization technique of stacking a 2D view along the z axis as the algorithm progresses is general purpose, and can be applied to many 2D views. It is reasonable to imagine that other hidden properties of algorithms will be exposed by examining 3D history of 2D views.

Related Work

This chapter is based on work that was done in the summer of 1992 and eventually published in 1993 [Brown 93]. At about the same time, Stasko and Wehrli did some very similar work, by extending the Polka algorithm animation system with 3D capabilities, designing a number of 3D animations, and classifying the various ways in which 3D added to their animations [Stasko 93c]. Interestingly enough, both our groups independently identified the same three uses of 3D.

Cox and Roman [Cox 92] used the Pavane program visualization system to create a 3D animation of a shortest-path algorithm similar to that shown in Fig. 1. Their work was developed independently of ours. The incorporation of 3D graphics was not central to their research.

GASP [Tal 95] is another algorithm animation system that uses 3D graphics. GASP was designed for animating algorithms that perform three-dimensional geometric computations; such algorithms typically have natural 3D views. However, Tal and Dobkin demonstrated that GASP is flexible enough to construct 3D animations of arbitrary algorithms.

Pictorial Janus [Kahn 92] integrates visual programming with program visualization. A program is a collection of nested two-dimensional closed contours (e.g. polygons and ellipses). During execution, the size and location of the contours are gradually changed according to a set of simple rules. A 3D view is created by stacking successive snapshots of the state of the program (each being a 2D view drawn in the xy plane) along the z axis, thereby capturing the history.

There are various examples of using 3D in program visualization. Lieberman [Lieberman 89] describes a 3D view of the execution of Lisp programs. The view shows the code for an expression in the xy plane on a block with some depth in the z dimension. As the program executes, each subexpression causes a new block to be displayed in front of the caller's block. When an expression is evaluated, its block (the frontmost) is removed. Koike's VOGUE system [Koike 92] provides a 3D visualization of class libraries: A conventional class hierarchy tree is drawn in the xy plane. Behind each node (in the z axis) are "floating" nodes for methods. Finally, Reiss has developed a 3D variation of a program call graph [Reiss 93], where the z coordinate (and the actual contents) of each node reflects some attribute of the corresponding procedure.

The scientific visualization community routinely uses interactive 3D graphics. Systems like AVS [Upson 89] support 3D visualizations of domain-independent data. The Information Visualization project at Xerox PARC [Robertson 93] has stimulated a flurry of interest in developing 3D views that show classical types of data organization (e.g., a tree) traditionally shown in 2D. Both scientific visualization and information visualization typically concentrate on a given set of numeric or relational data. We are concerned with visualizing the behavior of programs, which typically operate in subtle ways on abstract and complex combinatorial structures.

Summary

The potential use of 3D graphics for program visualization is significant and mostly unexplored. The examples in this chapter use 3D graphics for expressing additional information geometrically about a two-dimensional structure, integrating two nominally 2D views, and capturing a history of execution. Our use of 3D graphics is not to enhance the beauty of a program visualization; it provides additional, fundamental information.

Two of the examples stand out as being instances of general-purpose visualization techniques: In the Closest Pair example, we discussed using 3D for combining program control information with arbitrary 2D views of program data structures. In the Elementary Sorting example, we discussed using 3D for capturing a history of an arbitrary 2D view.

A great deal of experimentation is needed to better understand the strengths and weaknesses of using interactive 3D graphics for animating algorithms, and to develop a collection of 3D visualization techniques and metaphors to augment those that have been developed for using 2D, color, and sound.

Program Auralization

Marc H. Brown
and
John Hershberger

Recent advances in workstation and PC technology make it easy to generate digital sound, either internally or by interfacing to an external MIDI device. Although this is a recent trend in hardware, computer science folklore includes stories of programs that were debugged in the 1960s and 1970s using sound: by placing an AM radio on the computer!

Software visualization through sound, usually called *program auralization*, is the process of forming mental images of the behavior, structure and function of computer programs by listening to acoustical representations of their execution [DiGiano 92a].

Researchers have identified a number of reasons for using sound [Francioni 91]:

- Visualization is highly subjective, and what is insightful for one person is meaningless to someone else. Program auralization provides yet another "view" of a program; a view that might make some things obvious to some people. Furthermore, some types of information might just be difficult to represent graphically.

- Listening can be done passively. That is, one does not have to be paying strict attention listening to the normal behavior of a program in order to notice that some exceptional event has happened. Moreover, listening can be done in parallel with viewing.

- People have remarkable abilities to detect and remember patterns in sound (indeed, most people remember the melody of a song much sooner than they learn the words).

- Sound is a powerful medium for delivery of large amounts of data in parallel. This aspect of sound is especially useful for visualizing parallel programs; but even sequential programs can contain an enormous amount of data.

- Sound is inherently temporal, as are computer programs during execution.

Gaver, in his pioneering work on augmenting the Macintosh desktop with audio cues, advocated that audio information be used redundantly with visual information, so the strengths of each mode could be exploited and mutually reinforced [Gaver 89].

Baecker's seminal film *Sorting Out Sorting* (see Chapter 24) contains sound (in addition to narration), but it is not an example of program auralization. In that film, a musical score accompanies the sorting animations. The score repeats a short theme while an algorithm is running and plays a second theme just as the algorithm completes. Thus, the score is used to pass the time and to indicate the end of the algorithm. We don't consider this program auralization, because the music is not data or program driven. For instance, all runs of selection sort on N elements would sound *exactly* the same, regardless of the elements. Furthermore, selection sort would sound exactly like insertion sort, which would sound exactly like quicksort, except for the length of time that the main melody is played.

This chapter looks at the way that program auralization has been used in both program visualization and algorithm visualization.

Program Visualization

Francioni, Albright, and Jackson were among the first researchers to use audio for program visualization [Francioni 91]. The goal of their research was to provide a tool to help debug distributed-memory parallel programs. Their system collected traces of three types of program events: processor communication, processor load, and processor event flow. These program events caused a unique note or melody to be played using a particular timbre mapped to each processor. Their experiments confirmed that auralization of parallel program behavior could be a useful debugging and performance aid. They concluded that auralization should not replace visualization, but rather, visual portrayals could be enhanced by sound.

LogoMedia was the first system we know of that supported user-defined code and data program auralization [DiGiano 92a][DiGiano 92b]. In LogoMedia, programmers could annotate their code with control or data probes. A control probe allowed sound commands to be exececuted just before a line of code was executed, or upon procedure entry or exit. A data probe could be associated with an arbitrary expression, such that changes to any of the variables in the expression would trigger sound commands as well. The probes could be inserted with a graphical editor, and various sound commands could be specified using dialog boxes provided by the graphical editor.

The goal of the CAITLIN project is to determine whether musical feedback can help novices to debug programs [Vickers 96]. CAITLIN is a preprocessor for Pascal, and allows a user to specify an auralization for each type of program construct (e.g., a WHILE loop, an CASE statement). The auralization consists of three parts: a tune to denote the commencement of the construct, a structure representing the execution of the construct (i.e., the musical scale, default note length, instrument, and so on), and a tune to signal exit from the construct. Preliminary experiments indicate that subjects could follow the execution of simple programs; that is, they could identify the key constructs in the program using CAITLIN. Most of the problems were that subjects simply forgot the tune corresponding to each construct.

CAITLIN, unlike LogoMedia, does not allow auralization of data. CAITLIN also does not allow a user to selectively decide which lines of code, or procedure calls, should be auralized.

Algorithm Visualization

The only work we know of for using auralization as part of algorithm visualization is our own. This section describes our experiences using audio in algorithm animations in four distinct areas: for reinforcing visuals, for conveying patterns, for replacing visuals, and for signaling exceptional conditions.

Figure 1. Auralization of insertion sort running on 20 elements. Each vertical gray line in the staff indicates the completion of one pass through the array.

Reinforcing Visuals

Our first use of audio, and perhaps its most obvious use, was simply to reinforce what was being displayed visually. For example, in the hashing animation of Figure 2b in Chapter 7, each table has a pitch associated with it. Inserting an element into a table produces a tone of the corresponding pitch. In a sorting animation (like the one in Figure 1a in Chapter 7), each comparison or movement of an element produces a tone whose pitch is linearly related to the element's value. The musical score in Figure 1 shows the notes generated while sorting a file by insertion sort.

Conveying Patterns

Sorting algorithms produce auditory signatures just as distinctive as the visual patterns of moving sticks or dots. Compare the signature of bubble sort in Figure 2 with that of insertion sort. (A fair length comparison is given by looking at just the top staff.)

Bubble sort works by making passes through the array. During each pass, it compares adjacent elements and swaps them if they are out of order. Thus, during the kth pass, the bubble sort moves the kth largest element into its final position at the right end of the array. Most other elements to its left move left one position.

The two staves show the participants in each comparison. The top staff shows the large elements moving to the right, and the bottom staff shows the other elements moving one position to the left. By playing the two staffs with different instruments, one can easily hear two different themes.

Figure 2. Auralization of bubblesort running on 20 elements. Each vertical gray line in the staff indicates the completion of one pass through the array.

The idea of using multiple instruments to display multiple events in a program is further explored in the auralization of selection sort, whose score appears in Figure 3. Of course, the choice of instruments for each "voice" is important, as are the parameters (such as volume) that govern the instrument. In selection sort, the instruments that gave a pleasing auralization were a muted clarinet for the

Figure 3. Auralization of selection sort running on 20 elements. Each vertical gray line in the staff indicates the completion of one pass through the array.

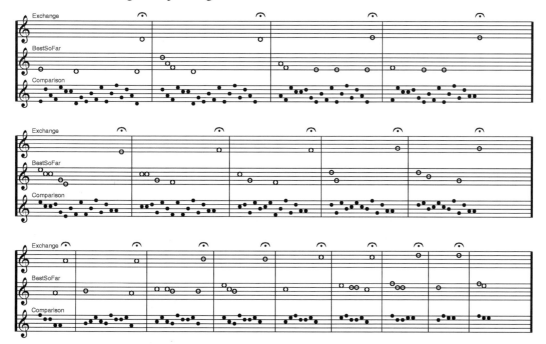

Figure 4. Auralization of a parallel topological sweepline. The top score corresponds to the regular arrangement of lines in Figure 4c of Chapter 7, and the bottom score to the less orderly arrangement in Figure 4b of Chapter 7.

Compare event, a loud gong (with lots of sustain) for the Exchange event, and a xylophone (with moderate volume and sustain) for the BestSoFar event.

People can hear relations in data that are never seen or displayed (and vice versa). Because sound is intrinsically time dependent, it is not surprising that sound is very effective for displaying dynamic phenomena, such as running algorithms.

Replacing Visuals

We've used audio representations to replace what can easily be displayed visually. This lets the user focus full visual attention on other visual views. For example, in the parallel quicksort algorithm in Figure 1a in Chapter 7 and in the parallel topological sweep in Figure 4c in Chapter 7, the sound-effects "view" produces a tone whose pitch rises with the number of active threads. We could easily print this number as text or display it graphically as a bar chart. However, because users receive the thread information through a nonvisual channel, they can focus full visual attention on the algorithm at work. The scores in Figure 4 compare the thread information for two sets of topological-sweep input data.

Signaling Exceptional Conditions

It was no surprise to find that audio was very effective for signaling exceptional conditions. After all, computers have beeped at users for years. However, an algorithm animation is different from an interactive program that, say, beeps when the user tries to do something illegal. In algorithm animations, long periods pass while the user passively watches the algorithm in action. In this situation, the user can easily "turn off" the visual input channel by looking away, looking at the wrong part of a display, or becoming "hypnotized" into complacency by the normal case. It is harder (though certainly not impossible) to turn off one's audio input channel.

For example, in the multilevel hashing algorithm described in Figure 2 of Chapter 7, inserting an element into a table makes a tone whose pitch depends on the table. Thus, the executing algorithm sounds notes within some chord.

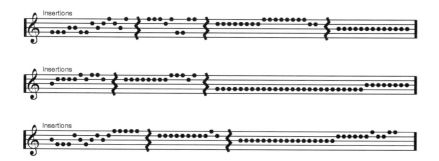

Figure 5. Auralization of multilevel adaptive hashing. The score shows the same hash-table history recorded visually in Figure 2c of Chapter 7. The wavy vertical bars denote the synthesized sound of a car crash.

However, when a new element collides with old elements in all tables, the animation plays the sound of a violent car crash, underlining the idea of a collision. The score in Figure 5 shows the same hash-table history recorded visually in Figure 2c of Chapter 7.

It is easy to dismiss this use of real-world sounds as overly cute. We refer the skeptic to Gaver for a thorough discussion of how and why everyday sounds can and should be integrated into computer programs [Gaver 89].

Summary

As noted in Chapter 7, designing an enlightening animation is a tricky psychological and perceptual challenge. What information should be presented and how? At present, creating effective dynamic visualizations of computer programs is an art, not a science.

We have found that sound is more difficult to use than, say multiple views or color (see Chapter 7), smooth animation (see Chapter 8), or even 3D graphics (see Chapter 9). Perhaps this is simply because we have less practice (and training) composing music than drawing diagrams. Or perhaps it is because sound is a more difficult medium to master, with many parameters (e.g., frequency, volume, attack and decay rates, duration, timbre, reverberation, brightness, and stereo placement [Iverson 92]), and poor use of sound is less forgiving than poor use of color, animation, or 3D.

Despite the challenges of using sound effectively, it is a valuable tool for software visualization.

Acknowledgments

Parts of this chapter are based on [Brown 92] and are used with permission.

User Interface Issues For Algorithm Animation

Peter A. Gloor

This chapter discusses user interface issues for algorithm animation. It is based on practical experiences collected when building the "Animated Algorithms" system [Gloor 93] which is described later in the book in Chapter 27.

In order to provide a algorithm animation system which is both easy to use and quick to learn, the design of the user interface is of fundamental importance. There are two aspects of the user interface requiring standardization: the consistency of object and motion, and the consistency of the control interface. The first aspect means that animation objects should always move the same way (consistency of motion) and that similar algorithm variables should be represented uniformly (consistency of object). To address the second aspect, Animated Algorithms offers a consistent control interface employing the VCR controller metaphor (Fig. 1).

The VCR controller is always the frontmost window on the screen and allows control over the stepping through or playing through of algorithms. Where appropriate we have added controller elements that emphasize the main steps of the algorithm and allow the student to proceed consciously from one logical algorithm step to the next (Fig. 2).

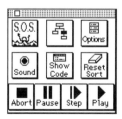

Figure 1. VCR Controller for sorting animations

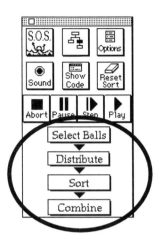

Figure 2. Controller emphasizing the main steps of bucket sort

These added controller elements emphasize the main steps of the algorithm and allow the student to step consciously from one logical algorithm step to the next.

Based on our experience with Animated Algorithms, this chapter discusses the "ten commandments of algorithm animation":

1. Be consistent

2. Be interactive

3. Be clear and concise

4. Be forgiving to the user

5. Adapt to the knowledge level of the user

6. Emphasize the visual component

7. Keep the user interested

8. Incorporate both symbolic and iconic representations

9. Include analysis and comparisons

10. Include execution history.

These points have been identified while making many mistakes and rebuilding many different versions of the Animated Algorithms user interface and animations. Obviously they go from general concepts to very algorithm animation specific requirements. They will now be discussed in detail by the example of Animated Algorithms.

1. Be consistent:
This aspect is true for the user interface of any system, but is especially important for educational algorithm animations. As discussed previously, we request consistency of object and motion, and consistency in the control interface.

2. Be interactive:
A high degree of interactivity is necessary to keep users interested and improve their understanding of the inner workings of an algorithm. Basically users should be forced to interact with the system at least every 45 seconds. Additionally, users also should be able to select their own input. For novice users, on the

other hand, a predefined input data set should be offered. In Animated Algorithms, controller elements emphasizing the main steps (fig. 2) force the user to interact with the animation by starting the next logical step of the algorithm.

3. Be clear and concise:

The essential points of the algorithm have to be presented clearly and to the point. Complexity can, e.g., be hidden by a hierarchical substructure. Access to this substructure is made possible by a *"step into"* button.

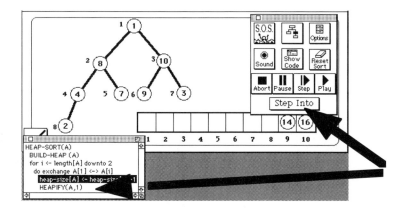

Figure 3. "Step into" button for heap sort

Figure 3 illustrates the "step into" button for the heap sort algorithm where the user is about to step into the **heapify** procedure. This technique permits the user to learn fundamental concepts first and then to expand into complexity. By highlighting the currently executed pseudocode line the user is able to always see exactly how the animation relates to the algorithm. It is also important to demonstrate where the algorithm breaks, i.e., to show under which boundary conditions the algorithm is inefficient or won't work.

Important *logical algorithm steps* can not only be emphasized by means of a separate controller (see figure 2), but they should also be accentuated in the animation by transitions from one step to the other. The student can get explicit pointers to the logical steps by hypertextual or voice annotations.

4. Be forgiving to the user:

The system has to be generous and forgiving to erroneous user manipulations.

This means that it allows only meaningful actions and alerts users if they are in the process of executing a meaningless action. Users are, for example, only allowed to define an input set that makes sense for the current algorithm. Also, the system should make sure that controller elements may only be used in correct order.

5. Adapt to the knowledge level of the user:
The system has to be adaptable to the knowledge level of the user. We have paid attention to this by allowing the user to set the animation speed himself. We also provide extensive built-in on-line help and permit stepping into or out of an algorithm where appropriate.

6. Emphasize the visual component:
Since animation is a graphical process, visualizations should be as self-explanatory as possible. This means that elements should not needed to be interpreted further. For example, elements to be sorted could be differently sized bars or balls instead of letters of the alphabet; one should use slider bars for setting the animation speed, or employ colored arrows in a hash table to indicate its fullness.

Figure 4. Different visual representation of data elements

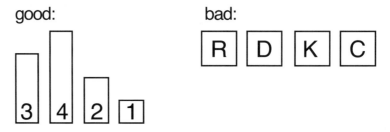

The requirement for consistency of motion means that similar actions should always be animated in similar ways. This allows students to recognize repetitive steps more quickly, even when they choose to perform a previously unseen action. Figure 5 shows the animation of the generic insert operation for the hashing algorithms, which is animated similarly independent of the particular addressing method.

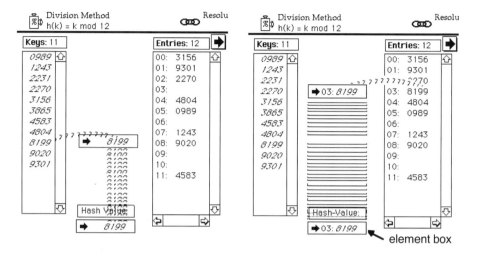

Figure 5. Generic animation of the insert operation for the hashing animation

7. Keep the user interested:

An animation should not only capture the initial interest, but keep the user's attention during the whole execution. Keeping the user interested also means that an animation can be aborted at any time. This is advantageous if, for example, a large data set would keep the algorithm executing for a long time while the user has already understood all concepts. It means also that frequent stopping points for single stepping have to be foreseen. Voice annotations are another useful means of keeping the user interested.

An animation should definitively not offer humor at any price, but good real world examples for the explanation of theoretical concepts help keep the user interested and improve the learning effect.

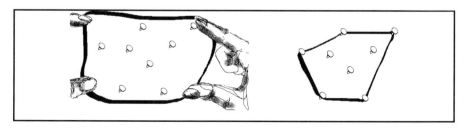

Figure 6. Real word example explaining the convex hull

Figure 6 demonstrates on an real world example how to find the convex hull of a set of points in a plane using an elastic rubber band.

8. Incorporate both symbolic and iconic representations:
The user should have the option of watching the execution of an algorithm in parallel as animation and as pseudocode. Figure 7 shows the animation window of an animation of the longest common subsequence algorithm.

Figure 7. Longest common subsequence animation containing both symbolic and iconic information

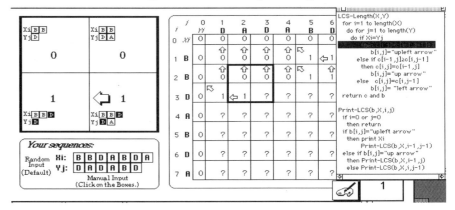

The right side of figure 7 is a symbolic representation of the algorithm in execution and the left side is the iconic representation of the same action.

9. Include algorithms analysis:
Wherever appropriate, analysis of the algorithm's behavior should also be included. Once an algorithm is run several times, it would be useful for the student to be able to see how different options affect the operation of the algorithms. These options can be either parameters to the algorithms itself, or variations in the input to the algorithm. Analysis information can be collected during the execution of the animations. Figure 8 displays the hashing analysis card allowing the student to view the collected data.

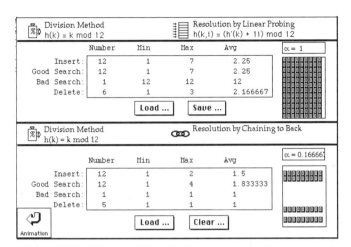

Figure 8. Hashing analysis card

Visual comparisons between different similar algorithms further deepen the understanding of the student. Figure 9 displays the sorting comparison animation of Animated Algorithms, allowing to comparing the different sorting algorithms with different input data sets.

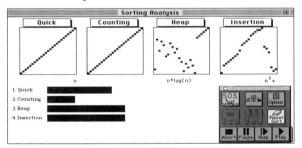

Figure 9. Comparison of sorting algorithms

10. Include execution history:

One of Marc Brown's three dimensions of algorithm animation [Brown 88a] demands that the animation give a temporal context for the momentary action. Ideally, an animation always keeps some sort of history that shows why the current action is happening based on a snapshot of past actions.

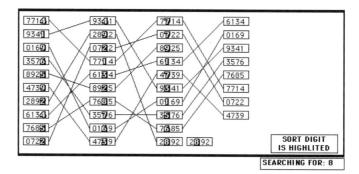

Figure 10. Radix sort containing history of actions

The snapshot of the radix sort animation in figure 10 illustrates the history concept. The fourth digit is currently being sorted, but the sorting sequence of all previous digits is still visible in the animation window.

Of course, an algorithm animation should also be implemented in a way such that it does not overstretch the built-in limitations of the hardware and operating system. This means, for example, that it was impossible to have full-color three dimensional animations on the Motorola 68000-based Macintosh-line that Animated Algorithms was designed for. It is more important for the student to have a system that *runs at acceptable speed smoothly* than a potentially dazzling system that is only capably of jerky motion on not top-of-the-line systems.

The ultimate requirement, of course, is to optimize the learning effect. Applying the above listed "ten commandments", algorithm animation system designers should be capable of designing educational systems hopefully avoiding the perils and pitfalls that our team ran into when developing Animated Algorithms.

Joining Pictures to Code: How to Specify a Visualization

Section

III

This section contains chapters that discuss how a piece of software connects to its visualization, and how such a visualization is constructed. Not represented here is the fundamental approach typified by many data structure display systems: a designer hand-crafts visualizations using a graphics library, and the visualization is generated at execution time by a unit of code that examines the data state and displays the appropriate visual depiction. The techniques described in this section offer alternatives to that basic approach.

The first two chapters discuss techniques for generating the visualizations based on program actions. Chapter 12 ("Interesting Events") describes the *interesting event* approach pioneered by the BALSA system and now common in most algorithm animations. The programmer identifies key points in a program that correspond to fundamental operations of its underlying algorithm. When those points are reached during execution, a parameterized event is dispatched to the visualization component of the system. Chapter 13 ("Declarative Visualization") describes an alternative approach that utilizes a formal program state to visualization state mapping. A designer constructs this mapping before execution. Then, as the program executes, changes in the program state trigger updates to the graphical view of the program. The chapter describes the Pavane animation system that uses this approach.

Finally, Chapter 14 ("Building Software Visualizations through Direct Manipulation and Demonstration") focuses on how software visualizations are constructed. Rather than depending on coding with a graphics toolkit, it advocates an approach whereby the designer sketches out graphically, via direct manipulation, the desired appearance of the visualization. This involves a limited form of visual programming in which the interaction environment closely mirrors the desired resultant visualization. The chapter describes the DANCE and LENS systems that follow this approach.

Interesting Events

**Marc H. Brown
and
Robert Sedgewick**

**Chapter
12**

Most *program visualization* displays (static and dynamic visualizations of code and data) can be created automatically, whereas most *algorithm visualizations* (static algorithm visualizations and algorithm animations) cannot. This chapter first examines why this is, and then presents *interesting events*, the approach that most algorithm animation systems have adopted for annotating algorithms with additional information that is communicated to views for creating displays. Interesting events are important both to users interacting with an algorithm animation system (as a way to control the execution of algorithms) and to programmers developing animations (as a way to simplify the process of implementing an animation). This chapter explores both of these topics.

Dynamic displays require two types of information: the *entity* to be displayed and a *delta* describing the change in the entity. Static displays need only information about the entity.

Dynamic and static displays of static or even executing code can be created automatically because the set of entities and deltas is well-defined and can be accessed directly by a display routine (which is typically part of the programming environment). The entities are derived from the source code, and the deltas from the changes in the program counter. Examples of code entities are procedures, statements, files, and blocks; examples of deltas are advancing to the next line of code, entering or exiting a procedure, and entering or exiting a block. Most contemporary commercial programming environments provide

**Automatic Program
Visualization Displays**

visualizations of code automatically, highlighting the line of code currently being executed, showing calling stacks, and so on.

Dynamic and static displays of data can also be created automatically, and indeed, most modern programming environments have a variety of (usually textual) displays of data that are updated as the program executes. The entities are the data structures to be displayed, and the deltas can be inferred by examining the data each time it is accessed or modified. A routine to display a static picture of the data structure automatically can access the data through the runtime environment. It needs to be told by the user how the data is represented in the program (i.e., a mapping into a canonical representation) and what type of display is desired (i.e., a display technique for the canonical representation).

Although canonical displays can be created without modifying the program, they are not always very informative, especially for non-trivial data structures. Moreover, dynamic displays created automatically cannot show the delta in the way the change is conceptualized because only the "before" and "after" conditions of the data are known. Thus, the display can do nothing more than interpolate between the two states.

Most algorithm animation displays cannot be created automatically because they are essentially renderings of the algorithm's fundamental *operations*; an algorithm's operations cannot be deduced from an arbitrary algorithm automatically but must be denoted by a person with knowledge of the operations performed by the algorithm. In addition, there are problems relating to real-time *performance* and to *informative displays*.

In terms of the taxonomy presented in Chapter 3, the only algorithm animation displays that can be created automatically are those with *direct* content which use *discrete* transformations. Views with direct content (be it of code or of data) are characterized as "program visualization" rather than "algorithm visualization" in Chapter 1. Nonetheless, such views appear in many algorithm animation systems.

In the next section, we discuss the difficulties with creating algorithm animation displays automatically. Following that, we describe the solution of instrumenting programs with *interesting events*, first introduced by BALSA [Brown 84b], and adopted by most subsequent algorithm animation systems.

We now examine in detail the problems with creating algorithm animation displays automatically.

Problem 1: Capturing operations

Algorithm operations do not necessarily correspond to each access or modification of the algorithm's data structures. In particular, (a) accessing a particular variable has different meanings at different locations in the algorithm, and (b) an arbitrary number of accesses and modifications (including zero) results in a single operation.

The following fragment of Quicksort illustrates these two problems:

```
procedure Quicksort(l, r: integer);
 var …;
 begin
 if r-l <= M then
   for i:= l+1 to r do
     begin
     v:=a[i]; j:=i;
     while (j>l) and (a[j-1]>v) do
       begin a[j]:=a[j-1]; j:=j-1; end;
     a[j]:=v
   end
 else
   begin
   v:=a[r]; i:=l-1; j:=r;
   repeat
     repeat i:=i+1 until a[i]>=v;
     repeat j:=j-1 until a[j]<=v;
     t:=a[i]; a[i]:=a[j]; a[j]:=t;
   until j<=i;
   a[j]:=a[i]; a[i]:=a[r]; a[r]:=t;
   Quicksort(l, I-1);
   Quicksort(i+1, r)
   end
 end
```

Note that this is not a vanilla version of the algorithm. It uses Insertion sort to process small subfiles

Two fundamental operations are being performed on the array: "set value" (in the **then** part) and "exchange" (in the **else** part). These operations should be illustrated differently.

However, a monitor cannot not know which accesses to array **a** constitute a "set value," and which an "exchange." Even if this problem were eliminated, say, by re-coding the Insertion sort phase using only exchanges, a second, more difficult, problem remains: how can a monitor infer which accesses comprise an exchange? It is the result of a variable number of modifications to the array. In the 7th line from the bottom, an exchange is the result of every second modification to the array. However, in the 5th line from the bottom, two exchanges result from every three modifications to the array. Of course, one could always change the Quicksort code fragment to guarantee that every exchange is the result of exactly two modifications. However, this would conflict with a primary goal of algorithm animation systems: minimal intrusions into the algorithm's original source code.

The second aspect of the problem, that of an arbitrary number of accesses and modifications resulting in a single operation, was also seen in the **Partition-Tree** view in Figure 1. A vital operation being displayed in that synthetic display is one we call "ElementInPlace." To simplify the discussion, assume that Insertion sort is not used for the small subfiles. That is, in the code fragment above, remove all code except the body of the **else** statement. After the resulting fragment code has been executed, the value stored in a[i] finalized. At this point in the Partition-Tree, the square boxes corresponding to elements l through r are replaced by a dark circle corresponding to element i. That node has two children: the left are elements l through i-1, and to the right, i+1 through r. This abstract operation cannot be inferred by simply monitoring variables: it is a conceptual operation that is essentially triggered by the control flow.

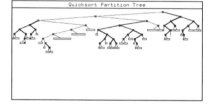

Figure 1. The Quicksort Partition Tree. In this binary-tree view of the partitioning process, each node represents an element in the array being sorted. Each subtree represents a subfile being sorted recursively, and the subfile is partitioned into two group separated by the root of the subtree. The color and thickness of the edges indicate which subfiles have been processed. (The edges turn from thin red lines to thick blue lines once processed.) In this implementation, small files are sorted using insertion sort, resulting in the unexpanded boxse connected by the thick blue edges. See also Figure 4 in Chapter 3.

Problem 2: Real-time performance

In general, the data being accessed or modified may be costly to identify, resulting in unacceptable performance. For example, knowing which node in a tree is being modified may lead to costly computation to determine its parent, siblings, and children. Just because a task is expensive does not mean that it is impossible; however, for interactive algorithm animation systems, performance is a real issue. One cannot just hope for faster hardware or more clever display algorithms, since for every increase in hardware or more clever display algorithm, the complexity of the algorithms and the size of the data that one will wish to animate is bound to also increase.

Problem 3: Informative displays

Many displays necessitate detailed knowledge about the algorithm's runtime behavior and the specific data upon which the algorithm will be run. For example, only because the Partition-Tree view in Figure 1 knows that the height of the tree will be about equal to the binary logarithm of the number of elements in the corresponding array, can it allocate that much vertical space from the start and the resulting tree will usually fit nicely in the window. However, it cannot know the *exact* height until the algorithm runs. In fact, the exact optimal size and layout parameters for this display would require the algorithm to be run twice!

Towards Automatic Algorithm Animation Displays

Algorithm operations must be identified by a programmer. Languages that support abstract data types are particularly well-suited to this approach. For example, in object-oriented languages, entities and their deltas are defined by objects and the messages they react to. Given a properly modularized object-oriented program, one just needs to specify how the objects and messages map into entities and deltas. This approach was followed by Duisberg's Animus using SmallTalk [Duisberg 86a][Duisberg 86b].

This approach is not limited to object-oriented programming. In algorithmic programming languages, such as Pascal or C, one could encapsulate the operations in procedure calls (there would be a one-to-one mapping between the procedure calls and messages in an object-oriented language), which could then be monitored automatically.

For example, the **else** clause in the Quicksort code fragment from above looks like this:

```
...
begin
v := a[ r] ; InitLeftPtr(l-1); InitRightPtr(r);
repeat
  repeat IncLeftPtr(i); until Compare(a[ i],v,">=");
  repeat DecRightPtr(j); until Compare(a[ j],v,"<=");
  Exchange(a[ i],a[ j]);
until j<=i;
Exchange(a[ i],a[ j]); Exchange(a[ i],a[ r]);
ElementInPlace(i);
Quicksort(l, I-1);
Quicksort(i+1, r)
end
...
```

It is tempting to believe that such a strategy is a panacea. However, algorithms from textbooks and journals are given in "straight-line" code; they are not broken into procedures. Even if the code is broken into procedures, the procedures may not be the appropriate ones. For instance, why would a programmer think to insert the procedure ElementInPlace in the code above since it does nothing? It is impossible to take straight-line code and infer automatically the correct abstractions to form the encapsulations.

The difficult issue of annotating an algorithm is one of identifying the phenomena of interest in the program; the appropriate syntax for enunciating the abstractions may or may not be directly supported in the implementation language.

Interesting Events

The approach taken in BALSA, and followed most general purpose algorithm animation systems (e.g., TANGO [Stasko 90b], ANIM [Bentley 91a], Zeus [Brown 91], and CAT [Brown 96)]) is to annotate algorithms with *interesting events* rather than forcing an algorithm to be radically proceduralized so that each meaningful operation is encapsulated. These events are in turn forwarded by the algorithm animation system to all views. Each view responds to the interesting event by drawing appropriate images. In the case of object-oriented algorithm animation systems such as Zeus, each view is a subclass of a window with additional methods to handle each interesting event.

Thus, the three lines before the first recursive call to Quicksort in the first version above would become:

```
...
t:=a[ i] ; a[ i] :=a[ j] ; a[ j] :=t;
InterestingEvent(Exchange, i, j);
until <= I;
a[ j]  := a[ i] ; a[ i]  := a[ r] ; a[ i]  := t;
InterestingEvent(Exchange, i, j); InterestingEvent(Exchange, i, r);
InterestingEvent(ElementInPlace, I);
...
```

The BALSA approach minimizes the changes to the algorithm, since the algorithm is augmented, not transformed. Of course, if one is willing to procedurize the algorithm, events can be inferred "automatically" by a rather simple preprocessor that inserts an annotation as the first statement of each procedure. The parameters of the event would be the name of the procedure, followed by the arguments of the procedure.

Some algorithm animation systems, such as TANGO [Stasko 90b], provide an editor so that events can be added in a structured way without actually changing the source code. The editor modifies the source code to include the annotations before it is run, never showing the modified source code to the programmer.

Interesting events also help to solve the second and third problems mentioned above. First, data that may be costly to identify automatically can often be readily identified by the algorithm; the data can be associated with an event and hence improve real-time performance. Second, "hints" concerning the characteristics of the algorithms (known by the algorithm but not by displays) can be associated with events.

There are numerous additional pleasant properties of this model for animating algorithms. A view can be debugged and exercised independent of any algorithm, by feeding it a stream of events generated by hand (or even randomly). Similarly, an algorithm can be debugged independent of any views. Because views are implemented external to algorithms, it is easy to reuse views among related algorithms. An algorithm being animated need not be implemented in any particular language as long as it is callable by the algorithm animation system, nor are there any restrictions on the data structures used in the algorithm.

If the stream of events generated by an algorithm are saved as the algorithm runs, then algorithms can run "backwards" by feeding the views the events in reverse order, with an additional flag indicating that the algorithm is in "reverse" mode. BALSA had this feature (see Figures 1 and 2 in Chapter 3: the scrollbar that looks like a bowtie just to the right of the BALSA logo allowed the user to set the speed and direction of the animation). Another reason to maintain the events is to enable a user to open a new view while an algorithm is running. The system brings the new view into synch by forwarding to the view all of the events that have already happened.

Finally, in an interactive setting, a user exploring an algorithm can specify events for setting breakpoints, for setting granularity of single stepping, for marking how much time each event should take to execute, and for synchronizing multiple algorithms. The next section shows how this was done in the BALSA-II [Brown 88b] system.

Interesting Events for Controlling Execution

The BALSA-II algorithm animation system allows execution to be controlled in terms program-specific units, namely the interesting events with which a programmer has annotated the algorithm. For each event, the user can specify whether it should be used as a *stoppoint* or as a *steppoint*. A stoppoint is analogous to a breakpoint in conventional debuggers: when the specified event has occurred the specified number of times, the interpreter pauses execution. A steppoint is a generalization of a conventional debugger's notion of "step to the next line." That is, when a user issues the "single step" command, the interpreter advances to the next event that is specified as a steppoint

The Stops command in the Run menu brings up the dialog box shown in Figure 3 for observing and specifying this information. Algorithms can be run in one of the four styles shown in Figure 4: Go stops at the next stoppoint; GoGo pauses at stoppoints; Step stops at the next steppoint; and StepStep pauses at steppoints. The Reset command terminates the execution of the selected algorithm.

Simply watching an algorithm in action may, at times, lead to mistaken impressions concerning its performance because the time required by the graphics performed in each view may dwarf the algorithm's computation time. Moreover, as more view windows are opened, the algorithm appears to run slower!

To precisely measure an algorithm's performance, we can find out the number of times each interesting event has occurred by issuing the Show Counts command found in the Stops... dialog in Figure 3. This information is shown in the left

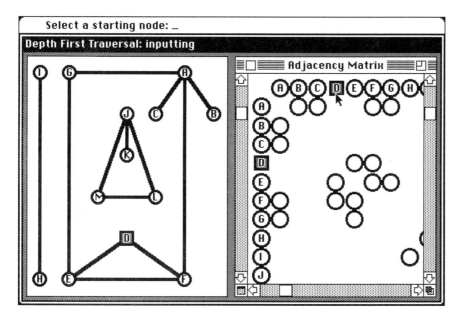

Figure 2. Depth-first Traversal of an Undirected Graph. The view at the right displays the adjacency matrix that defines the graph shown at the left. When this screen dump was captured, the algorithm had just finished its initialization and has paused, awaiting user response to identify a starting vertex. The selected vertex is D, highlighted in both views.

In both views, the display state of each vertex and edge indicates its state. Hollow circles are vertices that have not been visited, gray squares are vertices ready to be visited in the near future, and black squares are vertices that have been visited. Figures 4 and 6 show different graph traversal algorithms on larger graph during execution.

column of numbers in Figure 5 (the right column will be explained in a moment). In practice, interesting events correspond to an algorithm's fundamental operations, and these numbers are of immediate interest to people studying an algorithm's performance.

We can specify a *cost* for each event; intuitively, the cost is a measure of how much computer "time" the interpreter should allocate for the event. Figure 6 shows two instantiations of Kruskal's minimal-spanning tree algorithm on the same undirected graph. The algorithms have progressed at different rates because different costs have been assigned to the events. This feature is useful for simulating the algorithm on two different models of computation: for example, in one model, data movement might be expensive relative to data access, whereas in another model, these operations might have the same relative cost.

BALSA-II schedules the multiple algorithms in a round-robin fashion. During each time-slice, an algorithm executes until it reaches an event and then that event is broadcast by BALSA-II to all views so they can update themselves. By default, the cost for all events is 1. Changing the cost of event *e* for algorithm *a* to 3, say, would mean that whenever algorithm *a* generated event *e*, that algorithm would wait until all other algorithms generated 3 more events.

Figure 3. Costs, stops, and steps. The dialog box shows the interesting events for graph traversal algorithms. The check box immediately to the left of each event indicates whether that event is a steppoint. The typein boxes are the stoppoint (middle) and the cost assigned to each event (left).

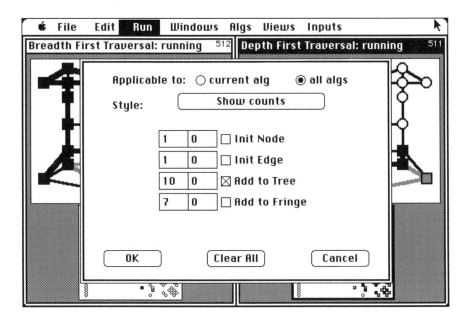

Figure 4. Execution Styles. The algorithm at the left is a breadth-first traversal of a graph, and the algorithm at the right is depth-first.

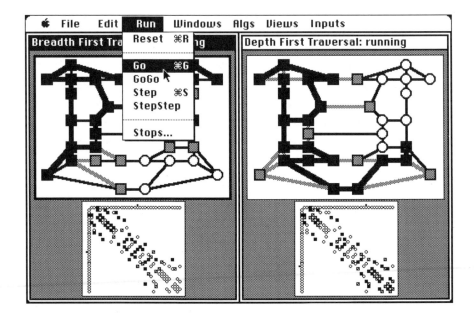

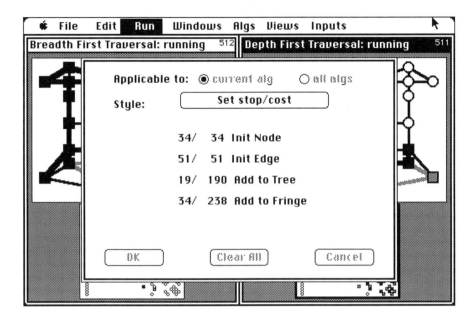

Figure 5. Event Costs. This dialog box is displayed as a result of selecting the "Show Counts" button in the dialog box from Figure 3. For each interesting event, the dialog show the number of times the event has occurred (left), and the time attributed to that event (right).

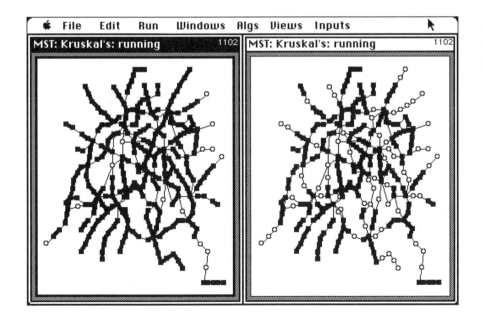

Figure 6. Synchronizing Multiple Algorithms. The number in the upper right corner (1102) is the "time" that each algorithm has used thus far.

Interesting Events for Animating Algorithms

This section gives a complete example of preparing an algorithm animation using the model of interesting events. The example uses JCAT, a Web-based algorithm animation system recently developed by Brown, Najork and Raisamo [Brown 96b], based on the CAT system by Brown and Najork [Brown 96a]. A JCAT "textbook" consist of passive multimedia material combined with interactive algorithm animations. The passive multimedia is specified using HTML and can exploit the expressive power of Web pages (e.g., text, audio, and video). The animations are prepared using a full-fledged algorithm animation system implemented in Java.

From the user's point of view, there are multiple views of the running program, each is updated simultaneously as the program runs. In addition, there's a control panel for starting, pausing, single-stepping (in units of interesting events) and stopping the animation, for adjusting its speed, and for giving input data to the algorithm.

Each view in JCAT, as well as the control panel, is implemented as an applet. Moreover, because JCAT is based on Java's RMI technology for allowing applets to communicate with each other, the views of algorithm can reside on any machine. Thus, in an electronic classroom, an instructor can control an animation on his machine (specifying input, stepping the program to some point, and so on), and each student in the class can see views of the program on their machines by pointing their browsers at the appropriate page.

The framework for animating an algorithm follows the model pioneered by BALSA, and discussed earlier in this chapter: Strategically important points of an algorithm are annotated with procedure calls that generate "interesting events" (e.g., a "swap elements" in a sorting algorithm). These events are reported to an event manager, which in turn forwards them to all registered views. Each view responds to interesting events by drawing appropriate images.

The task of animating an algorithm in JCAT consists of four parts: defining the interesting events; implementing the algorithm and annotating it with the events; implementing one or more views; and finally, creating Web pages that make use of the algorithm and views. The Web pages are prepared using HTML; the events, algorithm and views are implemented in Java.

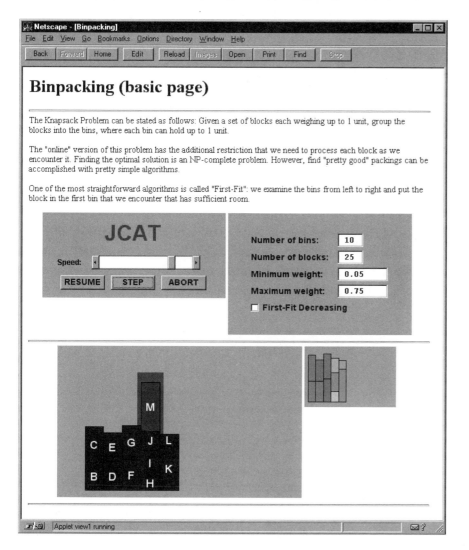

Figure 7. A page from a prototype JCAT textbook on binpacking algorithms.

The top-left applet is the JCAT control panel. It allows the user to start and stop the program, advance the program step-by-step, and adjust the speed of the animation. The JCAT control panel is algorithm-independent; this applet is used to control all algorithms in the JCAT system.

The applet at the top-right is an algorithm input dialog that is used for specifying input to the algorithm. This applet is specific to each algorithm. The algorithm input dialog used for binpacking algorithms allows users to specify the number of bins available for packing, the number of blocks to pack, the dimensions (in between 0.0 and 1.0) of each block, and whether to sort all of the blocks into decreasing order before trying to pack them.

The two applets below the horizontal line are view applets. The large applet on the left is a "Probing View"; it shows each block as a vertical bar whose size reflects the weight of the block. As the algorithm examines the bins from left-to-right, the new block is graphically shown on the bin being examined. Once a bin is found with enough room for the new block, the color of the new block changes from gray to blue. The smaller applet on the right is a "Packing View;" it shows how the blocks have been arranged into the bins. Color is used to redundantly encode the size of each block.

The Interesting Events

There are four interesting events for binpacking algorithms. The `setup` event is called once at the beginning to tell the views how many blocks will be processed by the algorithm and the maximum number of bins available. The `newBlock` event is called each time that the algorithm encounters a new block to pack. The parameter to the event is the weight of the new block. The `probe` event is called each time that the algorithm checks if the new block can be packed into the bin specified as a parameter. The `pack` event is called to signal that the last bin that was probed is where the new block will be placed.

The "interesting events" are specified as a Java interface. Here are the interesting events for binpacking algorithms:

```
public interface BinPacking_Events
{
  void setup(int numBins, int numBlocks);
  void newBlock(double wt);
  void probe(int bin);
  void pack();
}
```

The name of the interface is magical: JCAT will use this interface to create some additional objects that are needed for the algorithm and views to communicate. We've put the name "Binpacking" in bold here and in the places in the example algorithm and view where auxilary objects have been created based on this interface.

It is important to realize that there is nothing magic about these specific events or the parameters to them. Another programmer implementing a binpacking algorithm animation might have chosen a different set of events or different parameters. The choice of events and parameters will affect how much additional state each view much maintain, since views do not have access to the algorithm's data.

The Algorithm

An algorithm is a Java object that is a subclass of the JCAT class `Algorithm`, which in turn is a subclass of Java's `Applet` class. More specifically, an algorithm is a subclass of the type of algorithm for which it can generate interesting events. In this example, the first-fit binpacking algorithm class is a subclass of "`BinpackingAlgorithm`", which means, essentially, that it's an algorithm that can generate the events defined in the `Binpacking_Events` interface.

The actual algorithm appears in the method called "`algorithm.`" The following code shows the gist of the first-fit binpacking algorithm. The event annotations are shown italics.

```
public class FirstFit extends
  BinPackingAlgorithm
{
 void start() { . . .}
 void algorithm(BinPacking_Events z)
 {
   int numBins =
     readIntParameter("numBins",10);
   int numBlocks =
     readIntParameter("numBlocks",25);
   double totals[]=new double[numBins];

   z.setup(numBins,numBlocks);
   for (int b=0; b<numBlocks-1; b++) {
     double amt=nextBlock();
     z.newBlock(amt);
     int bin=0;
     while (bin<numBins) {
       z.probe(bin);
       if (totals[bin++]+amt <= 1.0) break;
     }
     if (bin==numBins) break;
     totals[bin] +=amt;
     z.pack();
   }
 }
 }
```

The algorithm method makes use of a few internal procedures (not shown) for retrieving the input data specified by the user.

The `start` method (also not shown) is defined by virtue of an `Algorithm` being a subclass of an `Applet`. This method is used to initialize the graphical user interface of the algorithm control panel.

A View

A view is Java object that is a subclass of the JCAT class `View`, which in turn is a subclass of an `Applet`. More specifically, a view is a subclass of the type of view to which interesting events it can respond. In this example, the views are subclasses of "`BinpackingView`", which means, essentially, that they also implement the `Binpacking_Events` interface.

Here is the actual code for the "Probing View" seen in Figure 7.

```
public class ProbingView extends BinPackingView {
  GP qp = new GP();
  Vertex v;
  double currWt;
  double totals[];
  int id, numBlocks, lastProbe, blockWidth;

  static Color ProbingColor = Color.darkGray;
  static Color PackedColor  = Color.blue;
  static Color LabelColor    = Color.white;

  public void init() {
    super.init();
    add(qp);
  }

  public void setup(int numBins, int numBlocks) {
    this.id = 0;
    this.numBlocks = numBlocks;
    this.totals = new double[numBins];
    for (int i=0;i<numBins;i++) totals[i]=0;
    qp.clear();
    qp.setWorld(-2.0, numBins+1.0, 2.1, -0.1);
    qp.redisplay();
  }

  public void newBlock(double wt) {
    id++;
    v = new Vertex(qp);
    v.setSize (1.0, wt);
    v.setPosition(-1.0, wt/2.0);
    v.setColor(ProbingColor);
    v.setShape(Vertex.RECTANGLE);
    v.setBorder(Vertex.HORIZONTAL);
    if (numBlocks <= 26) {
      v.setLabelColor(LabelColor);
      Character c = new Character('A'+id-1);
      v.setLabel(c.toString());
    }
    currWt = wt;
    lastProbe = -1;
    qp.redisplay();
  }
  public void probe(int bin) {
    v.move((double)bin, totals[bin]+currWt/2.0);
    qp.animate(speed);
    lastProbe = bin;
  }

  public void pack() {
    totals[lastProbe] += currWt;
    v.setColor(PackedColor);
    qp.redisplay();
  }
}
```

Each view implements the methods that are defined in the interesting event interface. The body of each method is responsible for updating the screen in a way that is meaningful for the view.

The class GP (not shown) is a rich, high-level animation package based on the metaphor of a graph consisting of vertices and edges [DeTreville 93]. Each vertex has various attributes associated, such as position, size, shape, color, border width, and label. An edge connects two vertices and has attributes such as color and thickness. Vertices can be repositioned, and such movement can be shown by smooth animation, inspired by the TANGO system [Stasko 90a] (see Chapter 8).

Parts of this chapter is based on [Brown 88b], [Brown 88c], and [Brown 96b], and are used with permission.

Acknowledgments

Declarative Visualization

Gruia-Catalin Roman

Flexibility, generality, and expressive power are critical to the rapid development of custom visualizations. Declarative visualization is a technique which provides the animator with the ability to construct complex visual representations of executing programs by defining abstract mathematical mappings from program states to graphical objects. The approach [Roman 89], which has been instrumental in the design of a system called *Pavane* [Roman 92], marks the first significant paradigm shift in program visualization since the introduction of interesting events. Figure 1 shows sample animations built with Pavane. While the latter technique can be implemented readily in any language with no tool support, the more abstract and less operational nature of the declarative approach requires some compilation mechanism to translate the abstract specification into a computation. In other words, much of the burden of managing the visualization process is shifted away from the animator to the visualization environment. Furthermore, the programmer can develop the visualization without examining the algorithm since only knowledge of the state representation is required.

Introduction

This chapter provides a tutorial introduction to declarative visualization, explains some of the technical reasons that led to the development of the technique, shows how declarative visualization can express a wide range of computing problems important in program visualization, and reviews briefly the manner in which the declarative paradigm is instantiated in *Pavane*.

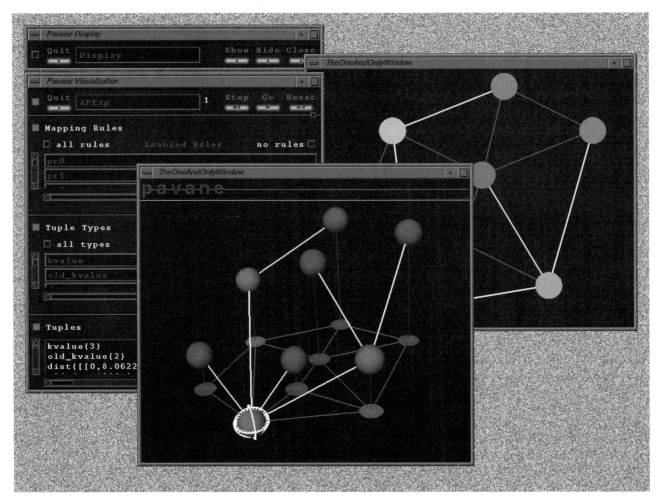

Figure 1. The animations shown in this chapter have been produced using a system called Pavane. Two views of an animation of a shortest distance program and some of the Pavane control panels appear above.
See Plate 3

In the declarative paradigm (figure 2) visualization involves three parties: a programmer, an animator, and a viewer—of course, one person may assume any or all three roles. The programmer develops the code without regard to the fact that it will be visualized; the animator defines the mapping from program states to graphical objects; and the viewer examines the results of the visualization either passively or actively. In the latter case, the viewer may choose to navigate through the visualization, alter the presentation style and contents, and even interact with the underlying computation. Our discussion of declarative visualization focuses on the animator and the manner in which one specifies the mapping from states to graphical objects. For simplicity, we assume that the program is already written and that the viewer is passive. Operationally, one can think of an execution model where every time the program changes state the display is altered to reflect the new state. The question is how one specifies the mapping and whether the notation is powerful enough to conveniently express a sufficiently broad range of visualization styles. We consider the specification issue first.

Simple mappings

The game of life is a mathematical game which simulates the life-cycle of colonies of organisms. The game starts with a grid whose cells may be empty or occupied and on each step births occur in empty cells that have the right number of neighbors (three) and deaths take place in occupied cells which have too few (less than two) or too many (more than three) neighbors. A program implementing the game might use a two dimensional Boolean array G of size n by n to encode the grid. A simple visualization may use dots to represent empty cells and spheres to depict the live organisms (figure 3). The most direct way of specifying such a visualization is via a function *Vis* which maps Boolean arrays to pictures consisting of dots and spheres, actually sets of graphical objects belonging to a predefined graphical vocabulary understood by the display system:

$$Vis(G,n) \Leftarrow \{ \textbf{dot}[position(i,j,0)] \mid 1{\le}i{\le}n \land 1{\le}j{\le}n \land \neg G(i,j) \} \cup$$
$$\{ \textbf{sphere}[position(i,j,0)] \mid 1{\le}i{\le}n \land 1{\le}j{\le}n \land G(i,j) \}$$

where all the unspecified graphical object attributes (e.g., color and size) assume default values.

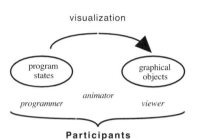

Basic Definition

Figure 2. The declarative paradigm treats visualization as a mapping from program states to graphical representations.

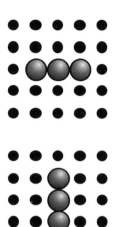

Figure 3. Two successive configurations in the game of life.

The notation can be further improved. The function name can be omitted. The function definition can be decomposed by cases with the separate results being combined by an implicit union operation. The explicit set notation can be dropped. Finally, the input domain can be treated as a set of tuples, i.e., the array element $G(i,j)$ can be viewed as a tuple $G(i,j,b)$ where G is the tuple type and b is either *true* or *false*—this way both the domain and the range of the functions are sets of objects. The result is a more compact notation reminiscent of rule-based programming:

$$G(i,j,false) \Rightarrow \textbf{dot}[position(i,j,0)]$$
$$G(i,j,true) \Rightarrow \textbf{sphere}[position(i,j,0)]$$

where all the free variables are universally quantified by convention.

It is important to note that the algorithm governing the game of life plays no role in specifying the visualization. The updating of the cells can be done synchronously or asynchronously and can be carried out by one or more processes; changes in the complexity or details of the algorithm do not affect the visualization, unless the state space changes. The same visualization works in all cases and the animator does not need to actually see the code. This is typical of the declarative paradigm and is its most attractive feature.

Technical Motivation

The motivation behind the declarative paradigm originates with the need for rapid development of abstract visualizations of complex concurrent computations. The notation introduced so far is not completely adequate for this purpose but some important technical implications of the paradigm are worth exploring before considering further extensions to the basic mapping notation. Throughout this section we use a trivial example to illustrate some of the ideas; the example, the performance monitor shown in figure 4, produces a bar chart representation of the utilization factor for a group of parallel processors. Given a processor k, the performance parameter is denoted by $P(k,u)$ and a basic visualization can be specified as

$$P(k,u) \Rightarrow \textbf{box}[position(k,0,0),height(u)]$$

Decoupling the visualization and programming tasks

The idea of annotating interesting events represents an important first step towards separating the programming and the visualization activities. The declarative paradigm goes one step further. In principle, the animator does not need to have access to the code of the software being visualized; a formal specification of the state representation is sufficient to construct the mapping. *Pavane* visualizations of Swarm [Roman 90] programs, for instance, require no access to the code. On the other hand, visualization of arbitrary C++ programs with *Pavane* does involve annotation of data declarations as well as markers to indicate completion of logically atomic operations—simple preprocessors can eliminate even further the need to access the code. In these kinds of situations the best strategy is to have the programmer decide what aspects of the program state are being exported to the visualization system and when, thus allowing the animator to deal strictly with the definition of the visualization mapping.

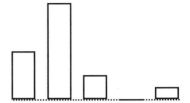

Figure 4. A simple processor utilization chart.

This separation of concerns simplifies the visualization process by insulating it from the complexities of the processing logic and its changes. The visualization need not be altered when the code changes or when very different algorithms (using similar data) are being tested out. During validation and testing, a visualization derived directly from the requirements specification and without knowledge of the operational details of the program is more likely to act as an effective black box testing instrument. In the case of the performance monitor, for instance, the visualization specification is not altered by the manner in which the parameter $P(k,u)$ is computed; it can be updated automatically by the hardware (no code), it may be derived from internal clock readings (a few lines of code), or it may be computed using a complex clock synchronization protocol (a complex subsystem involving many procedures and interprocess communication).

Accommodating concurrency

Understanding the full potential of the declarative paradigm requires one to consider the problem of visualizing concurrent computations (parallel or distributed). As it is the case with sequential algorithms, the initial state of the computation must be available to the visualization software, whether one uses interesting events or declarative visualization. In the declarative paradigm, however, since the visualization is based on the current state, it becomes possible for visualizations to be started up at any time. This feature is essential if one is to visualize non-terminating or long-running computations. Moreover, the birth and death of processes or even transient communication failures have no effect on the complexity of the visualization. By contrast, the loss or out-of-order delivery of a single interesting event may confuse completely the visualization without hope of recovery. Also, if the interesting events are not local to a process, i.e., involve data across multiple processes or sites, it is not at all clear where the annotations ought to be placed at all. Finally, it is often the case that the visual effects of an event cannot be determined from the event description alone, i.e., the visualization system must maintain some image of the program state anyway in order to interpret events properly.

If the performance monitor, for instance, needs to display in gray only the highest utilization (figure 5) a simple change in the mapping suffices

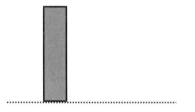

Figure 5. A maximum utilization chart.

$$P(k,u) \land u=\langle \textbf{max } u',k' : P(k',u') :: u' \rangle$$
$$\Rightarrow \quad \textbf{box}[position(k,0,0), height(u), color(gray)]$$

(the three-part construct used above applies the operator **max** to the multiset of utilization values u' obtained by considering all instances of tuples $P(k',u')$ in the state space). In an event-based strategy the animator needs to maintain a copy of the state since the graphical objects do not actually provide sufficient information to process each arriving utilization update. The declarative approach is clearly more abstract thus removing some of the animator's burdens at the price of a more complex visualization environment. Implicit in the type of mappings discussed so far is the ability to acquire a global snapshot of the underlying distributed computation. This is not available directly in distributed computations. However, composite mappings (discussed later in the chapter) provide reasonably abstract ways of computing global states.

Facilitating new kinds of abstract representations

Traditionally, program visualizations tend to have a very strong operational flavor, i.e., they show the mechanics of *how* an algorithm works without explaining *why* the algorithm works. One way to convey the latter is by visualizing not the operational and structural details of the algorithm but key formal properties encountered in the verification of the algorithm. The approach is called *proof-based visualization*. Our experiments with this technique focused on classical concurrent processing algorithms. The declarative paradigm's emphasis on states turns out to be a particularly good match for working with assertional proofs in the style of UNITY [Chandy 88]; invariant properties, for instance, can be easily captured graphically in terms of geometric and coloring relationships.

Because in concurrent programming proofs often rely on the use of auxiliary variables (variables which are not part of the program but are used to reason about its behavior), proof-based visualization revealed the need for the visualization mappings to maintain historical information. Moreover, proofs often deal with the notions of what is *feasible* to happen next or what is bound to *eventually* happen given the current state of the computation. These issues, in turn, lead to the emergence of speculative and anticipatory visualizations whose role is to prepare the viewer for what is to come. The generation of these kinds of visualizations must rely on state information since it involves implicit references to events which will or may arrive in the future.

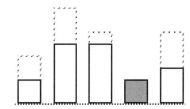

Figure 6. A visualization which anticipates the correct behavior of a program can help discover algorithmic errors.

The performance monitor can be used again to illustrate these ideas. Let's assume, for instance, that the scheduler was designed to always allocate the next task to the processor with the lowest utilization. This means that, if the system works correctly, only the lowest utilization can increase while all other utilization values may only decrease. For utilizations that can decrease one may want to show their previous values using dashed lines; utilization values that may increase can be highlighted by a change in color (figure 6).

The notation introduced earlier in this chapter is inadequate for the development of complex visualizations. By eliminating the function name we lost the power of recursion. There is no mechanism for specifying smooth animations. Historical information, if needed, must be maintained explicitly by the underlying algorithm. Multiple views of the same algorithm cannot be specified. In this section we discuss ways of addressing these and other apparent limitations and show that declarative visualization is a powerful and convenient tool for the serious animator. All the features outlined below are available in the current version of *Pavane* and the sample visualizations have been generated using *Pavane*. However, the discussion is general and brings up issues that are important to any visualization system.

Modular Specification of Complex Visualizations in Pavane

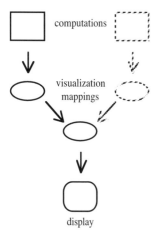

computations

visualization
mappings

display

*Figure 7. Compositionality
promotes reuse. A single
visualization can be used to validate
requirements and later debug the
delivered software. Such was the case
with the elevator visualization shown
in figure 8.*

*Figure 8. Each floor and the cabin
could be treated as composite objects.
*See Plate 3**

Composition

In the declarative approach the simplest visualization involves three components: the computation, a visualization mapping which implements the visualization rules, and a display which renders the graphical objects on the screen. Since the mapping ties the state representation to the graphical presentation, any change in data representation is likely to affect the mapping. This is one of the reasons for introducing composite mappings.

A first mapping can be used to create a general representation of the program state which, in turn, is provided to a second mapping whose role is to define the visualization proper (figure 7). Thus, only the first mapping is affected by changes in data representation.

Composition can be accomplished by simply identifying the output of one mapping with the input of the next. No new notation is really needed if the mappings are associated with distinct modules and mechanisms are provided for expressing the fact that one module feeds its output to the next.

Compound graphical objects

A byproduct of compositionality is the ability to construct increasingly more abstract views of the program state from one mapping to the next before reaching the point when a concrete visual representation is generated. When defining the graphical representation, it is desirable to work at an appropriate level of abstraction as well. This is feasible if the animator can define graphical objects tailored specifically to the task at hand (see figure 8). The basic graphical vocabulary recognized by the display must be expandable by allowing compound objects to be constructed from basic ones. In an elevator application, for instance, one should be able to control the cabin as a single entity whose structure, in terms of rectangles, is defined separately.

Camera controls

Navigation through the visualization is generally left at the discretion of the viewer. There are instances, however, when is it is advantageous to have the animator control the viewpoint (figure 9). To accomplish this in a declarative manner, the output range of the mapping must be extended to include a *camera* object. When the display observes the presence of a camera object, the viewer controls may be inhibited and the viewpoint may be determined by the position of the camera. This is simple enough but somewhat tedious since the camera attributes must be set again and again every time the mapping is recomputed. A better approach is to introduce the notion of a persistent object. The attributes of a persistent object are remembered by the display and, once the object is created, it continues to exist even if not present in the output of the visualization mapping. Persistent objects are useful not only for camera control but also if the visualization is extended to include auralization—once a musical piece is started it is desirable to let it have an independent existence and refer to its attributes only if and when they are to be changed. Since the camera is unique no identifier is required to refer to it. In other cases persistent objects must be assigned unique identifiers.

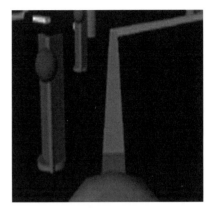

*Figure 9. By placing the camera over the nose of the train, one can show the conductor's view of the simulated railroad layout. *See Plate 3**

History recording

Animators often use color coding to communicate the age of a graphical object as a way of maintaining a focus of attention for the viewer (see Chapter 7). Since the underlying computation is unlikely to maintain this information, the mapping has to compute and manage it (figure 10). Formally, the previous configuration of the output must be made available as an input to the mapping rules next time around. If we assume that the types of tuples present in the input and output spaces of a mapping are disjoint, no notational changes are needed. One only needs to allow the mapping rules to refer to output tuples, which are assumed to have been produced by a previous application of the rules. This mechanism was introduced in *Pavane* originally due to the need to compute and visualize auxiliary variables critical to the verification of distributed algorithms.

*Figure 10. In the game of life the age of the cells (not computed by the program) is encoded in shades of blue. *See Plate 3**

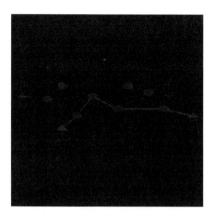

Figure 11. The closing of a connection (an event) in this simulation of an ATM network may require the selection of a new connection to be shown to the viewer.

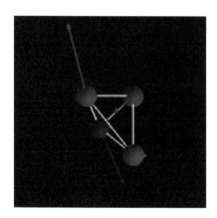

Figure 12. Smooth movement of the atoms can be accomplished by interpolation over multiple frames inserted between two consecutive program state representations.

Event recognition

Even though our approach to declarative visualization places a strong emphasis on program states, there are instances when events must be detected and visualized. Since an event is formally a pair of successive states, a visualization mapping can detect any event if allowed to compare its current and previous inputs. In *Pavane*, a one step history of all inputs and outputs to all mappings is maintained for this purpose and references to tuples appearing in the previous state are qualified by the prefix *old*. Testing for the loss of a connection between nodes *i* and *j* (figure 11) could assume the form (a comment is used as a place holder for the output):

$$\textbf{old}.\text{connection}(i,j) \wedge \neg\text{connection}(i,j)$$
$$\Rightarrow \quad \textit{select a new connection to display this time}$$

The addition of this feature makes it possible to extend the declarative paradigm beyond mapping states to graphical objects. Events detected by mappings or supplied by the computation can now be mapped to visual events, i.e., to changes in the scene being displayed. In visualizing distributed systems is advantageous to create an abstract global view of the entire computation and to detect global events at this abstract level, a task easily accomplished in the declarative paradigm.

Smooth animation

Event detection plays an important role also in the way declarative visualization handles smooth animation, as a visual event decomposition. A state change is mapped into a sequence of animation frames by generating graphical objects whose attributes are time dependent (in the number of frames). For instance, a rule that generates smooth movement of a sphere over *k* frames from position *p* to *q* may be generated using *ramp*, one of several built-in functions supporting animation (figure 12):

$$\textbf{old}.\text{atom}(i,p) \wedge \text{atom}(i,q)$$
$$\Rightarrow \quad \textbf{sphere}[\textit{center}(\textit{ramp}(0,p,k,q))]$$

For each state transition, the display establishes how may frames are needed to generate all the smoothly animated objects and for each frame evaluates all the frame-dependent attributes. Arbitrarily complex presentations can be choreographed to fill the space between consecutive states. The animator can use this capability not only to create continuity in the display but also to convey semantic information about the algorithm or to attract the viewer's attention.

Fixpoints

In introducing any formal notation, such as the one proposed here for declarative visualization, one must be careful not to restrict inadvertently the computational power of the model. We discovered, for instance, that the absence of recursion makes it impossible to generate certain kinds of displays, e.g., trees which can change in arbitrary ways, because in each state the position of a node depends upon that of its parent. To avoid this, one can add explicit recursion in the notation or introduce fixpoint rules—they are applied repeatedly until the output remains unchanged. This is the solution adopted by *Pavane*.

> **fixpoint**
> $node(x) \wedge root(x) \Rightarrow node\_height(x, 0);$
> $node(x) \wedge parent(x, y) \wedge old.node\_height (y, h)$
> $\qquad \Rightarrow node\_height(x, h + 1);$

These two fixpoint rules compute the height of all nodes in a tree. The first rule asserts that the height of the root is 0. The second rule establishes the height of a child as one greater than its parent's height.

Multiple views

Complex visualizations and direct comparisons among algorithms working on the same data require multiple views (e.g., figure 13 and Chapter 7). In *Pavane*, as in most visualization systems today, each view is associated with a separate window. To facilitate this, the linear composition of mappings can be extended to a tree whose root is a computation and whose leaves are distinct windows. By convention, all windows appearing on the same physical display are synchronized. Every time the computation changes state, the mappings along the path lying between the computation and each of the windows are composed together. When all the windows (being displayed on the same screen) receive new inputs, they start painting one animation frame at a time and they move on to the next frame together. When two windows appear on different display devices they are not synchronized at the frame level but they may be synchronized at state level. This is accomplished by disallowing the computation from taking another step until all the windows finish their current animation sequence. In *Pavane*, this is called synchronous visualization.

Distributed visualizations

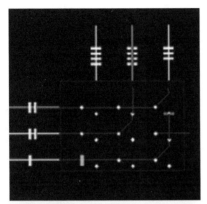

Pavane visualizations can be a lot more complex than suggested so far. Each mapping can be compiled as a separate module, can be linked at runtime to multiple other modules on both the input and the output sides, and can be placed on any available machine in the local area network. When this happens, the mapping uses as input the union of all its inputs and passes its output to all the modules that need it. On the input side, the animator may specify which subset of the inputs is required before the next application of the mapping takes place thus forcing the module to behave synchronously with respect to some modules on the input side and asynchronously with respect to the rest of them. On the output side, the animator may specify if the mapping must block in order to allow some other mapping to accept the results produced. Buffers can be used to tie mappings together when it is desirable to insulate them from each other.

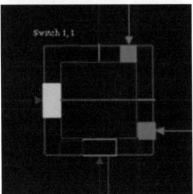

Support for distributed visualizations is natural for a system designed to facilitate the visualization of concurrent computations executing on a multiprocessor or across a local area network. One useful strategy is to allow each process in the underlying computation to supply its state to an initial set of mappings whose role is to filter the state information. The next layer of mappings can function as an abstraction mechanism. Included among its tasks is the construction of a consistent global state from which all the desired visualizations can be generated.

Figure 13. A message router and a detail view of one of its switches.

Interactions

Through-the-screen interactions are particularly important for complex visualizations because they allow the viewer to exercise control over what is being shown, when, and at what level of detail. This makes the visualization more responsive to the viewer's interests and saves valuable screen real estate. The current version of *Pavane* offers the ability to interact with the visualization system through viewing controls shown in figure 14 and by clicking on graphical objects on the screen. The information about such screen events is treated as the output of the display module associated with the respective window and can be communicated to mappings and to the underlying computation as well.

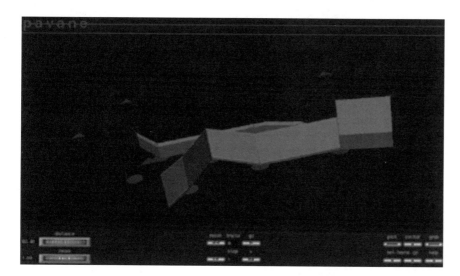

Figure 14. A Pavane *window and its viewing controls.*

A rich repertoire of declarative features, a compiler that translates the rules to C++ code, arbitrary graph structures, dynamic linking, through-the-screen interactions, and distributed execution provide the *Pavane* animator with the tools needed to go beyond visualizing algorithms to constructing complex visualization applications.

Experience to date

The successful development and application of *Pavane* to a wide range of visualization problems (concurrent algorithms, computer architecture simulations, scientific visualization, rapid prototyping, etc.) demonstrates the viability of the declarative paradigm. A formal study of the rule-based notation showed its computational power [Cox 94]. At a more practical level, the most important result of evaluating *Pavane* was the fact that competent programmers with no prior exposure to visualization are able to grasp the approach rapidly and are capable of animating already developed programs with three to six hours of effort. This is very encouraging when one considers the custom nature of the visualizations produced and the start-up effort associated with learning any new system. Even more encouraging is the fact that most of the visualizations built using *Pavane* require less than two dozen rules with three to ten being quite common. The rapid visualization capabilities of the approach make it highly suitable for exploratory work by enabling the animator to investigate a broader set of visualization alternatives in the same amount of time. Because of their compact representation and simple semantics, declarative visualizations are more easily debugged and maintained. The applicability of the approach to the development of industrial-grade applications is currently under evaluation. The distributed design of *Pavane* and the addition of through-the-screen interactions provide two features that are essential to this kind of effort. It is likely that in industrial applications performance will emerge as an important new evaluation criterion.

Conclusions and related work

The declarative approach to visualization is attractive because visualizations are specified and modified easily and because visualization is decoupled from the program code. *Pavane* [Roman 92][Roman 93] was instrumental in establishing the declarative approach as a distinct program visualization paradigm and led to the most extensive study of the declarative methods to date. Nevertheless, *Pavane* is not the first system to employ declarative notions in program visualization. *PROVIDE* [Moher 88] and *PVS* [Foley 86], for instance, make use of simple mappings from variables to icon attributes. *Aladdin* [Helttula 89] employs a declarative approach to define the relationship between program variables and the image, but combines this with an annotative approach which indicates at what points in the program the image should be updated; the annotations are specified graphically. *Animus* [Duisberg 86a] uses the declarative approach in two ways: each object can have a graphical representation that is automatically updated in response to changes in the object; more significantly, the animator can declaratively specify constraints on the relations among objects. More recently, rule-based specifications of animations have been incorporated in several systems including *TRIP* [Takahashi 94].

Acknowledgments

This work was supported in part by the National Science Foundation under the Grant CCR-9217751. The U. S. government has certain rights in this material. The author would like to thank Delbert Hart for his careful review of this chapter and valuable help with the layout and image editing.

Building Software Visualizations through Direct Manipulation and Demonstration

John Stasko

John Stasko

One of the most challenging aspects of developing a software visualization is creating the graphics portion of the visualization. This is particularly true when the visualization is to have sophisticated graphics and animation in it. To build software visualizations, developers typically use low-level graphics toolkits such as Xlib for 2-D and OpenGL for 3-D. Alternatively, they sometimes use special purpose visualization libraries with primitives particularly tailored for the types of displays seen in software visualizations [Stasko 90a] [Brown 91] [Stasko 93b] [Glassman 93] [DeTreville 93].

Introduction

Support libraries such as these are useful and appropriate when a crafted software visualization is being developed for a particular purpose. But even the simplest of these libraries still requires textual programming and has a moderate learning curve; developing visualizations with graphics toolkits simply takes time. One alternative to the programming approach is to design and implement software visualizations by direct manipulation and demonstration. Since the eventual "output" of a software visualization is graphical in nature, why not design the visualization using the same medium? This approach potentially can be easier to learn and use, and is thus appropriate for software visualization contexts where speed of construction is of the essence. Two examples of individuals who would benefit by being able to develop their own software visualizations very rapidly are instructors who are preparing algorithm animations and who have little spare time, and programmers who are debugging their code.

Computer animation systems have long used demonstration and interactive sketching for building new visualizations. One of the first of these systems, GENESYS [Baecker 74], allowed designers to sketch animation keyframes by hand and use visual depictions of path-descriptions to describe how the objects in the keyframes should move and change. In algorithm animation, Duisberg's prototype Gestural system [Duisberg 87] captured user gestures made while using a mouse to manipulate a picture of a program. The system resulted from earlier work on the Animus system [Dusiberg 86] that used temporal constraints to help animate program behaviors. Both systems functioned in the Smalltalk environment. Recently, the "by demonstration" approach has proved useful in many different domains and is growing in popularity. See [Cypher 93] [Myers 92] for an excellent overview of example work in this area.

The remainder of this chapter will describe two systems that provide direct manipulation, demonstrational operations to develop software visualizations. The first system, Dance, supports the creation of algorithm animations, and the second system, Lens, supports the creation of software visualizations useful for visual debugging.

The DANCE System

The Dance (Demonstration ANimation CrEation) system for designing algorithm animations by demonstration includes a direct manipulation style graphical editor that allows designers to sketch out animation scenarios, then it automatically generates the appropriate animation design code that will carry out the desired actions. The design code is used as input by the Tango algorithm animation system [Stasko 90a] for creating animated views of computer programs.

Dance supports the design of algorithm animations by demonstration [Myers 92] because it creates generalized animation routines that can be adapted to particular program executions. This also distinguishes the system from other direct manipulation tools, many commercial products, that create "hard-coded" animation scenarios. The types of algorithm animation routines built using Dance are dependent upon run-time information from a driving program that dictates how the animation should appear.

Dance supports simplified animation design by freeing developers from writing code. In addition, the system also serves as an interactive tutorial for the animation paradigm it supports. Early users of Dance reported that its visual paradigms helped to illustrate the underlying animation principles of the Tango system.

Tango uses designer-created animation description code to display algorithm animations. Designers identify key points in application programs, which when reached, activate the appropriate animation description routines. Dance provides a way to generate the animation description routines via direct manipulation, relieving the burden of manual text type-in.

Animation sequences in Tango are based on the path-transition paradigm [Stasko 90b] and Chapter 8 in this book. The paradigm is composed of four abstract data types: location, image, path, and transition. Locations identify particular geometric positions of interest within the animation coordinate system. Images are the graphical objects that undergo changes to create the frames of an animation. Paths are sequences of relative (x,y) control points that manage image modifications. Each offset in a path corresponds to a new animation frame. Transitions are the logical units of action or change in animations and are defined by a type, the image affected, and the path controlling the modification. Transition types include *move*, *resize*, *color*, *fill*, *raise*, *delay*, and *alter visibility*. Designers create and manipulate instances (objects) of the four data types in order to create animation sequences. Sets of operations are organized into logical animation actions called *animation scenes*.

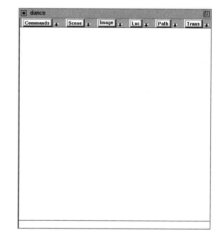

Figure 1. Overview of Dance user interface.

Data type operations and parameters

From a user's perspective, Dance is organized much like a typical graphical editing tool with a main graphics window and a set of pull-down menu choices above. (See Figure 1.) At any moment, the design of only one animation scene is active. During a particular session, however, animation scenes can be written out to multiple, different files at various times.

Animation scenes used by Tango consist primarily of sequences of path-transition data type operations. Each operation returns an object, which is typically then used as a parameter to a subsequent operation. In the C implementation of the path-transition paradigm, the data type operations are implemented as procedures with the data type instances being assigned as the

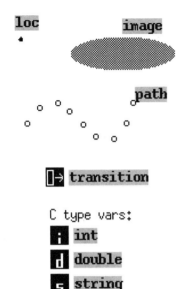

Figure 2. Depictions of the different variable types in Dance.

return values (variables in C) of the procedures. In the Dance window, variables of different types have their own unique visual depiction as shown in Figure 2. Locations are represented as small filled circles. Images utilize their natural graphical object type (lines, circles, rectangles, ellipses, text, splines, etc.) Paths are represented by two-dimensional tracks of small hollow circles, simply interpreting the path's *x* and *y* offsets under the geometry of the window. Transitions are represented by small icons appropriate to the transition type. Tango design code commonly includes integer, double, character, and string variables too, so each of these types is represented by a small icon of the first letter of the type.

Variables' names are displayed with their visual depictions. Variables local to the animation scene (C procedure) being defined have a yellow name label background. Global variables have a green background. Later, we shall see how these labels can be "picked" in order to use the variables as parameters to other operations. Location, image, and path variables can exist anywhere in the graphic window. The positions that locations and images occupy are important, that is, they have a natural geometric interpretation with respect to the animation coordinate system. Paths are purely relative, however, so they can be placed anywhere without changing their interpretation. For organizational purposes, transitions are placed in a column in the upper right of the window, and C-type variables go in the upper left.

Operations upon the four path-transition data types come from the pull-down menus at the top of the window. Designers invoke an operation by making the appropriate button choice from a particular data type's menu. All of Tango's operations are implemented.

When an operation is selected, its parameters must be specified. For example, the transition *Create* operation requires type, image, and path parameters. For parameters taken from a set of choices such as the type parameter, Dance provides selections from dialog boxes. To select the image and path parameters for this operation, Dance allows the designer to pick an existing variable label, via the mouse, in order to select the desired parameter. If a designer selects a variable not of the correct type, Dance identifies the error and allows a new selection. Finally, the system prompts the designer to name the resulting created variable, which then appears in the window and is available for later actions. When the C code for this procedure is generated afterwards, Dance fills in all the appropriate variable declarations.

Invoking design operations

The menus at the top of the Dance edit window provide both general editing capabilities and specialized path-transition operations. The *Command* menu includes the usual undo, refresh, and stop actions, as well as a choice for writing out all defined animation scenes to a file name specified by the designer. The *Scenes* menu supports animation scene initiation and termination.

Each of the four path-transition data types has its own menu. To create images, the designer specifies size and position with the mouse, and other attributes such as color and fill via dialog choices. Dance also allows arguments such as image position to be specified in different ways. For example, the x and y positions (real-valued numbers) can be specified by selecting existing double variables, by positioning relative to an existing location variable, or by typing an arbitrary C expression.

Designers create paths by "press-drag-release" and "sequence-of-click" mouse actions, or via selecting a predefined path pattern. Existing paths can be modified via direct manipulation as well. Menus for operations from two auxiliary Tango packages, the Twist macro facility and the Association data storage and retrieval facility, also exist, as does a menu of miscellaneous Tango operations such as user input of coordinates and images.

Because animation scenes in Tango are just C procedures, Dance supports the inclusion of various C language constructs and statements. The C menu includes buttons for declaring local and global variables and for defining macros. In addition, animations typically contain mathematical code for calculating spacing, ratios, etc. Code such as

```
spacing = 0.8 / (n + 1);
```

is quite common. Hence, the C menu also includes a button which allows a designer to type in an arbitrary string that will be placed in the resulting C procedure. This command is useful for entering comments and procedure calls too. Because Dance provides graphical mechanisms for performing programming related activities, it exhibits elements of a simplified visual programming system [Chang 87] [Shu 89].

In addition to invoking operations from menu selections, Dance provides implicit aids for animation code development. As mentioned earlier, the system enforces that parameters (selected by designers) to operations be of the appropriate type. The system also warns designers of attempts to reuse an existing variable name for another purpose. Additionally, Dance provides menu operations that summarize current attributes of the design session such as the transitions that have been performed, the associations available for use, and the types of composite images that have been created.

Example animation design

To better understand how Dance facilitates animation development, it is useful to examine some example designs of animation scenes. For a simple yet thorough introductory example, see [Stasko 91a]. Here, we will describe the design of an *exchange values* animation scene common in sorting algorithm animations. The animation depicts the array of values to be sorted as a row of rectangular blocks; the height of a block corresponds to the magnitude of the corresponding array value. The scene to be developed corresponds to a swap of two values in the program: Exchanging two elements that are out of order is shown by simultaneously moving the blocks in clockwise paths to the other's prior position. Figure 3 shows how the Dance window will appear after all of the specifications for this scene. It is a useful reference to help follow the subsequent design description.

Note that when we are designing the exchange scene with Dance, we must assume that earlier scenes in the animation will prepare the exchange scene to operate. In particular, an initialization scene will take the original set of data values and draw them as the row of blocks. In Tango, pertinent data objects such as this row of blocks are stored in associations, hash-like storage and retrieval mechanisms. The initialization scene also will store the blocks under an association whose key is its array index. The driving sort program provides two index values to the *Exchange* animation scene as parameters. The scene uses those two values as keys to the association, and it retrieves the two appropriate image variables.

To begin the Exchange scene design, we specify the name, parameters, and parameter types of the function being created. Selecting the *Define* choice from the *Scene* menu opens a series of dialog boxes for making those definitions.

Our exchange scene will receive two integer parameters named *p1* and *p2* from the sort driver program. The parameters are the indices of the array elements being switched. Each parameter is just a local integer variable, so they have yellow pickable labels to help select them as parameters to subsequent operations.

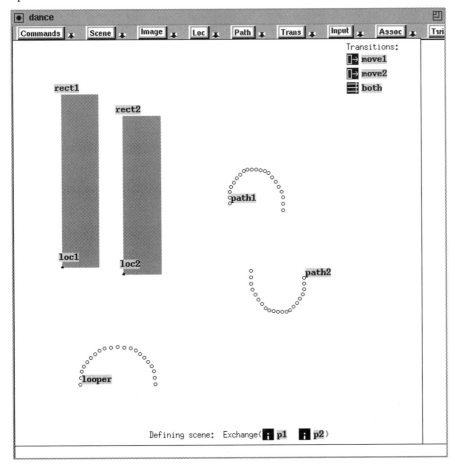

Figure 3. Design of the exchange value sorting animation scene prior to transition performance.

The first action of the scene body is to acquire the block images of the two array index parameters. In the sorting animation, the blocks will already be on the screen when this animation scene is called. But, because this scene is its own unit, we need to acquire the C variables referencing the two pertinent images. As mentioned above, data values in Tango are stored in associations. So here, we perform two association retrieval operations (choose the *Retrieve* command from the *Assoc* menu). After allowing us to enter the resultant variable names, we'll use *rect1* and *rect2*, and association string name (*ID*), Dance prompts us to pick parameters to the association via the mouse. These parameters are simply the two scene parameters, *p1* and *p2* respectively. Finally, because no animation is actually running, Dance must find out what types of objects will be retrieved. It prompts us to choose the object type being retrieved. We pick image objects, then Dance allows us to draw two rectangles that act as place-holders and will appear roughly as they would in the animation. Precise positioning and sizing is not important because all subsequent actions in the animation will be relative to the actual run-time rectangles retrieved.

Once the blocks are in place, we select the *Loc* command from the *Image* menu in order to acquire two location objects corresponding to the lower left (southwest) corners of the rectangles. These locations, named *loc1* and *loc2*, will be the endpoints of the paths that the rectangles will move along. Dance provides a dialog box with possible compass positions, and we follow the southwest selection by picking the blocks' variable labels to designate the image objects.

Next, we choose the *Type* command from the *Path* menu to instantiate a predefined *clockwise* path. It is a semi-circle path moving from left to right in a clockwise direction. We name this path *looper* and Dance allows us to specify where the path should be placed on the display. It really can be drawn anywhere in the window because it is a relative modifier to be applied to images with absolute positions. Note, however, that this path probably will not move the left block to the right block's exact position as desired: the path moves a predefined amount in the *x* direction, but the two blocks may be arbitrarily spaced depending on how many values are being sorted on a particular execution. Consequently, we choose the *Example* operation from the *Path* menu. It utilizes an existing path as a pattern or prototype, but also takes two locations specifying beginning and ending positions of a new path. Dance provides a dialog box for specifying the resultant path variable name (we choose *path1*), then it prompts us to select, via the mouse, the example path to use and the two location endpoints. We simply select the yellow labels of the appropriate items, *looper*, *loc1*, and *loc2* in order, then Dance displays the resultant path. This path, when applied to *rect1* in a move transition, will move *rect1* to *rect2's* position. At animation runtime, *path1* may take on many different sizes due to the array elements being exchanged. But, due to its dependence on locations taken from the pertinent images, it is guaranteed to always move blocks correctly.

The final path operation we make is to create a path that is a 180 degree rotation of *path1*. This new path will move *rect2* to *rect1's* position. To do this, we simply select the *Rotate* operation from the *Path* menu, then pick *path1* with the mouse when prompted, and enter 180 as the rotation value into a dialog box prompt. We name the new path *path2*.

After creating paths, we must create two move transitions. To do this, we select the *Create* command from the *Trans* menu and designate the transition name (we choose *move1* and *move2*), the transition type (move), and then pick the appropriate image and path labels when prompted to do so. Transition *move1* uses *rect1* and *path1*, and *move2* uses *rect2* and *path2*, the rotated path. Next, we need to make a new transition which is simply both of these movements occurring concurrently. In Tango, this is known as transition composition. So, we select the *Compose* transition menu operation and Dance prompts us to select the transitions to be composed. We use the mouse to select *move1* and *move2* and provide the resulting transition name, *both*.

To make the animation actually occur, we choose the *Perform* operation from the *Trans* menu and pick the *both* variable label when prompted by Dance to do so. Dance then illustrates the resulting animation and interchanges the two blocks. Finally, we wrap up this animation scene by storing (*Store* operation under the *Assoc* menu) the two image objects under their new, switched indices in the association mapping maintained in the animation.

Once the Exchange scene has been demonstrated in this fashion, its animation description can be written out to a file. Figure 4 shows the actual C code that Dance produced for the scene. The code will compile correctly, and the resulting object file can be dynamically loaded by Tango for use in animating programs.

Figure 4. Tango animation code that Dance generated for the exchange scene.

```
     void Exchange(p1,p2)
     int p1;
     int p2;
{
     TANGO_LOC loc1, loc2;
     TANGO_IMAGE rect1, rect2;
     TANGO_PATH looper, path1, path2;
     TANGO_TRANS move1, move2, both;

     rect1 = (TANGO_IMAGE) ASSOCretrieve("ID", p1);
     rect2 = (TANGO_IMAGE) ASSOCretrieve("ID", p2);
     loc1 = TANGOimage_loc(rect1, TANGO_PART_TYPE_SW);
     loc2 = TANGOimage_loc(rect2, TANGO_PART_TYPE_SW);
     looper = TANGOpath_type(TANGO_PATH_TYPE_CLOCKWISE);
     path1 = TANGOpath_example(loc1, loc2, looper);
     path2 = TANGOpath_rotate(path1, 180);
     move1 = TANGOtrans_create(TANGO_TRANS_TYPE_MOVE, rect1,
                 path1);
     move2 = TANGOtrans_create(TANGO_TRANS_TYPE_MOVE, rect2,
                 path2);
     both = TANGOtrans_compose(2, move1, move2);
     TANGOtrans_perform(both);
     ASSOCstore("ID", p1, rect2);
     ASSOCstore("ID", p2, rect1);
}
```

Summary

The Dance system provides a number of benefits to the developers of algorithm animations.

- **Ease of design:** Animation developers can shift their focus from the details of design language syntax to the more important matter of creating interesting, visually informative algorithm animations. Although familiarity with the underlying path-transition animation paradigm principles is still necessary, Dance frees designers from low-level syntactic concerns.

- **Program development support:** Dance, through design-time warnings and automatic code generation, helps eliminate common program development errors such as type mismatches, use of undeclared variables, and simple syntax errors.

- **Rapid prototyping:** Because designers develop animation visually, Dance promotes rapid prototyping. Designers can save time by experimenting with the look and style of various graphical effects without having to enter the traditional program development cycle. Without this type of demonstrational design, developers must code, compile, and run an animation repeatedly in order to converge on a desired animation view.

- **Ability to fine-tune:** In using Dance, animation designers still have the option of examining the code it produces and editing or "tweaking" the code as necessary. The ability to modify or override the designed code is an important feature for detailed animations that must look "just-so."

- **Paradigm illustration:** Dance provides a visual metaphor for the path-transition animation paradigm—this metaphor has proven useful for explaining how the different types of objects in the paradigm function and interact.

An area in which Dance could be improved is increased graphical editing support. The use of rulers, grid lines, gravity, etc., would allow Dance to achieve the high level of sophistication found in current graphical editors. Another useful addition would be support for a concurrent view of the animation code as the demonstrational design is performed.

Our experiences with the Dance system motivated us to examine this approach to building software visualizations further. In particular, we wondered if the direct manipulation approach could be simplified even more and adapted for use as a type of visual debugging tool. If programmers could interactively and rapidly create visualizations of their code, they could use the resulting display during program execution to trace and evaluate their programs. Further, if this was done in the context of a traditional debugger, a new style of program debugging might emerge.

We felt that a system should use a direct manipulation design style as exhibited by Dance to provide such capabilities. But we also believed that the system must be even easier to learn and use, not overwhelming the programmer with a great number of primitives and commands. To achieve this goal, we studied over 40 algorithm animations created with the Tango system by a wide variety of authors in order to identify a core set of constituents that were repeatedly used in visualizations of programs. We sought to identify both the common graphical objects used in the animations and the common actions that the objects made.

The LENS System

We found that only lines, rectangles, circles, and text were routinely used in these animations and that six operations commonly occurred:

- Move an object to a particular absolute position, by a relative amount, or to a position relative to another object

- Change the color of an object

- Change the fill style (outline or filled) of an object

- Make an object flash

- Make two objects exchange positions (a special combination of movement actions)

- Delete an object or make it invisible

For further details on the identification of these "kernel" capabilities, see [Mukherjea 93] [Mukherjea 94]. Our intention was to use these capabilities as the basis for a visual debugging system. It should allow designers to instantiate objects graphically through direct manipulation and the use of a graphical editor, and to specify animation actions through a set of menu-based commands where each choice corresponded to one of the core actions we identified.

Using Lens

Once the set of core operations had been established, we began development of a visual debugging system called Lens that would embody these operations. The system is implemented on top of UNIX, the X Window System, the XTango algorithm animation system, and the debugger dbx. Its target language is C.

In this section, to provide a better "feel" for how Lens works, we describe how programmers interact with the system. To begin a visual debugging session, a programmer issues the command,

```
% lens foo
```

where *foo* is the name of an executable program that has been compiled with the appropriate debugging flags. The entire Lens display window then appears as shown in Figure 5. After start-up, the user selects an initial source file to view via a selection within the *File* menu (it may be any source file such as *foo1*.c or *foo2*.c used to build the binary *foo*), then Lens loads and displays this source and awaits the entry of animation commands. (Other source files can be subsequently loaded as well.) In the Lens window, the left area presents program source code, the upper right area is the graphical editor for designing objects' appearances, and the lower right area is for issuing debugger commands.

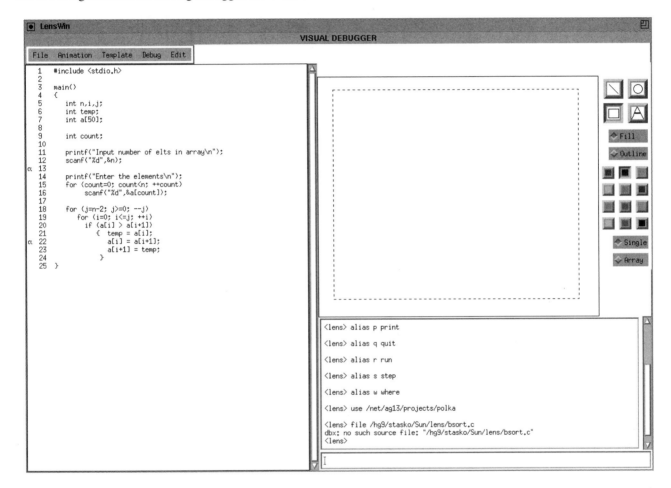

At this point the programmer can issue normal debugger commands or designate the special animation commands at particular points in the source code. To do this, the programmer chooses commands from the *Animation* menu above the source code. It has nine options that correspond to the kernel of algorithm animation constituents found in our study of algorithm animations: 1) Define coordinate system 2) Create graphical object 3) Create location marker 4) Move 5) Fill 6) Color 7) Flash 8) Exchange 9) Delete.

Figure 5. Lens display presented to a programmer. The left section shows source with animation annotations, and the right section contains the graphical editor and debugger command window.

When either the *Create graphics* or *Create location* command is chosen, the programmer is prompted to enter the variable name of the object or location marker being depicted. The variable name is subsequently used to identify the object for the action commands. This is a key advantage of Lens: a programmer works in the context of familiar program entities, not graphics primitives. After a name has been entered, Lens asks the programmer to use the graphical editor to design (draw) the object or location's appearance and/or position. The design is structured according to the object specifications that were discovered in our earlier research on existing animations. For example, when a line is created, its position can be specified using the mouse, it can be specified relative to another object (by name or by picking a graphical object), or it can be specified to relate to the value of a program variable. All these choices are made via a dialog box entry or by graphical direct manipulation. Once the design of the object's appearance is complete, Lens asks the user to designate, using the mouse, the source code line at which object or location creation should occur. Lens indicates the presence of animation commands by showing an 'a' beside the code line. The presence of multiple commands per line is designated by an 'A'.

When a programmer chooses one of the six action commands, Lens asks for the name of the variable(s), and consequently graphical object(s), to which the action should apply. The programmer simply types in a variable name such as x or a[i][1], Lens notes the choice and saves the association in an internal database. Finally, the programmer selects the source code line on which to place the command. Programmers also can examine existing animation annotations simply by clicking on a source code line containing them. Lens pops up a dialog box or boxes summarizing the animation command(s) that has been designated there. Every animation annotation also can be deleted, thus supporting trial and experimentation. Figure 6 shows both a question dialog used for specifying a "Move" action, and the summary dialog shown when the same Move annotation is queried later.

---

[1] The system supports single variables, pointer variables, or an array variable with an expression as its index, but not arbitrary C code.

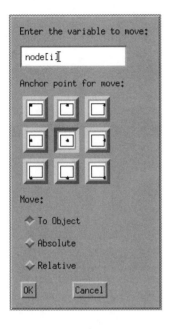

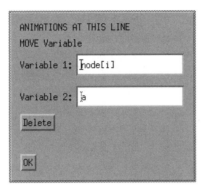

Figure 6. Dialog boxes used by Lens to designate a Move action and to summarize the same action.

When the programmer wishes to execute the program and see its animation, he or she chooses the *Run* command from the *Debug* menu or simply types "run" in the debugger command shell. Lens then pops up an animation window and displays the animation that corresponds to the programmer's design and this particular execution. Whenever execution encounters a line holding an animation command, the corresponding action is performed. Lens uses the routines from the XTango system to generate the animations it presents.

If the animation is not sufficient or not what the programmer wanted, the programmer can go back, add or delete animation commands, and rerun the animation, all without leaving the Lens environment. Full dbx capabilities are supported within the lower right command window also, so the traditional power of the debugger can also be utilized.

To add extra debugging support, Lens provides "templates" for common data structure visualizations. A template is a predefined graphical data structure depiction, much like those shown in Incense [Myers 83] or VIPS [Isoda 87] [Shimomura 91]. Lens provides templates for scalars, arrays, linked lists, and binary trees. To instantiate a template, let's take the linked list as an example, the programmer merely specifies the pointer into the list, the name of the field in the structure used as the "next" pointer, and some "value" field of the nodes to graphically present. Through its communication with dbx, Lens can traverse the list and render an image of the list's state at that moment. A sample list depiction is shown in Figure 7.

Figure 7. Lens' template depiction of a linked list shown in an XTango animation window. The icon buttons to the left are for panning and zooming the view, and the buttons on the bottom are XTango animation controllers. The scrollbar to the right controls the relative speed at which the animation runs.

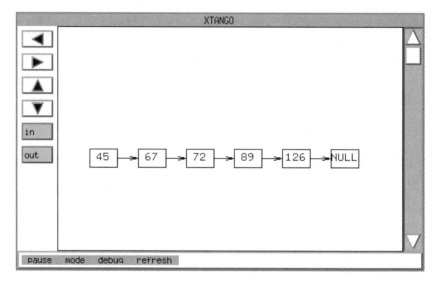

Additionally, Lens supports saving animation annotations defined during a session, so that program debugging can be resumed at a later time using the same animation context.

To learn more about the details of how Lens works and to find a number of example animation definitions, please see [Mukherjea 93] [Mukherjea 94]. The system is also available via anonymous ftp at the site `ftp.cc.gatech.edu` in the file `pub/people/stasko/lens.tar.Z`.

Remaining difficulties

The simplicity and ease of use of Lens was not without a cost. Although the system is capable of creating many sophisticated visualizations, we often wanted to design new visualizations that were simply beyond its scope. In particular, the following difficulties often arose:

• **Conditional and repeated executions of animations** — Lens has no mechanism to specify conditional or repeated occurrences of animation commands. If the appropriate programming construct is not in the program being visualized, a designer has no way of specifying these control operations.

- **Specifying the layout of graphical elements** — There is no way in Lens to do sophisticated graphical object layout such as trees and graphs.

- **Depicting the visual representation of programming variables** — Often, it is difficult to define the mapping from program entities to graphical objects. This can be from the lack of constructs in the program to serve as the basis for the mapping or from an inadequate graphical vocabulary in Lens.

For further details about these limitations and others, see [Mukherjea 94].

Challenges and difficulties such as those mentioned above illustrate the limitations of a direct manipulation, demonstrational approach and the sheer power and utility of programming for building software visualizations. Both the Dance and Lens systems make some initial steps toward being able to create software visualizations interactively, but further research and development is necessary to fulfill the promise that this approach holds.

Acknowledgments

Sougata Mukherjea assisted in the development and implementation of the Lens system. This research was supported in part by the National Science Foundation under contract CCR-9109399. Portions of this chapter are reprinted, with permission, from [Stasko 91a] Copyright 1991 ACM and [Mukherjea 94] Copyright 1994 ACM.

Visualization for Specialized Domains

This section covers the visualization of specific domains, each offering novel challenges for SV designers. The first two chapters cover the visualization of AI languages. AI languages tend to have relatively complex execution models and relatively simple data structures. This is reflected in the systems described, which focus on showing control flow rather than data flow.

Chapter 15 ("The Truth about Prolog Execution") concentrates on The Transparent Prolog Machine (TPM). TPM uses an augmented AND/OR tree notation to show the execution of Prolog programs. The chapter describes how TPM fulfilled the twin challenges of, on the one hand, showing very detailed views of execution, and, on the other, showing the execution space of very large programs.

Chapter 16 ("Visualizing Knowledge Based Systems") provides an overview of the visualization work carried out within the Knowledge Based Systems community. The chapter describes a variety of approaches to visualizing inference systems from simple text based tracers through to systems which use 'knowledge level' models.

Chapter 17 ("Visualizing Concurrent Programs") describes the problems of visualizing concurrent programs, which are inherently large and complex and thus produce vast quantities of data. The chapter discusses how the visualization construction tasks of data collection, data analysis and display need to be adjusted to cope with the added complications of concurrency.

The Truth about Prolog Execution

Marc Eisenstadt
and
Mike Brayshaw

Introduction

When The Transparent Prolog Machine (TPM) was first conceived in the mid-1980's, debugging logic programming was still at an early stage. At that time there were two existing schools of thought. From a more formal perspective the emphasis had been placed either on a deep understanding of the declarative semantics — the static and logical meaning of a collection of axioms and rules (e.g. [Shapiro 82]) — or on reasoning about the rationale underlying the debugging process [Pereira 86]. Alternatively a more procedural tracing model had been put forward by Byrd [Byrd 80] which gave an account of the execution behaviour of running Prolog programs. Most commercial implementations at this stage featured some variant of Byrd's 'Box' model, although the amount of information made available to the user varied greatly, and access to certain fine-grained details was generally held not to be possible. The situation that we faced from a logic programming perspective was therefore one where the programmer was often short of information and blinkered by the perspectives that were on offer.

In parallel to the above, work in the human-computer interaction community had been evolving towards a consensus about the importance of clear and consistent models of program execution (e.g. [Eisenstadt 83] [duBoulay 81]). The benefits of such models were both pedagogical and practical: the whole development/debugging cycle could be streamlined when the programmer was equipped with facilities for clearly visualizing and monitoring program execution.

TPM was an attempt to bring together these ideas and produce a clear, consistent, and information-rich picture for Prolog programmers. In the mid-1980's graphical workstations were clearly the way ahead. Thus, we were not shackled by 'glass-teletype' environments and instead sought to find the best notations to explicate program meaning and execution. The results are presented below. To the notations themselves we added means of dynamic interaction: below we discuss program animations, searching, and manipulation techniques that allow TPM to scale-up to handle large programs. First we consider the project domain in more detail and discuss why Prolog should require a tool of this sort.

Prolog overview

Prolog as a language has a series of notable features which differentiate it as a programming tool. A Prolog program consists of a series of 'predicates' or 'relations' organised into facts and rules, such as those shown in Figure 1. A program is run in the conventional sense by posing a query. A query is like a question that is asked of the rules and facts. The question is answered by a search, resulting in a **yes** for a successful outcome and **no** otherwise. The query itself is taken as a goal to be proved, and this is done by a precise sequence of 'clause head matching', explained in some detail in the caption to Figure 1. This may be done by either matching it against a fact or alternatively reducing the goal to its subgoals using an existing rule, and then recursively proving the subgoals. Thus, in Figure 1, the unary (i.e. one-argument) relation human(X) can be regarded as a sub-goal of the unary relation mortal(X). These subgoals are then searched left-to-right in a depth-first fashion. The program successfully terminates when all subgoals can be reduced to leaf nodes which match an existing fact or built-in primitive statement that is true. If all can be proved, then the top goal (query) can be proved. Prolog will return the answer 'yes' and show the binding of any variables contained in the query (Figure 2).

```
1   human(plato).
2   human(socrates).

3   mortal(X):- human(X).

4   ?- mortal(socrates).

5   yes
```

*Figure 1. Two Prolog facts (lines 1 and 2), one Prolog rule (line 3) stating that 'for all X, X is mortal if X is human', one Prolog query (line 4) asking whether Socrates is mortal, and the output of execution (line 5). Lines 1-3 are also known as **clauses**: mortal(X) is the **head** of clause 3, and human(X) is its **body**. The query in line 4 is said to match the head of clause 3, which is precisely why it gets selected for execution. A fact such as line 1 could also be rewritten as the trivially-true rule: 'human(plato):-true'.*

In proving a query, if there are alternative possibilities in the search, Prolog takes the first option. If a goal fails subsequently, Prolog backtracks to the immediately proceeding choice point, and selects an alternative. A primitive, called the 'cut', may be used to stop this process in specific instances. Additionally, a powerful pattern matcher allows variable substitutions to be made when proving goals. These substitutions can be undone on backtracking. Data structures are made out of logical terms or lists. There are no iterative control constructs (e.g. for, while, case, loop) — instead the programmer has to employ the built-in search engine using recursion or backtracking. Thus, in using Prolog programmers have to grasp a complex execution story involving search, backtracking, and variable unification, in addition to learning how to represent the problem solutions in this potentially idiosyncratic manner. These idiosyncrasies motivated the logic programming community to find better ways of conceptualising Prolog to make it easier to understand and use.

Bundy and his colleagues at the University of Edinburgh provided an excellent account of the many trade-offs involved in trying to develop a good 'Prolog story' which could be used both for teaching Prolog and for providing a view of execution in the context of writing and debugging large Prolog programs [Pain 87]. The basic tenet of the 'Edinburgh Stories' school, as we shall refer to it, is that an AND/OR tree (Figure 3) provides the best overall account of what is happening during Prolog execution, but that it needs to be combined with a view of the database and a resolution table to explicate the links to the user's original code and to the all-important variable instantiations which occur during execution. The Edinburgh Stories account argued that although there is not normally enough room to show the execution of very large programs, this might be solvable through the principled use of multiple-window displays.

The problem of designing a purpose-built graphical tracer for Prolog programs was addressed by Dewar and Cleary [Dewar 86]. Their system attempted to provide an intuitive zooming facility for examining Prolog execution in detail. Although it incorporated a very nice display of clause head selection (study the caption to Figure 1 for an explanation of this process) and the active goal/subgoal hierarchy, it suffered from four deficiencies: (a) Every goal invocation involved a complete replication of the icons depicting the relevant portion of the database, so the space they occupied rapidly grew out of all proportion to their importance in understanding the behaviour of the running

```
1   human(plato).
2   human(socrates).

3   mortal(X):- human(X).

4   ?- mortal(Z).

5   Z = plato;
6   Z = socrates
```

Figure 2. Same facts and rules as Figure 1, but this time the query at line 4 uses a variable. The output of the query at line 5 shows the first binding or instantiation of variable Z. If we force backtracking by entering a ';' at line 5, we obtain another alternative, as shown on line 6. Variables in rules are universally quantified (e.g. 'for all X' in line 3), whereas variables in queries are existentially quantified (e.g. 'does there exist a Z' in line 4).

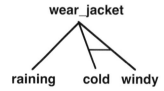

Figure 3. AND/OR tree depicting natural-language commonsense rule: 'wear a jacket either if it is raining or alternatively if it is cold and windy'. The horizontal line indicates a conjunction.

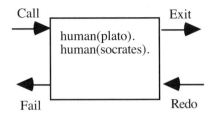

Call   Exit

human(plato).
human(socrates).

Fail   Redo

Figure 4. Byrd's box model of Prolog debugging. This expresses the various control situations under which a predicate can be invoked. In this view, the predicate 'human' is a procedure which exits upon success, but can be 'redone' later if appropriate (as seen in line 6 of figure 2).

```
PTP: zoom(4).

 4  > split([1],2,...) {1}
 5    @ 1<2
 6    ++1<2
        &
 7    ? split([],2,_44,_45)
 8    -~split([],2,_44,_45)
 9    ^ 1<2
10    -^1<2
11  < split([1],2,...) {1}
```

Figure 5. Snapshot of PTP (Eisenstadt 1984, 1985) using 'retrospective zooming' to debug a program. Each of the symbols between the line number and the code is a precise descriptor of program behaviour. For example, '>' on line 4 means 'entering a subgoal', '@' on line 5 means testing a primitive, '-~' on line 8 means 'failure due to lack of unification'.

program; (b) the logical structure of the AND/OR tree, acknowledged by Dewar and Cleary to be important, was sacrificed for practical reasons; (c) the mapping between the user's source code and the running invocations was sacrificed in order to provide user-defined icons; (d) the actual implementation ran too slowly to be used on anything other than 'toy' examples. Although we are in complete sympathy with the need to pursue important theoretical and design issues within the realms of small test examples, we feel very strongly that solutions to toy problems simply do not scale up to the enormity of serious logic programming applications. Large scale problems are themselves therefore of fundamental importance to work of the type described herein.

Our own earlier work (PTP: [Eisenstadt 84b] [Eisenstadt 85a], and the work of Plummer [Plummer 88] (Figure 6), concentrated on enhancing the Byrd's 'Box' model of Prolog execution [Byrd 80] (see Figure 4) to the point where it would give more precise symptomatic information so that the programmer could home in more readily on trouble spots. PTP distinguished 19 different fine-grained execution behaviours, including 7 different causes of predicate failure, thus giving programmers a very close-up view of the action (Figure 5). In [Eisenstadt 85a] we added a top-level supervisory program which could detect characteristic symptom clusters or 'trace footprints' produced behind the scenes by the trace package in order to spot bugs. TPM sought to build upon this experience but in the context of the notationally richer environment afforded by the more powerful graphical workstations of the late 1980's. Moreover, our approach incorporated ideas gained from the parallel development of teaching material [Eisenstadt 88a], and thereby we sought to provide facilities in a clear and consistent manner so that they would be useful to experts and novices alike.

The work described below started with two premises: (i) it is essential to show the full execution space of large Prolog programs; (ii) it is essential to base a tracing package on an 'extended execution model' which discriminates between clause head matching and clause body execution (as illustrated in Figure 1). We have stuck with these two premises partly because of the challenge of resolving their underlying contradiction: premise (i) involves a global view of things, while premise (ii) involves a very close up view. Our aim has been to reconcile these differences without losing the advantages provided by either. We feel strongly that different levels of detail (i.e. different grain-size of analysis) involve different conceptual views of what is happening, and therefore a simple 'aerial view/close-up zoom' facility (such as that used in the tracer of Dewar and Cleary, [Dewar 86]) does *not* provide a magical solution, particularly when programs other than toy examples are involved. It is nevertheless possible to accommodate both premises. The key insights which enable this accommodation, and which drive the whole of the work described in this chapter, are the following:

• When a Prolog programmer is debugging a program which he or she has personally been developing over a period of weeks or months, an overall graphical view of the execution space of that program is highly meaningful to that programmer, because it conveys its own gestalt. (We have a strong hunch that this is true up to a limit of several thousand nodes, although this needs to be tested empirically.)

• The concept of a 'node' in a traditional AND/OR tree is needlessly impoverished. With just a few enhancements, and for a very small computational overhead, a simple node can become a 'status box' which concisely encapsulates a goal's history, including detailed clause head matching information.

• The traditional AND/OR tree does not reveal the difference between one clause containing a disjunction and two separate clauses. More specifically, the distinction between clause head and clause body is not shown in AND/OR trees, despite the overwhelming importance of the head/body distinction to the debugging of Prolog programs. A minor notational variant enables us to overcome this problem.

Section 2 describes the underlying principles involved in the design and development of our view of Prolog execution, which we dub 'The Transparent

Prolog Machine' (TPM). TPM served as the basis for our own textbook and video material [Eisenstadt 88a] as well as providing the underlying execution model for our graphical tracer.

TPM's notation has two central ideas. The first is that the overall trace structure and dynamics can be shown via an animated AND/OR tree. This captures the program's search procedures, including the concept of *backtracking* to find alternative solutions to goals. Secondly, information can be divided into coarse-grained and fine-grained views. This allows users to have details when they

(0) 0 p([1,2,a,b],3,A)
       p([1,2,a,b],3,⇒[B|C]):-
                    D is 3 -1,
                    !,
                    q(1,B),
                    p([2,a,b],D,C).

Figure 6. Plummer (1988) demonstrated another enhanced Box model debugger. Unification was shown in a step by step manner (for each argument), with an arrow ⇒ indicating the current step.

The Transparent Prolog Machine: underlying principles

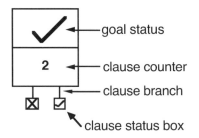

Figure 7. A procedure status box.

require them in the context of broader long distance views. TPM allows users simply to switch between the two in order to obtain the total picture. In this section we describe an idealised fine-grained account of Prolog execution. Later we will show how this integrates with the coarse-grained model and then discuss additional information-organising principles used in TPM.

The Procedure Status Box

We follow the common practice of using the name *procedure* to refer to the collection of clauses defining a given predicate or relation (e.g. the two clauses of *human* in Figure 1 can be regarded as a procedural definition). The cornerstone of our notational convention, illustrated in Figure 7, is the *procedure status box*. This box replaces the simple AND/OR tree 'node' in our display of the execution space. The upper part indicates the *goal status*, and informs us whether the goal is currently being processed (a question-mark), whether it has succeeded (a tick, sometimes called a 'check'), whether it has failed (a cross, sometimes called an 'X'), or whether an earlier success was followed by failure upon backtracking (a tick/cross combination). The number in the lower half of the procedure status box is a *clause counter* which tells us which of several clauses for a given procedure is currently being processed.

The small 'legs' dangling down underneath the procedure status box are called *clause branches*, and correspond one-for-one to the individual clauses comprising the definition of a relation in the database. The leftmost branch corresponds to the first clause, and the next branch corresponds to the second clause, etc. The small boxes at the bottom of Figure 7 are *clause status boxes*, used to indicate the outcome of processing of each individual clause. The clause status box may contain any of the four symbols used to indicate the main goal status (question mark, tick, cross, and tick/cross). Alternatively, a clause branch may simply terminate in a horizontal 'dead-end bar' when the head of that clause fails to unify with the current goal.

Let's now observe the execution of a trivial Prolog program in slow motion to see how the procedure status box is used. Consider the three-clause database presented in Figure 8. Suppose that the following query, corresponding to 'Who eats rubbish?', is posed:

$$\text{?- } \textbf{eats(X, rubbish).}$$

1   eats(joe, hamburgers).
2   eats(fred, X).
3   eats(X, bread).

Figure 8. Three clauses defining the relation **eats**. Clause 2 can be read 'Fred eats anything', and clause 3 can be read 'anyone, indeed anything, eats bread', i.e. 'for all X, X eats bread'.

Figures 9(a)-9(d) show the 'innards' of execution. In Figure 9(a), we see the main goal displayed alongside the procedure status box. The goal status symbol is a question-mark, there are three clause branches corresponding to the clauses in the definition of eats, and the '0' indicates that no clauses have yet been 'inspected'.

Figure 9(d) shows the moment when processing is complete. The clause status box for clause 2 has been marked with a tick. Precisely because there are no descendants emanating from this clause status box, we can tell at a glance that this was a trivial success, i.e. an ordinary Prolog fact. The clause branches formally correspond to disjunctive choices, so if *any* of them succeeds, the procedure as a whole succeeds. Therefore, the goal status indicator becomes a tick as well, indicating that the goal has succeeded.

The four-step unification sequence depicted in Figures 9(a)-9(d) is of most use to us in teaching Prolog. Once this account has been shown to students (both in textual form and in an animation on our accompanying video material), we ask them to fill in the details in empty 'status boxes' alongside various examples. In order to capture this behaviour in our tracer, TPM includes an animation control panel (sometimes called a *replay* panel). This allows users to step forward and backwards through such sequences to see the dynamics of Prolog in action.

Fine-Grained Views

AND/OR trees (Figure 3) are a frequently used and highly expressive way of describing the execution of logic programs, and Prolog programs in particular. [Pain 87] concluded that AND/OR trees offered the greatest potential in terms of clarity of explanation, but that they suffered from several deficiencies, as summarised here:

    1. It is not immediately clear when a call has been successful;

    2. It is difficult to see what subgoals are outstanding at any moment: the current goal is not immediately obvious;

    3. The output substitution is not clearly displayed, but must be calculated by combining the unifiers along the winning branches;

    4. To keep the different environments of recursive calls clear, the variables have to be renamed: their origins are not always clear;

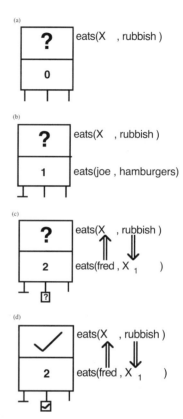

Figure 9(a-d). Four-step detailed execution snapshots, given the new query

?- eats(X, rubbish).

(a) Initial pending goal.

(b) A copy of clause 1 of eats is inspected, but the head does not unify with the goal.

(c) A copy of clause 2 is inspected, and its head does unify, as shown. Variables in clauses which are copied and inspected are automatically renamed by adding an appropriately-numbered subscript. At this instant, the interpreter does not know that clause 2 is a winner.

(d) End of processing. The clause status box for clause 2 shows that it is a winner (trivially), and thus the main goal wins.

5. There is no direct link to the clauses in the database; and

6. In the general case, it is complicated to see which parts of the tree should be scribbled out by the cut.

We were motivated by this account to try to improve matters. We reasoned that the 'node' in a traditional AND/OR tree was a needlessly impoverished representation, and that by enriching it in appropriate ways we could have our cake and eat it too. In other words, we wanted to have an intuitively clear AND/OR-style account of execution while providing all the details that a traditional AND/OR tree leaves out. The missing link is precisely the procedure status box described above. These boxes can be used in place of simple AND/OR tree nodes providing fine-grained views, with the clause branches representing OR choices, and subgoal branches (borrowed from the standard AND/OR tree notation) representing AND 'siblings', i.e. conjunctions of subgoals. The combination has led us to refer to our diagrams as *AORTA Diagrams* (AND/OR Tree, Augmented).

The overall structure of AORTA diagrams (and indeed the AND/OR trees from which they evolved) is inherently simple when the chronology of execution maps trivially onto the left-to-right/top-to-bottom branching structure of the diagrams. In other words, as long as control flow is straightforward, graphical representation of control flow is also straightforward. In Prolog, backtracking immediately alters this trivial mapping because it can lead to new invocations of goals caused by the re-satisfaction of previous choice points and subsequent re-execution of sibling goals. Nevertheless, AORTA diagrams offer a solution. A procedure status box concisely encapsulates in one (two-dimensional) place the execution history of a single *invocation* of a procedure. During the course of that invocation, all sorts of things may happen, but the net result is maintained in the individual clause status boxes. If a goal fails, it may be re-invoked later at what amounts to the same location in the execution space. We can use a third dimension (i.e. depth) to cater for the distinction between older and newer invocations at the same place in the execution space. When there are two or more such invocations, the latest invocation appears normally, but prior invocations are depicted schematically in the form of a shaded *ghost* status box 'underneath' the latest invocation. In effect, the ghost is just an icon meaning 'there was (at least) one prior invocation here'. In our textual displays, the ghost just serves as a reminder, but in our graphical tracer implementation, the ghost is actually a mouse-sensitive item which allows the user to examine what happened at the appropriate point in the execution history.

The cut

In addition to handling multiple invocations of a goal, the other major extra-logical control problem to deal with is the cut. Recall that the cut is a way of stopping backtracking into a particular choice point. Using AORTA diagram notation, this is surprisingly easy. Bearing in mind that the cut (depicted by a '!') is itself a subgoal which has ancestors and (typically) siblings, the following three things happen when a cut is encountered:

1. older sibling goals and their descendants are 'frozen' (enshrouded in small cloud which makes them unalterable on backtracking)

2. upcoming clause branches of the cut's parent goal are chopped (future 'step-fathers' are eliminated).

3. the cut succeeds, just like any ordinary Prolog goal.

To illustrate the way AORTA diagrams deal with the cut, Figure 10 presents a small program and sample interaction contrived to illustrate a large number of AORTA diagram features in a small space. The program depicts the circumstances in which some X has a party. Figure 11 shows a TPM screen snapshot following successful termination of the query ?- **party(Name).**

For the moment, we concentrate just on the lower half of Figure 11, which shows the AORTA view. We can see that **happy** succeeded initially on clause 1, but unification with either clause of **birthday** was not possible. This failure caused the backtracking into **swimming**, which itself failed upon backtracking (no further clauses to attempt), as indicated by the tick/cross combination appearing in the top of its status box. This is also the case with the **!** (cut) goal, which is displayed as a circular node to indicate that it is a system primitive. Notice the frozen cloud[1] around the cut's older siblings **hot** and **humid** and the scissors-plus-jagged-edge icon showing the elimination of the

---

[1]Our convention is that the frozen cloud is shown in light gray when it first occurs, and in darkened gray once an attempt has been made to backtrack into it.

```
%have party if you are happy
%and it is your birthday,
%or to cheer up sad friend:

party(X):-
        happy(X),
        birthday(X).
party(X):-
        friends(X,Y),
        sad(Y).

happy(X):-              %X is happy if
        hot,            %it's hot
        humid,          %and it's humid
        !,              %but only if
        swimming(X).%X is swimming
happy(X):-
        cloudy,
        watching_tv(X).
happy(X):-
        cloudy,
        having_fun(X).

cloudy.     %'it is cloudy'
humid.
hot.

having_fun(tom).
having_fun(sam).

swimming(john).
swimming(sam).

watching_tv(john).

sad(bill).     %'Bill is sad'
sad(sam).

birthday(tom).
birthday(sam).

friends(tom,john).
friends(tom,sam).

?- party(Name).
Name = sam
```

Figure 10. Program contrived to illustrate a large number of AORTA diagram features in a small space. The program specifies the circumstances in which X has a party.

remaining clause branches under the procedure status box of the parent goal **happy**. The parent's failure is further indicated by the tick/cross in the top part of its status box. The failure of clause one of **party** led to clause two being attempted. The **friends** goal succeeded on clause one, i.e. **friends(tom, john)**, but **sad(john)** failed in its first invocation. Upon backtracking, **friends** succeeded on the second clause, namely **friends(tom, sam)**, and a brand new invocation of the **sad** goal occurred, hence the ghost status box showing the previous invocation of **sad**. We can also see in Figure 11 that X_3 was instantiated to **tom**, Y_3 was instantiated to **sam** and that this instantiation was passed to the goal **sad**. The goal **sad(Y_3)**, with Y_3 instantiated to **sam**, matched directly against the fact **sad(sam)** in the database. This led to the success of the goal **sad** and consequently of the main goal **party**, at precisely the moment captured in Figure 11.

The Coarse-Grained View

A practical tracer poses an interesting set of constraints for the Prolog environment designer. The execution space for serious Prolog programs can be enormous, and may thwart the designer who has a nice 'toy' paper and pencil execution model.

The coarse-grained view (CGV), shown in the top part of Figure 11, is designed to allow users retrospectively to analyse the behaviour of a program. It shows the *execution space* of the program (as opposed to the full search space) and the final outcome of attempted goals. This is done by means of a schematised AND/OR tree in which individual nodes summarise the outcome of a call to a particular procedure. Each node is conceptually a collapsed procedure status box, just showing the top half. A white box (or green in our colour version) shows a successful goal, black (red in colour) shows failure, grey (pink) shows failure on backtracking following initial success, while a thick-rimmed box indicates a pending goal on the stack. System primitives are shown as circles instead of squares.

All the views can be animated via a replay panel, which allows users to see the dynamics of their programs in action. This greatly facilitates the understanding of the complexities of backtracking. The full Figure 11 represents a screen snapshot of an Apollo workstation implementation of TPM. The replay panel is on the right with the query button. Selective highlight is at the top left.

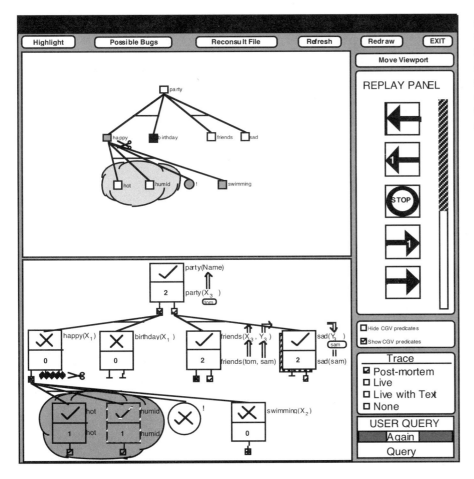

Figure 11. Snapshot of the Apollo version of TPM. A query could be traced in a variety of modes (either live or via retrospective post-mortem analysis). To run a query users clicked on the bottom right button. Various other display options are shown around the graphics area.

Clicking on a CGV (top graphics area) node gives either a one-ply (*quick zoom*) or three-ply-(*full zoom*) AORTA view of that node. Here we can see a CGV of the **party** program of Figure 10. The bottom view shows a *full zoom* in to the fine-grained (AORTA) view, with the data-flow for **party**, **friend**, and **sad** depicted. Clicking on other nodes could also reveal (a) their data-flow, (b) variable binding histories, or (c) origin of variable instantiations.

TPM could also deal with much larger examples, as shown in Figure 12. A scaled version of the coarse grained view is depicted at the top of the figure. A selected window on that view is highlighted and then shown in more detail at the bottom of the figure.

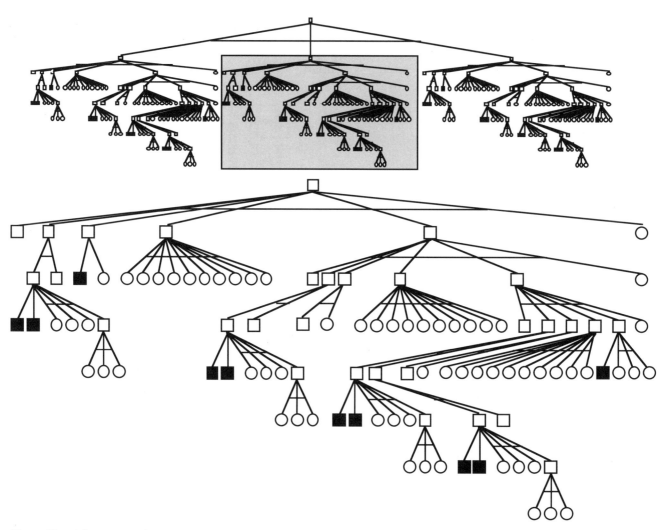

Figure 12. A large execution space, and the accompanying 'full-screen viewport' to show where the CGV fits within the full space. A 'selective Highlighting' facility allows the user to pinpoint items of interest in the display.

The execution space at the top of Figure 12 contains 310 nodes. Our current display can cope comfortably with 2,500 nodes at the same resolution as that depicted in Figure 12. As an example of the powerful gestalt effects possible even in an unlabelled diagram, notice first the cluster of three circular nodes (depicting primitive calls) at the deepest level of nesting of the tree. Now try to find the same pattern of three 'circular sisters' elsewhere in the tree. Finally, put yourself in the position of a programmer who has been developing the associated code over a period of days, and has become accustomed to the repetition of certain familiar shapes. Our point is that locating 'items of interest' in the tree is surprisingly easy. Such items of interest can, of course, be inspected more closely, even while preserving a considerable degree of surrounding context. In order to help the programmer locate items of specific interest, TPM has a 'selective highlighting' facility by which one can highlight (using a characteristically eye-catching diamond surround) nodes in the tree which satisfy some particular constraint or behavioural description (see Figure 13).

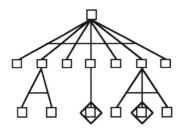

Figure 13. The effects of the TPM highlight request on the AND/OR tree. Nodes that matched the parameters as stated in the highlight menu are highlighted by surrounding diamonds.

Seeing the wood from the trees: four navigation methods

Tracing a program can potentially produce very large amounts of information. This problem is not limited to large programs: small programs that use a lot of backtracking or workhorse predicates can also overload the user with too much information. No matter how big the display, only so much information can be displayed at an intelligible level of resolution. This creates an artificial 'horizon' over which one can't see. Thus, if n levels of detail are displayed, but there is crucial information at level $n+1$, then that crucial information is simply beyond the current horizon. Our approach is to acknowledge the problems of the horizon but to provide the user with a large number of manipulation and customisation aids that allow great freedom both in constructing an appropriate view and in manipulating the current view. Our four basic manipulation techniques are described briefly below (for a fuller treatment see Brayshaw and Eisenstadt, 1989). All of these manipulations are fully integrated with the animation tool and selective highlighting.

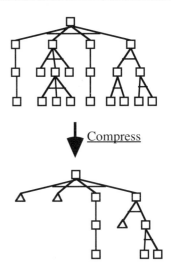

Figure 14. Compressing the CGV (top view) to display only the information that the programmer wishes to work with (bottom view).

• *granularity*: this is our distinction between coarse-grained (CGV) and fine-grained (AORTA) presentations which we described earlier.

• *scale*: a given coarse-grained presentation may itself need to be re-scaled for a 'far-away' look, as in the moving viewport feature which we use for extremely large programs.

• *compression*: this allows user-defined collapsing of large program traces into meaningful segments. We use triangles to indicate the compressed tree. The user can select nodes for compression either at runtime or in a source file. Debugging information may be kept for later inspection or thrown away. Major efficiency gains can thus be made by not storing (post-mortem) trace information about compressed nodes or their children. If the debugging information is optionally stored however, then a compressed node may be expanded retroactively by a single mouse click.

• *abstraction*: user-defined representations provide a movement away from fidelity to the raw Prolog code and towards a representation closer to the programmer's own plans and intentions. Users specify a top level mapping from the program behaviour to a higher level schematic about how they want to see the trace. These higher-level formatting instructions can bring out new information and help users abstract away from pure trace information details. Often, as in Figure 15, they allow users to move from a code perspective to a more functional or domain based view.

Conclusions

Running implementations of TPM have been created for Macintosh, Apollo, Symbolics, and Sun workstations, built directly in Prolog or Lisp. TPM can be summarised as having the following key features:

• It could trace all the language and provide specific information that users need (e.g. the number of a clause head, scope and effects of a 'cut', variable renaming, origin of variable instantiations, and detailed models of complex unifications).

• Its distinction between fine-grained and coarse-grained views allowed it to scale up to large programs.

• Program animations gave a clear model of the dynamics of the language, allowing users to investigate what their program actually did. Backtracking in particular was well shown.

• Rapid location devices, via Selective Highlight, allowed the user to find a particular item of interest without the tedium of stepping through a large execution sequence.

• A good overall picture of program execution was given, allowing users to understand the context of particular calls.

• It had a basic model of information engineering which allowed it to scale up to sizeable information spaces.

- It was customisable.

The work in TPM continues in MRE [Brayshaw 93a] [Brayshaw 93b] [Brayshaw 96]. MRE extends TPM's information engineering model presented above into a full *Information Manager* which allows even further manipulation of views. Coarse and Fine-grained views are rationalised and others added to show different aspects of the virtual machine linked through a common execution story. Agents can be programmed to help users sort through all the information the programmer is presented with. Hybrid views which incorporate algorithm visualisation techniques can be viewed alongside software visualisations views. Lastly, authoring tools allow users to define agents which then let them create their own custom visualisations. The MRE architecture is currently being ported to other non-programming based information spaces, like those found on the Internet.

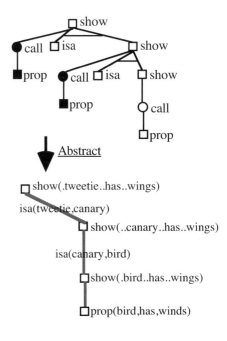

Figure 15. An example of abstraction. Users can move from code style views to ones that map much more onto domain representations.

This work was originally funded by SERC grant numbers GR/C/69344 and GR/E/2333.3, as part of Alvey Project IKBS/161, undertaken collaboratively with Expert Systems International Limited.

Acknowledgments

Visualizing Knowledge Based Systems

John Domingue

In this chapter I shall provide an overview of the visualization work carried out within the Knowledge Based Systems (KBS) community. A KBS typically performs tasks normally carried out by some human expert within some domain (e.g. medical diagnosis or financial market speculation). The creation of a KBS involves eliciting and analysing knowledge from a knowledge source (usually a human expert) and encoding the knowledge into a machine executable form. Conventional software engineering methodologies and techniques are not applicable for KBS construction because a specification can not be easily created. The reason for this is that in the domains tackled algorithmic solutions are not known. Instead human experts tend to rely on rules of thumb or heuristics. Within a KBS knowledge is typically represented in two formalisms. Declarative knowledge is represented by frames and procedural knowledge is represented by rules. Frames can be thought of as structures (slots with values) with (sometimes complex) inheritance not too dissimilar from object oriented programming languages. Most commercial KBS development environments contain graphical browsers to view frame hierarchies and inspect individual frame slot values.

A KBS will contain an *inference engine* which performs inferencing over rules. Two types of inferencing can occur over rules: forward chaining or backward chaining. Backward chaining is goal driven, reasoning backwards from a toplevel goal via subgoals and subsubgoals. The execution model for backward chaining

Introduction

systems is usually very similar to or identical to that of Prolog. As this is covered in Chapter 15, I will not discuss it further here. The rest of this chapter will concentrate in the main on forward chaining visualization systems.

Forward chaining systems are data driven, inferring forwards from data. Since forward chaining systems are not commonly used, before describing some SV systems, I shall give a quick overview of the forward chaining execution model.

The Forward Chaining Execution Model

The figure below shows the basic components of a rule.

Figure 1. The components of a rule.

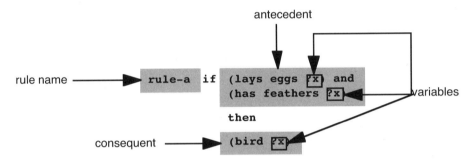

The execution of a set of rules consists of repeated *match/fire* cycles. On each cycle the *antecedent* of each rule is compared with *working memory,* where working memory is a list of working memory elements. Each element is a pattern similar to the antecedent and *consequent* of a rule, except that elements do not contain variables.

The matching rules create a set of *instantiations* which enter a *conflict resolution set.* In an instantiated rule the variables are replaced by the corresponding terms within the matching working memory element. Various conflict resolution strategies are used to select a single instantiation to *fire* from the conflict set. When a rule fires its instantiated patterns within the consequent are added to or retracted from working memory.

The execution model is summarised in the diagram below:

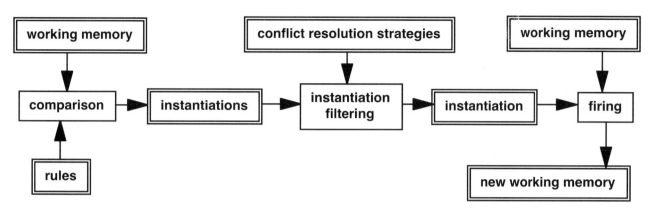

Figure 2. The forward chaining execution model. The boxes within a single line are processes and the boxes within a double line are data. The lines indicate dataflow.

I shall now illustrate the execution model with a small example. Consider the rules and initial working memory shown in figure 3.

In the first match/fire cycle the instantiations shown in figure 4 would be created for rule-a and rule-b.

At this point conflict resolution strategies would be used to determine which instantiation would be selected to fire. Each strategy behaves like a filter taking a set of instantiations as input and returning a (possibly) reduced set. Typical common conflict resolution strategies include:

- choosing instantiations depending on rule order,

- choosing instantiations which were created by matching against newer working memory elements, and

- not choosing instantiations which have previously fired.

Assuming the first instantiation in figure 4 was chosen to fire, working memory would become:

```
((bird robin) (lays eggs robin) (has feathers robin)
 (lays eggs crocodile) (has scales crocodile))
```

```
rule-a: if (lays eggs ?x)
              and
           (has feathers ?x)
              then
           (bird ?x)

rule-b: if (lays eggs ?x)
           (has scales ?x)
              then
           (reptile ?x)

rule-c: if (bird ?x)
              then
           (flies ?x)
```

```
((lays eggs robin)
 (has feathers robin)
 (lays eggs crocodile)
 (has scales crocodile))
```

Figure 3. Three rules and an initial working memory.

```
if (lays eggs robin) and
   (has feathers robin)
      then
   (bird robin)

if (lays eggs crocodile) and
   (has scales crocodile)
      then
   (reptile crocodile)
```

Figure 4. The instantiations created from figure 3 in the first match/fire cycle.

In common with other Artificial Intelligence (AI) languages forward chaining systems have the following features (see section introduction for further discussion on this topic):

- a relatively clean execution model (e.g. only one type of control flow),

- complex control flow,

- programs developed declaratively,

- relatively simple data structures,

- (initially) used within a rapid prototyping development methodology,

- the language is programmable, and

- automatic memory allocation and garbage collection.

These features had several consequences. Because of the emphasis on rapid prototyping the environments of the early eighties (e.g. the Symbolics™ Genera™ environment) provided good debuggers coupled with tools to speed up the edit/load/run cycle. The debuggers enabled programmers to inspect/modify a program's current state (e.g. the stack, data structures) and control and data flow from within break points.

Creating SV systems was made relatively easy by the fact that AI languages have a clean execution model and are programmable. By programmable I mean that a language is highly extendible (up to the point of becoming a new language). An interesting discussion on this property, in relation to Lisp, can be found in [Sandewall 90]. AI languages also often have inbuilt hooks to the interpreter/compiler or are provided with complete sources.

Rule bases are developed in a declarative fashion. That is inter-rule control flow is not considered when the rules are written. In fact there are no explicit means for specifying control flow within a set of forward chaining rules. This means that the developer will not be able to predict the order of rule firing. Clearly any system which can clearly display control flow will be of benefit.

The remainder of this chapter contains descriptions of some sample forward chaining SV systems. The first system is a simple text based trace from a popular public domain system. The following systems are all graphical, mostly using node-link diagrams to represent parts of rules or working memory (or both).

The CLIPS Tracer

CLIPS™ is a public domain system[1] which contains a object oriented system, a Lisp like procedural language and a forward chaining rule system based on OPS5 [Forgy 82]. A Knowledge Engineer (KE) can select the granularity of the trace before running a program. Figure 5 below shows a small portion of a set of rules, solving the 'monkeys and bananas puzzle' within the CLIPS™ system with the finest-grained trace.

Forward Chaining SV Systems

```
FIRE   37 drop-object-once-moved: f-17, f-54, f-49
Monkey drops the ladder.
<== f-54    (monkey (location t7-7) (on-top-of floor) (holding
ladder))
==> f-55    (monkey (location t7-7) (on-top-of floor) (holding
blank))
==> Activation 0      drop-object-once-moved: f-17,f-55,f-49
==> Activation 0      hold-object-to-move: f-17,f-49,f-55,
<== f-49    (thing (name ladder) (location held) (on-top-of
held) (weight light))
<== Activation 0      drop-object-once-moved: f-17,f-55,f-49
<== Activation 0      hold-object-to-move: f-17,f-49,f-55,
==> f-56    (thing (name ladder) (location t7-7) (on-top-of
floor) (weight light))
==> Activation 0      drop-object-once-moved: f-17,f-55,f-56
==> Activation 0      climb-ladder-to-hold: f-16,f-7,f-56,f-55,
==> Activation 0      already-moved-object: f-17,f-56
<== f-17    (goal-is-to (action move) (arguments ladder t7-7))
<== Activation 0      already-moved-object: f-17,f-56
<== Activation 0      drop-object-once-moved: f-17,f-55,f-56
FIRE   38 climb-ladder-to-hold: f-16,f-7,f-56,f-55,
==> f-57    (goal-is-to (action on) (arguments ladder))
==> Activation 0      climb-directly: f-57,f-56,f-55
```

Figure 5. A small portion of a finest-grained trace from a CLIPS program solving the 'monkey and bananas' problem.

The first line of figure 5 indicates that the 37th rule to fire was `drop-object-once-moved` which relied on the working memory elements `f-17` (which is `(goal-is-to (action move) (arguments ladder t7-`

---

[1]CLIPS runs on PCs, Macintoshes and Unix platforms and is available via anonymous ftp from ftp.ensmp.fr (192.54.148.100) or from ftp.cs.cmu.edu (user/ai/areas/expert/clips).

`7)))`, `f-54` and `f-49`. The second line is output produced by the program. The subsequent lines indicate that when `drop-object-once-moved` fired:

- the working memory elements `f-55` and `f-56` were added to working memory,

- the working memory elements `f-54`, `f-49` and `f-17`, were retracted,

- new instantiations were created for `drop-object-once-moved` (2 instantiations using `f-17`, `f-55`, `f-49`, and `f-56`), `hold-object-to-move` (using `f-17`, `f-49` and `f-55`), `climb-ladder-to-hold` (using `f-16`, `f-7`, `f-56` and `f-55`) and `already-moved-object` (using `f-17` and `f-56`), and

- instantiations for `drop-object-once-moved` (2 instantiations), `hold-object-to-move` and `already-moved-object` were deleted.

The next rule to fire was `climb-ladder-to-hold` which relied on `f-16`, `f-7`, `f-56` and `f-55`. `Climb-ladder-to-hold` added `f-57` to working memory and a new instantiation for `climb-directly` was created.

As you can see although fine-grained information is provided by the CLIPS trace even a moderate sized program would be hard to follow.

Tree Based Visualizations

During the 1980s a number of systems (GEETREE [Lewis 83], DTree [Mott 87], KEE and GUIDON-WATCH [Richer 85]) used tree based visualizations. Most of the systems used depicted individual rules as 'and' trees. The GUIDON project at Stanford University investigated how KBS could provide a basis for teaching programs. One KBS developed within the project was NEOMYCIN [Clancey 84] a medical consultation system. To aid medical students a graphic interface to NEOMYCIN providing multiple views on a knowledge base and on the reasoning process during diagnostic problem solving was developed. The interface called GUIDON-WATCH [Richer 85] presented the execution of a KBS using a variety of views each displayed within a separate window.

The KEE™ system from IntelliCorp™ contained a tree-based rule tracer which displayed rules that were *tickled* by the rule interpreter. A rule was said to be *tickled* if it partially matched against a new working memory element. In the trace each displayed (*tickled*) rule was connected to the rule that deposited the matching working memory element. This provided a *spreading effect* trace, which can best be demonstrated by an example. A

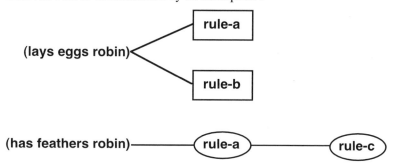

Figure 6. A KEE trace of the rules from figure 3. An oval indicates that a rule was tickled and fired. A rectangle indicates that a rule was tickled but did not fire.

trace of the rules in figure 3 with working memory (`(lays eggs robin)` `(has feathers robin)`) would have the appearance of figure 6 above.

A rectangle indicates that a rule was *tickled* but did not fire and an oval indicates that a rule was first *tickled* and then fired. This style of trace provides little temporal information, concentrating instead on the logical links between working memory elements and rules. The graph is also quite bulky, a typical trace of four or five rules over ten cycles would fill a landscape screen.

The MCC System

The system developed by [Poltreck 86] at the MCC contained a number of views to graphically display the static and dynamic relationships between rules and facts in a forward and backward chaining rule system. Figure 7 shows a screen snapshot from the rule and fact ('fact' is synonymous with 'working memory element') display after the rules (which find the routes between two cities) have fired 29 times. Rules are represented by arrows, forward chaining rules pointing to the right and backward chaining rules pointing to the left. The layout algorithm for the display places rules in columns with the facts in between. The first rule within the knowledge base is assigned the first column, and all the rules it could possibly interact with are displayed in the second column. Facts are grouped by predicate (the first term in the pattern) and are represented by an oval. The number within the oval indicates the number of facts present for the predicate. Initially, before execution begins, there are no lines connecting rules to facts. When a rule fires directed lines connect the rule to its antecedent and consequent facts.

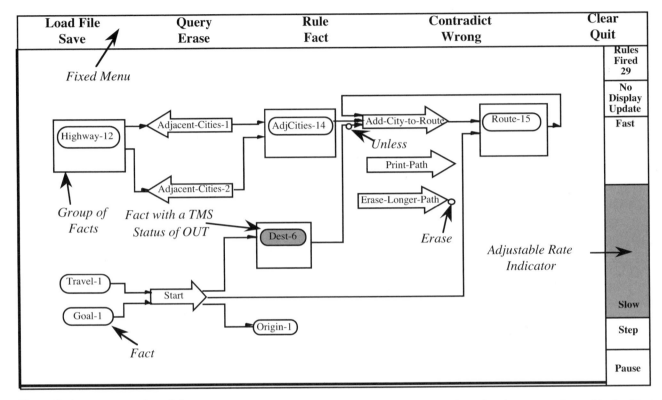

Load File	Query	Rule	Contradict	Clear
Save	Erase	Fact	Wrong	Quit

Fixed Menu

Rules Fired 29

No Display Update

Fast

Group of Facts

Fact with a TMS Status of OUT

Adjustable Rate Indicator

Slow

Step

Pause

Unless

Erase

Fact

Figure 7. A screen snapshot of the fact and rule display from [Poltreck 86].

A Truth Maintenance System (TMS) (referred to in connection with the Dest-6 node in figure 7) keeps track of which facts led to a particular fact being asserted. If any of the supporting facts are retracted then the status of the supported fact changes from IN to OUT and the fact can no longer match against a rule.

In addition to the fact and rule display two other views were provided. The first displayed potential interactions between rules, that is rules whose antecedents and consequents overlapped. The second view contained a fish-eye display focusing on the execution path to and from a particular fact.

KEATS

The KEATS project [Eisenstadt 90b] [Motta 91] aimed to provide methodological and software support for the whole knowledge engineering life-cycle. The KEATS toolkit provided dynamic visualizations of a forward and backward chaining system and of a truth maintenance system. The forward chaining visualization system, called TRI (Transparent Rule Interpreter)

[Domingue 88] [Domingue 89], used a 'musical score' metaphor to show coarse-grained behaviour. Figure 8 shows the TRI graph for the rules and working memory in figure 3.

Figure 9 shows a full screen snapshot of TRI in use. The left uppermost window shows the rule graph displaying the complete coarse-grained history of rule execution. If a firing rule invoked the backward chaining system the cross is replaced by a triangle. All windows beneath the rule graph provide fine-grained views of selected (from the rule graph) slices of the history. The three small windows at the upper right of the figure show three slices of working memory for particular (user-selected) predicates. Each pattern is mouse sensitive, enabling either the relevant node in the rule graph to be highlighted, or a more detailed description of the pattern to be displayed. The two large windows at the bottom left and bottom centre show two slices of the conflict resolution set. The top part of each of those windows contains the definition of the rule; the bottom part shows all the instantiations the rule had in the conflict set for a particular cycle. Each instantiation is mouse sensitive, allowing operations such as displaying or editing the deleting conflict resolution strategy. Each working memory clause is also mouse sensitive, enabling either the relevant node in the rule graph to be highlighted, or a more detailed description of the pattern to be displayed. If a rule involves backward chaining, an additional mouse click is sufficient to bring up a display of the backward chaining execution history (proof tree), as can be seen in the lower right hand corner. Each node in the tree corresponds to a goal, which may or may not have been successful, within the execution. The display of proof trees is based on [Eisenstadt 88a] (See Chapter 15 on the Truth about Prolog Execution in this book): a white node indicates a success, a white node containing a cross indicates a (trivial) success by matching against a working memory element, a black node indicates a failure and a grey node indicates failure due to backtracking. It is possible to abstract the tree both by zooming out and by allowing robust backward chaining rules to be 'black boxed' away, facilitating the display of thousands of nodes in a large proof tree. Each node in the tree is mouse sensitive. Clicking on a node displays more detailed information (the window above the proof tree window) including: the rule the goal was called from; the source code version of the call; and the actual call, in which variables are likely to have been renamed.

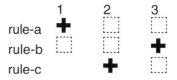

Figure 8. A TRI graph showing the execution of the rules rule-a, rule-b and rule-c from figure 3. The + means that a rule fired, a box means that a rule entered the conflict resolution set but did not fire. The rules fired in the order: rule-a, rule-c then rule-b. Rule-c entered the conflict resolution set during the last 2 |cycles| only.

TRI has proved to be a useful tool for debugging knowledge bases. The rule graph display was adopted by IntelliCorp in their ProKappa product and by Harlequin in the KnowledgeWorks product.

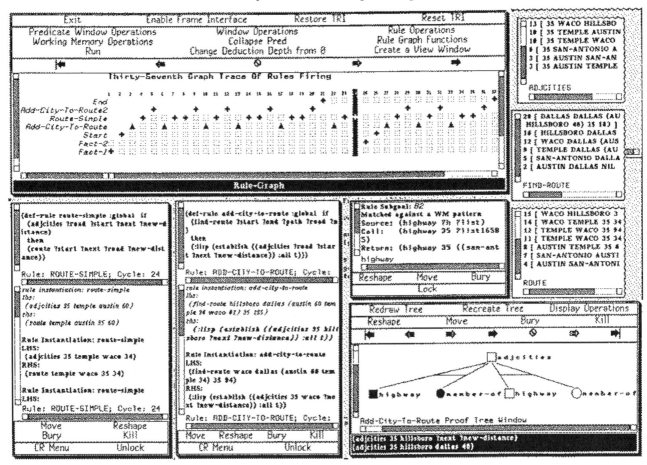

Figure 9. A full screen snapshot showing typical interaction with TRI.

VITAL

KBS development can be seen as a process of model transformation. Psychological techniques are used to elicit knowledge from a knowledge source. The elicited knowledge fragments are organised into a conceptual model (a "model of expertise" [Weilinga 84]). The conceptual model is transformed into a design model where non-functional requirements, from a requirements specification, are taken into account. The design model is at the same level of abstraction (termed the knowledge level) as the conceptual model, but is oriented to describing the system to be built rather than the knowledge extracted. The final transformation is from the design model into executable code.

Within the VITAL project [Shadbolt 93] an effort was made to integrate SV technology into the VITAL KBS development methodology. The work was aimed at providing support for KBS verification and validation. By verification I mean 'was the system constructed correctly' and validation as I mean 'was the right system constructed'. Verification is carried out by comparing a KBS model against its predecessor (e.g. an implementation against a design model). Validation is carried out by comparing an implementation against an initial model (either a requirement specification or a conceptual model).

A summary of how SV was used within the VITAL project is shown in figure 10. The left column in figure 10 shows three of the four phases of KBS construction within the VITAL methodology. The right column shows how SV technology is used within VITAL. At the conceptual modelling stage a knowledge engineer can attach images to concepts. The mapping between the images and concepts can be as simple or as complex as desired. Once a mapping has been established a domain dependent scripting tool is automatically generated. Using this tool an expert can, with a knowledge engineer, by direct manipulation create an Expert Scripted Visualization (ESV) which represents a single case. The graphics and layouts within the ESV can then be hooked up to the KBS implementation providing a KBS domain visualization. Validation is carried out by comparing the ESV with the KBS visualizations. Verification is carried out by comparing design and code level visualizations against the domain visualization. The design visualizations are provided by highlighting the currently executing task within a control and data flow diagram. Code level views of a task execution using visualizations based on TPM (see The Truth about Prolog Execution in this book) and TRI (see above) are also provided. The three levels of visualization are synchronised and can be replayed in parallel.

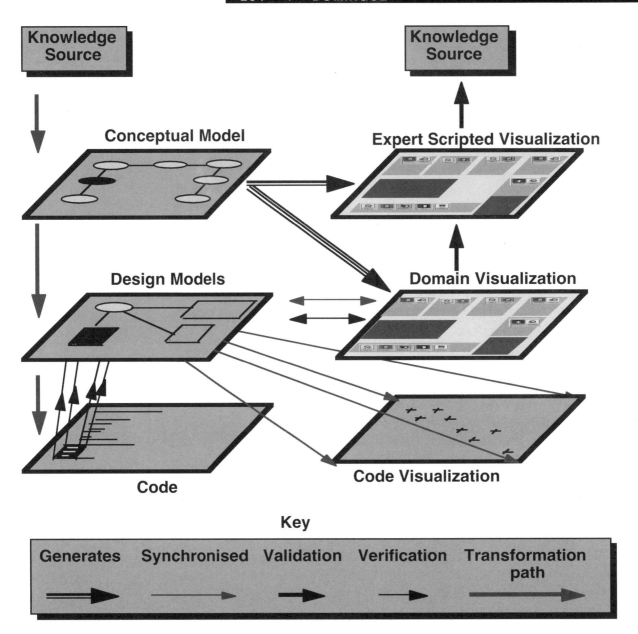

Figure 10. The SV based verification and validation support provided by VITAL.

All the systems reviewed in this chapter aim to help KEs debug their KBs. Before finishing it is worth considering for a moment exactly what sort of information KEs are likely to require from an SV system during the debugging task. An incorrect conclusion from a KB means that a buggy inference occurred somewhere in the execution. At a fine-grained level an incorrect inference in a forward chaining system means that the wrong instantiation fired. This could be due to:

- the conflict resolution strategies choosing the wrong instantiation,

- a buggy instantiation (which had a higher priority than the correct instantiation) was created, either because of a buggy working memory element or because of a buggy rule,

- the correct instantiation was not created because one (or more) of the necessary working memory elements was missing.

SV systems should allow the above information to be gleaned easily.

According to [Eisenstadt 93a] the single biggest problem for general programmers is the *cause-effect chasm*. It is the large temporal distance between observed symptoms and underlying causes which makes bug finding hard. When debugging a KB the KE has to track back from a 'symptomatic' incorrect inference (series of rule firings/working memory assertions) to the buggy inference which actually caused the error. Thus an SV system should enable KEs to navigate potentially large 'inference spaces'. One way of enhancing navigability is to provide a high level abstraction. A potential source of abstraction can be found in the knowledge level models, that is in the design model or the model of expertise. Inferences can be chunked according to the source knowledge fragment i.e. a set of rule firings can be represented as a single task execution. VITAL used this technique to some extent but there is scope for further work. For instance, one of the current research topics in KBS is that of knowledge reuse. The idea is that it should be possible for parts of a conceptual or design model from one KBS to be reused within the development of another. To this end libraries of problem solving methods and domain ontologies have been created. It should be possible to incorporate skeletal SV into these libraries. Views would then be attached to problem solving methods and domain specific icons to elements within a domain ontology. The skeletal SV would be used to provide 'knowledge level visualizations' of the executing KBS. For example, the

Conclusions

hierarchy of possible categories within the 'classification' problem solving method lends itself to a tree based visualization.

KBS development relies on a large amount of interaction with non-computer experts (for knowledge elicitation and validation). I believe that SV technology has the potential to play a large role in facilitating communication between KEs and human experts by providing a rich dynamic interactive medium.

Visualizing Concurrent Programs

Eileen Kraemer

Introduction

Understanding the behavior of concurrent programs is more challenging than understanding the behavior of sequential programs. Concurrent programs are by nature large and complex and may produce vast quantities of data. Instead of a single process, there are multiple threads of execution interacting in complex and possibly unforeseen ways. Threads or processes communicate, compete for resources, periodically synchronize, and may be dynamically created and destroyed. The coordination of these many threads of execution is complex, and may result in unexpected interactions. Execution may be non-deterministic. That is, multiple executions of the same program may result in varying program behaviors. Debugging is complicated by this problem with reproducibility, as an incorrect output may occur only once in hundreds or thousands of executions.

A further complication results from obstacles to the collection of data. In a purely sequential program, a breakpoint can be set at which the program's execution is momentarily suspended and a "snapshot" of the program's state can be collected and studied. Producing a snapshot of program state is more complex in a concurrent program - multiple threads must be stopped, and messages in transit must be considered in calculating the global state. Memory may be distributed, and messages in transit may be difficult to access. Further, communication delays between processors may be large, and may vary greatly. Finally, system clocks may not be synchronized across the multiple processors involved in the computation, and may "drift" at different rates.

These factors make it difficult both to understand concurrent programs, and to collect and analyze the data necessary to evaluate their correctness and performance. Traditional tools for debugging, performance monitoring, and program comprehension are generally not sufficient for locating errors and inefficiencies in concurrent processes, keeping track of the activities that may lead to synchronization errors or deadlocks, and explaining the execution and interactions of these processes.

For example, the voluminous output of concurrent programs can quickly overwhelm textual tracing facilities that work well for serial programs. While many parallel debuggers exist that allow programmers to set breakpoints, suspend processes, and examine the local states, the presentation generally consists of disjoint snapshots of small subsets of the program state, in which events of interest can easily be missed and from which higher-level information about distributed data may be difficult to extract. The static analysis tools prevalent in the program comprehension arena also are generally not equipped to deal with problems of concurrency such as complex synchronization interactions and the difficulties with reproducibility brought on by non-determinism.

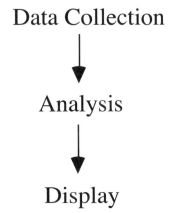

Figure 1. Tasks involved in the visualization of a concurrent program.

Graphical visualization can be a powerful tool for understanding and explaining complex tasks such as parallel computation. Visualization can assist the user in grasping the concurrency of the program and in managing the large number of objects likely to be found in parallel and distributed programs. Interactive, graphical displays can also assist with a critical component of concurrent programming: understanding the interactions between processes, both those that occurred and those that *could have* occurred in an alternate feasible program execution. Appropriate displays of concurrent programs can help the viewer develop intuition about performance and correctness problems that stem from unanticipated interactions between processes.

In creating a visualization of a parallel program, a number of inherent tasks are present. These tasks include data collection, analysis, and display. In the following paragraphs we will discuss each of these tasks in the context of the visualization of concurrent systems.

Data Collection

In both serial and concurrent systems some form of instrumentation is used to collect the data to be analyzed and visualized. This instrumentation may be in hardware or in software. It may be inserted for purposes of visualization and then removed from the production version, exist permanently within the system and be enabled and disabled dynamically, or it may be dynamically inserted using lightweight debugger techniques.

Any form of instrumentation will *perturb* the system to some degree. That is, the existence of this instrumentation will affect the performance of the program, and may affect the order in which the program events occur. The extent of the perturbation, or probe effect, varies according to the volume of information collected, the monitoring method, the system architecture and system software, the level at which the instrumentation occurs, and the programming paradigm. Further, the programmer's tolerance for perturbation of the system will vary with the task being performed.

The goal of performance evaluation is to provide an accurate depiction of the efficiency of execution of the program and its components, and to locate performance bottlenecks. Instrumentation of the program to collect the necessary data can affect the program's performance and distort the performance statistics. Thus, there is a low tolerance for perturbation in performance evaluation tasks, and a major goal of instrumentation for performance evaluation is to minimize perturbation. Programmers performing debugging tasks will tolerate greater performance losses, as their main interest is correctness rather than performance. However, programs that contain non-deterministic constructs (whether intentional or unintentional) may exhibit a different event order in the instrumented mode. This may bring out errors that were previously undetected - a good thing in a debugging situation. However, this altered event order may also mask errors - not a desirable feature. Thus, the goals of debugging systems will differ from those of performance evaluation systems. For example, controlled execution and the ability to specify the instrumentation points at run-time are desirable features for debugging. Further goals, such as the detection of non-determinism and the calculation and forced execution of alternate feasible orderings may also be of interest for debugging, but will require interaction with analysis components of the tool.

Hardware level instrumentation tends to introduce the least perturbation. However, not all systems have monitoring hardware in place, nor can all events of interest be easily captured at a hardware level. Information that can be collected at the hardware level includes measures of single process and total process CPU times, elapsed time, program counter samples, cache misses, memory and switch traffic, and instruction and data address samples. Such information is useful in calculating performance evaluation metrics. Higher-levels displays such as algorithm-specific performance displays or algorithm animations require higher-level events, and thus employ software level instrumentation.

Software instrumentation, the insertion of small pieces of code that report *interesting events*, values of interest, may be performed at the level of the operating system, the run-time system, or at the level of the application program. Instrumentation at the operating system level can be used to collect information such as message sends and receives, process creation, scheduling, and termination, page faults, context switching, memory access, and system calls. Visualizations based on these types of events can portray the execution of the operating system itself, and highlight the interactions between the system software and the hardware. Of particular interest for concurrent systems are those values that can be used in analyzing load balancing, contention for resources, data placement, and tradeoffs between parallel and serial execution of particular sections of code.

Instrumentation of the run-time environment can provide information such as the state of various run-time queues, the acquisition and release of locks, entry to and exit from parallel sections, arrival at and departure from synchronization barriers, the dispatching of loop chunks, and procedure calls and returns. This type of information can be used to associate performance bottlenecks with specific actions of the application code, and to visualize aspects of the run-time system itself. Analysis and visualization of this data can be useful in evaluating the correctness of the flow of control, in understanding the execution of existing programs, detecting errors in the logic of the synchronization structure that coordinates the various threads of control, gaining intuition about the cause of load imbalances, and in selecting procedures for further optimization.

Instrumentation of the application program itself can provide information about abstract, high-level, and user-defined events. This information can feed a variety of displays, including algorithm-specific performance visualizations and debugging displays that are detailed enough to allow the viewer to verify the correct execution of all or a portion of the program. Further, this type of instrumentation can provide the association between operating or run-time system events and particular portions of the source code.

How does the data collection process in concurrent systems differ from the data collection process in sequential systems? Concurrent programs run on multiple processors, tend to be long-running, and are often sensitive to changes in timing. The long-running, multi-process nature of these programs leads to increased volumes of data. The distribution of data across separate memories may make it difficult to access remote values and to determine globally consistent states. This increased volume, coupled with possible non-determinism, causes concurrent programs to be more sensitive to perturbation. Also, in addition to the data collected for a serial program, it may be necessary to collect data that will permit the reconstruction of a consistent event order, investigation of alternate event orderings, detection of some non-deterministic constructs, or estimation of the effects of perturbation. This additional data may provide information about the causal relationships between events or may consist of a timestamp or corrected timestamp. The calculation of this additional data, whether a timestamp or event-relationship information, further adds to the overhead of data collection and the resulting perturbation of the program.

The large volume of data produced by concurrent programs requires that the instrumentation to collect the data be inserted selectively and intelligently. This is required both to reduce perturbation and to limit the size of the collected data, which can quickly become unmanageable. There are several approaches to "intelligent" data collection, and decisions must be made about whether, when, and where to reduce, store, analyze and display the collected data. In the following paragraphs we discuss these decisions and the costs and benefits that must be weighed.

Should visualization be performed on-line (concurrent with the program's execution) or post-mortem (after the program has terminated)? On-line visualization provides the benefit of an up-to-the-moment view of the computation's progress and can reduce the overhead of data storage (assuming that the data are not needed after visualization). However, the visualization can not be too detailed, as the viewer would find it difficult to comprehend such a rapidly updating, highly detailed display. Also, on-line visualization can add overhead in several ways. The collection of data requires both storage space and

CPU time. If the visualization is performed locally, it will compete for CPU time with the program under study. However, if the visualization process is remote, the task of forwarding the collected data to the remote monitoring station will require both CPU time and communication bandwidth.

Post-mortem visualization provides the opportunity for a more detailed display that can proceed at a user-specified pace, and generally will perturb the program to a lesser degree than on-line visualization. However, it does not entirely eliminate contention for CPU time, as the data must still be collected and stored. The volume of data produced by a concurrent program is likely to require that the data be written to disk, rather than kept in memory, again competing with and perturbing the program of interest. Filtering and reduction of this data can reduce the volume. Performing data reduction by filtering, statistical analysis or other methods involves tradeoffs between the execution overhead of performing the data reduction, and the now reduced overhead of transmission and/or storage of the reduced data set. If such filtering and data reduction is to be performed, it may be done locally (at each process or processor) or the data may be forwarded to some central site for filtering, reduction, and storage. The decision of whether to perform the data reduction locally or centrally must be carefully analyzed for the particular architecture, reduction method, monitoring scheme, and the class of application program under study.

In speaking of concurrent systems, we include both shared memory and distributed systems. In a shared memory system, each processor can access any variable residing in the shared memory. Multiple processors can access the shared memory simultaneously if the memory locations they are trying to read from or write to are different, but synchronization operations are required to prevent simultaneous access to the same location. If one processor wishes to pass information to another processor, it simply writes into a shared variable. The other processor would then read from the shared variable. Again, a synchronization operation would be required to ensure that the write precedes the corresponding read.

In a distributed memory system, each processor has its own private memory that is not accessible from any other processor. Data communication takes place using message passing via an interconnection network. The data of interest and the problems involved in accessing these values will differ between shared and distributed memory systems. In shared memory systems, access is straightforward. Distributed systems require more overhead to access a value "owned" by a remote process. The extent of this overhead will vary with the characteristics of the interconnection network. However, distributed systems may provide an advantage in selecting interesting values - the contents of a message or perhaps a particular type of message may be easily identified as "interesting". In shared memory systems this can be more difficult - we probably *don't* want to record *every* access to shared memory. There would be too many accesses, and most of them would not be of interest. Which values are interesting to collect? This is a more difficult decision that generally requires higher-level instrumentation such as a specialized library of synchronization calls, or user-directed modification of the application program.

Determining event order is a problem in both parallel and distributed systems. Collection of data from concurrent programs differs from the collection of data from serial programs in that there are multiple streams of data. These streams must be ordered and merged for analysis and visualization. Although timestamps are often used as a means of ordering, these values must be accurate and consistent to produce a reliable ordering. In the absence of synchronized clocks running at the same rate and with adequate resolution, additional analysis must be performed to determine a *consistent* event order. Lamport[Lamport 78] defined a consistent ordering of events in a distributed system in terms of the *happened-before* relationship, a partial ordering of the events in the system. *Happened-before* is the smallest relation satisfying three conditions: 1) If *a* and *b* are events in the same process and *a* comes before *b*, then *a happened-before b*. 2) If *a* is the sending of a message by one process and *b* is the receiving of the same message by another process, then *a happened-before b*. 3) If *a happened-before b*, and *b happened-before c*, then *a happened-before c*. A consistent ordering of events is one which does not violate the *happened-before* relationship.

The data collection phase must collect the information needed to consistently order events. Some systems rely on clock-correction schemes to produce synchronized timestamps of adequate resolution, for example, Bugnet[Wittie 89]. Other, systems have built-in instrumentation that will produce consistent timestamps. For example, Xab[Begeulin 93] uses a causality-based timestamp correction scheme. The Conch Network Computing System[Topol 95a], can produce either Lamport-style timestamps that adhere to a partial ordering based on causal relationships, or physical timestamps.

Analysis

After the data collection phase has produced a stream of data describing the program's execution, the analysis phase may then process the data before passing it on to the display phase of the visualization system. This processing may be as simple as format conversion or the calculation of statistics, or as complex as the detection of higher-level abstract events from a stream of lower-level events. In parallel and distributed systems, this analysis may also include the determination of global states, and the ordering of events.

The analysis phase of a typical performance visualization system will compute performance metrics and statistics. In a post-mortem visualization system, the analysis and display may be simplified by the preprocessing of the trace file to determine parameters such as time scale and number of processors. Values such as message traffic totals and averages, CPU utilization, and load balance may also be computed.

In general, the amount of analysis that may be performed in on-line visualization systems is limited due to time constraints. However, in some systems there is a "feedback loop" in which performance data is analyzed for the purpose of making on-line dynamic changes to a parallel or distributed program[Gu 95]. These on-line changes may be automated or under user control. The extent of this analysis is limited by the relationship of the overhead incurred to the performance gains realized by the resulting adaptations.

Many systems create intermediate data structures such as procedure call, synchronization, and other flow graphs, as part of the analysis process. For example, IPS-2[Miller 90] performs critical path analysis on the execution graph which it creates. This determination of the longest time-weighted path through the graph produces information useful in performance evaluation and tuning.

The analysis phase may be user-directed, as in Pablo[Reed 91]. This system provides a set of performance data transformation modules that the user can manipulate and interconnect graphically to form an acyclic, directed data analysis graph, and thus specify the analysis to be performed.

The level of instrumentation is a determining factor both in the types of displays that can produced, and in the analysis that must be performed to transform the data from the form in which it is collected to the form necessary to feed the displays. For example, if the instrumentation is collecting lower-level system events, and the displays require knowledge of higher-level, algorithmic events, the analysis phase may be called upon to detect these higher-level events from the stream of lower-level events. One such analysis tool is the event recognizer module of the EBBA, Event Based Behavioral Abstraction, tool[Bates 89].

EBBA is a high-level debugging tool that allows the user to specify models of program behavior consisting of abstract and primitive events. An event detection tool examines the stream of primitive events from the program, and applies a pattern-matching algorithm to construct user-specified abstract events. The techniques for performing this modeling are called *clustering* and *filtering*. Clustering is used to hierarchically define higher-level behaviors as aggregates of primitive and other previously defined high-level events. Filtering is used to elide from the data stream those events not relevant to the behavioral model under study. The program's behavior is then compared to the model to determine correctness. Several notes of caution regarding this method: A larger volume of data must generally be collected than if the instrumentation were performed at the higher level, and the analysis involved is significant. Additionally, there are limitations on the ability of any analysis system to correctly detect abstract higher-level events from a stream of low-level events.

The detection of non-determinism is an important analysis function for concurrent systems. One tool for detecting non-determinism is TraceViewer[Helmbold 90]. Given a sequential trace, a trace analyzer component parses the trace file, and constructs an event history graph. A time vector value is calculated for each event. The trace is then analyzed to determine the shared objects referenced between synchronization events. All of this information is then used to find unordered or concurrent events and variable access conflicts, and report on these race conditions.

Static analysis, another method for detecting non-determinism, generates all possible concurrency states, and it can be used to detect deadlock and race conditions. However, such analysis of an arbitrary program has been shown to be NP-hard and it does not deal well with dynamically created objects. Techniques for *folding*, the grouping of equivalent concurrency states into classes[Helmbold 91], have simplified this process.

Other systems attempt to negate or minimize the effects of non-determinism in visualization. For example, Instant Replay[Leblanc 87] [Leblanc 90] and Bugnet[Wittie 89] record enough information from one run to allow replay in the same, or "almost the same," order on subsequent runs. Bugnet bases its ordering on physical time(timestamps) rather than causal relationships. The Instant Replay system uses data gathered from one run of a program to guarantee that subsequent runs within the system occur in an equivalent logical order. Further refinements of the data collection process have been developed to reduce the volume of the traced data[Netzer 95].

One form of analysis common to all of the purposes of visualization discussed here, yet peculiar to parallel systems, is the determination of the order of events. Displays that fail to adhere to a consistent order of events may be misleading, fail to provide the user with the most informative perspective on the program under study, or may fail completely. For example, a visualization that shows a message *Receive* occurring before the corresponding *Send* would be confusing to the viewer. Similarly, any statistical calculations based on such an event stream could be misleading. For example, a calculation of messages-in-transit (number of messages sent - number of messages received) could result in a negative number if the event stream is out-of-order.

At the simplest level, the calculation of a consistent order may involve the assignment of timestamps to events. If all processes have access to a global clock, the system may order the events based on physical time. Physical time provides information not only about the order of events, but also about the elapsed time between events.

The calculation of a consistent causal ordering (e.g., one that does not violate the Lamport *happened-before* relationship) involves the determination of the order of events at each processing node (condition 1 of *happened-before*), the determination of the interprocess events and their relationships to one another (condition 2), and the calculation of the transitive closure of the causal relationships (condition 3). Such an ordering is often referred to as a *logical time* ordering.

The Animation Choreographer[Kraemer 94] is an analysis tool that allows users to view, manipulate, and explore the set of alternate feasible orderings of the program execution under study, both through a specialized form of execution history graph, and in the context of user-defined and user-selected visualizations, thus providing the user with a variety of temporal perspectives on the computation. That is, the user may view the program's execution based on timestamps, or may view a serialized ordering, an ordering that illustrates the maximum concurrency, or an ordering in which the timestamps have been adjusted so that they do not violate causality.

Displays of concurrent programs must address the same basic concern as displays of sequential systems - the creation of *effective* displays. That is, displays that use space, color, shape, and text well, that present sufficient detail but do not overwhelm the viewer, and that allow the user to navigate through a hierarchy of related views to find the view that presents the most interesting perspective for the user's current question about the program's execution. Displays of concurrent programs differ in that the problems in dealing with scale are exacerbated and problems dealing with temporal issues are introduced.

Display

The most critical issue in the visualization of a concurrent program is the ability to convey knowledge and intuition regarding the dynamic behavior the program. Of particular concern are the interactions between processes with respect to synchronization and communication. Effective displays must be capable of representing these interactions and their relationships; they must be capable of concurrently displaying events that were (or could have been) concurrent in the program.

Another complex problem for displays is the scalability problem. For small scale executions, simple views based on time, processing elements, interactions, and subtasks are adequate. For massively parallel executions, such displays are largely ineffective. For these executions, we may be dealing with hundreds or thousands of processes, each of which may produce tens of thousands of event records. A simple execution history graph that provides the ability to pan, zoom, and scroll is not sufficient to create an effective display. Instead, displays must be created whose format, size, meaning, and effectiveness are independent of the number of processing elements involved.

Figure 2. This animated program call graph view from the Gthreads package is dynamically constructed as threads are forked, functions are called, and the point of execution of a thread moves from function to function.

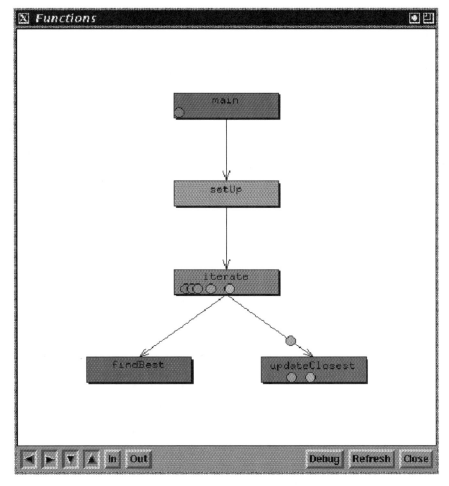

The most effective displays are those that map well to the programmer's mental model of the computation. Of course, the types of mental models that people form will vary by individual and by user group. In addition, many facets of the display task are determined by the *purpose* of the visualization. For example, debugger displays attempt to provide some view of program state. Often, this is a highly specialized view of some particular aspect of the computation, such as the pattern of access to shared memory, the interprocessor communication of a particular distributed memory architecture, or the order in which subroutines are called. Performance visualization tools generally provide a graphical representation of standard metrics such as processor utilization or communication load. Algorithm animation systems provide highly application-specific views of the program's data structures and the operations which update these data structures, or some more abstract representation of the computation and its progress. These visualizations are often useful not only in understanding the actions of the computation, but also in debugging and performance evaluation. Graphical displays similar to those used in performance evaluation and algorithm animation systems have been used in program specification systems and simulation systems as well.

In the following paragraphs we will describe the various types of displays that have been created for the visualization of concurrent systems, and discuss the purposes for which they are best suited. These displays include program graphs, communication graphs, statistical displays, memory access displays, barscope views, and xy plots.

Many systems display program graphs, in which the vertices represent program entities and the arcs represent call relations or temporal orderings, similar to the graph shown in Figure 2, from the Gthreads[Zhao 95] library for the visualization of threads-based parallel programs. Often, these displays can be animated by highlighting the current node. This type of display can be useful in debugging and program visualization, displaying the order of execution of subprograms, and allowing the viewer to detect unexpected sequences, or unexecuted subprograms. This type of display may also convey the relative time spent in various subprograms, useful information in performance evaluation. The task display of ParaGraph[Heath 89] [Heath 91] can be used in this way.

A number of systems use a graph to represent the concurrency of the computation. For example, the concurrency map[Stone 89] displays the event histories of processes on a grid. Viewers of the display can derive the set of alternate feasible event orderings. Makbilan's[Zernik 91] causality graph also represents the temporal relationships among the events in a parallel computation. Color coding is used to partition nodes of the graph into past, present, and future in relation to some selected node.

The HeNCE system[Begeulin 91], Heterogeneous Network Computing Environment, contains an integrated, graphical toolkit for creating, compiling, executing, and analyzing PVM programs[Sunderam 90]. As the program executes, HeNCE can display an animated view of the execution via a program graph. The nodes of the program graph change color to indicate the occurrence of various trace events. Another system for the visualization of PVM programs, PVaniM[Topol 96], is an enhancement package for PVM 3.3 that produces animations of the execution of PVM applications. PVaniM provides a general purpose set of views that work with all PVM applications, and provides support for users to build custom, application-specific animations. The two main components of PVaniM are a tracing library and a general purpose set of animations that work with all PVM applications.

Figure 3. Processes are arranged around the outside of the circle. Messages are shown as colored disks that move into the center of the circle when sent and out the receiving process upon receipt. Undelivered messages conspicuously remain in the center.

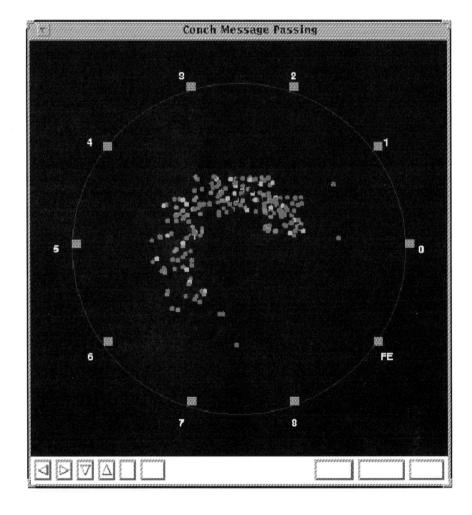

A number of systems present displays that represent connections and communication among processors. Figure 3 is a message passing view from the Conch system[Topol 95a]. Processes are arranged around the outside of the circle, and messages are represented as colored disks that move into the center of the ring when sent and out to the receiving process upon receipt. Figure 4, from the AIMS system[Yan 95] represents the topology of the system under study. These types of displays are useful in observing communication patterns, detecting anomalies in those patterns, and in evaluating the mapping of processes to processors. Belvedere[Hough 87], a pattern-oriented parallel debugger, also displays patterns of communication. The viewer observes these patterns for deviations from a model of expected behavior in order to detect bugs. Similar displays can be found in Bugnet[Wittie 89], Voyeur[Socha 89], SDEF[Engstrom 87], and Radar[Leblanc 85].

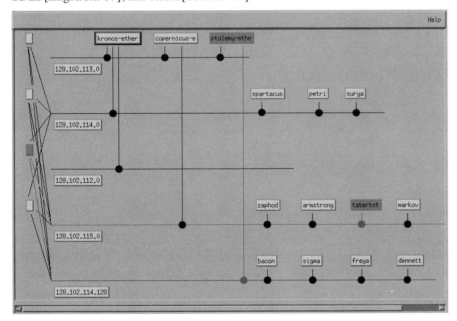

Figure 4. The AIMS View Kernel display of network topology.

Many debuggers provide time-process diagrams that present a running display of communications over time. Generally, one axis represents time, and individual processes are drawn along the other axis. Message traffic is depicted by lines connecting processes in pairs. The space-time diagram(Figure 5), from the ParaGraph system[Heath 89] [Heath 91] shows communication between processors over time. As time progresses, the display scrolls off to the left. IDD[Harter 85], the Interactive Distributed Debugger, the process-time diagram of Moviola[Leblanc 90], and PVaniM[Topol 96] provide similar displays.

Figure 5. A time-process communication graph from the ParaGraph system. Similar displays are provided by IDD and Moviola.

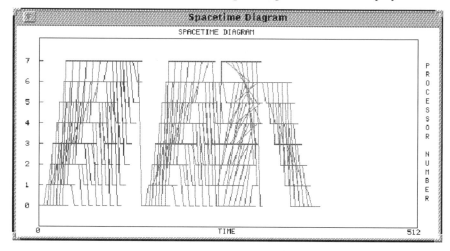

A number of performance evaluation systems provide displays of statistical information. Tapestry[Malony 90] displays include dials, bar charts, kiviat diagrams, and matrix views. ParaGraph[Heath 89] [Heath 91] provides bar graphs and kiviat diagrams to display processor utilization statistics, and a matrix view to show message traffic and volume. Figure 6 shows a kiviat diagram representing the CPU utilization of each of the processors involved in a parallel computation.

SHMAP[Dongarra 90], the Shared-Memory Access Pattern program, is designed to aid in the study of memory access patterns, cache strategies, and processor assignment on matrix algorithms in a FORTRAN setting. The main display uses two windows - one to show loads from main memory, one to show stores to main memory. Memory is represented two-dimensionally. Each memory access results in the illumination of the corresponding memory element. Gradual fading over time is used to aid the user in recognizing the recently accessed elements. A similar display is used for cache accesses.

SIEVE.1[Sarukkai 92], which relies on a spreadsheet of data collected from the program, can be used to create a number of XY plot displays. Columns from the program spreadsheet are assigned to the X and Y axes. Lines and rectangles are used to connect the data points. Color coding may be used to represent processor ID or other attributes, and to create displays such as that shown in Figure 7. Although created with POLKA[Stasko 93b] rather than SIEVE, the figure shows a view of an execution of parallel quicksort in which the Y axis represents time, and the X coordinates represent the indices of array elements that have been swapped. Vertical lines have been drawn between swapped elements, and color has been used to represent the ID of the processor performing the swap.

Application-Specific and Abstract Displays

Thus far, we have discussed *generic* rather than *application-specific* visualizations. That is, the general appearance of the views remains constant across varied application programs. A number of other displays are application-specific; visualizations of different programs will have different appearances. This type of visualization will generally require some extra effort on the part of the user, but will result in a display which more closely matches the user's mental model of the computation. Systems for the creation of application-specific visualizations include Voyeur, PARADISE, BALSA, Tango, Pavane, and POLKA.

Voyeur[Socha 89] attempts to simplify the task of building views through use of a class hierarchy. The base class contains the basic structure of a display window - a title bar, menus, status area, buttons, and a scrollable drawing area. Associated with the base class are simple mechanisms for specifying the contents of these interaction devices and for associating them with the desired routines. Displays as diverse as a load-balancing algorithm animated as sharks and fishes moving across a grid, a program trace view, a linked-list view of the load-balancing algorithm, and a vector view of an Applied Math problem may all be created using these base classes.

PARADISE[Kohl 92] [Kohl 91] is a *meta-tool* for generating custom visual analysis tools. It provides an abstract object-oriented, visual modeling environment in which the user creates a tool to process and display a stream of events from the system under study.

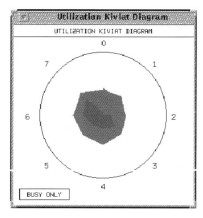

Figure 6. A kiviat graph from the ParaGraph system. Each vertex of the dark shape in the center indicates a particular processor's current CPU utilization, with the center indicating 0% and the edge of the circle indicating 100%. The outer, lighter colored shape represents the "high-water-mark" of CPU utilization for each processor.

*Figure 7. A plot representing the progress of a parallel quicksort program over time. (created with POLKA) *See Plate 4**

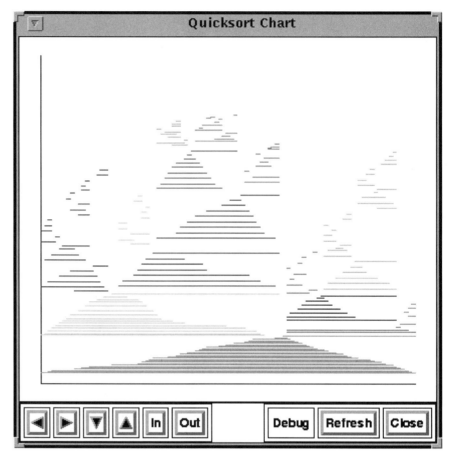

Program visualization and algorithm animation tools for parallel systems generally achieve an abstract view through user specification and software-level collection of high-level abstract events. This is also the case in tools for the animation of sequential programs, such as BALSA[Brown 88b] and TANGO[Stasko 90b].

The Pavane system[Roman 92], which operates on a shared-memory tuple space architecture, supports formal mappings from a program space to an abstract animation space that can later be rendered. This model supports highly application-specific program views. To describe a visualization, programmers must construct the mappings, which are similar to those in formal proof systems. In PARADE[Stasko 95c] the events of interest for visualization may be received via event calls from the program under study, received through a pipe, or read from a file or database. These events may be automatically generated control, message, and synchronization events, or programmer annotated application-specific program events. An *animation choreographer* gathers the events logged for each processor and orders them for visualization according to user specifications. That is, the events may be chronologically ordered according to timestamp, logically ordered according to observable precedence relationships, or otherwise ordered according to user specifications. POLKA[Stasko 93b] a general purpose object-oriented software visualization and animation methodology, is used to create the graphical displays. A 2-D version based on the X11 Window System and a 3-D version based on the GL graphical library have been implemented. POLKA focuses on supporting continuous animation scenarios representing the concurrency of parallel programs.

Conclusion

The trend in high performance computing is toward greater concurrency and distribution. The increased volume and distribution will cause this data to be more expensive and difficult to collect. Thus, techniques to minimize the amount of data collected, to perform filtering and reduction of data, and to intelligently balance the burden of data collection and analysis between distributed and central agents will become increasingly important.

With increased concurrency and distribution comes increased complexity. In the absence of fully automated tools for the detection of timing-dependent errors, visualization will be useful in helping programmers develop intuition about non-deterministic constructs and programming errors, and in locating these problems and relating them back to the source code. In debuggers, perturbation effects which may obscure errors or bring new errors to light will require the application of causal ordering strategies such as those described in this chapter.

More highly distributed data will tend to increase the variation in latency across a more complicated hierarchy of memory structure, thus increasing the importance of decisions regarding data placement because of their effects on the nature and volume of inter-processor communications. Similarly, the way in which the program is decomposed into tasks will greatly affect performance. Visualizations of the placement of data, task decomposition, and the effects on performance will be essential to writing efficient parallel programs. Visualization will continue to be useful in conveying information about how well a program is performing, and in conjunction with analysis tools, in investigating and predicting performance on alternate problem sizes and architectures.

Compiler technology may ease some of the burdens of understanding program correctness and performance, while introducing other problems. Compilers may be used to automatically insert code for software instrumentation and to control hardware instrumentation and to collect information that will assist in revealing the effects of contention for resources, task synchronization, and the overhead of parallel resource management. The use of automatically parallelizing compilers may ease some of the burden of programming. However, this automatic parallelization will also obscure the relationship between source code constructs and performance. With appropriate compiler hooks, visualizations can be produced that will assist the programmer in making the connection between generated code and program performance.

In summary, the trend toward greater concurrency and increased distribution will lead to greater complexity and a greater need for graphical visualization to help with debugging, performance monitoring, and program comprehension. However, the tasks associated with visualization - data collection, analysis, and display - will themselves be complicated by the increased concurrency and distribution.

Visualization for Software Engineering

Section

V

This section describes perhaps the largest application domain for software visualization technology--its use for software engineering and program development. The chapters discuss how software visualizations can make program design, debugging, testing, understanding, optimization, and maintenance easier, faster, and maybe even more fun.

Chapter 18 ("Visualization for Software Engineering -- Programming Environments") describes the FIELD programming environment which utilizes a number of different types of software visualizations. The system provides views of data structures, memory usage, cross referencing, file dependencies, and many other attributes of a comprehensive programming environment. Chapter 19 ("ZStep 95: A Reversible, Animated Source Code Stepper") focuses on one particular component of a programming environment, the debugger. It shows how the addition of graphical views can make debugger usage easier and more natural.

Chapter 20 ("Visualization of Dynamics in Real World Software Systems") introduces a software visualization system that has been used to debug, test, and optimize large, real-world software systems. It describes how the visualizations were useful to identify particular problems and bottlenecks in different software systems. Chapter 21 ("Maintenance of Large Systems") presents the SeeSoft system and a novel visualization technique it utilizes to assist with the maintenance of large software systems. This technique is useful for communicating information about many different software engineering metrics such as test code coverage, code authorship, bug location and recency, amidst others.

The final two chapters present work aiding program development and analysis in two particular domains. Chapter 22 ("Visualizing Object-Oriented Software Execution") describes a software visualization system for object-oriented programs. The system introduces visualizations for depicting critical class, instance, and method operations and statistics from a program execution. Chapter 23 ("Visualization for Parallel Performance Evaluation and Optimization") describes how software visualizations can be used for performance evaluation and optimization of concurrent programs. Visualization appears to be a valuable way of communicating performance data back to programmers.

Visualization for Software Engineering — Programming Environments

Steven P. Reiss

FIELD, the Friendly Integrated Environment for Learning and Development, was developed from 1986 through 1992 as an attempt to use workstations effectively for UNIX-based programming [Reiss 90a] [Reiss 90b] [Reiss 94a]. It integrated a wide variety of UNIX tools into a common framework. This framework was enhanced with new tools developed for the environment, both tools for programming support and tools for program visualization.

An example of the environment can be seen in Figure 1. The window at the upper right is the control panel showing the available tools. The principal viewing tool for the source is an annotation editor shown in the lower right. The debugging tool, shown in the middle left of the figure, has both a textual and a visual front end, as well as a data structure displayer, display, shown in the upper right and displays of the current debugger state such as the stack display shown in the center. The configuration management front end is shown in the lower left. A textual display of information from the cross-reference database is shown in the upper right.

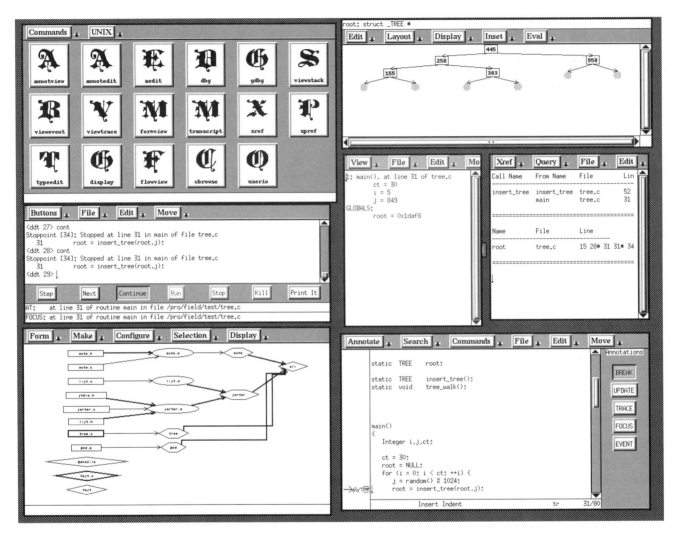

Figure 1. Overview of FIELD.

FIELD integrated the various programming tools using a message-based integration mechanism [Reiss 90b]. This mechanism uses a central message server that the tools (or appropriate tool wrappers) talk to. When the tool starts up, it registers with the message server patterns that describe the messages it is interested in. As it runs, messages are sent to the message server and are redistributed according to these patterns to all interested tools. Messages are typically of two types, commands that request action from another tool, and information that provide data from one tool that might be of potential interest to other tools.

To augment the existing set of UNIX programming tools and to provide a basis for program visualization, FIELD provided several new tools or extended tool wrappers that offered data about a program to other tools through the message server. The primary such tool was the cross-reference database. This tool gathered information about the syntax and semantics of a program and stored it in a relational database for querying by other tools. The information, gathered either by scanning the source or using compiler-generated data, included references, definitions, scopes, calls, include dependencies, function descriptions, class hierarchy links, and class member data. Other tools included a wrapper around both configuration management (*make*) and version control (*rcs*) tools that offered query facilities, and a generic wrapper for the various UNIX profiling tools that again allowed querying by other tools.

In addition to these tools for analyzing static data, FIELD provided a library-based monitoring facility that utilized the message server to provide information about a program's execution while the program was running. This tool worked by inserting its own library between the application and the system libraries to catch calls related to memory allocation or to input/output. It then sent messages describing each allocation or input/output event so that other tools, primarily dynamic visualizations, could display the program in action.

In addition to demonstrating how the computation power of workstations could be used to integrate a wide variety of programming tools, FIELD attempted to demonstrate how the graphical capabilities of workstations could facilitate program visualization. FIELD offered program visualizations both to provide a better interface to existing and newly developed tools and to offer the programmer insights into program structure and behavior.

FIELD's Visualization Tools

The earliest visualization tool provided by FIELD was the annotation editor. The FIELD annotation editor provided a common front end to the program source for both editing a visualization. It was a full-function text editor augmented with an annotation window to the left of the text as can be seen in Figure 2. Annotations were displayed in this window as a descriptive icon. Text associated with an annotation could be displayed at the user's request. Annotations were derived from messages received from the message server so that tools could request an annotation by sending an appropriate message. The editor could be set up to automatically display the line containing the annotation, changing files or position as needed to do so. It could also be set up to display a particular type of annotation by highlighting the corresponding line rather than using an icon. The annotation editor provided both static and dynamic visualizations. Static visualizations included a display of where breakpoints were located in a file and information about errors and warnings from compilation. Dynamic visualization showed the program executing either by a moving icon or by continually highlighting the currently executing line.

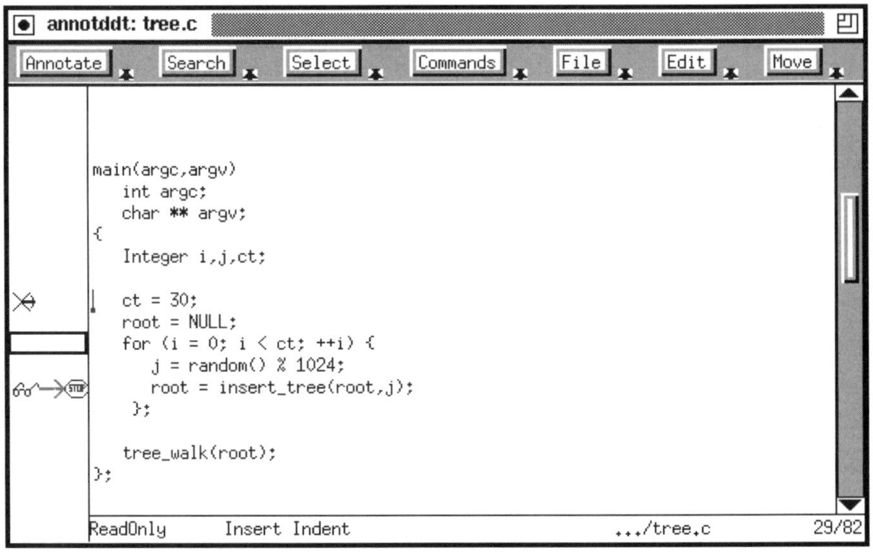

Figure 2. FIELD annotation editor showing a cross reference annotation as well as a focus (eyeglasses), execution (arrow), and break (stop sign) annotations on a simple program.

The next set of visualization tools offered by FIELD were diagrammatic based on a general purpose structure visualization package originally developed for the GARDEN programming system [Reiss 87]. This package, GELO, was designed to as a generic means for displaying 2D structured diagrams [Reiss 89]. It provided a simple framework based on simple boxes, arcs, rectilinear tilings, and arbitrary layouts. It included constraint satisfaction methods for managing tilings and a variety of placement and routing algorithms for handling layouts. Three FIELD tools were written using GELO directly: the call graph browser *flowview*, the class hierarchy browser *cbrowse*, and the make dependency browser *formview*.

PLATE I

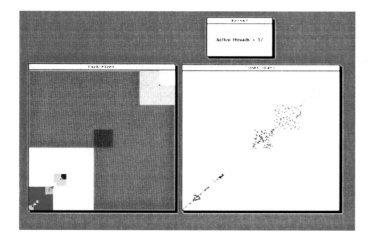

Figure 1a.

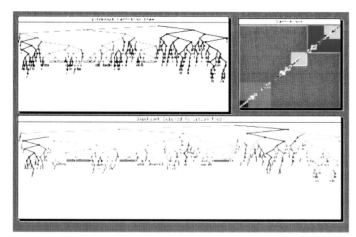

Figure 1b.

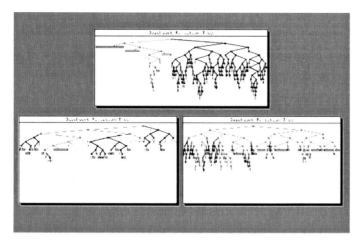

Figure 1c.

Figure 1 from Chapter 7: Quicksort. See pages 90–91 for discussion.

PLATE II

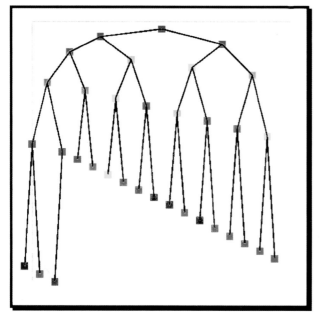

Figure 3a.

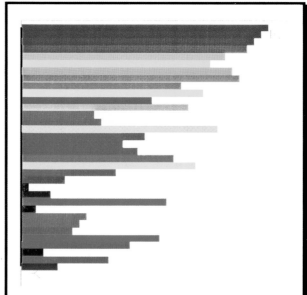

Figure 3b.

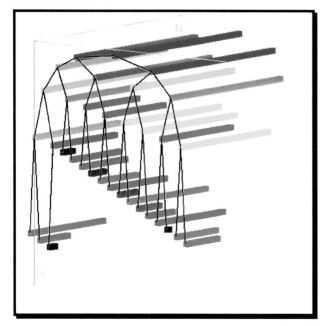

Figure 3c.

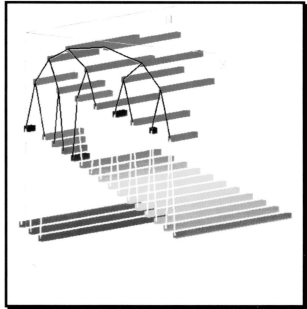

Figure 3d.

Figure 3 from Chapter 9: Heapsort. See pages 126–127.

PLATE III

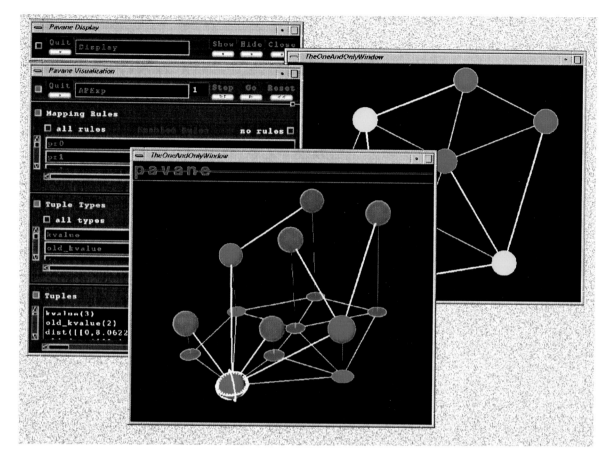

Figure 1 from Chapter 13: Animations built with Pavane. See pages 173–174.

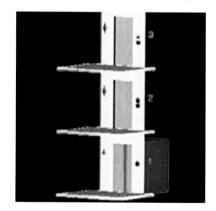

Figure 8 from Chapter 13: Compound graphical objects. See page 180.

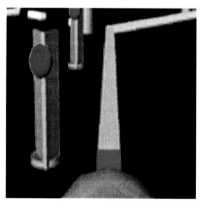

Figure 9 from Chapter 13: Camera controls. See page 181.

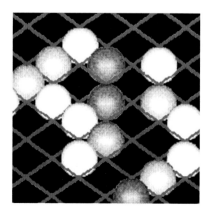

Figure 10 from Chapter 13: History recording. See page 181.

PLATE IV

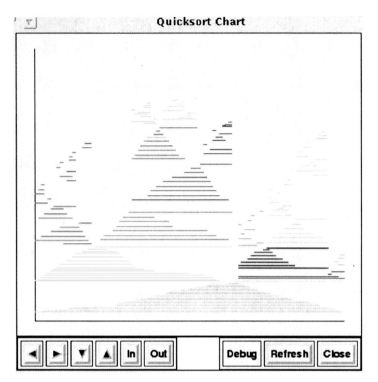

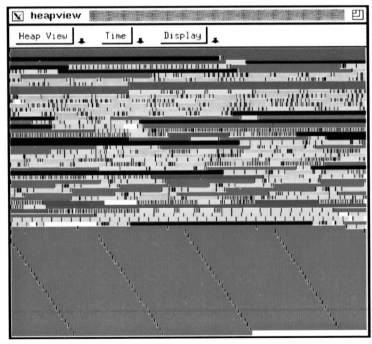

Figure 7 from Chapter 17: Quicksort (created with POLKA). See page 254.

Figure 7 from Chapter 18: FIELD heap visualization tool. See page 267.

PLATE V

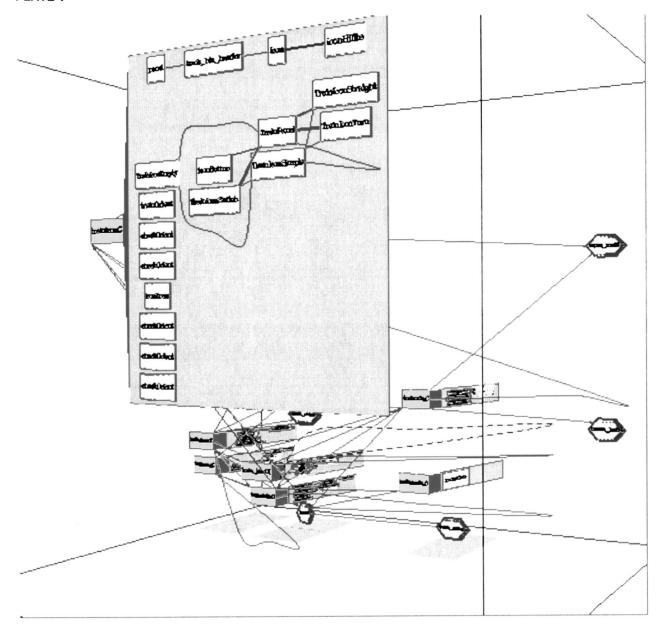

Figure 10 from Chapter 18: Sample 3D call graph display. See page 276.

PLATE VI

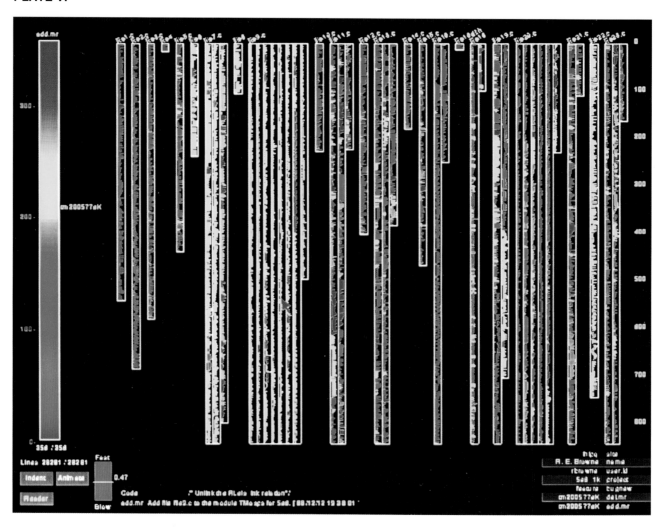

Figure 1 from Chapter 21: SeeSoft code display. See page 319.

PLATE VII

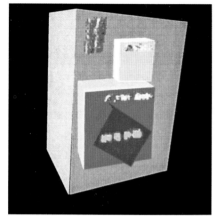

Figure 12 from Chapter 19: A 3D program representation. See page 289.

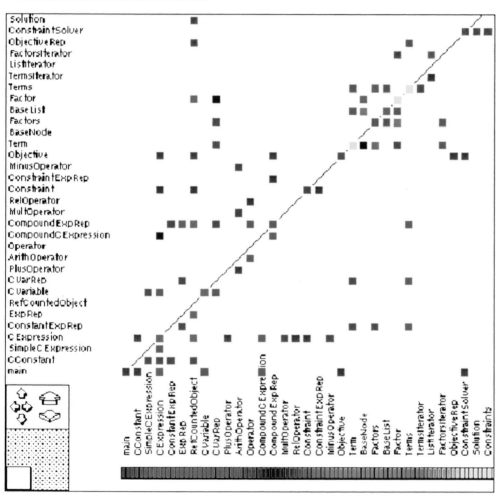

Figure 3 from Chapter 22: Inter-class call matrix. See page 334.

PLATE VIII

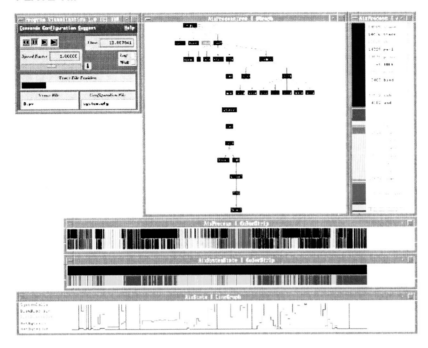

Figure 2 from Chapter 20: The PV system configuration. See page 300.

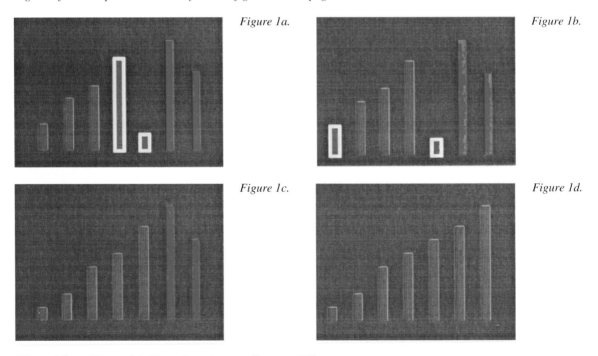

Figure 1a.

Figure 1b.

Figure 1c.

Figure 1d.

Figure 1 from Chapter 24: Linear insertion sort. See page 372.

The flowview tool provided a hierarchical view of a program's call graph as seen in Figure 3. This tool gets information about functions and calls from the cross-reference database. It organizes the information in a hierarchical fashion by grouping functions into files, files into directories, and directories into their parent directory. It provides a variety of browsing techniques aimed at allowing the programmer to focus on particular items of interest. If offers detailed information through a textual information window. It also provides a dynamic view of the program by highlighting nodes as they execute. For example, in Figure 3, the currently executing node is shown in red and the other nodes active on the call stack are shown in green.

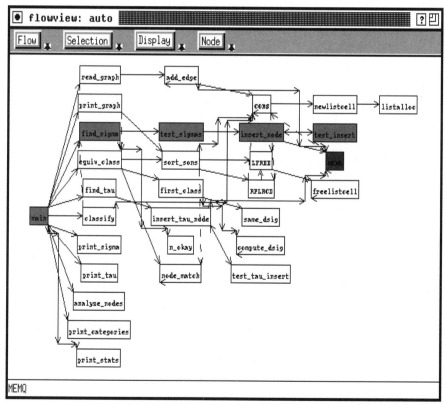

Figure 3. Dynamic call graph display from FIELD. The currently executing routine (MEMQ) is in red while the other active routines are shown in green.

The second diagrammatic visualization displays the class hierarchy for C++ or Object Pascal programs as shown in Figure 4 [Lejter 92]. This tool also obtains its information from the cross-reference database. It displays information about both the relationships between classes and the methods and fields of each particular class. It provides a variety of browsing techniques to allow the user to focus on a particular class or member. It uses different visual encodings to illustrate the contents of a class and the different relationships. For example, color is used to indicate the selected member and the relationship of that member in related classes — whether it is inherited, redefined, etc. This tool also provides a textual information window with detailed information about the selected class and dynamic highlighting of methods as they are executed.

Figure 4. Class Hierarchy Display from FIELD. The two classes, EMPLOYEE_RANK and EMPLOYEE and the member function systemCost have been selected. Color is used to indicate the relationship of various classes to the selected field. Information encodings are used to differentiate between different protectiuon levels as well as methods and data. The dark outline of the class PROGRAMMER indicates that it represents a collapsed hierarchy.

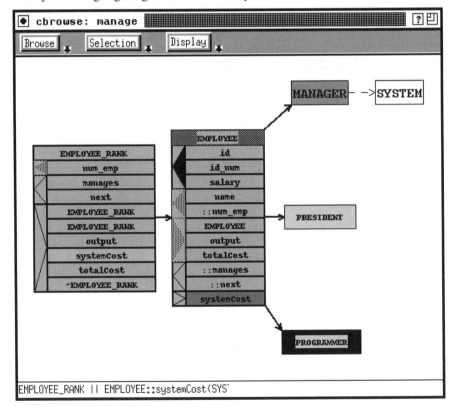

The third visualization tool provided by FIELD used the wrapper around *make* and *rcs* to gather information about file and build dependencies and put up a corresponding display. This display, as shown in Figure 5, showed the dependencies and the current state of each file. It uses color to indicate which files are out of date and which targets need to be rebuilt. The type of border around a file box indicates the current check-out state of the file. Different shape nodes indicate different types of targets. The window is interactive in that the user can browse to select targets of interest and can initiate check-in, check-out, and build operations from the display.

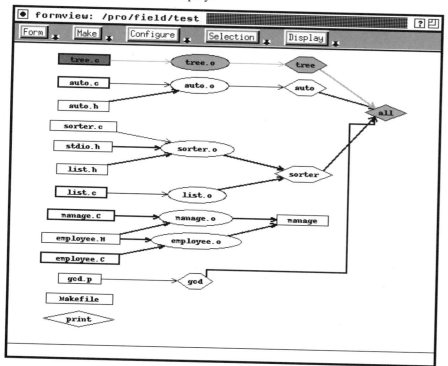

Figure 5. Make dependency display from FIELD. tree.c is shown in green to indicate it is out of date. Its successors are shown in thistle (violet) to indicate they need to be rebuilt. Thick arcs represent explicit dependencies while thin arcs represent implicit ones. Thick outlines around a file box indicate that the file is checked out from the version control system.

A fourth visualization tool in FIELD that uses GELO displays user data structures. This tool comes in two pieces; in addition to the actual display of the data structure, there is a visual editor that allows the user to define how the data should be displayed. For example, the first image in Figure 6 shows the default display of a linked tree structure while the second shows the display after the user has used the visual editor to cause the structure to be displayed as a tree. The data for this display was obtained from the system debugger through the message server. This view of the data structure also served as an editor, allowing the user to change the data while the program was being debugged.

Figure 6. Views of the data structure visualization tool from FIELD. The first diagram shows the default display of a tree while the second shows the user-defined display of the same tree.

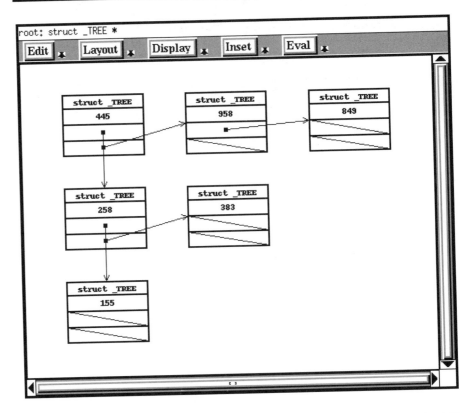

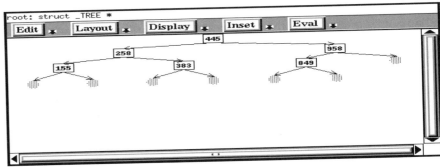

In addition to the diagrammatic visualizations based on the GELO package, we introduced several more abstract visualizations to illustrate program execution. Three such visualizations were developed, a view of the memory allocation and the heap, a view of file input and output, and a graph of various performance statistics. The heap visualizer, shown in Figure 7, provided a color-coded map of user-allocated memory. Colors could be used to show block size, when the block was allocated, or where the block was allocated from. By clicking on a block, the user could get detailed information about when and where it was allocated. This view has been used to find memory leaks and other anomalous program behavior in a variety of programs. The second tool offered a view of file I/O. In addition to showing the status of all attempted opens, it showed how files were read and written. Colors were used to show either I/O time or block size; fill patterns were used to differentiate reads from writes. An example is shown in Figure 8.

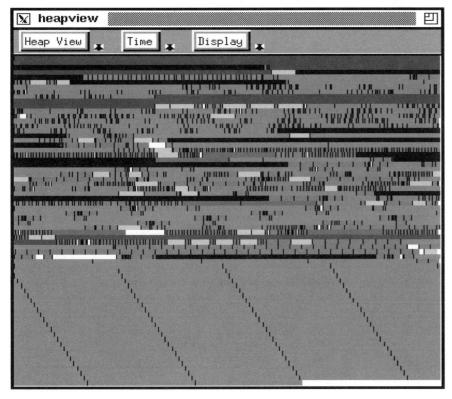

*Figure 7. FIELD heap visualizatrion tool. Here, color is used to encode the size of the blocks. The large blue area at the bottom indicates a memory leak in the application being monitored. *See Plate 4**

Browsing Techniques

While diagrammatic visualizations are common in describing software, they are not particularly good at displaying large amounts of data. The binary for the bulk of the FIELD system, for example, consists of about 7,000 functions and 22,000 calls. It is almost impossible to put up a meaningful display of the resultant graph on a small screen. The effectiveness of the diagrammatic visualizations for moderate-to-large scale software systems then depends on providing effective techniques for providing the "right" display. This means allowing the programmer to easily focus on the part of the overall graph that is of interest to the current situation and providing as much information as practical within the limits of the display. FIELD's GELO-based browsers attempt to do both. The former is done by providing a range of powerful browsing capabilities. The latter is done through a variety of information encodings.

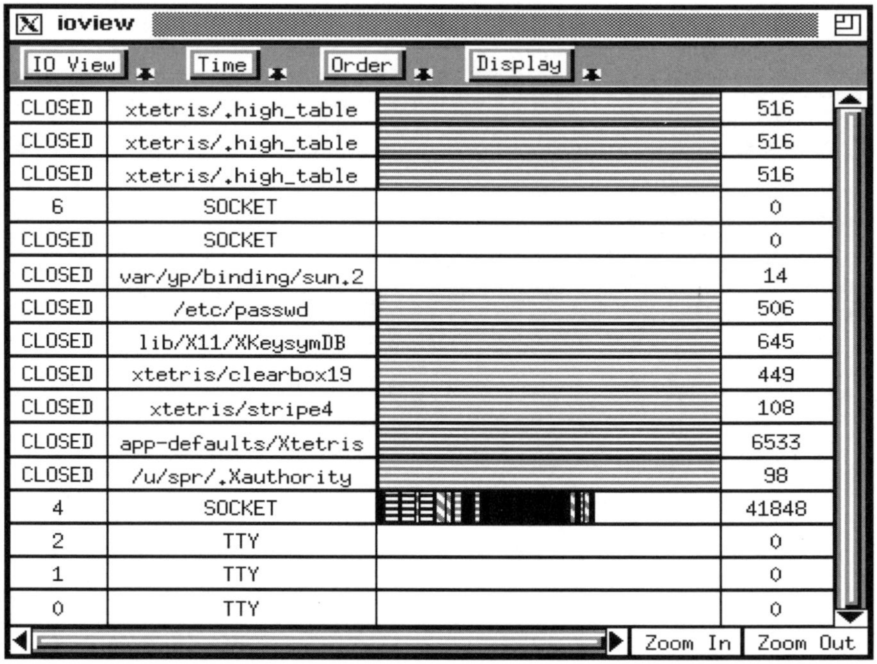

Figure 8. Input/output visualizer from FIELD. The colored areas reflect file reads and writes, with reads indicated as horizontal lines and writes as diaganols. Color is used to encode the size of the I/O operation. The number on the right indicates either the file size or the amount of I/O done depending on the type of file.

Browsing in the three diagrammatic visualization tools is based on three techniques: exploiting hierarchy, using names and name patterns, and considering only connected graphs.

Of these techniques, exploiting hierarchy is the most effective, allowing the programmer to quickly focus on the items of current interest. Most large software visualizations can be viewed hierarchically. The class graph hierarchy was derived directly from the superclass-subclass relationship. The call graph hierarchy was derived by grouping functions into the file they are defined in, files into their directory, and directories up the UNIX directory hierarchy. The dependency hierarchy was determined by the use of recursive invocations of *make*. Where there hierarchies are not unique (as in a class graph with multiple inheritance), the tool used depth-first search to identify a hierarchy that was then used. In addition to these natural hierarchies, the call graph browser allowed the user to define new hierarchies on the fly. These hierarchies were defined by name patterns, one pattern to identify candidate names and a second pattern to determine the parent of a given node. These were used to group all methods or to group all methods with the same method name.

Once a hierarchy was established, the various browsers provided the ability to easily collapse and expand nodes. In general three techniques were provided. The mouse could be used to expand or collapse a particular node. This was typically done by having control-Right button collapse a node and selecting an already selected node expand that node. Secondly, one or more dialog boxes were provided where the user could browse over the various nodes being displayed and choose which should be expanded or compacted. The call graph browser presented these options using the hierarchy; the other browsers just presented the nodes directly. Finally, the user could specify as part of the drawing options that all nodes should be expanded.

The system also provided automatic means for managing the hierarchy. When the initial display is computed, all nodes are assumed to be compacted. The system then expands nodes one at a time until an appropriate number of objects exist on the display. When a node is selected, which can be done by name or from another tool through an appropriate message, the system insures that all parents of that node are expanded so the node can be displayed.

The second technique we use, allowing the user to select which nodes should be displayed and which should be ignored, is also quite effective, especially when combined with the use of hierarchy. The system provides three mechanisms whereby the user can eliminate or include nodes. First, nodes can be eliminated from the display using a shift-left button click on the node. If the node represents a hierarchy, the whole hierarchy is removed. Secondly, the user can pick and choose which nodes should be displayed or ignored using the same sequence of dialog boxes used for indicating which should be expanded or compacted. Finally, the user can provide regular expression patterns of names to include and exclude. These patterns can be applied additively (i.e. a name is included if it matches the pattern, but not excluded if it doesn't match) or completely.

The tool provides several convenience functions for managing whether nodes are displayed or not. It will insure that any current selections and their parents are not ignored so that the selections will be displayed. It also provides menu buttons to include all nodes and to exclude or include system nodes (i.e. those that come from system libraries and not the user's application).

The final browsing option allows the user to focus on a subgraph of the overall display that is induced by the current set of selections. Here the user can specify the number of levels to consider and whether paths leading into the selected nodes, out of the selected nodes, or both should be used. If the user asks for the local graph, the tools will start with the selected nodes, identify all nodes that are reachable using only the given number of links, and display the resultant subgraph. This allows the user to use the overall browsing techniques to find the nodes of interest and then to see subgraph induced by those nodes. A special case of this technique is used in the call graph display. Here, an additional option of only displaying nodes that are reachable from the main program is provided. This is useful when there are significant numbers of nodes that are defined but not used that would otherwise clutter up the display.

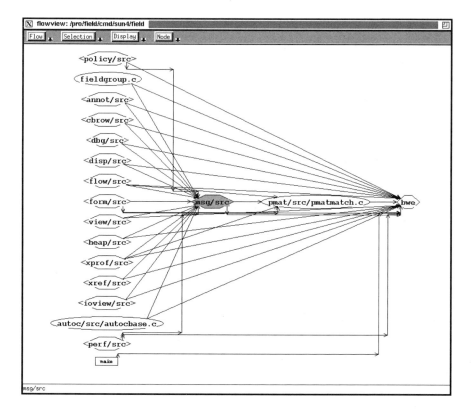

Figure 9. Call graph displays of FIELD. Functions are represented as rectangles, files as ellipses, directories (or directory hierarchies in the case of BWE) are shown as hexagons. Color indicates the current selection. Note that the overall structure of FIELD, with various tools using the central message server and all tools using the BWE user interface toolkit, is readily apparent.

The overall effectiveness of these browsing techniques can be seen in Figure 9. This is a call graph display of the main FIELD binary and represents about 200,000 lines of C code. The initial display consisted of two nodes, one representing the FIELD directory hierarchy and the other representing the X11 toolkit used by FIELD, BWE. The *bwe* node in the display was left untouched (it represents about five-eighths of the code). The *field* node was expanded to get the various directories shown in the display. Note that where the directory only contained one file (as in pmatmatch.c), the system automatically expanded the directory into the file. Next we selected the main program to cause the corresponding directory to be expanded down to the file level and the main file down to the function level. We then manually removed the other files and functions from this directory. Finally, we selected the node representing the FIELD message server, *msg/src*, and restricted the display to the induced subgraph. The resultant display provides a good overview of the structure of

FIELD relevant to the message server. On the left are the various FIELD tools, each of with uses both the message server for communications and the BWE toolkit [Reiss 90c] for its display. The pattern matcher, central to the use of selective broadcasting in the message server, is used by the message server as well as some of the tools.

Information Encodings

In addition to providing the user with the tools needed for identifying the information of current interest, the FIELD visualization tools attempt to provide as much information as possible through information encodings and associated windows.

Textual information is provided both in the visualization display and in a separate information window on the class and call graph browsers. The status line at the bottom of the diagrammatic visualizers contains two names: the one on the left represents the currently selected item while the one on the right designates what the cursor is currently pointing to. This latter is updated continually as the user moves around the display. The information window is updated each time the user makes a new selection to contain a description of the current selection. This window is active in that the user can click on relevant parts of the display to get additional information or select objects.

Other information is encoded in the shapes of nodes, the line styles and thickness of arcs, using colors, and with text as part of the display. The class browser shown in Figure 4 shows several of these encodings. Color is used both to show the selected classes (light blue) and the selected member (systemCost in EMPLOYEE, green). Color is also used to show the relationship of this member to the corresponding member in other classes. Here pink indicates a redefinition, yellow a inherited instance, thistle (light purple), an instance between this member and its definition in a superclass, orange the defining instance of the member if it is inherited from a superclass, and cyan represents a redefinition. Where a class has been collapsed to only show the name and not the members (as is done here at the user's option for all non-selected classes), the member encoding is used to color the class. The fill style for the class or the class name if the class is expanded, provides additional information. If the class is abstract then it has a halftone fill. If the class represents a collapsed hierarchy, a solid fill is used. The triangles on the left of the member names indicate either method (pointing right) or data (pointing left) and the protection, with solid indicating private, shaded protected, and hollow public. Friend and static members are indicated by a box with an X rather than a triangle. Arc styles indicate either public or private inheritance via arc thickness and friend relationships via dashed lines. Virtual inheritance would be indicated by an arrowhead with a bar. Member names that begin with a double colon indicate inherited members.

Additional information would be encoded and displayed if desired. Different arc styles are used to express the client-supplier relationship, the type relationship, the calls relationship. Members can be displayed with an additional textual field that contains one or more of the key letters I for inline, V for virtual, v for implicitly virtual, P for pure, C for const, S for static, and F for friend. If the user wants members display for all classes, then the selected classes are indicated both by color and by increasing their size.

The other diagrammatic editors used similar techniques to encode the information that is particular to their display. Similarly, the heap and input/output visualizer displays use color and fill patterns. In the heap display, color can encode, at the user's option, the size of the block, the time the block was allocated, the type of the block (if the information is available), or the source of the allocation. In the input/output visualizer, color can denote either block size or the time the input/output operation was done. Here fill patterns distinguish reads and writes in such a way that overlapping I/O operations can be easily detected.

The visualizations provided by FIELD were designed to accomplish several goals. The simplest was to provide a reasonable, visual interface to the underlying UNIX tools. This is best seen in the *formview* browser which serves as a front end to both *make* and *rcs* (i.e. commands to both of these tools can be issued through the graphical interface). Similarly, the call graph and class hierarchy browsers provided a front end to the cross-reference database, while the data structure display tool provided a partial debugger interface. This goal, to the extent it was attempted, was quite successful.

Visualization Effectiveness

A second goal was to provide program understanding. This can be divided into two parts — understanding the dynamic behavior of a system and understanding the static structure. The views that offered insights into the dynamic behavior, have been successfully used and valued for a variety of systems, both large and small. *Heapview* has been used to find memory leaks, allocation anomalies, and related memory problems in large (200K line) systems as well as in understanding the memory behavior of system libraries (Sun's XGL). The data structure display tool has been widely used in introductory programming classes both to provide an understanding of the student's data structures and to facilitate object-oriented debugging.

The tools have not been as successful at providing insight into the static structure of a system. While the class browser and call graph displays have been used, they have not been widely used for program understanding. An experiment we ran to evaluate their effectiveness for program understanding showed only a marginal improvement from using the tools. This unintuitive result can be explained several ways. A large part of the problem was speed — the time it took to generate the data for the visualizations (especially for C++ programs) was such that they could not be used for one-shot questions. Moreover, the time needed to become comfortable with all the features of the tools was a significant barrier. A second problem was the lack of resolution on a 2D display of a large system and the difficulty in achieving the "proper" visualization for a given question. Another problem is that the information conveyed by the diagrammatic browsers was known to the programmer a priori (since it was typically used on their own program), and did not offer much in the way of insights.

The diagrammatic tools were not unsuccessful, however. They have been widely used and relied on as a browsing mechanism within the environment. The tools provide a convenient way of locating code for a particular routine or method — in FIELD, whenever the user clicked on a node in the call graph or the class browser or a file in the dependency display, the corresponding code would be brought up in an editor. This became the primary means for the student programmers for navigating around their programs.

Related Work

Visualization has been applied to programming environments ever since there were workstations and display that could be used. Many of the early workstation programing environments, while primarily exploring incremental compilation and immediate programmer feedback, provided visual interfaces. PECAN [Reiss 84] [Reiss 85]provided multiple views of the program syntax, semantics, and execution. Magpie [Delisle 84] extended the Smalltalk [Goldberg 83] notion of a browser to provide a visual interface for procedural programming. Later implementation of the Cornell Program Synthesizer[Teitlebaum 81], Poe

[Fischer 81], Gandalf [Notkin 85], and Mentor [Donzeau-Gouge 84] all featured visualizations of either the code or the execution. Visualization in programming environments has now become relatively standard so that it is included in most commercial environments (e.g. HP's SoftBench, Sun's SPARCworks, ObjectCenter, SGI's CodeVision, Lucid's Energize, and ParcPlace's ObjectWorks), and is used in recent versions of experimental environments such as Marvel [Kaiser 88], Arcadia [Taylor 89], and Proteus [Graham 92].

Visualization of particular aspects of a program has also proliferated. The PV system [Brown 85b] provided general visualization for simple programs. Data structure visualization was pioneered by Myers [Myers 83] and has been implemented in several other systems [Baskerville 85] [Ding 90] [Isoda 87] as well as GARDEN, FIELD, and most recent commercial systems. Call graph and class browsers are now standard in commercial C++ and Smalltalk environments. Performance visualization is also quite prevalent, including such work as [Appelbe 89] [Guarna 89] [Moher 88] [Snyder 84].

Another rich source of work in program visualization comes from reverse engineering tools. Systems such as RIGI [Muller 92] make extensive use of visualizations as a key to understanding and reorganizing existing software systems.

Conclusions

Visualizations for programming environments are many and varied. FIELD demonstrated a wide variety of visualizations for different applications: as front ends to existing UNIX tools, as visualizations to show the static structure of a system, and as visualizations to show a system in action. FIELD demonstrated the effectiveness of such visualizations and pointed out their weaknesses. It illustrated a variety of techniques for using the limited screen space to display the large quantities of information inherent to a programming environment, both in terms of browsing and in terms of information encoding.

Work on visualizations for programming environments is continuing. Our current efforts involve extending our packages for 2D visualization to three dimensions. Here we have developed a general engine that supports a wide variety of 3D visualizations including layouts, tilings, file views, 3D trees, scatter plots, multiple-hierarchy displays, time-based displays, and cluster plots [Reiss 95]. It is connected to a powerful browsing engine that provides hierarchical browsing using user-specified hierarchies and supports all the

*Figure 10. Sample 3D call graph display with grouped files and arcs. Hexagonal boxes represent collapsed files. The selected file is shown in front with a fully expanded layout while other files are shown as tags and a compressed layout. Red arcs between files represent groups of calls and their thickness is proportional to the log of the number of calls. The blue dashed arcs represent accesses of global variables from a function. In the diagram the depth of a node is determined by its distance from the currently selected file. *See Plate 5**

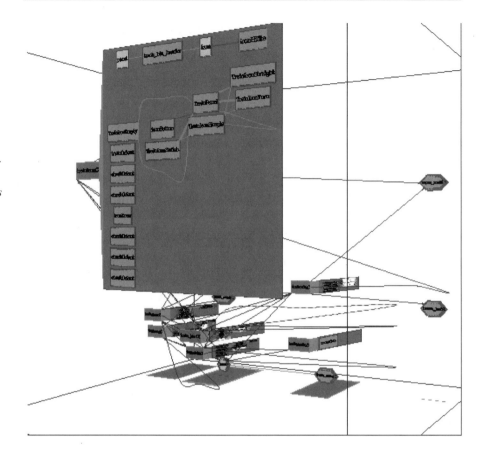

browsing techniques available in the FIELD visualizers. The engine is being used for displaying call and class hierarchy graphs as shown in Figure 10, as a general front end for project management, and to provide three different visualizations of profiling data.

Other current related efforts are aimed at providing a high quality textual and graphical hyper-linked interface to all software artifacts, from design documents, to code, to user interface diagrams, to static and dynamic visualizations. Another effort is aimed at addressing one of the weakness of the diagrammatic visualization tools of FIELD by providing the programmer with a high-level, interactive visual query interface for quickly defining both what information should be visualized and how it should be displayed.

ZStep 95: A Reversible, Animated Source Code Stepper

Henry Lieberman
and
Christopher Fry

ZStep 95 is a program debugging environment designed to help the programmer understand the correspondence between static program code and dynamic program execution. Some of ZStep 95's innovations include:

Introduction

- An animated view of program execution, using the very same display used to edit the source code
- A window that displays values which follows the stepper's focus
- An incrementally-generated complete history of program execution and output
- "Video recorder" controls to run the program in forward and reverse directions and control the level of detail displayed
- One-click access from graphical objects to the code that drew them
- One-click access from expressions in the code to their values and graphical output

Programming is the art of constructing a static description, the program code, of a dynamic process, the behavior which results from running the program. In that sense, it is analogous to composing music. The program code is like a musical score, whose purpose it is to cause the performer [in the programming case, a computer] to perform a set of actions over a period of time.

Supporting the cognitive tasks in programming

Figure 1. A screen snapshot of ZStep 95 in use.

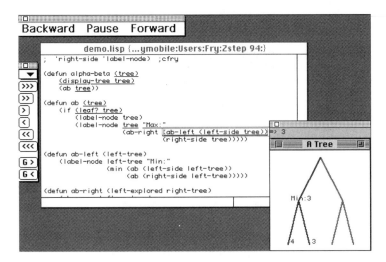

What makes programming cognitively difficult is that the programmer must imagine the dynamic process of execution while he or she is constructing the static description, just as a composer must "hear the piece" in his or her head, while composing. This puts a great burden on the programmer's short term memory. What makes programming even more difficult than composing is that a musical composition usually specifies a single performance, whereas a program may be executed in a wide variety of conditions, with different resulting behavior.

Many, if not most, non-syntactic program bugs result from a discrepancy between the programmer's imagining of the desired behavior in a given situation, and the actual behavior of the program code in that situation. [In the case of a design problem, the program may behave as "intended", but the problem may be that the original intention is wrong.]

Once program code is written, the problem remains of verifying that the code written actually expresses the programmer's intent under all circumstances of interest. Interactive tools such as debuggers and program visualization systems can be invaluable in bridging that gap. Instead of trying to imagine how the events in a program unfold over time, why not have the machine show them to you?

We have designed a program debugging environment to explicitly support the problem solving methodology of matching the expectations of a programmer concerning the behavior of code to the actual behavior of the code. This environment is called ZStep 95.

Two principal activities in debugging that can be assisted by tools in the programming environment are instrumentation and localization. Instrumentation is the process of finding out what the behavior of a given piece of code is, the software analog of attaching oscilloscope probes to a hardware component. Traditional tools that assist instrumentation are trace, breakpoints, and manually inserted print statements: trace instruments all calls to a function, a breakpoint or print statement instruments a specific function call. The problem with using trace and breakpoints in debugging is that they require some plausible hypothesis as to where the bug might be, so you know where to place the instrumentation. They are not of much help when you have no idea where a bug might be, especially when there are too many possibilities to check individually.

Localization is the process of isolating which piece of code is "responsible" for some given undesirable behavior of a buggy program, without any prior knowledge of where it might be. Among traditional tools, a stepper is potentially the most effective localization tool, since it interactively imitates the action of the interpreter, and the program can in theory be stepped until the error is found.

However, traditional steppers have a fatal interface flaw: they have poor control over the level of detail shown. Since the programmer's time is too valuable to make looking at every single step of an evaluation feasible, only those details potentially relevant to locating the bug should be examined.

Traditional steppers stop before evaluation of each expression and let the user choose whether or not to see the internal details of the evaluation of the current expression. If the user chooses to see all of the details, they must wade through a lot of irrelevant information. On the other hand, if they attempt to speed up the process by skipping over [presumably working] code, they are likely to miss the precise location of the bug.

The user can't make the decision about whether to see the details of an expression if he or she doesn't know whether this expression contributes to the bug. This leaves the user in the same dilemma as the instrumentation tools -- they must have a reasonable hypothesis about where the bug might be before they can effectively use the debugging tools!

Problem solving processes in debugging: localization and instrumentation

20-20 hindsight: Reversible control structure

The solution adopted by ZStep 95 is to provide a reversible control structure. It keeps a complete, incrementally generated history of the execution of the program and its output. The user can confidently choose to temporarily ignore the details of a particular expression, secure in the knowledge that if the expression later proves to be relevant, the stepper can be backed up to look at the details. Thus, ZStep 95 provides a true localization tool.

There has been a considerable amount of past work on reversible program execution [Agrawal 91] [Balzer 69] [Lieberman 84a] [Lieberman 87] [Moher 88] [Zelkowitz 73], but this work has concentrated on the details of minimizing the space requirements of the history and tracking side effects to data structures, both of which are important, but secondary to the user interface aspects which are the emphasis of this paper. It is important not only to "back up" variables to their previous values, but also to "back up" a consistent view of the user interface, including static code, dynamic data, and graphical output so that the user "backs up" their mental image of the program execution.

The reversible control structure aspects of ZStep 95 are discussed in more detail in [Lieberman 87]. We will address the issue of the computational expense of the history-keeping mechanism later.

ZStep 95's main menu uses a bi-directional "video recorder" metaphor. The single-arrow "play" and "reverse" correspond to single-step in a traditional stepper, and the "fast-forward" and "rewind" operation go from an expression to its value and vice versa, without displaying details.

It is important to note that ZStep 95's expression-by-expression stepping is not the same as statement-by-statement or line-by-line stepping found in many steppers for procedural languages. Individual lines or statements may still contain complex computations, and it is a severe limitation on the debugger if the granularity cannot be brought down finer than a statement or line.

The two "graphic step" operations G> and G< are an innovation that lets the user step *the graphic output of the program* back and forth, rather than control the stepper in terms of the expressions of the code. This will be discussed below.

Figure 2. ZStep 95's "control menu"

Go to end of program ———————— ▽ ⟫⟫
Show value of expression, without stopping ⟫
Single step ———————————————— ⟩
Single step backwards ———————— ⟨
Back up from value to expression ——— ⟪
Go to beginning of program ———— ⟪⟪

Single step "graphically" ——————— G ⟩
Single step backwards "graphically" ——— G ⟨

ZStep 95 also has a "cruise control" mode, in which the stepper can run continuously, in either direction, without user intervention. The distance of the cursor from the center of the panel controls the speed. The user can stop it at any point when an interesting event appears, and run the stepper in either direction at that point.

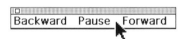

Figure 3. ZStep 95's "cruise control"

A crucial problem in designing an interface for program debugging is *maintaining the visual context*. Because programming is an activity in which many items of interest have complex temporal and spatial relationships to other items, it is important to present each item with its context clearly identified.

Keeping the debugging problem in context

Items such as the expression currently being evaluated, the value of a variable, or graphics drawn by the code may have almost no meaning outside their proper context. The programmer wants to know:

- *Where* in the code was that expression evaluated?
- *Which* instance of the code was it?
- *When* did the variable have that value?
- *How* did that graphic appear on the screen?

If the item and its visual context are spatially or temporally separated, a new cognitive task is created for the user -- matching up the item with its context. This new cognitive task creates an obstacle for debugging and puts additional burden on the user's short term memory. Linear steppers or tracers that simply print out the next expression to be evaluated create the task of matching up the expression printed to the place in the code where that expression appears. "Follow the bouncing ball" interfaces that point to an expression and print out a value in another window lead to "ping-ponging" the user's attention between the code display and the value display.

Follow the bouncing window

Because most programmers input their code as text in a text editor, the primary mental image of the program becomes the text editor's display of the code. Thus, to preserve the WYSIWYG property, ZStep 95 always use the text editor's display to present code during debugging.

To maintain visual continuity, it is important that the exact form of the user's input be preserved, including comments and formatting details, even if they are not semantically significant. As the interpreter's focus moves, the source code of the expression that is about to be evaluated, or has just returned a value, is highlighted.

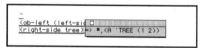

Figure 4. The value window moves through the code.

Steppers always have the problem of how to show code expressions and their values simultaneously. In ZStep 95, as the editor's focus moves from expression to expression, we use a floating window to display the value. The display of the value is always exactly aligned with the expression to which it corresponds, so that the visual association between an expression and its value is obvious. The floating value window is colored light green to indicate if the expression is about to be evaluated, light blue to indicate a return value, or yellow if it has caused an error.

Our approach is to integrate instrumentation tools directly into the stepper. We provide two facilities for pointing at a piece of code and inquiring about the behavior of the code. Rather than inserting breakpoints or print statements into the actual code and resubmitting the code to the interpreter or compiler, we let the user simply point at the desired expression, then run the stepper until that expression is reached. This is called *Step to Mouse Position*. This is like a breakpoint, but an advantage is that the stepper is runnable both forward and backward from the point where the program stops, and all information about the computation remains available.

Even more dynamic is *Show Value Under Mouse,* which is like a continuously updated Step to Mouse Position. The user simply waves the mouse around the code, without clicking, and the expression currently underneath the cursor displays its value window.

We also provide a facility to track the behavior of a given expression over different execution histories. The operation *Current Form History* allows the user to point at an expression and bring up a menu of the past values of that expression.

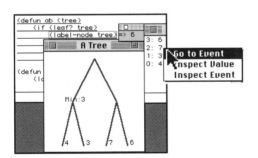

Another history facility is the Values Filter, which brings up a menu of all returned values in the history satisfying a condition. Clicking on one of the values returns the stepper to the corresponding event. We could also provide a filter on the expression executed, which would correspond to a traditional trace.

What did that code do?

```
ZStep Current Form
Eval Defun for ZStep
_____Modes_____
Show Value Under Mouse
Step to Mouse Pos
_____Navigation_____
Go to First Stepped Form
Go to Current Stepped Form
Go to Last Stepped Form
_____Misc_____
✓Auto-position Value Window?
Print Event Trace?
Current Form History
Make Values Filter
Delete Events After Current
Inspect Current Event
Help
```

Figure 5. ZStep 94's pull-down menu

What has that code done?

Figure 6 The history of values of an expression

ZStep 95 has a stack display that is updated continuously with each event, animated in tandem with the source code animation. Each stack frame is itself a menu item, and clicking it returns you to that frame. All graphic display and other context is restored exactly as it was when that stack frame was first entered.

What code did that?

One of the most essential, but also most difficult, tasks in debugging is being able to reason backward from the manifestation of some buggy behavior to the underlying cause. Even when the bug is visually apparent in the application's user interface, the programmer must work backwards from an incorrect display to the code responsible. Traditional tools do not make any special provision for debugging programs with graphic output; worse, the user interface of the debugger often interferes with the user interface of the target program itself, making it impossible to debug!

ZStep 95 maintains a correspondence between events in the execution history and graphical output produced by the current expression. Considerable care is taken to assure that the graphic output always appears consistent with the state of execution. When the stepper is run forward or backward to a certain point in the execution, the graphic display is also moved to that point.

Figure 7. Clicking on a graphical object backs up the stepper to the event which drew it

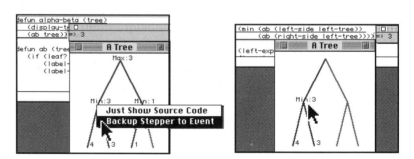

Furthermore, individual graphical objects on the display also are associated with the events that gave rise to them. We allow the user to click on a graphical object, such as a tree node in our example, and the stepper is automatically positioned at the event which drew that node. Just as in our other operations like

Step to Mouse Position, the stepper is active at that point, and the program can be run forward and backward from that point.

In reasoning from the behavior of the program to the code, it is useful to be able to *step the behavior* rather than step the code. The user conceptualizes the behavior of the program as a set of graphic states that unfold over time, as the frames of an animation. The increments of execution should be measured in terms of the animation frames rather than execution of code, since events that happen in the code may or may not give rise to graphic output.

ZStep 95 provides two operations, *Graphic Step Forward* and *Graphic Step Backward*, that run the stepper forward or backward, respectively, until the next event happens that results in significant graphic output. Below, each graphic step results in an exploration of the next branch of the tree.

Each graphic step runs the stepper forward or backward until it is pointing at the event which was responsible for the graphic output, and the stepper remains live at all times. While stepping non-graphic code, the effects of previous graphic operations remain visible, just as they do in a normally-running program.

We could also provide graphic step operations analogous to "graphic fast forward" and "graphic rewind". Because the stepper can be run from either the code or the graphics at any point in time, the user can easily move back and forth between the different points of view.

Trial and error is a tried and true strategy for solving all sorts of problems, but it's not a great strategy. It's inefficient, and can even be dangerous if the trial itself contains risks. It is the debugging strategy of last resort, but it is far better than having no strategy at all.

Let's see that again, slowly

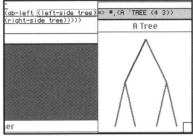

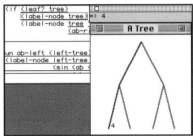

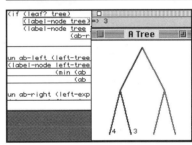

Figure 8. Three successive "graphic steps"

Programming by Error Message

By understanding how trial and error works in debugging, we can provide support for this strategy in the programming environment. Interpretive environments, which let you perform the "edit, run, test" loop quickly, are one way to facilitate this rather dumb approach. Compiler warnings of traditional programming environments can also be quite useful, but they rarely pinpoint the expression that failed. ZStep 95 implements several improvements that can drastically decrease the number of trials.

Traditionally, errors during program execution are disruptive. If you run some giant program and you get "error number -127" you have no idea which part of the program was responsible. Some environments put the user into a breakpoint loop, from which special commands can examine the error, and the stack can be inspected. In either case, errors disrupt execution and often lose information about partial computations which may have finished correctly.

Having an accurate mapping between the source code and the error is crucial. In ZStep 95, an expression which results in an error simply displays the error message in place of the value of the subexpression most relevant to the error. The value window is colored yellow to indicate the error condition. The stepper remains active, all intermediate values are preserved, and the program can be run backward to examine the history that led up to the error.

Figure 9. Programming by Error Message

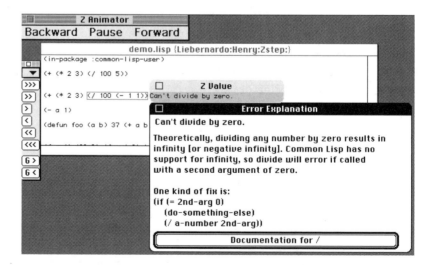

Let's use (/ 100 (- 1 1)) as an example program fragment. If an error occurs you'll see the expression highlighted, with a floating window containing the error message immediately to the right. We can back up to pinpoint the source of the error.

Now, we have confidence that we know just where the error is coming from, but we might not yet know how to fix it or how to avoid getting it in the future. If we ZStep forward to see "(/ 100 (- 1 1)) Can't divide by Zero" again, we can then click on "Can't divide by Zero" to get a dialog box with more information. This includes the full text of the error message, a brief explanation of the theory of the error [Dividing by zero would result in infinity and Common Lisp can't represent infinity], some examples of correct calls to the function "/" and perhaps some counter-examples. Finally you can click on a button to get additional documentation on the divide function itself.

Knowing exactly where an error occurred will often allow an experienced programmer to fix the bug. But a good error message can inform the inexperienced *why* it occurred, allowing them to not just fix the current error but to prevent creating such errors in the future. With really great error messages you can imagine typing code while knowing very little about a programming language. Your first fragments will be syntactically incorrect and you'll be told why. After you've got the syntax down, you'll be getting semantic errors. These may require several levels of explanation that ultimately extend to the architecture of algorithms.

ZStep 95 facilitates the repair phase, since it leaves you in the text editor with the cursor pointing to relevant code. Furthermore, you are then just one click away from restarting the entire computation after the edit. However, we cannot support restarting the computation from any point in ZStep's history after the edit, because editing a running program cannot guarantee consistency of the event data structures.

ZStep 95 has implemented support for only a tiny number of such error messages. A complete system would support all of the functions in the base language and let the programmer easily enter in support for their own functions. To further the "Programming by Error Message" concept, the documentation for the function that errored [divide in our example] would contain links to other arithmetic functions as well as descriptions of the data types that they operate on, i.e. numbers. Extended examples that contain calls to the function in question *in context* as well as explanations of the algorithms being used would round out the ideal "Programming by Error Message" environment.

Debugging the ZStep idea: Evolution from ZStep 84

ZStep 95 is an evolutionary descendant of steppers we have been working on since ZStep 84 [Lieberman 84a]. We have been "debugging" the ZStep idea through informally testing different alternative interfaces and implementations. We present here just a few of the interesting aspects of ZStep 84's interface to illustrate some design alternatives.

Figure 10. ZStep 84's interface: before (left) and after (right) evaluating the expression `(fact (1- n))`

ZStep 84 displayed code in two windows simultaneously. The top window contained an unmodified copy of the source code, annotated just by highlighting the current expression about to be evaluated or just evaluated. The bottom code window also showed the same code, but with the expressions replaced by their values as they are evaluated. In the right half of the illustration, the expression `(fact (1- n))` is replaced by its value, `2`.

Substituting a value for its expression has the advantage of being consistent with an intuitive "evaluation is substitution" conceptual model of the evaluation process, and also shows return values in their context. However, we prefer the single floating panes approach, since it reduces the "ping-pong" effect of splitting the user's attention between two windows.

Instead of the "tape recorder" controls of ZStep 95, ZStep 84 used a single menu, which dynamically changed the names of the items depending on whether it was in the state of just about to evaluate an expression or just about to return a value. The current interface now uses the color of the floating window to indicate whether it's in an eval or a return state, and the control button arrows are more intuitive than reading the names of the operations.

There is no reason why we have to limit ourselves to textual representations of programs. In most of our implementations of ZStep, we have refrained from changing the physical appearance of program code, simply to keep the focus on debugging interfaces and not launch debates about visual programming. But we are sympathetic to the idea that graphical representations of program code might prove to be helpful in debugging. A graphical representation of programs, especially if it is animated as the stepper runs the code, might make bugs more visually apparent than by linearly reading program text.

Graphical representation of programs

Figure 11. A function call tree representation of program code

We have done several experiments along these lines. The illustration above shows a program represented as a tree of function calls, again with the values for expressions that have returned a value substituted in place. Returned values are rendered in a different color from program code expressions. The current execution point, the list ((1 4) 5 (9)) in Figure 10, is also displayed in a different color.

This function call graph is also animated by the stepper as the program runs, and can be seen simultaneously with a more conventional textual code display.

More radically, we have also worked on three-dimensional animated representations of code [Lieberman 89]. This three-dimensional representation uses boxes and other 3D forms to represent program elements and smooth animation of program execution.

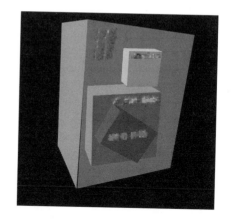

*Figure 12. A 3D program representation. *See Plate 7**

By now, many readers will be thinking: isn't all this history-keeping and use of special-purpose interpreters ridiculously expensive? Histories eat up enormous amounts of storage, and interpreting code is slow. The answer is: yes, it can be expensive. But, compared to what?

There's nothing slower than a program that doesn't work yet!

First of all, we have to keep in mind that the purpose of the stepper is to debug programs that don't work yet, and so worrying about optimizing execution is silly. Even in an extremely large program, where keeping a complete history is infeasible, judicious testing can often isolate a fragement of the code which is not too large to run ZStep on. Nevertheless, we admit that there may be bugs that appear only after long runs involving large amounts of code, and so our techniques may be inappropriate in these cases. However, we conjecture that the vast majority of bugs are relatively shallow, and the productivity improvements from finding simple bugs quickly will far outweigh slower execution during testing.

Second, the key to making these techniques feasible over a wider range of programs are tools for selectively turning on and off history-keeping mechanisms. A simple way to automate selective processing of history in a common case would be to run the program normally until an error occurs. Then a program could use the stack inspector to determine what functions were involved in the error, and history-keeping would be turned on selectively for those functions. The problem would then be run again from the beginning.

Another common objection to our approach is that it is not guaranteed to work in the presence of programs that have side effects. First, we should observe that certain kinds of shallow side effects do in fact work without any special provisions. Incrementing a variable will, because of the history, preserve the values both before and after the operation. More complex side effects involving shared data structures will not work, but one is no worse off than with conventional debugging techniques. More elaborate history-keeping mechanisms such as those studied in the simulation literature could alleviate this problem.

A wonderful use of our stepper is in educational applications, where execution efficiency is not of much concern, but interactive control and data visualization are paramount. One of the best ways to teach programming to a beginner would be to have the student step through example programs. In general, a stepper is an excellent tool for understanding code written by others.

Implementation

ZStep 95 was implemented in Macintosh Common Lisp 2.0. It is a prototype, and not a production implementation in several respects. First, it works with only a subset of Common Lisp. Second, no attempt was made to optimize speed or space constraints. Third, we did not perform any formal user testing, besides getting feedback from both experienced and novice programmers. Our main goal was to experiment with novel interfaces to dynamic program visualization.

Adapting ZStep 95 concepts to C would be possible, but challenging. A complete parser and unparser for C syntax would be required and care would have to be taken to assure the C interpreter or compiler kept enough type and run-time information.

The lesson for design of languages and environments is to consider debuggability as a primary criterion. If the goal of a new environment is to make programmers more productive, nothing could contribute to this goal more than introspective features that provide the foundation for sophisticated debuggers.

We're sad to report that there is not as much related work in this area as there should be. Even recently implemented programming environments seem to provide only the same set of tools that have been around for the past 30 years: trace, breakpoints, stack inspection, and perhaps a line-by-line stepper.

Related work

The Transparent Prolog Machine [Eisenstadt 88a] provides an innovative graphical view of program execution, and an interface carefully designed with Prolog's more complex execution model in mind. An innovative stepper for Lisp which shares some of the principles described here was recently implemented by Watt [Watt 94].

Many of the elements of our approach do have a long history. Reversible debuggers have been explored as far back as 1969 [Balzer 69], and more recently by Moher [Moher 88]. However, these debuggers did not provide reversible animations of both the code and its graphical output, nor connections between individual code expressions, values and individual graphical objects.

The field of visual programming [Glinert 90a] uses graphical objects to represent the elements of the program, such as variables, functions and loops. The best of these environments also provide some animation of the graphical representation during execution. The pioneering work on animated visualization of program code in a single stepper was done by Ron Baecker [Baecker 75].

Animation of visual representations of data manipulated by programs often appears under the name *algorithm animation* [Brown 88c] [or *scientific visualization* if the algorithm represents a physical process]. Animations of data help a programmer visualize the dynamic effects of a program as it runs. But most visual programming and algorithm animation systems confine themselves to visualizing and animating either the code or the data, but not both.

No one of these approaches -- reversiblity, animation of code, or animation of data -- by themselves will lead to a satisfactory set of debugging tools. ZStep 95's contribution is to integrate reversibility, animation of code, and correspondence between code expressions, values and graphic output, all under unified interactive control. Using the control structure of a stepper to control visualization of data helps solve one of the fundamental problems of software visualization: establishing the correspondence between data that looks faulty and determining the code that corresponds to the error. Adding data visualization facilities to the code visualization that steppers provide solves the problem of determining the effect of a particular piece of code upon the [sometimes complex] program state.

Acknowledgments

Support for Lieberman's work comes in part from research grants from Alenia Corp., Apple Computer, ARPA/JNIDS, the National Science Foundation, and other sponsors of the MIT Media Lab, and for Fry's work from Harlequin, Inc. The authors would like to thank Marc Brown, John Stasko and Blaine Price, who ran the CHI 94 Workshop on Software Visualization, and John Domingue for helpful suggestions. Portions of this paper appeared in "Bridging the Gap Between Code and Behavior in Programming", Henry Lieberman and Christopher Fry, CHI '95, reprinted by permission, Copyright ACM 1995.

Visualization of Dynamics in Real World Software Systems

Doug Kimelman,
Bryan Rosenburg
and
Tova Roth

Visualization of Software Behavior

To truly understand any realistically complex piece of software, for purposes of debugging or tuning, one must consider its execution-time behavior, not just its static structure. *Actual* behavior is often far different from expectations, and often results in poor performance and incorrect results. Further, the ultimate correctness and performance of an application (or lack thereof) arises not only from the behavior of the program itself, but also from activity carried out on its behalf by underlying system layers. These layers include user-level libraries (e.g. dynamic memory allocators, I/O packages, communications libraries, concurrency facilities, graphics systems), the operating system, and the hardware. Finally, problems often become apparent only when one considers the interleaving of various kinds of activity, rather than cumulative activity summaries at the end of a run. Thus, for debugging and tuning applications in a realistically complex environment, one must consider behavior at numerous layers of a system concurrently, as this behavior unfolds over time.

Clearly, any textual presentation of this amount of information would be overwhelming. A visual presentation of the information is far more likely to be meaningful. Information is assimilated far more rapidly when it is presented in a visual fashion, and trends and anomalies are recognized much more readily. Further, animations, and views which incorporate time as an explicit dimension, reveal the interplay among components over time.

With an appropriate visual presentation of information concerning software behavior over time, one can first survey a program execution broadly using a large-scale (high-level, coarse-resolution) view, then narrow the focus as regions of interest are identified, and descend into finer-grained (more detailed) views, until a point is identified for which full detail should be considered.

Further, displays which juxtapose views from different system layers in order to facilitate visual correlation, and which allow these views to be navigated in a coordinated fashion, constitute an extremely powerful mechanism for exploring application behavior.

PV — A Program Visualization System

PV, a prototype program visualization system originally developed at IBM Research,[1] embodies all of the visualization capabilities proposed above. Success with PV in production settings and complex large-scale environments has verified that these capabilities are indeed highly effective for understanding application behavior for purposes of debugging and tuning.

Users often turn to program visualization when performance is disappointing — either performance does not match predictions, or it deteriorates as changes are introduced into the system, or it does not scale up (and perhaps even worsens!) as processors are added in a multiprocessor system, or it is simply insufficient for the intended application.

With PV, users watch for trends, anomalies, and interesting correlations, in order to track down pressing problems. Behavioral phenomena which one might never have suspected, or thought to pursue, are often dramatically revealed. A user continually replays the execution history, and rearranges the display to discard unnecessary information or to incorporate more of the relevant information. In this way, users examine and analyze execution at successively greater levels of detail, to isolate flaws in an application. Resolution of the problems thus discovered often leads to significant improvements in the performance of an application.

PV shows hardware-level performance information (such as instruction execution rates, cache utilization, processor element utilization, delays due to branches and

---

[1] PV is currently available as a "technology demonstration" from IBM Software Solutions on CD-ROM, Order No. SK2T-1159-05.

interlocks) if it is available, operating-system-level activity (such as context switches, address-space activity, system calls and interrupts, kernel performance statistics), communication-library-level activity (such as message-passing, inter-processor communication), language-runtime activity (such as parallel-loop scheduling, dynamic memory allocation), and application-level-activity (such as algorithm phase transitions, execution time profiles, data structure accesses).

PV has been targeted to shared-memory parallel machines (the RP3 [Kimelman 91]), distributed memory machines (transputer clusters running Express), workstation clusters (RISC System/6000 workstations running Express), and superscalar uniprocessor workstations (RISC System/6000 with AIX [Kimelman 94]).

PV is structured as an extensible system, with a framework and a number of plug-in components which perform analysis and display of event data generated by a running system. It includes a base set of components, and users are encouraged to add their own and configure them into networks with existing components. Novice users simply call up pre-established configurations of components in order to use established views of program behavior.

The figures accompanying this chapter show some of the many views provided by PV. The section on "Experience with PV" describes some of these views in detail and discusses their use.

PV is trace-driven. It produces its displays by continually updating views of program behavior as it reads through a trace containing an execution history. A trace consists of a time-ordered sequence of event records, each describing an individual occurrence of some event of interest in the execution of the program. Typically, an event record consists of an event type identifier, a timestamp, and some event-specific data. Events of interest might include: sampling of a cache miss counter, a page fault, scheduling of a process, allocation of a memory region, receipt of a message, or completion of some step of an algorithm. A trace can be delivered to the visualization system live (possibly over a network), as the event records are being generated, or it can be saved in a file for later analysis.

AIX Trace

The standard AIX system (IBM's version of the UNIX operating system), as distributed for RS/6000s, includes an embedded trace facility. AIX Trace [IBM AIX Performance], a service provided by the operating system kernel, accepts event records generated at any level within the system and collects them into a central buffer. As the event buffer becomes full, blocks of event records are dumped to a trace file, or dumped through a pipe to a process, e.g. for transmission over a network. Alternatively, the system can be configured to simply maintain a large circular buffer of event records that must be explicitly emptied by a user process.

Comprehensive instrumentation within AIX itself provides information about activity within the kernel, and a system call is provided by which user processes can provide event records concerning activity within libraries or the application. On machines incorporating hardware performance monitors, a device driver can unload hardware performance data, periodically or at specific points during the execution of an application, and generate AIX event records containing the data.

The variant of PV that is targeted to AIX workstations is based on AIX Trace. Unless otherwise noted, all of the applications discussed in this paper were run on AIX RS/6000 workstations with AIX Trace enabled. Traces were taken during a run of the application and saved in files for later analysis.

For the applications discussed here, tracing overhead was negligible — less than 5% in most cases. In no case was perturbation great enough to alter the behavior being investigated. Trace file sizes in all cases were less than 16 megabytes.

Views in Action — Experience with PV

This section describes some of the many views provided by PV, and explains their use, by way of examples of actual experience with PV. This section also gives a bit of the flavor of the overall use of PV for software visualization.

PV has been applied to a number of different types of applications across a number of domains, including: interactive graphics applications written in C++, systems programs (compilers, etc.) written in C, computation-intensive scientific applications written in Fortran, I/O-intensive applications written in C, and a large, complex, heavily-layered, distributed application written in Ada.

Views of Process Scheduling and System Activity

In one example, the developers of "G", an interactive graphics application,[2] were concerned that it was taking 12 seconds from the time that the user entered the command to start the application, until the time that the main application window would respond to user input. They suspected that a lot of time was being lost in the Motif libraries. Their PV sessions proceeded as follows.

Overview of the Entire Run

Visualization typically begins with a global view of the system and a review of the entire run in order to get oriented. Working from the outside in, the developers first examined a view that shows the tree of all of the processes in the AIX system as it changes over time.

Figure 1 shows this view in a window titled "AixProcessTree | DGraph". Processes are colored according to the time they have taken *recently*, not simply the time they have accumulated since the beginning of the run. This is achieved by maintaining a sliding time window, e.g. the most recent 2 seconds, and coloring processes according to the time taken within that window. (To reduce time and space requirements, the sliding window is approximated by exponentially decaying the time accumulated so far for each process.) Process colors range from blue,[3] to indicate a small amount of time, through green, yellow, orange, and finally red, to indicate a large amount of time. An important aspect of this display is that it shows processes playing off against one another over time. Some processes glow red ("heat up") first, then fade back to blue as others heat up. For example, this view can show how execution alternates between the X server and an X client application during interaction with the user.

For application "G", the developers observed that first a shell comes alive and forks off a process "Gfront" (seen near the bottom of the view in Figure 1). Gfront is a front-end process responsible for interaction with the user, and we see that it seems to alternate periods of high activity with the X server. This is

---

[2] "The stories you are about to hear are true. Only the names have been changed to protect the innocent."

[3] Color reproductions of the figures in this chapter are available from any of the authors as an IBM Research Center Technical Report, or in [Kimelman 94].

likely to be the time during which the control panel is created and first appears on the display. Gfront then appears to fork off a second shell, which forks off a process "Gback" — a back-end process responsible for computing images. Thus, the multiple process structure of "G" rapidly becomes apparent from this view.

About 12 seconds into the run, the "Idle" process (near the top left of Figure 1) lights up. This process is a system process which runs when no other process is ready. In this case, time spent in Idle suggests that the application has completed its initialization phase and is now waiting for user input. As the run progresses, a sequence of activity appears repeatedly: Gfront and the X server heat up a bit as user interaction takes place, then Gback glows red monopolizing the processor as it generates a new image, and finally the X server heats up as the image is displayed.

Thus, from having seen this view, and from having observed the run during which the trace was taken, a good deal is evident about the overall structure and sequence of execution within this multiple-process application. This would be the case even for a developer unfamiliar with the application (but perhaps responsible nonetheless for understanding its poor performance).

Figure 2 shows a complete workstation display from a session in which PV is being used to analyze a run of application "G". The view to the right of the process tree is a histogram showing how much time each process has accumulated between the beginning of the run and the current point in the replay of the run. Each process in the system is represented by one segment of the histogram bar, and the process to which a segment of the bar corresponds is indicated by its color. A legend or "key" at the side of the bar provides the mapping from colors to process names and numeric identifiers. This mapping between color and processes is also used by a number of the other views.

At the end of a replay of this run of application "G" (not shown), the process time histogram shows that the process Gfront accumulated 12 seconds over the course of the entire 97-second run, the process Gback accumulated 18, the X server 8, and the idle process 51. The rest of the time was scattered among a number of other processes.

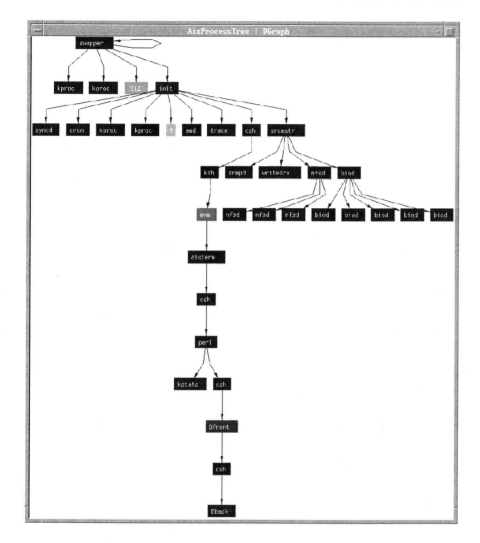

Figure 1. The PV process-tree view.

Thus, this end-of-run summary showed that 51 seconds out of the 97-second run were spent idle, but this summary provided no indication of how many of these idle seconds were in fact warranted, perhaps spent simply waiting for user input, and how many were somehow on the critical path for the application. Cumulative summaries of execution time spent in various functions, as provided at the end of a run by conventional profilers, or perusal of thousands of lines of detail in textual reports, would have been of no additional help.

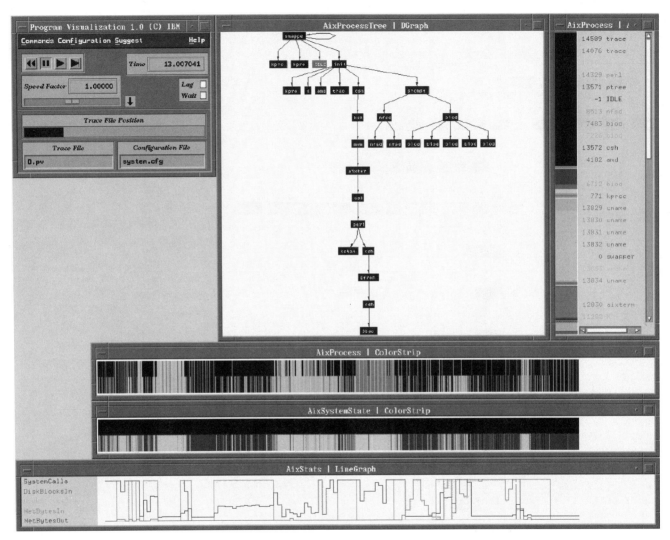

*Figure 2. The PV system configuration, showing activity on the system as a whole. * See Plate 8 ***

Focus on Application Startup

Having taken an overview of the entire run, and with the concern being, as described above, that the application requires 12 seconds to get started, the developers replayed execution yet again, this time suspending the replay after 13 seconds (as indicated by the "Time" field in the PV control panel at the top left of Figure 2).

The process time histogram in Figure 2 shows that in fact `Gfront` (light pink) directly consumed only 3 of the 12 seconds required to get started. The X server (light green) consumed half a second, two C-shells (magenta and dark green) consumed a total of 2 seconds, and `Gback` (salmon color, near the bottom) consumed a third of a second. The system was idle (dark purple) for 5 of the initial 12 seconds.

Thus, it was apparent that the two processes of application "G" were not even running for much of the 12 seconds that they should have been rushing to establish the main application window(!). Further, it wasn't even the X server process that was running instead of them (for graphics applications, the X server must run periodically on behalf of the application, in order to satisfy graphics requests made by the application). Altogether, the application seemed to be responsible for less than a third of the startup time. In fact, the system was idle much of the time. It was also surprising to see that C-shells were consuming a full 2 seconds.

To understand where, and perhaps why, the idle time and C-shell time occurred, the developers turned to a more detailed view showing the actual sequence of process activity making up this 12 seconds.

The wide short window titled "AixProcess | ColorStrip" in the middle of Figure 2, consists of a strip of color which grows to the right as time passes. Color at any instant in time indicates which process is currently running (using the same mapping between colors and processes as the process time histogram described above). When the strip hits the right edge of the window, it scrolls to the left as more data is added at the right. With the time scale and window size that the user has chosen in this case, this strip shows the most recent 15 seconds of activity. (A facility exists for zooming into any region of particular interest along the strip in order to display greater detail with finer resolution. Half-height black notches along the top of the strip mark areas where there is more detail than can be displayed at the current resolution.)

The process strip shows that as the run begins, a C-shell (magenta) starts and is active for about a second. `Gfront` (light pink) then starts, but another second later the system goes idle (dark purple) for about 2 seconds, except for brief and intermittent activity by network file system and auto-mount daemons. About 5 seconds into the run, `Gfront` again becomes active, alternates with the X server (light green) for a second or so, and then gives way to a second C-shell (dark green). This C-shell runs for one and a half seconds before spawning the Gback process (salmon). Shortly after Gback starts, there is a 1 second interval during which the system is mostly idle. Then Gfront runs again briefly. There follows another 2 second interval of idle time, and finally, the startup sequence completes with a last bit of activity in Gback.

At this point it becomes clear that of the 51 seconds of idle time incurred during the run, the 5 seconds just observed during startup are, in fact, on the critical path for this application. These 5 seconds are contributing to the delay in getting the application started, and are not simply time spent waiting for user input later in the run. This fact would never have been apparent from conventional profiling tools.

Investigation of Critical Idle Time

To understand the reason for this critical idle time, the developers next inspected a view showing what system activity is taking place over time, and they focused on the points in time where the system was going idle.

The wide short window titled "AixSystemState I ColorStrip", beneath the "AixProcess I ColorStrip" window in Figure 2, is a strip in which the color at any instant in time indicates what system-level activity is taking place (e.g. system call, clock interrupt, page fault, I/O interrupt, process running in user-mode, etc.). (A key can be popped up to give the mapping between colors and activities. Alternatively, clicking anywhere on the strip pops up an information box giving the name of the system activity represented by the color at that point, as well as the time corresponding to that point in the strip.)

Beneath the second strip in Figure 2 is another wide short window titled "AixStats I LineGraph", which plots a number of kernel performance statistics over time. Each statistic is plotted in a different color, with the mapping between colors and statistics given at the left of the graph.

The two color strips and the line graph are configured so that they show the same time spans. As well, the three views are aligned so that a point in one view corresponds to the same instant in time as the points immediately above or below it in the other views. Further, the three views aligned in this way can be navigated in a coordinated fashion — when the user zooms in on any of these views, expanding a region of interest in order to reveal greater detail, the other views expand the same region of time automatically.

(PV provides a number of other views which can be aligned and navigated in the same fashion, including views showing hardware performance statistics, and views showing which loop of a function is currently active, or which user-defined phase of an algorithm is currently being executed.)

Following along the process strip until the first major block of time where application "G" goes idle (dark purple), zooming in to show greater detail, and then dropping down to the system state strip, shows that the idle time begins with Gfront making a stat() system call. After .6 seconds of idle time, handling of the stat() system call is completed, at which point Gfront begins a long series of open() and read() system calls, each of which causes Gfront to be suspended and the system to go idle again. The idle periods dominate the time required to handle the system call itself. During this time, the statistics graph shows a large amount of data arriving over the network (cyan), and AixSystemState shows periodic ethernet interrupts, while AixProcess shows amd (the auto mount daemon) and biod (a network filesystem daemon) running periodically (thin slivers of cyan and blue).

Thus, the nature of this idle time was revealed: system calls to examine a number of files were incurring large network delays.

Having used graphic views to narrow their focus to a very small period in time (where individual file access system calls were occurring), the developers turned to a textual view for details concerning which files were resulting in the large access delays. The trace report view (not shown in the figures) shows a textual report giving the full detail of each event. As each event is displayed graphically in other views, this view highlights the corresponding line in the report. By suspending the visualization displays when the system calls of interest appear on the system state strip, and then examining the lines highlighted in the detailed report window, the names of the files being accessed can be determined.

From the name of the directories and files being accessed, it was immediately obvious to the application developers that Gfront was scanning for startup information. This information was scattered across a number of files, which in general could (and in this instance did) reside in filesystems which are remote-mounted over a network. Once it was apparent how much time this remote file access was actually consuming, it was a simple matter to devise an alternative scheme whereby the startup information was collected into a single local file which could be accessed quickly.

Eliminating the idle time due to accessing these startup files improved startup time by about 15 percent.

Thus, in uncovering a problem with application "G", consideration of system dynamics — the sequence of events and interactions — allowed developers to isolate the significant points in the execution (and disregard insignificant ones) in a way that no end-of-run summary could. Further, the use of graphic displays to continually re-examine execution at successively greater levels of detail, with a continually narrowing focus, allowed developers to home in quickly on questionable behavior, where painstaking perusal of textual trace reports alone would be unlikely to provide any feel for "the big picture" at any point in time (the "can't see the forest for the trees" syndrome). Finally, without the visual correlation facilitated by juxtaposition of views and coordinated navigation, it would have been much harder to make the connection between the various aspects of this performance problem. At the very least, it would have taken much longer by any less direct means.

Further Opportunities for Improvement

Similar detailed investigation of the other blocks of idle time that were deemed to be significant revealed that another 15 percent of the startup time was spent waiting for a standard system utility to simply determine the amount of physical memory available on the host machine, and that a further 10 percent was spent waiting for page faults incurred while loading `Gback`. Both of these blocks of idle time constitute significant opportunities for performance improvement.

From the process color strip discussed above, it also became apparent that the time spent in the two C-shells described above was occurring in single blocks prior to starting up `Gfront` and `Gback`. Most of this time was spent in user mode, rather than in system calls or other system activity. This immediately implicated the lengthy shell scripts used to launch the application. These scripts were subsequently simplified, resulting in another 15 percent improvement in the application startup time. Here, the ability of PV to show components of the surrounding environment, in this case the C-shells, without any special preparation helped developers understand the overall progress of the application in ways that process-specific tools could not.

Thus, overall, PV was invaluable in helping the developers of application "G" review its behavior, focus on suspect areas, and ultimately home in on flaws in the implementation.

Views of Memory Activity and Application Progress

In another example, PV views (shown in Figure 3) revealed a number of memory-related problems in "A", a compiler. Each view in this case is rectangular, with each position along the horizontal axis corresponding to some region of a linear address space (the size of the region depends on the scale of the display). In one view, color is used to represent the size of a block of memory on the user heap. (In Figure 3, this view is the first of the two windows titled "AixMalloc I OneSpace".) In another view, color is used to represent the source file name or line number that allocated the block. (Figure 3, second window titled "AixMalloc I OneSpace".) In a third view, color is used to represent the state of each page in the data segment of the user address space. (Figure 3, window titled "AixDataSeg I OneSpace".) For purposes of correlation, the views are configured to show the same range of addresses, and they are aligned so that a given address occurs at the same horizontal position in each view. As well, zooming in on a region in one view automatically causes the corresponding zoom operation in the other views.

Each of the OneSpace views in Figure 3 is split into an upper half and a lower half, each representing part of the data segment of the address space of compiler "A". The left edge of the upper half represents address 0x24200000; successive points to the right along this half represent successively higher addresses; and the right edge represents address 0x24600000. Thus, the upper half of these views represent 4MB of the data segment. Similarly, the lower half of these views represents an expanded view of the 248KB from 0x2448E571 to 0x244CAE35. The black guidelines show where the region represented by the lower half of a view fits into the region represented by the upper half.

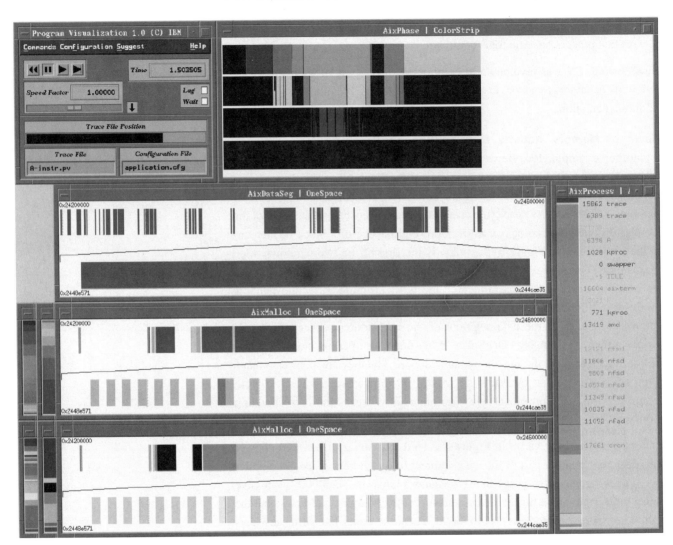

Figure 3. The PV application configuration, showing program phases, the data segment, and the heap for a user-specified target process.

These views showed a number of wastes of memory, none of which could technically be classed a "leak". Rather, they were "balloons" — still referenced, but largely full of empty space. In one case, the heap views showed that every second page of the heap was not being made available to the end user (shown in Figure 3 in the upper "AixMalloc | OneSpace" as alternating green and white blocks in the lower half of the view), yet the corresponding positions on the data segment view showed clearly that *every* page was being faulted in (shown in the lower half of Figure 3, "AixDataSeg | OneSpace", as all magenta). The heap views also showed that all of the blocks in question were of the same size. Having identified blocks of a particular size as being problematic, the source code for the allocator was quickly inspected, with particular attention to the treatment of blocks of the problematic size. It rapidly became apparent that, in certain situations, half of the heap was being left empty due to an unfortunate interaction between user code, the heap memory allocator, and the virtual memory system.

In another case, a static array was declared to be enormous. This was felt to be acceptable because real memory pages were never faulted in unless they were required for the size of the program being compiled. However, the data segment view emphasized that the array *did* occupy address space, and this became noteworthy when the compiler could not be loaded on smaller machine configurations, even though only moderate-sized programs needed to be compiled.

Finally, late in the run of this compiler, pages began flashing in and out of the data segment view, indicating that pages were repeatedly becoming inactive, then becoming active again and being zero-filled. Glancing at the system activity view (described earlier), during the time that the page flashing was occurring, allowed this behavior to be correlated to periods of excessive disclaiming and subsequent reclaiming of pages by the compiler: the compiler was in fact giving pages back to the system (using a `disclaim()` system call), then immediately faulting them back in. This suggested that a memory block caching strategy might be employed to great advantage.

An application phase view, which provides a roadmap to the progress of an application, allowed this thrashing in the address space to be attributed directly to the offending phase of the compiler. (In Figure 3, this view is the window titled "AixPhase | ColorStrip".) The application phase view consists of a number of strips of color, as in the process scheduling and system activity views described earlier. The strips are stacked one on top of the other, and they grow to the right together over time. The color of the top strip shows which user-defined phase of the application is in progress at any instant in time. (A key can be popped up to give the mapping between colors and phases.) The color of successively lower strips shows successively deeper sub-phases nested within the phases shown at the corresponding positions on the higher strips.

This view is driven by instrumentation in the form of simple event generation statements. The statements are inserted manually or automatically into the source to indicate where major and minor phases of computation begin or end. Alternatively, procedure entry and exit event statements can be inserted automatically using object code insertion techniques.

In the case of compiler "A", correlation in time between the application phase view and the data segment view immediately made it clear that a back-end code generation phase (shown in Figure 3 as light green) was responsible for the excessive paging activity.

In another example, these memory-related views revealed a number of actual memory leaks in "F", a large Ada application. Due to the visual nature of these views, it was immediately apparent that particular leaks were flooding the address space (which was bleeding full of the color of the allocators in question) and hence required immediate attention. It was just as apparent that other leaks were inconsequential (they were small and growing slowly) and hence could be ignored until after a rapidly approaching deadline. This is something which would not be readily apparent from the textual report of conventional special-purpose memory leak detectors.

Without concurrent display of system- and user-level activity over time, the behavior discovered here would have been virtually impossible to detect in any convenient fashion.

Views of Hardware Activity and Source Progress

Finally, in an example involving "T", a computation-intensive scientific application, a view showing which loop of a program was active over time, in conjunction with views of hardware performance statistics over time, highlighted opportunities for significant improvements in performance. These views are shown in Figure 4.

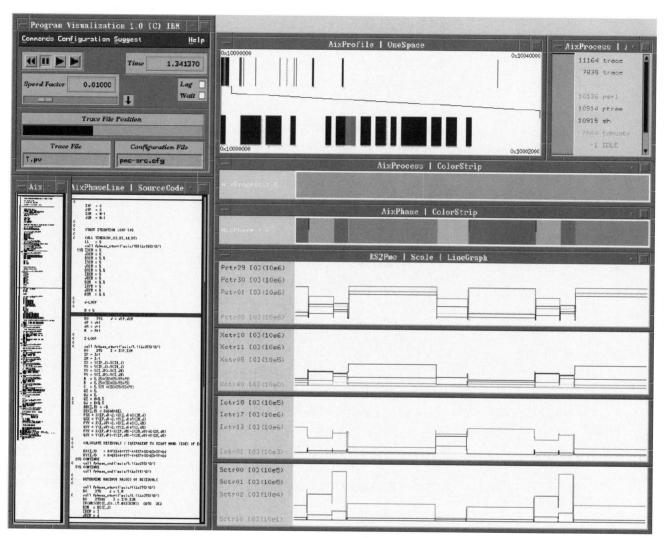

The program loop view is simply the application phase view described earlier, with color used to indicate which program loop is active at any instant in time (rather than which arbitrary user-defined phase is active). (In Figure 4, this view is the window titled "AixPhase | ColorStrip".) The hardware performance view consists of a stack of linegraphs growing to the right over time. (Figure 4, window titled "RS2Pmc | Scale | LineGraph".) Hardware-level performance metrics (instruction-execution rates, memory-access and cache-miss rates, etc.)

Figure 4. The PV performance-monitor *configuration, showing hardware performance metrics for a user-specified target process.*

are sampled at loop boundaries and plotted on the various graphs. In this case, the two views showed the same time span and were aligned for purposes of correlation and navigation. Thus, the program loop view shows the history of loop execution over time, in a way that allows it to be correlated easily with hardware performance data.

These views allowed programmers to easily identify the longer-running loops (the loops with the wider bands in the loop view — the teal loop and the blue loop), and they allowed programmers to correlate execution of a particular loop (the blue loop) with a dramatic decrease in MFLOPS. The hardware view showed that the loop was not cache-limited and was not a fixed point loop, yet one floating point unit was seldom busy, while the other was extremely busy but completing very few instructions. To understand the behavior of this particular loop, a number of additional views were opened to show the program source.

Each source view highlights a line of source at the beginning of the major loop currently being executed. One of the views is, in effect, a "very high altitude" view of the source (as in [Eick 92c]), in which the entire source of the program fits within the single window. Although the code is illegible due to the "very small font", the overall structure of the program is apparent, and the overall progress of the application can be tracked easily. The code in the second view of the source is legible, but the view can only show a page of source at a time and must be scrolled in order to view different parts of the program. (These two source views are shown side by side at the left of Figure 4, beneath the PV control panel.) The third view shows the assembly language source, as generated by the compiler, with the same form of highlighting as the other two source views. (In figure 4, this view is hidden behind the other windows.)

For application "T", glancing at the source views confirmed that, for the loop in question, a divide instruction was in fact causing one floating point unit to remain fully busy while not completing very many instructions. The assembly view showed that the reason for the second floating point unit not even keeping busy was an unnecessary register dependence in the generated code. Thus, the problem turned out *not* to be a cache problem, but rather one of unbalanced processor utilization — not keeping *both* floating point units busy. Using these views for feedback, the programmer was able to experiment rapidly with manual source transformations, and ultimately to achieve a 12% improvement in the performance of application "T".

Overall, through experience with PV in these situations and many others, the visualization capabilities proposed above have proven tremendously effective for debugging and tuning, often in cases where traditional methods have failed.

Trace-based software visualization can often be more readily adapted to realistically complex environments than can more tightly coupled approaches (such as those based on debugger technology). Experience with application "F" illustrates how quickly trace-based visualization can be brought to bear on realistically complex applications.

Application "F", introduced briefly in the previous section, was in fact a complex, distributed Ada system consisting of a number of software layers built one upon another. Its developers faced serious performance and stability problems, and deadlines were approaching rapidly.

Key components of the language runtime libraries were instrumented in less than a day, by inserting event-record generation system calls at crucial points. This allowed the developers to quickly achieve a good overall picture of certain aspects of the behavior of their system. They then inserted additional instrumentation, where required, for more detailed inspection of suspect areas. In this way, with the views described in previous sections, PV revealed a number of instances of anomalous behavior, including the memory leaks discussed earlier, excessive context switching, and processes consuming far more time during startup than anyone realized. As in the case of the memory leaks, PV helped focus and prioritize tuning activity, and ultimately, visualization was regarded as having been a significant contributing factor in achieving system goals.

In other cases, the views described in previous sections were used to to deal with memory problems involving a custom user-level memory allocator. Conventional special-purpose memory leak detectors were of no help because they had no knowledge of the custom allocator and were not extensible. The custom allocator could, however, easily be instrumented to generate the small amount of trace information required to drive the PV views of memory activity.

Conventional tools for debugging or performance analysis, and special-purpose language-specific utilities, could never have been adapted as quickly in these

Adaptability of Trace-Based Visualization

complex production environments, and could not have provided as broad a collection of capabilities from a single facility in return for the adaptation effort. Even facing imminent deadlines, developers deemed it worthwhile to divert from "core" tuning efforts, to devote time to connecting PV to their application, and to running and inspecting visualization displays.

Thus, trace-based software visualization has proved to be readily adaptable and widely applicable in addition to being an extremely powerful tool for presenting program behavior.

Future Research

The user interface is bound to be a severe limitation of *any* current software visualization system. Typical displays of software are crude approximations, at best, to the elaborate mental images that most programmers have of the software systems they are developing. Opening, closing, and aligning windows on a relatively small 2-dimensional screen is a cumbersome means of manipulating a few small windows onto an elaborate conceptual world.

With the advent of sufficiently powerful virtual reality technology, a far more effective facility for software visualization could be achieved by mapping multiple-layer software systems onto expansive 3-dimensional terrains, and providing more direct means for traversal. Traversal could involve high-level passes over the terrain to obtain an overview, and descent to lower-levels over regions of interest for more detailed views. The system could also provide the ability to maintain a number of distinct perspectives onto the terrain. The panorama could include both representations of the software entities themselves, as well as derived information such as performance measurements, and more abstract representations of the entities and the progress of their computation.

Related Work

The notion of program visualization per se [Price 93] [Stasko 92] first appeared in the literature more than ten years ago [Herot 82]. Much of the initial work in program visualization, and many recent efforts, are concerned solely with the static structure of a program. They do not consider dynamics of program behavior at all.

Algorithm animation work [Brown 88b] [Stasko 90b] has focused strictly on small algorithms, rather than on actual behavior of large applications or on all of the layers of large underlying systems. Further, algorithm animations often require large amounts of time to construct (days, weeks or even months). This is acceptable in a teaching environment, where the animations will be used repeatedly on successive generations of students, but is unacceptable in a production software development environment where it is critical that a tool can be applied readily to problems as they arise.

Recently, there has been much work in the area of program visualization for parallel systems [Kraemer 93]. This work has in fact been concerned with dynamics, but much of it has been confined to communication or other aspects of parallelism. Little consideration has been given to displaying other aspects of system behavior. PIE [Lehr 89] shows system-level activity over time, but its displays are limited primarily to context switching. Other system-level activity and activity from the application and other levels of the system are not displayed simultaneously for correlation.

The IPS-2 performance measurement system for parallel and distributed programs [Hollingsworth 91, Miller 90] does integrate both application and system based metrics. However, system metrics are dealt with strictly in the form of "external time histograms", each describing the value of a single performance metric over time, as opposed to more general event data. Thus, where non-application data are concerned, IPS-2 is limited to strictly numeric presentations, such as tables and linegraphs. Dynamic animated displays of behavior, such as those showing system activity over time, or memory state as it evolves, are not possible with IPS-2. Program hierarchy displays are used primarily only for showing the overall structure of an application, or for specifying the program components for which performance measurements are to be presented.

Some vendors provide general facilities for tracing the system requests made by a given process. However, these facilities tend to apply to a single process rather than the system as a whole, and hence are not useful for showing the interaction between a process and its surrounding environment. Furthermore, these facilities tend to have very high overheads.

Profiling tools, such as the UNIX utilities "prof" and "gprof", have existed for some time, but these utilities simply show cumulative execution time, at the end of a run, on a function by function basis.

A number of workstation vendors have recently extended basic profiling facilities or debuggers by adding views to show time consumption and other resource utilization graphically. Many of these tools now report utilization with granularity as fine as a source line, and many allow sampling during experiments which can cover some part of a run rather than just an entire run. None of these tools, however, supports the notion of general visual inspection of continuous behavior and system dynamics at multiple levels within a system.

Some debuggers are now including views of behavior in the memory arena, but none of these tools provides the power and generality of PV.

The power of PV, and its novelty, lie in its combination of a number of important properties. PV provides *both* quantitative and animated displays, and it presents information from *multiple* layers of a program and its underlying system. Further, PV facilitates *correlation* and *coordinated navigation* of the information displayed in its various views. Finally, PV presents views which address important concerns for software behavior on mainstream *workstation* systems, not just clusters or parallel machines. PV embodies all of these capabilities and it provides effective industrial-strength support of *large-scale* applications (even hundreds of megabytes of address space and hundreds of thousands of lines of code).

Conclusion

In production settings, over a wide range of complex applications, PV has proven invaluable in uncovering the nature and causes of program failures. Developers facing serious performance problems and imminent deadlines have found it worthwhile to invest time to connect PV to their application, and to run and inspect visualization displays.

Experience with PV indicates that concurrent visual presentation of behavior from many layers, including the program itself, user-level libraries, the operating system, and the hardware, as this behavior unfolds over time, is essential for understanding, debugging, and tuning realistically complex applications. Systems that facilitate visual correlation of such information, and that provide coordinated navigation of multi-layer displays, constitute an extremely powerful mechanism for exploring application behavior.

Maintenance of Large Systems

Stephen G. Eick

Introduction

This chapter describes a new graphical technique for displaying computer source code and an interactive system *SeeSoft* embodying the technique.[1] The motivation for inventing this technique comes from studying a large database of computer source code from a real-time telephone switch. The database contains several million non commentary lines, and has been written by several thousand programmers over the last two decades. There are currently several versions of the system deployed with annual releases and ongoing development for two future versions.

A huge problem for the programmers involved with large software systems is to understand all the code. The code listing for a 1,000,000 line program, printed 50 lines per page, would require 20,000 pages! With the amount of ongoing maintenance activity and new development, any listing would soon be out of date. Programmer productivity for large systems is abysmal. It can take weeks of detailed study for a programmer, unfamiliar with a particular section of the code, to find a software fault (bug) and figure out how the existing code works well enough to fix it without breaking any current functionality. This is particularly a problem when the programmers doing maintenance are not those who wrote the code originally. The process of trying to understand code is called discovery and takes between 70% of an experienced programmer's time and 90% of a new programmer's time when fixing bugs.

---

[1]An early version of this paper appears in the 1992 ASA conference proceedings.

Understanding the code is critical for several other areas in the development process. Project managers need to track code milestones to ensure that customer deliverables are met. With all large developments there is staff turnover. New programmers must be trained. Software engineers must design new feature code to have minimal impact on the existing code. Management needs to know files that are difficult to change and projects that are hard so they can assign difficult tasks to their best people. As part of ongoing maintenance activities, code is continually being reorganized. The reorganization may be around functional areas, features, or departmental structures. Analysts involved with restructuring studies and code archaeology try to determine when files are becoming too complex and when directories are becoming too big. Complex files may be simplified by rewriting them and large directories may be split. Dead code (not reachable) must be identified and deleted. Performance analysts study code execution traces to ensure that it executes efficiently. Testers are interested in knowing if their test suites exercise the new features in a release.

The current practice in code analysis is to use code browsers such as *Cscope* [Steffen 85] and *CIA* [Chen 89]. These tools enable users to search for textural patterns, find variables' references, and display code fragments in windows, among other things. They are effective, but more is needed. With current tools programmers can only see one screen of code at a time, at most 100 lines on a large monitor. This makes it difficult to get an overall perspective on the code. Further, there is no display of the temporal evolution of the code from the change history.

For production software systems the source code is kept in change management systems. The most common change management systems for UNIX^{TM} computers are the *Revision Control System* [Tichy 1985] and *Source Code Control System* [Rochkind 1975]. These systems maintain a complete change history and can recreate the code as it existed at any point in time. Change management system usually contain many additional statistics besides the source to help manage the project. The statistics include variables such as the date a change was made, change abstract, responsible programmer, user id, affected feature, reason for the change, whether the change fixes a bug or adds a new feature, etc. The change history is a rich, underutilized, resource of information about the system.

By processing the change management files it is possible to create data sets containing statistics associated with each line of code. The data set consists of lines of code broken into files, and variables associated with each line. The variables may come directly from the change management database (i.e. who wrote the line, when was it last changed, what feature was it for) or may be derived from other sources. For the C Language [Kernighan 78] the statements may be classified into different types: declarations, C preprocessor statements 's, (#defines's), and block comments, C control structures (if, for, while, switch and case), assignment statements, or function calls. Code profiling tools such as prof [Hume 90], gprof [Graham 82], or lcomp [Weinberger 84] create execution counts and CPU cycle usage's for each line. These statistical data sets can be extremely large, as there are data items for each line of code.

Traditional statistical analysis techniques are useful, but better methods are needed. To analyze this class of data my colleagues and I have developed a new graphical method and implemented it in the SeeSoft visualization tool. The remainder of this paper describes our technique in detail and applies it to visualizing production code.

Visualizing Line Oriented Statistics

SeeSoft displays line oriented code statistics using a rectangle to represent each file and colored[2] rows within the rectangle to represent the statistics associated with the lines of code. The position of the rows corresponds to the position of the lines within the file and the size of the rectangles to the size of the file. The file names are shown above each rectangle. If a file is longer than can fit in a single rectangle, multiple adjacent rectangles are used. The color, indentation, and length of each row may be tied to statistics associated with the corresponding code line. When the row indentation and length are tied to the code indentation and length, the display looks like an extremely reduced representation of code printout that has been typeset [Baecker 90a, p. 235].

Figure 1 shows a SeeSoft display for 23 C language files from one directory. The length and indentation of each row corresponds to the code and the color (gray level) to the date each line was added. Figure 2 shows the same data without the row indentation, so that all rows are displayed using the full width

---

[2]In the black and white version of this paper "color" is to be interpreted as gray level.

of each column. This gives the same visual prominence to the short rows as the long rows and is easier to see on printed gray scale output. The most recent changes are in red (black) and the oldest in blue (light gray), with a rainbow [Foley 90] color spectrum (gray scale) between. On the left-hand side there is a mouse sensitive slider with a distinct color for each change. In gray scale printouts the color levels blur together, although they are actually distinct. The '356 / 356' and '28281 / 28281' printed underneath the slider shows that there have been 356 changes in this directory and altogether there are 28,281 lines of code. Currently all 356 changes and all 28,281 rows are displayed. At the bottom there are buttons and a slider that controls the display and in the bottom right-hand corner is a list of statistics: site, name, user.id, bugnew, project, del.mr, and add.mr. The current statistic is add.mr (adding modification request), or change that added each line. The statistics are arbitrary and depend on the data being analyzed. The mouse is pointing at a row in file file9.c. The code corresponding to this row is printed at the bottom along with its the change abstract. The values of the other statistics for this row are also printed next to their names in the lower right-hand side. This particular row is a C comment statement for a new feature, added in 1988 by change tm200577eK by programmer R. E. Browne, whose user id is rbrowne.

An experienced C programmer can pick out the C language control structures in Figure 1. By convention, C code is indented along its control structures. These patterns are clearly visible on a standard high-resolution (1280x1024) workstation monitor, although difficult to see in the figure. Saw tooth patterns correspond to C case statements and indentations to C if statements. The sizes of the rectangles show the length of the files. The largest file, file9.c, spans eight columns and contains 6,384 lines. Other large files are file16c, five columns and 4,433 lines, and file7.c, three columns and 2,480 lines.

Figure 2 shows the same data as Figure 1 except the mouse is in a different location and indenting has been turned off. There has been recent change activity in several files as indicated by the black regions. The solid color block of code are stable with the intensity indicating the code age. The file file1.c on the left is the oldest and has not been touched in years.

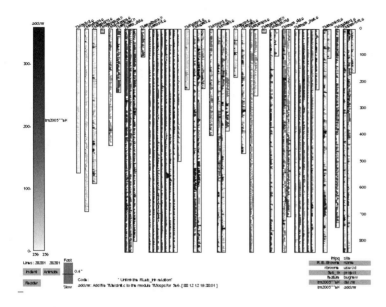

Figure 1. SeeSoft Code Display. *A SeeSoft display showing the change that added each line for files in one directory. The most recent changes are in red (black) and the oldest in blue (light gray), with a color spectrum (gray scale) between.*
* See Plate 6 *

Information Density

With SeeSoft's compact representation of data it is possible to comfortably display 35 files containing 50,000 lines of code on a standard high resolution (1280x1024) workstation color monitor. I have displayed 100,000 lines, although the rows are tiny. For each row it is possible to display three statistics coded in the row indentation, length, and color, although it is natural in analyzing software that the indentation and length correspond to that in the code. This technique maximizes Tufte's data-ink ratio [Tufte 83]. By manipulating the display, it is possible to interpret a huge volume of data.

Figure 2. SeeSoft Display With No Indentation. *This is the same data as in Figure 1 except the code indentation has been turned off and the mouse is pointing to a different row. Turning off indentation gives the same visual prominence to the short and long rows.*

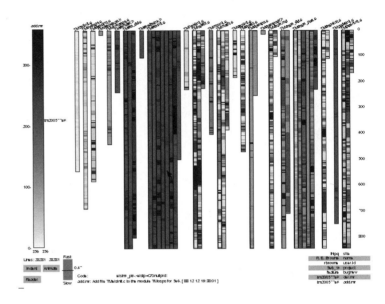

Direct Manipulation And Brushing

SeeSoft applies the direct display manipulation techniques and increases their effectiveness by performing the interactions in real-time. As the user moves the mouse around the display, the computer tracks the mouse and activates the rows under the mouse. Only active rows are displayed and in Figures 1 and 2 all rows are active. This technique is similar to brushing [Becker 87]. Holding down the left mouse button makes the activation permanent and holding the right button causes deactivation.

When the mouse touches a row, slider statistic value, or file name, all rows associated with that entity are activated. Activating a slider value activates all rows associated with that value. If the current statistic is the change as displayed in Figures 1 and 2, then all rows touched by that change are activated. Activating a row also activates its statistic value and thereby activates any other rows with the same statistic value. Activating a file activates all rows in that file. Figure 3 shows the same data as in Figure 2 except that only the code added in 1992 is active and one additional change from 1988. The 1988 change shows that the activated ranges are arbitrary and may be independently manipulated.

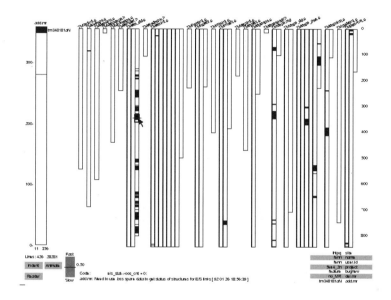

Figure 3A. Code Changed In 1992. A SeeSoft display showing the code added in 1992 and one change from 1988 with the row indentation deactivated. There have been 10 additions so far in 1992 adding 423 lines. The change in 1988 added 3 lines so that in total 11 changes and 426 lines are active. The mouse is pointing at code that was recently added by user id fenn for a new feature. The small box around the mouse position corresponds to a Browser window (Figure 3B).

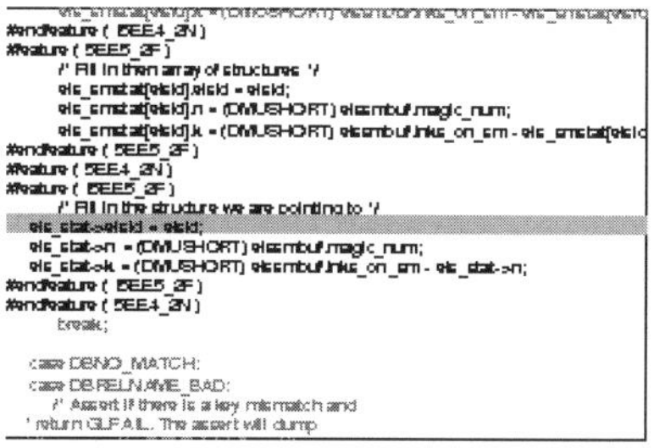

Code Browsing

Programmers discovering interesting patterns need to see the actual code. When the programmer depresses the Browser button at the bottom left-hand side of the screen two actions occur. A new window for displaying code using a 10 point font is created and a small colored "magnifying" box appears on the graphical display. In Figure 3 the magnifying box is at the mouse position and follows the mouse as it is moved around the display. The code underneath the box is displayed in the window. The size of the magnifying box is proportional to the size of the browser window. This enables the programmer to understand what fraction of the total is visible and where the code is in the file.

Multiple browser windows may be created and independently positioned. The border color on each browser window is the same as its corresponding magnifying box. The programmer manipulates and positions the boxes

Figure 3B. Browser Window. Code underneath the box on Figure 3A is displayed in a separate window using a readable font.

independently using the mouse and right mouse button. The browser windows enable the programmer to smoothly move between the condensed SeeSoft data representation and code. In this way a SeeSoft user can choose the best of either view.

Multiple Statistics

The current statistic determines the row colors in the display and is manipulated using the slider. A user may select a new statistic from those named in the lower right-hand side by pointing to the statistic and depressing the left mouse button. In Figure 4 the current statistic is programmer name and the mouse is on file file20.c. This activates all rows in the file. By activating all rows any users who added any of these lines are activated in the color scale. Activating users in the color scale activates any other rows that any of these users touched. This particular file has been changed by 24 of the 106 programmers working in this directory. Each statistic has an independent persistent slider. It is possible to study relationships between the statistics.

Statisticians concern themselves with interactions between variables. SeeSoft supports conditional inference by allowing the programmer to select a background or conditional variable. A SeeSoft user activates a conditional variable by pointing to it and depressing the right mouse button. This deactivates any rows in the current variable that are inactive in the background variable. Figure 5 shows the same data as Figure 4 except for the background variable bugnew. This categorical variable take two values: feature indicating new development, and bug indicating a bug fix. In Figure 5 only the bug value of the background variable bugnew is active. Thus the display shows all lines in any files that were added to fix bugs by any programmer who ever worked in file file20.c.

An effective display manipulation technique is to blink a background variable. Holding down the right mouse button on a statistic causes it toggle on and off as a background variable. The result is that the lines conditionally affected by this variable blink, giving a vivid visual display.

SeeSoft's mechanism for selecting the current and background statistics is a powerful mechanism for analyzing data. Data analytic queries are entered using the mouse and the results graphically displayed. The human-computer interface is natural. New users find it intuitive and easy to interact with their data.

Animation

The animate button and animate speed slider enable the user to scan over the current statistic. Depressing the animate button causes SeeSoft to sequentially activate and deactivate a continuous range of slider values. The animation speed is controlled by the slider. Animation is useful for scanning across large numbers of statistic values in search of interesting patterns. This technique is particularly helpful when the current statistic is related to time, as are code changes. The animation visually displays the time sequence of code changes, showing a movie of file activity as lines were added and deleted.

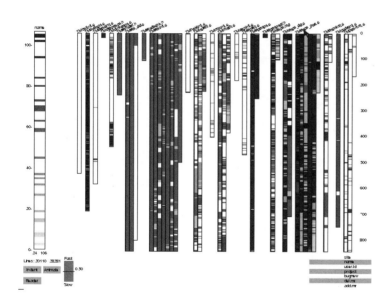

Figure 4. Programmers Who Touched One File. *This display shows programmers who have worked on the code in this directory. There have been 106 different programmers making changes and 24 touched the file file20.c. Any other rows touched by these programmers are also active.*

This section describes how SeeSoft might be used in a software engineering environment. For new programmers or programmers unfamiliar with a particular code directory, Figures 1 and 2 provide a high-level bird's eye view of the code. Programmers can easily identify the large files, C control structures,

Code Analysis Using SeeSoft

frequently changed code, and stable code. Using the code browser windows in Figure 3, programmers can see the actual code, declarations, variable assignments, and so on. This view is particularly important for new programmers undergoing training. When a programmer finds the lines that she thinks need to be changed, she can brush the mouse on the rows and look at the associated change abstracts to ensure that she is correct. By switching the displayed statistic to the programmer name or user.id, she can call or send email to the developer who originally wrote that code. In large software systems there is often duplicated code. By deactivating all lines and reactivating the lines of interest, she can look at the other lines touched by the same set of changes to find related code. By switching the current statistic to bugnew, she can check if there have been many bug fixes in the area. Switching to user.id will show how many other people had touched the code. Code touched by many people or code added to fix bugs may be more subtle than feature code and thus can serve as a warning flag for extra caution. Finally, after her changes are complete she can print out SeeSoft pictures showing the new code for her manager.

Project managers can use SeeSoft displays similar to Figure 3 to track current work. Using program differences it is impossible to follow source code changes, there are too many of them. Highlighting recent changes, changes related to individual projects, or changes by particular team members shows ongoing work. If the project manager discovers activity in files unrelated to the current feature, he or she can investigate further to figure out if there is a flaw in the feature design.

Certain files are harder to change than others. These files are often large, full of bugs, frequently changed, or changed by many people. SeeSoft can help managers identify these files by making displays showing how many different developers have touched each file, number of bug fixes, and the stability of the code. Managers can then assign their best people to work on difficult files. Since SeeSoft can identify how frequently files are changed, it can help managers balance workloads across their staff.

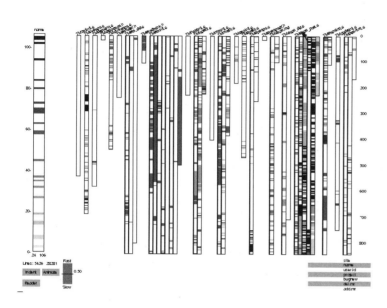

Figure 5. Code Fixing Bugs. *This figure is the same as Figure 4 except only rows added to fix bugs are shown. By blinking on and off the conditional variable, bugnew (impossible to do in a static medium such as this paper) it is possible to visually compare the bug fixes with the new features.*

One feature in SeeSoft (not shown) allows users to display multiple related statistics in split column mode. Each of the columns is split down the middle and the statistics are displayed side-by-side. One application of split column mode is to display adding and deleting changes with color indicating the change date. For files undergoing churn, many of the lines will be deleted soon after they are added. Another application of split column mode is to study "fix-on-fix" rates. A fix-on-fix occurs when code added to fix a bug causes other problems and has to be changed again. Both high levels of code churn and fix-on-fixes are indications to management of coding problems that need to be addressed.

In large projects analysts study the code to determine sections that need to be rewritten or reorganized because they are too complex, changed too many times, or have too many bugs. SeeSoft displays can be invaluable in identifying sections of code needing to be reworked. For example, Figure 4 shows that none of the changes to code in file20.c touched file1.c, or file10.c. This follows since the mouse is on file20.c which activates all changes touching file20.c and no lines in the two mentioned files are active. The set of changes touching the lines in file1.c also touched all lines in file2.c and file6 and almost all lines in file7.c, file9.c, file11.c, file13.c, file16.c because many of the lines in these files are active. Using SeeSoft it is obvious (particularly on a color computer monitor) that code in this directory was done in phases: the early code, a large development in 1988, and recent changes. The different phases are split over sets of files. Figure 6 shows the early code written before 1988. This code has been stable since the deactivated newer code is in different files. If this directory ever became too big, the code written in different eras would be candidates for separation.

Figure 6. Older Stable Code. This figure shows code written early in the development cycle. This code is concentrated in particular files.

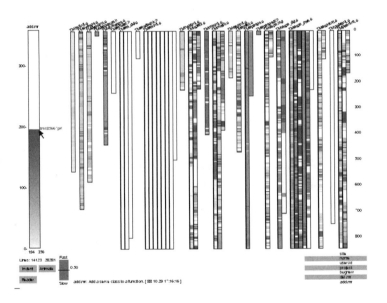

Performance analysts can use SeeSoft to identify "hot spots" in the code and testers can ensure that their test suites have sufficient code coverage. Eick and Steffen [Eick 92b] apply SeeSoft to the problem of analyzing line count profile execution data. Frequently executed blocks of code, hot spots, are shown in red and unexecuted code is shown in gray.

The current version of SeeSoft[3] is a 4,500 line C++ program running UNIX using the X11 and Motif widget set and on Silicon Graphics Iris workstations using the GL graphics library, and under MS Windows. The portability between UNIX and MS Windows is based on the *Vz* cross-platform library. Vz is a C++ class library emboding multiple views, tight linking between the views, and direct manipulation. SeeSoft's graphics and mouse manipulations are performed using color map animation [Foley 90] and do not need the high-performance graphics capability of workstations.

The reduced representation SeeSoft uses to display code was first introduced by Eick, Sumner, and Steffen [Eick 92c] to study the change history of code, applied to visualize hot-spots in program execution [Eick 92b], used to analyze complex log files [Eick 94b], and generalized to visualize arbitrary text [Eick 94a]. This representation has been widely copied and is used in Brown University's PLUM system [Reiss 94b], IBM's program visualization product [Kimelman 94], and DEC's FUSE product [Zaremba 95].

On a high-resolution (1280x1024) monitor it is possible to clearly display 50,000 lines of code but we have displayed 100,000 lines. Eventually the columns become too thin to perceive the lines. Although 50,000 lines is a lot of code, it is still only a small fraction of a multi-million line system. To display even more code, Baker and Eick [Baker 95a] use hierarchical space-filling techniques for displaying code that is subdivided into directories, subdirectories, and files and animate their displays to show the historical evolution of a large production software system. Their technique provides an overview of the complete system by aggregating, but loses the details for the individual lines.

Ball and Eick [Ball 96] generalize the reduced representation used by SeeSoft in three ways. Their *pixel* representation increases the information density by a factor of ten over SeeSoft by encoding each line with one (or more) pixels on the display shown in columns. They also introduce *block* and *summary* representations for showing and comparing statistics across a large number files.

This paper describes a new graphical technique and software system SeeSoft for analyzing statistics associated with lines in computer source code. The SeeSoft system implements the technique and applies interactive graphics methods to

---

[3]Written by Thomas Ball.

manipulate the display. The technique involves displaying files as rectangles and the code in the files as colored rows inside the rectangles. The method has been applied to analyze a large body of source code from a real-time telephone switch.

Traditionally statistical scientists have borrowed many techniques from computer scientists. This paper describes an example where statistical methods have direct application to solving difficult problems in software engineering. Software Visualization applies graphical methods to the problem of understanding software and, as this example shows, the results can be dramatic.

Future work involves extending the visualization technique used in SeeSoft to showing files within subsystems instead of lines within files. Visualizing lines within files is the right abstraction for programmers making changes. But for some software engineering problems, better abstractions involve files within modules and modules within subsystems. Similar display techniques may apply with the rows inside the rectangles representing characteristics of files and the rectangles representing software modules.

The display paradigm showing lines within files has wide applicability to other textual databases besides computer code. The technique applies to any text corpus or ordered database where there are statistics associated with each line or entity. Other applications include indexed text such as legal writings, software documentation, and transaction databases. For example, the books in a large library could be displayed on a SeeSoft screen. Each book might be represented by a row, the location of the row in the columns might correspond to the book's physical location on the shelves, the length of each row could be proportional to the number of pages in each book, and the color of each row to the number of times the book has been checked out.

Acknowledgments

I would like to gratefully acknowledge helpful conversations with David Atkins, Thomas J. Ball, and Graham J. Wills, and a careful proofreading by Mary L. Zajac. In particular, Eric E. Sumner and Joseph L. Steffen collaborated on the original version of SeeSoft.

Visualizing Object-Oriented Software Execution

**Wim De Pauw,
Doug Kimelman
and
John Vlissides**

Understanding the structure and internal relationships of large class libraries, frameworks, or applications is essential for fulfilling the promise of object technology. Moreover, discerning global and local patterns of interaction among classes is critical for tuning and debugging. Although the object-oriented paradigm lets programmers work at higher levels of abstraction than procedural approaches, the tasks of understanding, debugging, and tuning large systems remain difficult.

This difficulty has numerous causes. There is a dichotomy between the code structure (static hierarchies of classes) and the execution structure (dynamic networks of communicating objects) of object-oriented programs. The programmer must understand and map between these structures, a significant burden even after the programmer is familiar with them. Further, functionality tends to be dispersed across multiple classes, making it hard to see and predict the system's overall behavior. And the sheer number of classes and complexity of relationships in applications and frameworks makes these problems all the more acute.

Much is known about how to characterize programs statically. Contemporary programming languages and design formalisms embody countless lessons learned

Introduction

over nearly a half century of modern computing. On the other hand, much less is known about characterizing and manipulating the *dynamic* aspects of a program. Yet a program's dynamic aspects are just as important to its design, implementation, and refinement as its static specification. This is especially true of object-oriented programs, where the gulf between static specification and run-time behavior is particularly wide. Insight into the dynamic aspects is critical for understanding, tuning, and debugging object-oriented software.

We believe that tools that focus on dynamic behavior are essential to fulfilling the promise of the object-oriented paradigm. We also believe that visual tools are most effective for this purpose. Users are easily overwhelmed by a steady stream of text. The fields of scientific visualization and program visualization have demonstrated repeatedly that the most effective way to present large volumes of data to users is in a continuous visual fashion [Upson 89, Nielson 90, Kimelman 91, Jerding 95]. Animated visual displays let users assimilate information rapidly and help them identify trends and anomalies.

Previous attempts at visualizing object-oriented systems have depicted objects communicating using a variety of graphical notations. The trouble with this approach is that it does not scale. All but the simplest programs employ many hundreds or thousands of objects; and the more objects there are, the greater the need for visualization. But presenting such volumes of objects, even graphically, quickly overwhelms the user. More powerful visualizations are required.

This paper introduces a set of novel visualizations for displaying execution behavior of object-oriented programs. Our approach leverages object-oriented concepts to handle programs of realistic size and complexity. We organize visual information in terms of classes, objects, methods, messages, and relationships between them. The visualizations structure execution information into different levels of detail and let users navigate through the levels. Users can deal effectively with the large volume of execution information that even a simple program can generate. The set of views includes displays that cluster classes or objects according to the degree to which they interact, histogram variants showing class instances and their activity levels, and cross-reference matrices indicating the degree of various forms of inter- and intra-class references. A detailed description of the visualization environment's design appears elsewhere [De Pauw 93].

During the development process, a programmer turns to visualization either for general inspection to verify that a program is running smoothly or to track down the cause of a specific problem. Typically, the programmer examines high-level views first to get an overview of system behavior; then more specific views are used to focus on suspicious behavior.

This section presents actual experience with visualization in the development of QOCA, a constraint-solving toolkit [Helm 92]. We begin by examining a high-level view that shows overall patterns of communication.

Visualizing Communication

The **inter-class call cluster** provides a dynamic overview of communication patterns between classes. Figure 1 shows a snapshot of this view early in the execution of QOCA. This view shows class names as floating labels. The amount of communication between instances of two classes determines the distance between their labels.

The view is animated such that the more communication there is between classes, the more their labels gravitate towards each other and cluster together. Classes that communicate infrequently are repelled towards the edge of the view. The floating labels are colored according to the number of messages that the corresponding class received, from few (dark violet) to many (red). For QOCA, the classes Term, Terms, Factors, BaseNode, and BaseList (which are concerned with representing and manipulating constraints) clearly show strong interaction with each other.

This view also indicates the current call stack. It shows the classes of the instances that have received the messages currently on the call stack. A blue path leads from the label `main` through each of these classes, in call stack order. The last segment of the path, leading to the currently active class, is red. In Figure 1 the thread of control goes from `main`, through Objective, CompoundExpRep, Terms, Term, Factors, and finally to the currently active class FactorsIterator.

A Visualization Case Study

Figure 1: Inter-class call cluster

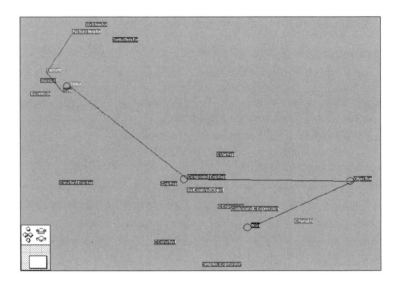

The inter-class call cluster focuses attention on the most active and most cooperative classes at any moment. These classes provide a good starting point for more detailed study either for optimization or understanding the structure of an application — clustered classes, for example, are likely to be tightly coupled or from the same subsystem [Wirfs-Brock 90]. The number of classes in a cluster is typically small, on the order of ten classes or fewer, probably because systems with broader interactions are exponentially more complex and are less likely to be developed in the first place.

Object-oriented programs often exhibit distinct execution phases. Most programs have at least one initialization phase as a precursor to a (much longer) communication phase; programs may have several such phases. Different phases become evident from the dynamics of the inter-class call cluster. The start of a new phase is often marked by many new classes bursting out of the center of the view. Some classes gravitate together quickly; others migrate to the edges of the view. The call stack path also reflects a new phase when its shape changes drastically after a period of relative stability. An execution hot-spot often manifests itself as a cluster of red class labels. The red (i.e., active) portion of the call stack path tends to dart between such classes. These are prime candidates for optimization. Paying particular attention to small but popular classes can be more effective than redesigning complex but infrequently used classes. In this example, the classes Term, Terms, BaseList, BaseNode, ListIterator, and FactorsIterator are good prospects for performance tuning.

Not all hot spots are revealed in this way, however, because there isn't necessarily a strong correlation between the number of calls and CPU usage. Some messages may invoke expensive methods, while others invoke cheap ones. The **time bar chart** offers another way to find hot spots in a program. It shows the cumulative CPU time spent per class (Figure 2). The time bar chart verifies that Term, Terms, BaseList, ListIterator, FactorsIterator are compute-intensive classes, whereas BaseNode apparently isn't. It also exposes the Factor class as a potential hot spot.

Figure 2: Time bar chart

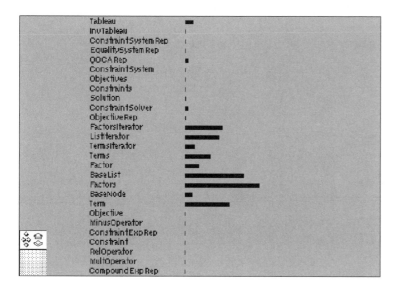

A Closer Look at Communication

While the inter-class call cluster offers insight into the dynamic messaging behavior of the program, the **inter-class call matrix** (Figure 3) gives cumulative and more quantitative information. Classes appear on the axes in the order in which they are instantiated. A colored square in this visualization represents the number of calls from a class on the vertical axis to a class on the horizontal axis. The color key along the bottom indicates relative number of calls. Colors range from dark violet, denoting fewer calls, to red, denoting more calls.

*Figure 3: Inter-class call matrix. *See Plate 7**

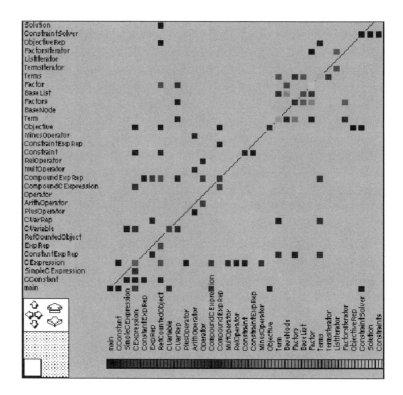

The red squares in this view confirm our impression from the inter-class call cluster that Term, Terms, BaseList, BaseNode, ListIterator, and FactorsIterator are called most frequently. As we've mentioned, it often pays to take a closer look at classes showing high activity. Such classes are often the key to understanding larger parts of the system and to optimizing its performance.

Moreover, unexpectedly high activity can be symptomatic of bugs in the program.

Many inter-class dependencies can appear as macroscopic features in the inter-class call matrix. Vertical stripes indicate classes that are called by many other classes; these tend to be key abstract classes in the framework or library. Horizontal stripes indicate a class that calls many other classes, typically the classes of its instance variables. Clusters close to the diagonal may indicate tightly coupled classes or subsystems. The appendix discusses this visualization in more detail.

The inter-class call matrix also supports a "zooming" capability that lets a user navigate to more detailed information on demand. When a user clicks on the square for a class *A* on the left and a class *B* at the bottom, another view appears: the **inter-function call matrix**. This subview displays the number of calls from each method of *A* (on the left) to each method of *B* (on the bottom).

Figure 4 shows the subview produced by clicking on the (Terms, Term) square in Figure 3. The subview shows the communication between Terms methods (on the left) and Term methods (at the bottom). The prominent blue square in the lower right of Figure 4 indicates that the most frequent communication between Term and Terms is the call from `Terms::Add` to `Term::SameVarsAs`.

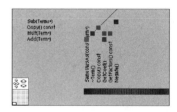

Figure 4: Inter-function call matrix subview for calls from Terms to Term

An important feature of our visualization system is its support for inspecting a phenomenon from multiple perspectives. For example, the inter-class call cluster and matrix views display essentially the same information; however, the cluster view conveys more of the dynamism of object communication, whereas the matrix view's stability makes detailed comparisons easier. By presenting the same information in more than one way, we exploit our various cognitive aptitudes more effectively.

Insight from Instances

The preceding visualizations emphasize the display of relationships between *classes*. Focusing on *instances* can reveal program dynamics at finer levels of granularity.

Figure 5: Histogram of instances

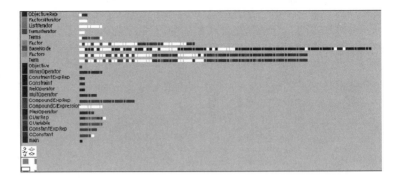

The **histogram of instances** (Figure 5) displays all instances of each class. Rows of small colored squares form the bars of the histogram. Each bar represents all instances of the class whose label appears to its left. Again, a square's color indicates the number of messages an instance has received. Colored squares appear and disappear as objects are instantiated and destroyed. White squares indicate objects that have been destroyed; these squares will be reused by newly created instances. This visualization lets us see how many instances exist at a given time and their level of messaging activity. It also shows relative object lifetimes and can reveal anomalies such as undesired copy constructor calls in C++, which show up as extremely short-lived objects.

Like the inter-class call matrix, the histogram of instances can also furnish more detail through navigation [De Pauw 94]. The user can click on squares to see more information about the corresponding instances and how they relate to each other. The user has a choice of viewing this information textually or graphically. For example, clicking on a particular instance *a* of class *A* can produce a textual subview (shown in Figure 6) that displays three sets of information:

• The messages that this instance received, from whom, and how many.
• The messages that this instance sent, to whom, and how many.
• The creator of this instance.

Alternatively, the user may want to see graphically how an object relates to the objects that it calls, the objects that call it, the object that created it, or the objects it creates. In this case, the histogram of instances can display any of

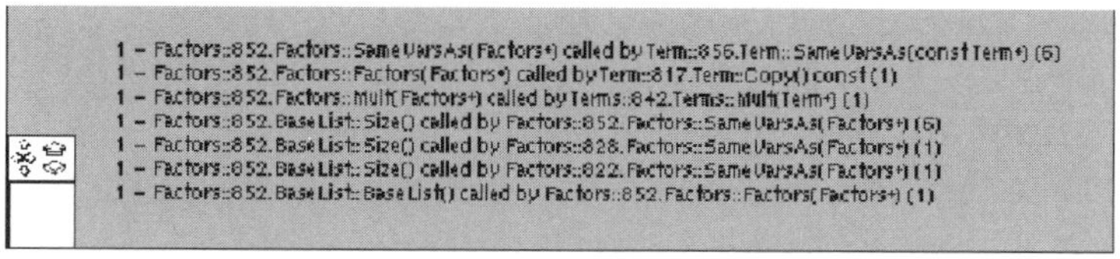

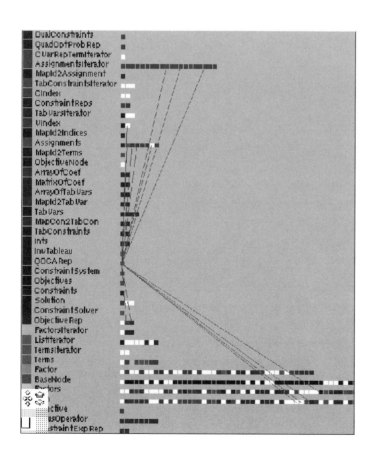

Figure 6: Textual subview with communication history of an object

these relationships by drawing lines between the relevant squares. Figure 7 shows the lines that indicate the objects that a QOCARep object allocated.

Figure 7: Red lines showing objects allocated by QOCARep object

Consider again the classes Term, Factors, and BaseNode. Previous views showed high activity for these classes. The instance histogram shows that these classes have unexpectedly large numbers of instances. Further, by watching the animation of this view as execution of the application progresses, we see that most of these instances are active for a brief period after they are created, but then remain inactive for the rest of the run. This is all indicative of a possible memory leak. Indeed, if we waited until the end of the application, we'd see that most instances of these classes are never reclaimed.

Pinpointing the Problem

To correct this memory leak, a first step might be to find the classes responsible for allocating these unreclaimed instances.

Figure 8: Allocation matrix

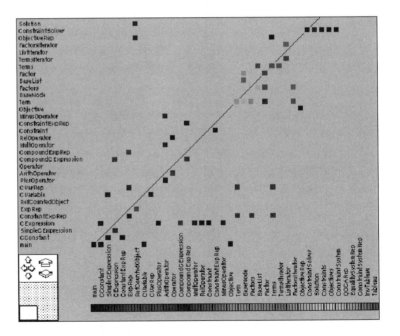

As we've seen, the histogram of instances lets us examine the allocation of instances by clicking on each one. A broader view of allocation patterns is given by the **allocation matrix** (Figure 8). It plots the classes that allocate new objects versus the classes they instantiate. This view shows allocation dependencies and the most frequently allocated objects at the class level. We can use this information to pinpoint the sources of allocations and subsequently reduce the application's storage and construction costs.

In this case it appears that Term is allocating most instances of Term and Factors. However, it is not necessarily the case that Term is responsible for deleting these instances. In fact, allocated objects are commonly passed to instances of client classes, and that the clients are responsible for deleting the allocated objects after making use of them.

To identify suspect clients, we glance back at the inter-class call matrix (Figure 3). We see that two classes send messages to Term most frequently: Term itself and Terms. Clicking on the square that represents the calls from Terms to Term pops up a more detailed matrix view (Figure 4). This "zoomed-in" view shows which member functions of the calling class (Terms) are invoking which functions of the called class (Term); calling functions are arranged along the vertical axis, and called functions are arranged along the horizontal axis. We see that `Terms::Mult()` makes heavy use of a number of functions of Term, *including* its destructor `Term::~Term()`. In contrast, `Terms::Add()` also makes heavy use of functions of Term, but makes no use of `Term::~Term()`. This suggests that `Terms::Add()` may be the culprit.

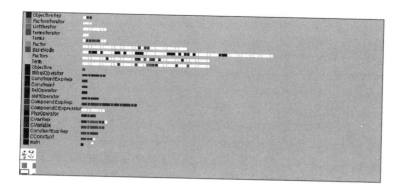

Figure 9: Histogram of instances (corrected code)

Inspecting the code we find that instances of Term are passed from Term to `Terms::Add()`, which never deletes them, but clearly should. Correcting this bug by adding a missing "delete" statement leads to the healthier histogram of instances in Figure 9, shown at the same point in the program's execution.

This section catalogs several of the views we have developed. We give an example of each view along with its name, a description of its purpose, its main graphical elements, and a discussion of how we interpret it both statically and dynamically. We also describe each view's support for navigation and its relationship to other views.

Allocation Matrix

See Figure 8.

Purpose

Reveals which classes instantiate other classes.

Elements

Classes appear along the left and bottom edges. Each square in the matrix denotes the number of instances of a class on the bottom that are allocated by a class on the left. A square's color reflects how many instances have been allocated. The color key at the bottom indicates the mapping of number of instances to color, from few (dark violet) to many (red). The color reflects the total number of instances created over the entire execution; the squares do not revert to dark violet when instances are destroyed. Therefore a square might be red even when the current number of instances is small.

Interpretation

• **Static:** The view shows the relative number of allocations among classes.
• **Dynamic:** Color changes indicate the time at which classes allocate instances and the rate of allocation.

Navigation

Clicking on one of the squares produces a more detailed view, as shown in Figure 10.

On the left are the methods of the class doing the allocation; at the bottom are one or more constructors of the class being instantiated. Each square in the matrix represents invocations of a constructor at the bottom by a method on the

Visualization Catalog

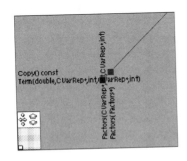

Figure 10.

left. The square's color represents the number of invocations, from few (dark violet) to many (red).

Related Visualizations

Patterns in the allocation views are related to call patterns in the inter-class call matrix, because normally a class will communicate with classes it instantiates.

Histogram of Instances
See Figure 5.

Purpose

Shows instances grouped by class and indicates their levels of activity. It can also indicate allocation and communication relationships among them.

Elements

Classes are arranged along the left edge. They appear when they are first instantiated. Each square in the view denotes an instance of the class to the left. A square's color reflects how many calls have occurred on the instance. The color key at the bottom indicates the mapping of number of calls to color, from few (dark violet) to many (red). A white square represents an instance that has been deleted. Thus the user can see all destroyed objects and use them for navigation. Alternatively, the user can choose to reuse white squares for new instances, thereby producing a more compact view.

Interpretation

• **Static**: Classes with similar or identical bars suggest close coupling or containment. Unexpectedly large numbers of instances may suggest a memory leak.

• **Dynamic:** Instances from different classes appearing and disappearing in unison are another indication of close coupling or containment. Bars that grow rapidly can reflect object creation in tight loops. Squares flashing rapidly between dark violet and white indicate short-lived objects, which might reveal an opportunity for optimization (e.g., stack versus heap allocation) or a bug (e.g., unintended copy constructor calls).

Navigation

The user may choose to see any of the following by clicking on a square:

- A line from the selected object to its creator.
- Lines from the selected object to the objects it created.
- Lines from the selected object to the objects it has called.
- Lines from the selected object to the objects that have called it.

For example, the view in Figure 7 shows an object connected by red lines to the objects it created. Clicking on a class name produces lines connecting all instances of the class to their respective creators, createes, callers, or callees, depending on the user's choice.

The user may also choose a textual view showing the communication history of a selected class or object as in Figure 6.

Inter-Class Call Cluster
See Figure 1.

Purpose

Provides a dynamic overview of the degree to which objects interact.

Elements

Classes appear as floating labels. The more two classes communicate, the closer they will appear; classes that do not communicate repel each other. Classes having an instance with a method on the call stack are connected by blue lines. A red line leads to the class with the currently active method. The color of a class label reflects the number of calls that have been received by this class, from few (dark violet) to many (red).

Interpretation

- **Static:** Clustered classes are likely to be tightly coupled and/or are part of the same subsystem. Hot-spots are indicated by red colored classes.
- **Dynamic:** Concentrated activity of the red line for long periods between elements of a cluster suggests an execution hot-spot. Any of the following phenomena may indicate a new phase in the program's execution: (1) many new classes bursting out of the center and coalescing into clusters; (2) a drastic change in the shape of the call stack path; and (3) major shifts in the positions of class labels.

Related Visualizations

The inter-class call matrix provides a cumulative record of communication patterns.

Inter-Class Call Matrix
See Figure 3.

Purpose

Provides a cumulative overview of communication summarized by class.

Elements

Classes are arranged along the left and bottom edges. The classes appear as they are first instantiated. Each square in the view denotes the number of method calls on the class on the bottom by methods of the class on the left. A square's color reflects how many calls have occurred. The color key at the bottom indicates the mapping of number of calls to color, from few (dark violets) to many (reds).

Interpretation

• **Static:** Vertical bands may reveal a base class that is heavily used, either through inherited code or by explicit calls from subclasses. Horizontal bands suggest classes that drive or contain instances of many others. Squares on the diagonal indicate calls to self. Clusters near the diagonal are a sign of classes that are instantiated together and are designed to work together. Red areas may indicate closely coupled classes.
• **Dynamic:** Many new classes appearing along the edge of the view may indicate a new execution phase. Noticeable color changes draw attention to classes that interact heavily.

Navigation

Clicking on a square produces a more detailed view of the communication between the two corresponding classes as shown in Figure 4.

On the left are the calling methods, and the methods they call are at the bottom. Each square in the matrix reflects the total number of method calls for the caller-callee pair. The square's color indicates the number of invocations from, few (dark violet) to many (red).

Related Visualizations

The inter-class call cluster reveals more of the dynamics of inter-class communication.

Time Bar Chart

See Figure 2.

Purpose

Shows CPU time usage per class.

Elements

Classes appear along the left edge as they are first instantiated. The length of the bar to the right of the class label is proportional to the amount of CPU time spent in the methods of the class.

Interpretation

• **Static:** Longer bars indicate computation-intensive classes.
• **Dynamic:** Bars that grow at the same rate may indicate closely coupled classes.

Navigation

Clicking on a class name will produce a new view showing the CPU time usage for each method in the class as shown in Figure 11.

The methods of the class appear on the left. To the right of each method label is a bar whose length is proportional to the CPU time spent in the method. The sum of the lengths of the bars in this view is equal to the length of the original bar.

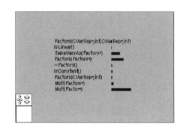

Figure 11.

Related Work

The notion of program visualization first appeared in the literature over a decade ago [Herot 82], and algorithm animation was popularized shortly thereafter [Brown 84b]. Work on visualizing the dynamics of program execution has flourished in the area of parallel systems [Kimelman 91, Heath 91], where the need is clear for a means of understanding the interactions among elements of a complex system.

More recently, the importance of program visualization for object-oriented systems has been recognized.

For purposes of debugging, Bocker and Herczeg [Böcker 90] introduce a "software oscilloscope" for visually tracking the detailed interactions between objects in a system. To inspect a program's dynamic behavior during execution, they introduce obstacles between objects and animate the flow of messages across these obstacles. At any point, execution can be suspended to inspect context with conventional browsers. However, focus is solely on debugging and microscopic program behavior. No consideration is given to higher-level program structure or more global behavior over time.

West [West 93] describes another system focused on microscopic behavior of object-oriented programs. Object hierarchies are animated, with objects appearing in a view as they are created and disappearing as they are destroyed. Object interactions are shown with dynamic arrows and message labels. An interesting aspect of this work is the set of strategies for laying out object hierarchies: "first-reference"—where an object is shown as a child of the object that first held a reference to it; "creation"—where an object is shown as a child of the object that created it; and "class-ordered"—where objects are simply grouped into columns according to class. To combat problems of scale, elaborate filtering mechanisms had to be introduced. The focus in filtering is on *exclusion*, under the assumption that it is more natural for a user to gradually remove irrelevant activity than to have to state initially what is to be displayed.

Wilde and Huitt [Wilde 92] suggest that a major barrier to maintaining object-oriented software is difficulty in program analysis and understanding, and they recommend that visual tools be developed to aid in these activities. In particular, the recommendations include tools based on dependency analysis, graphs, and clustering methodologies, which might help address the problems of comprehending high-level system structure, dynamic binding, and dispersed program structure, among others.

Davis and Morgan [Davis 93] introduce one formulation of a graph showing invocations between methods. Their primary interest is in revealing behavior reuse. Reuse of behaviors manifests itself as imbalance in the graph, with a preponderance of edges leading down and to the left. Low-level or basic behaviors drift to the bottom of the graph, and high-level or application behaviors rise to the top. While this view provides an excellent indication of reuse, it would be difficult to gain much understanding of overall system behavior or class-level interaction from its use in isolation.

Kleyn and Gingrich [Kleyn 88] address the need for understanding object behavior in order to facilitate code sharing and reusability. A tool is presented for concurrently animating a number of different graph-based views of the dynamic behavior of an object-oriented program. Structural views include excerpts of the inheritance and containment hierarchies. Behavioral views include graphs of invocations between methods as well as invocations between objects and invocations between methods associated with objects. However, animation is achieved solely by highlighting nodes on fixed graphs. The graphs themselves are not dynamic in that their form never evolves. Further, no consideration is given to presenting other aspects of run-time behavior, such as object allocation activity and object lifetime.

Conclusion

We have introduced novel views of the behavior of object-oriented systems. Our visualizations have already proved effective in our day-to-day work for understanding large, complex object-oriented systems and for debugging and tuning them.

A program's dynamic aspects are just as important to its development as its static specification. Object-oriented concepts like classes, instances, messages, and methods offer a sound basis not just for static modeling but for dynamic modeling as well. In a sense these concepts are *more* important to dynamic modeling, because they offer a way of managing the vast amount of information that can characterize even a simple program's execution.

We are continuing to define a comprehensive set of views dealing with a broad range of aspects of object-oriented system behavior. We are also expanding the set of object-oriented languages with which this system can be used. Moreover, we are investigating architectural support for navigation between views, exploration and elision of details within views, and new tools that will enable users to explore the internal state and structure of executing applications. We believe that visualization of object-oriented systems will be an effective and complementary addition to existing development tools. The views we have presented lay a foundation for these visualizations.

Acknowledgments

Richard Helm contributed to the design and implementation of several of the visualizations in this chapter.

Visualization for Parallel Performance Evaluation and Optimization

**Michael T. Heath,
Allen D. Malony
and
Diane T. Rover**

Introduction

The primary motivation for using parallel computer systems is their high performance potential, but that potential is often notoriously difficult to achieve in practice. Thus, users are often faced with the formidable task of analyzing and tuning the performance of parallel programs. Parallel systems can be instrumented to provide ample feedback on program behavior, but the volume and complexity of the resulting performance data often make it extremely difficult for users to interpret them properly to gain insight into program behavior and performance. To help reason about and understand parallel performance data, visualization has been recognized as an important and needed component in the development and application of parallel performance evaluation tools [Messina 93]. Many tools for parallel performance analysis have incorporated visualization techniques in a variety of ways (see [JPDC 93] for an overview of the field). The positive results from this work indicate that the visualization of performance data can offer helpful insights into the behavior of parallel systems..

Despite the opportunity for improving parallel performance evaluation, the technology of performance visualization (visual techniques and methods for applying them) has remained specialized and ad hoc. This is partly due to the fact that the design and use of parallel systems has continued to evolve, and parallel performance analysis tools are still mostly experimental. However, it is also true that the interpretation of performance data often involves artificial and abstract models of parallel computation that may have little or no direct meaning to the user and may be difficult to relate to application-level concepts represented by the user's program.

The challenge for performance visualization lies in visually representing the mental models users apply in attempting to understand performance information. Hamming's maxim "The purpose of computing is insight, not numbers" implies that understanding (insight) is accomplished only by representing numeric values (analytically or symbolically) in meaningful relations to the phenomena that the data represent. But what if the phenomenon represented reflects the nature of the computation itself?

As Miller [Miller 93] remarks, physical scientists have the benefit of physical reality to guide the design of, and provide a context for, visual representations that appeal to the viewer's intuition of how physical phenomena behave. The creations of computer scientists, on the other hand, are often artificial, involving several layers of abstraction in mapping problem domains onto software and hardware computation models. This is even more pronounced when considering parallel problem abstractions and parallel models of computation, especially when the nuances of how those models are implemented and are executed lie at the heart of the evaluation problem.

Although parallel performance data can characterize well-defined operational behavior of parallel execution (e.g., the time to send a message or the number of active processors), relating performance information back to the abstractions that the user understands is a challenge, particularly when a performance view that appeals to one person's mental model may have little in common with models held by others [Miller 93].

Herein lies the performance visualization conundrum: how can meaningful visual representations of performance data be created when the insight gained into parallel performance phenomena depends on the parallel computation abstractions that served to produce the performance data in the first place? The solution is that the visualization techniques and methods used to construct graphic displays of the data must be closely integrated with the models of parallel computation the data represent.

Despite the fundamental challenges in parallel performance visualization — the complex data sets, the artificial aspects of parallel computation, the need for integrated analysis and visual models for effective data insight, and the dependence on the user's mental perspective for data understanding — important concepts for visualization design and use have begun to emerge. In addition, performance visualization technology has now been through several generations of implementations.

In this paper, we discuss the visual display of parallel performance data from several perspectives.[1] First, we develop a high-level, abstract model for the performance visualization process and an underlying theory for applying visualization principles. Next, we provide a retrospective on the history of parallel performance visualization technology, focusing on those areas of technology development that have been most important in defining the role of visualization today. Last, we discuss the concepts and principles that have been important for effective performance visualization practice. Following these three perspectives, we present a few parallel performance scenarios using existing visualization tools that demonstrate some of the techniques and concepts.

In their paper "Analyzing Parallel Program Execution Using MultipleViews" [LeBlanc 90], LeBlanc, Mellor-Crummey, and Fowler emphasize the need to develop a general, unified approach to parallel program analysis that supports the creation and integration of multiple views of an execution and allows the user to tailor the visual display to specific analysis. Miller [Miller 93] also states a fundamental performance visualization requirement of integrating models of parallel system execution and performance with pictures designed to illustrate them effectively. If we are to focus on those visual display techniques that aid in revealing the meaning of parallel performance data to the user, we should regard the techniques as part of a parallel performance visualization process or methodology that includes performance analysis as a major constituent.

---

[1] This paper is derived, in part, from two the papers found in [Heath 95a] [Heath 95b].

A Parallel Performance Visualization Model

A proposed high-level model of parallel performance visualization highlights the architectural relationship between performance data analysis and performance display, emphasizing the different aspects of visualization development. The model, depicted in Figure 1, emphasizes the binding of performance analysis abstractions to performance visual abstractions. It is based on the following notions:

* *Performance analysis abstraction*: a specification of the performance characteristics to be observed from the data, the performance analysis to be performed, and the semantic attributes of the performance results.

* *Performance view*: a representation of a performance analysis abstraction in a form that allows its attributes to be mapped to a performance display.

Figure 1.

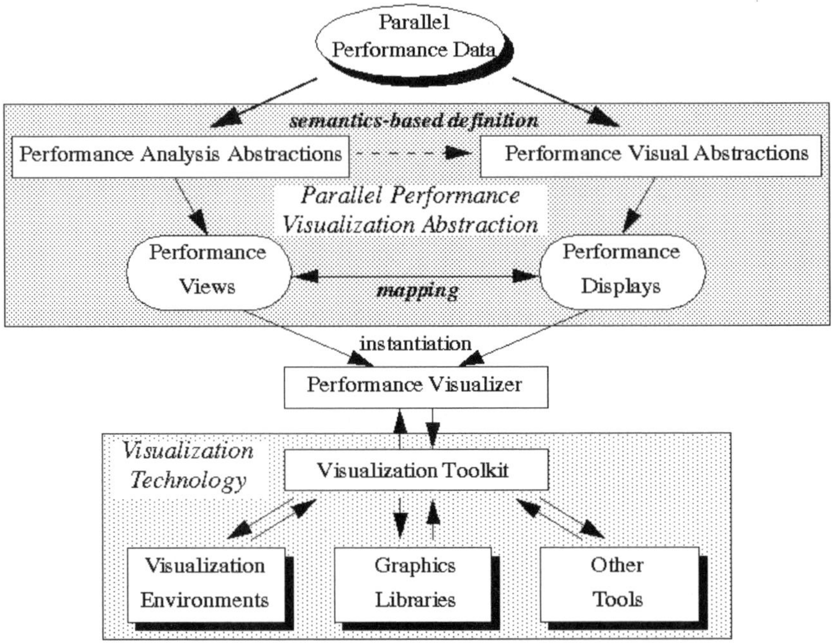

* *Performance visual abstraction*: a specification of the desired visual form of the abstracted performance data, unconstrained by the limitations of any particular graphics environment.

* *Performance display*: a representation of a performance visual abstraction in a form that identifies the visual properties to which the attributes of a performance view are mapped.

* *Performance visualization abstraction*: the mapping of a performance view to a performance display.

A key point in the model is that the performance visual design can and should incorporate knowledge of the performance analysis abstraction very early on, providing the basis for performance interpretation in the final visualization. The binding between performance analysis and visual abstractions is a mapping from the outputs of performance views to the inputs of performance displays. This performance visualization abstraction embodies the relationships between performance data and visual display that are important in revealing the performance meaning in the visualization.

To be useful, and to evaluate its effectiveness, a performance visualization abstraction must be instantiated in a performance visualizer tool that implements performance views, displays, and their mappings using environment-specific graphics technology, based on underlying graphics libraries, toolkits, and other resources. In the following retrospective on visualization technology, we can see how the abstract model evolved in tool implementations, and how it provides a framework for understanding visualization concepts and display techniques as applied in performance evaluation scenarios.

The development of parallel performance visualization technology has faced numerous challenging problems. Much of the early work dealt with the development of specific performance displays derived mostly from statistical graphics and adapted to represent performance data; Kiviat diagrams [Kolence 73] and Gantt charts [Gantt 19] are good examples. The importance of views of dynamic performance data and of the relations between events across multiple processors motivated the use of displays based on activity network and PERT chart concepts (e.g., the SCHEDULE displays [Dongarra 87]), or a generalization of the Gantt chart where time is associated with the horizontal axis (e.g., the Moviola displays [LeBlanc 90]). However, multiple performance displays were not generally available or well integrated in a single parallel performance tool.

Performance Visualization: A Retrospective History

The work of LeBlanc et al. on multiple views [LeBlanc 90] and Couch on graphical performance representations [Couch 88] began to define a theory of performance visualization, setting the tone for research on performance visualization environments that offered an integrated set of performance analysis and display techniques. Perhaps the most successful of these tools in terms of popular acceptance was ParaGraph [Heath 91], although many other tools also deserve recognition for contributing to the promotion of visualization as an important component of the performance evaluation process.

From an implementation standpoint, however, the integration and support for multiple views and displays, as implied by the nascent theory, represented a software engineering challenge. Initially, tool developers statically linked analyses to displays. As a result, tools tended to restrict the number and type of views and displays, and their combination, with little support for customization or extension based on user preferences.

The issue here lies at the heart of the parallel performance visualization problem: how and to what extent the user is involved in the performance visualization process? If a user gains insight into parallel performance behavior by looking at a performance display designed to reveal properties of a performance view, how ubiquitous will this insight be among other users? This issue was addressed directly by developing performance visualization environments that were able to accommodate new analysis and display modules; HyperView [Malony 89] was an early example of such an environment.

The environments also began to support more user interaction in selecting view-display combinations and in specifying view-display attributes. As a result of this work, performance environments not only became extensible, but retargetable to different performance evaluation scenarios. Pablo [Reed 91] took this research one step further by incorporating support for performance environment prototyping, which involves performance analysts directly in the creation of tools specific to their performance evaluation needs.

Because of the difficulties in developing performance displays, many performance visualizations used only simple graphic techniques to construct general-purpose displays with supposedly wide appeal. However, there was some practical evidence that suggested application-specific displays would be more beneficial:

In general, this wide applicability is a virtue, but knowledge of the application often lets you design a special-purpose display that reveals greater detail or insight than generic displays would permit [Heath 91].

This was mainly an issue of incorporating the semantic context of the performance analysis into the visualization. Several approaches, ranging from portraying data parallel program performance [Rover 93] to presenting full task invocation histories of fine-grained applications [Tick 91] successfully used semantic attributes in display design.

However, many application-specific displays were hard-coded by necessity and did not directly involve users in their construction. Furthermore, the visual display technology used in performance environments was not advancing as rapidly as might be expected, particularly in contrast to scientific visualization research. Recently, performance visualization research has shifted its emphasis to the technology required to generate application-specific performance visualizations that involve the user in rapid prototyping of performance displays. The three prime objectives of this recent work are:

- to exploit the perceptual capabilities of sophisticated graphics in the design of performance displays;

- to provide support for high-level performance visual abstractions and their instantiation through visualization languages, graphics libraries, and data visualization environments;

- to involve the user directly in prototyping and customizing performance displays so that meaningful performance visualizations can be readily constructed and evaluated.

There has been a increased awareness of the concepts and principles underlying good data visualization [Keller 93][Tufte 83]. With the progressive history of parallel performance tool development, we see some of these concepts proving useful in practice in the design of effective performance views and displays. Still other concepts, however, have arisen from the unique challenges of interpreting performance data. In this section, we attempt to classify and define the concepts and principles that are found across the range of performance tools cited in the literature [JPDC 93].

Visualization Concepts and Principles

Context

In order to present performance information in a meaningful way, some context must be established to which the user can relate that information:

- *Perspective*: the point of view from which information is presented. Typical perspectives for performance information include the hardware, the operating system, or the application program. A given perspective may emphasize states of processes or processors, or interactions among them, and the information may or may not be amalgamated over space or time.

- *Semantic context*: the relationship between performance information and the constructs and abstractions (e.g., data structures, control structures) in the application program. An example of semantic context is when the selection of a graphical element of an image causes the corresponding portion of the application program to be highlighted. This is demonstrated well in the AIMS system [Yan 93], where selecting a communication line between processors highlights the corresponding send and receive statements in the user program.

- *Subview mapping*: a mapping between a subset of a graphical view (e.g., a rectangular subregion) and the corresponding subset of the data being rendered (e.g., see [Couch 93]). The existence of such a mapping implies that the data can be reconstructed from the image, which would not be the case if the data are reduced in such a way that detail is lost.

Scaling

For scientific visualization in general, the scaling of graphical views as data sets become very large is a major challenge. This is especially true of performance visualization as the number of processors or duration of execution become very large. A number of techniques have been used to deal with the problem of scaling:

- *Multidimensional and multivariate representation*: a representation of data in which there are many attributes per datapoint. Performance data are typically multidimensional, with both space-like (e.g., processors, memory) and time-like dimensions, and other parameters (e.g., problem size) that may vary as well. Such a multivariate representation is conceptually compact, but the technical challenge for visualization is to represent as many dimensions as possible on a flat video screen. For example, two screen dimensions plus color can be used to depict three data dimensions: time, processor, and processor state.

- *Macroscopic and microscopic views*: the level of detail represented by a given view. A macroscopic view conveys the "big picture," while a microscopic view depicts fine detail.

- *Macro/micro composition and reading*: a display composition that allows perception of both local detail and global structure. In such a display, fine details are discernible, but the details accumulate into larger coherent features.

- *Adaptive graphical display*: the adjustment of graphical characteristics of a display in response to the size of the data set. The goal here is to reveal as much detail as possible without having the visual complexity interfere with the perception of that detail.

- *Display manipulation*: the interactive modification of a display, using techniques such as scrolling or zooming, to cope with large volumes of data and varying levels of detail. Scrolling and/or zooming along the time axis is often used to convey fine detail for long runs that would otherwise compress the time axis and lose detail.

- *Composite view*: a synthesis of two or more views into a single view that is intended to enhance visual relationships among the views and present more global information [Couch 93]. Examples include combining lower dimensional displays into a single higher dimensional display, or taking time along a third axis to construct a three-dimensional display from a two-dimensional animation.

User Perception and Interaction

Successful visual performance tuning depends on a synergistic feedback loop between the user and the visualization tool. The tool produces images that are interpreted by the user, and in turn, through the selection of views and options, the user helps guide the tool in detecting and isolating performance bottlenecks. Some important concepts in this category include:

- *Perception and cognition*: the development of an impression, awareness, or understanding of a phenomenon via the senses. Human visual perception has powerful abilities to grasp patterns, distinguish variations, classify objects, etc., through size, shape, color, and motion. A familiar example of the use of shape to convey information is the Kiviat diagram. Another example is the use of color in timeline displays to give an impression of dominant states of performance behavior.

- *Observing patterns*: the observation of spatial, temporal, or logical patterns of behavior, which are often indicative of important inter-relationships among models and data. For example, a repetitive pattern over time is often related to iterative loops in a program.

- *User interaction*: the selection among alternate views, levels of detail, and display parameters by the user. Such interaction enables the user to customize the visualization for a given situation to enhance understanding. For example, in a processor oriented display the user may select a particular layout or ordering of processors in order to make patterns and relationships more evident, or select only one specific processor to study in detail.

Comparison

Comparisons and cross-correlations between related views or representations can be a powerful tool in yielding insight into behavioral characteristics and their causes. Some graphical techniques for visual comparison include:

- *Multiple views*: the visual presentation of data using multiple displays from different perspectives. Any single visualization or perspective is usually capable of displaying only a portion of the relevant behavior of interest. Viewing the same underlying phenomenon from diverse perspectives gives a more well rounded impression and is more likely to yield useful insights [LeBlanc 90]. For example, one view might show load balance, while another gives a better indication of concurrency. Still other views, say of communication or data accesses, could convey additional perspectives on the same underlying behavior.

- *Small multiples*: a series of images showing the same combination of variables indexed by changes in another variable, much like successive frames of a movie. Information slices are positioned so that the viewer can make comparisons at a glance. Time-based animation is one example of this technique, but indexing can also be done by processor number, code version, problem size, machine size, and so on.

- *Cross-execution views*: the visual comparison of performance information from different executions of a program, which may differ in various ways, such as problem size or machine size.

A number of techniques have been developed for visually extracting useful information from a large, complex dataset:

- *Reduction and filtering*: the representation of raw data by statistical summaries, such as maxima and minima, means, standard deviations, frequency distributions, etc. This notion extends to graphical reduction, in which a visual display conveys general trends rather than detailed behavior.

- *Clustering*: multivariate statistical analysis and presentation techniques for grouping or categorizing related datapoints. The intent is to classify points, or identify outliers, in a multidimensional data space. Classical examples of clustering displays include scatterplots and frequency histograms.

- *Encoding and abstracting*: the use of graphical attributes such as color, shape, size, and spatial orientation or arrangement to convey information, such as additional dimensions. Such overloading can easily be abused, but when used appropriately, color-coding, etc., can be very effective in increasing the dimensionality of flat displays.

- *Separating information*: visual differentiation among layers of information through color highlighting, foreground/background, etc. For example, performance features associated with the critial path of a computation can be highlighted with unique colors.

We now present a few scenarios to illustrate some of the performance evaluation problems encountered and the range of possible visualization applications. These scenarios are not intended to be exhaustive. Rather, the purpose here is to show how the analysis and visual concepts and abstractions are applied in the practice of visualizing performance data. The reader is referred to specific articles in the bibliography for more complete and detailed visualization applications; see in particular [JPDC 93].

The earliest parallel performance visualizations were largely based on performance abstractions that were very close to the hardware, and these were usually mapped to very simple graphic displays that were already in use with conventional serial systems. Kiviat diagrams, for example, were already a well known device for depicting relationships among multivariate performance data, such as the utilization of various resources in computer systems [Kolence 73]. It was quite natural, therefore, to extend their use to display processor utilization or other performance data for parallel computer systems.

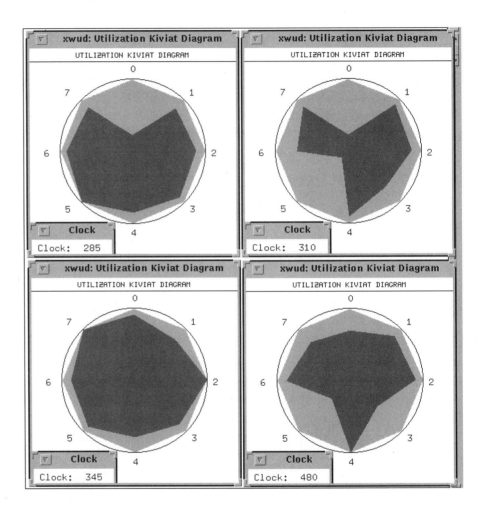

Figure 2.

The example in Figure 2 shows processor utilization in a parallel sparse matrix computation using a Kiviat diagram. Each processor is represented in the diagram by a separate radial axis, and its percentage utilization determines a point along this axis, from zero at the origin to 100% at the perimeter. Connecting these points by straight lines forms a polygon whose shape and size give a quick visual indication of overall efficiency, individual processor utilization, and the load balance across processors. A succession of these diagrams over time, either as an animation or using selected snapshots, shows how these quantities vary during the course of execution. This simple visual display makes effective use of a number of concepts, such as multidimensional representation, macro/micro composition and reading, small multiples, shapes, and patterns.

Of course, good parallel performance requires, among other things, that the computational work be spread evenly across the processors, that each processor's share of the work be done concurrently, and that there be a minimum of additional work beyond that required by a serial algorithm. Thus, the corresponding processor-oriented performance analysis abstractions -- load balance, concurrency, and overhead, respectively -- are of considerable interest in optimizing performance. In Figure 3(a), utilization data has been integrated over the lifetime of the computation and broken down into *busy*, *overhead*, and *idle* values, giving a quick and effective visual impression of load balance and overhead, but no insight into concurrency. Although this display can reveal the presence of poor load balance or excessive overhead, it does not pinpoint the specific time of their occurrence.

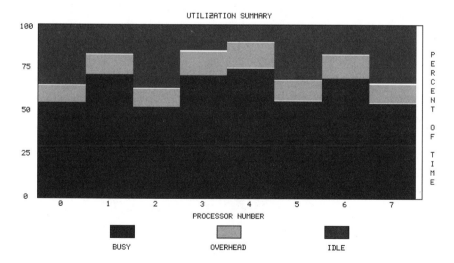

Figure 3a.

This deficiency is remedied by the timeline display shown in Figure 3(b), where the same information is now given as a function of time, so that specific periods of busy and idle activity on specific processors can be identified and correlated across processors. Note, however, that this more detailed view is less effective in providing an overall impression of the relevant performance abstractions. This simple example illustrates a number of points, such as the different levels at which data can be presented and the importance of multiple views.

Figure 3b.

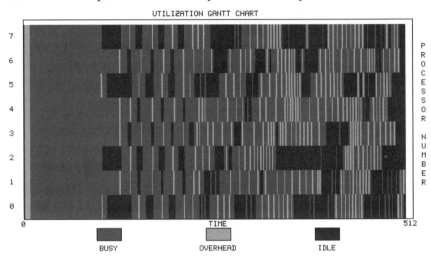

The Kiviat diagram and timeline display above demonstrate a tension that sometimes exists in performance visualization between views that try to convey impressions of overall performance behavior and those that support the presentation of detailed information. Although the principle of multiple views certainly helps to relieve this tension, it would be advantageous to derive visualizations that have both perceptual appeal and presentation of data detail; what we have termed macro/micro composition. For example, with more sophisticated graphics capabilities, the visual abstraction of the Kiviat diagram can be extended to show a history of processor utilization values in the form of a "Kiviat tube," formed from two-dimensional Kiviat "slices" layed out in time along the third dimension. As seen in Figure 4(a), for an entire program execution, and Figure 4(b) for a small time interval, the "shape" of processor utilization over time is apparent. Although the details of any particular time point are reduced, the three-dimensional visualization control could be used to zoom in on a time period or the visualization could be easily animated to show the values at a time point. The latter idea could be enhanced by displaying the complete tube as a transparent structure, keeping the Kiviat slices rendered in color. In constructing the visualization, several visualization concepts were used, including shape construction, composite views, and pattern observation.

Figure 4a-b.

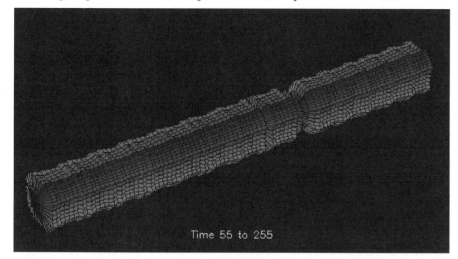

Time 55 to 255

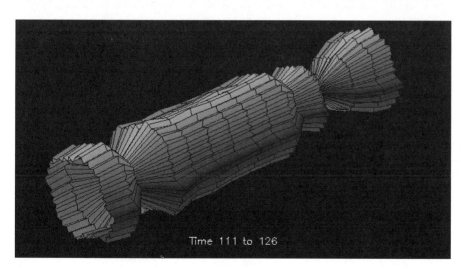

Time 111 to 126

Often, the potentially large amount of performance data to be navigated through for a large-scale program leaves the user bewildered as to where to begin searching for performance problems. Moreover, even if the user can be guided to

Critical Paths in Parallel Computation

the source of a performance problem by a tool, there remains a need to set up appropriate hypotheses and tests for the tool to use in its search process [Hollingsworth 93]. Though this is admittedly an iterative process, it becomes mere guesswork and trial-and-error if the user has no basis for his or her hypotheses and tests. In any case, graphical displays can give the user an overall sense of performance for a large-scale program by categorizing behavior, highlighting potential bottlenecks, and providing a quantitative description of the performance data.

As an example, the *critical path* is the longest serial thread, or chain of dependences, running through the execution of a parallel program. It is an important performance analysis abstraction because the execution time of the program cannot be reduced without shortening the critical path, and hence it is a potential place to look for bottlenecks. Of particular significance is the stability of the critical path across multiple executions of the program, since it may reveal the presence or absence of a systematic bias in the execution. By itself, however, the stability of the critical path does not tell us whether such a bias is good or bad, so it should be augmented by other views.

For parallel programs based on message passing, an appropriate visual abstraction for depicting the critical path is a minor modification of a spacetime diagram, since data dependences are satisfied by interprocessor communications. Figure 5 (a-d) shows the critical paths (highlighted in black) for a sequence of successive improvements in a parallel program for solving the shallow water equations on a sphere using a spectral transform method [Worley 92]. Time has been rescaled in each instance, so the time scale shown does not reflect the actual performance improvement, which is more than a factor of three overall. These performance improvements were actually achieved by analyzing the behavior of the program using utilization and task displays, but it is nevertheless instructive to observe the resulting behavior of the critical paths.

In the initial implementation, Figure 5(a), the performance is poor due to a substantial load imbalance, and the critical path, not surprisingly, stays on a single processor (the most heavily loaded one).When the load balance is improved, Figure 5(b), the critical path begins to spread out over more processors, as no single processor is now the bottleneck. Further improvement yields further spread in the critical path, Figure5(c). This would seem to agree

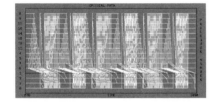

Figure 5a.

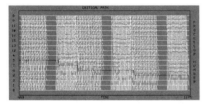

Figure 5b.

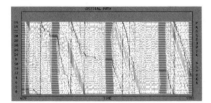

Figure 5c.

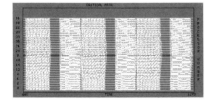

Figure 5d.

with the intuitive notion that a well balanced algorithm should produce a somewhat random critical path, due to slight vagaries of timing in the nearly equal tasks. After the final improvement, however, the critical path once again settles largely on a single processor, Figure 5(d). The explanation is that this implementation uses a carefully pipelined, ring-oriented algorithm that has had all of the previous load balance and communication anomalies removed, so that now the behavior is very regular, and hence the trailing processor in the pipeline is now consistently on the critical path.

Our last scenario considers data access patterns in parallel programming languages, such as High Performance Fortran (HPF) [Kimelman 95] or parallel C++ (pC++) [Malony 94], that incorporate data distribution semantics. Interprocessor communication in such languages is implicitly determined by the data distribution, and hence the selection of the distribution is the programmer's main control over parallel efficiency. An appropriate analysis abstraction, therefore, is the proportion of local versus remote data accesses required to support a given choice of data distribution.

Access Patterns for Data Distributions

For an application involving Gaussian elimination on a matrix, the relevant data structure is a two-dimensional array, which can form the basis for an effective performance view that relates easily to the application program. The visual abstraction, shown in Figure 6 (a-f), represents the data structure as a surface whose height and color are determined by the proportion of local data accesses for the corresponding position in the two-dimensional array. Color (grayscale in this paper) serves here to enhance the viewer's perception of the differences in data accesses within a single image, and it also helps unify the series of images. The changes in the surface could be animated over time, but perhaps even more effective is the use of a series of snapshots (small multiples) in conveying the changing data access patterns as the algorithm progresses. The concepts highlighted in the visualization include multiple dimensions, macro/micro composition (data points on a surface), double cueing (height and color), and encoding of data structure mapping in spatial arrangement.

Figure 6a-f.

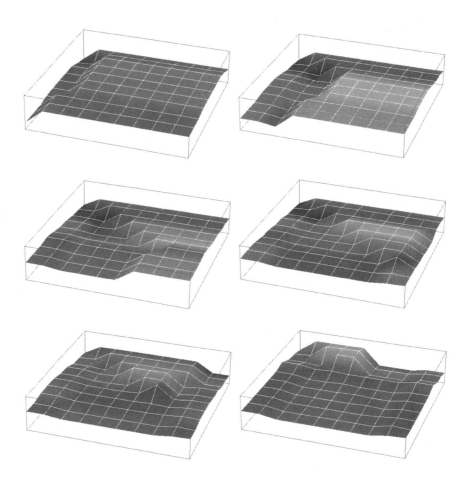

Conclusion

The technology for parallel performance visualization has evolved from a few simple statistical displays to visualization environments that can be extended with analysis and display modules supplied by tooldevelopers. More recently, there has been a focus on visualization systems that can incorporate the user's semantic perspective in visualization creation and application. However, even with developed concepts and principles for performance visualization design, and new advances in performance visualization technology, it is still a challenging undertaking to develop generally useful parallel performance visualizations. Miller addressed some of these concerns in his essay [Miller 93], where he listed criteria for good visualization. These criteria, like the concepts we have enumerated, help to define general requirements to guide the visualization designer in creating effective visual displays.

The increasing sophistication and complexity of parallel computing environments will continue to present new challenges to understanding the behavior and performance of parallel programs. The performance visualization model we have presented emphasizes the need for integrating performance evaluation models with performance displays to provide a foundation for developing meaningful visual abstractions. But the model also acknowledges the need for user involvement — in design, in interaction, and in evaluation — from which true performance insight is ultimately achieved.

Visualization for Education

The original impetus for SV research was an effort to aid novices attempting to understand standard computing algorithms or trying to debug their programs. This section describes the experiences, insights, successes and failures of several of the key SV research groups in using SV technology within their teaching over a period of about a decade and a half.

Chapter 24 ("Sorting Out Sorting: A Case Study of Software Visualization for Teaching Computer Science") describes the 'one that started it all' - *Sorting Out Sorting* (SOS). SOS is a 30-minute teaching film which describes nine sorting algorithms. Sorting algorithms sort the items within some data structure into a predefined order. The chapter discusses how various problems such as timing were overcome. Timing problems were derived from the fact that students initially need to see animations at a slow pace so that they can understand the underlying algorithm, but playing the whole animation at a slow speed would prove boring. This problem was further compounded by the need for the animation to be integrated with a narration, and the fact that the animation of some sorting algorithms slow down as they progress. It is almost an understatement to call the SOS film a milestone in SV history. The images were so compelling that even after fifteen years sorting algorithms are still the first choice among SV researchers for demonstrating their SV systems.

Chapter 25 ("Software Visualization in Teaching at Brown University") describes experiences in SV based teaching at Brown university since the early 1980s. SV based teaching at Brown is centered on a lecture hall where the lecturer and each student have their own high-specification graphics workstation. The environments (BALSA, MEADOW, Passe, Piper) have display sharing capabilities (either self contained or provided by an in-house display sharing tool XMX) enabling the students to see a replication of the lecturer's interface. The authors remark that although the visualizations are popular with students they require a considerable effort in their design, construction, integration and maintenance.

Chapter 26 ("Using Software to Teach Computer Programming: Past, Present and Future") discusses efforts at the Open University (OU) in aiding psychology students construct cognitive models in AI languages. The chapter describes the OU's 'change of heart', in the approach taken to aiding the students, from using AI based debugging aids to explaining the innards of a language's virtual machine. Initially a *cradle to grave* approach was adopted, that is, using a common environment to support novices and experts. It was argued that by providing multiple abstractions both groups could be supported. An integrated course including software, text books and video was produced. Unfortunately, recent empirical studies have showed that the visualization is problematic for very early novices. This has resulted in a *stage appropriate* approach to be adopted. In this approach students use a visualization appropriate for their current learning stage.

Finally, Chapter 27 ("Animated Algorithms") describes a relatively new system *Animated Algorithms*. *Animated Algorithms* is a Macintosh based system used by students to build visualizations combined with hypertext and digital video support on an introduction to algorithms course. The chapter discusses the educational benefits of the construction process.

Sorting Out Sorting: A Case Study of Software Visualization for Teaching Computer Science

Ronald Baecker

Like professional programmers, teachers and students of computer science frequently use pictures as aids to conceiving, expressing, and communicating algorithms. Instructors used to cover blackboards and themselves with chalk in drawing intricate diagrams of data structures and control flow, yet often made errors such as improperly estimating the space needed for a proper layout. Students try to improve their visualization of a program's behaviour by sketching representations of nesting of procedures, scope of variables, memory allocation, pointer chains, and organization of record structures.

Unfortunately, a program's behaviour cannot be described by a static drawing; it requires a dynamic sequence. We must trace control flow, bind variables, link pointers, and allocate memory. We must execute processes which mimic those of the machine. It is difficult for us to enact these dynamic sequences directly. Our drawings are inaccurate. Our timing is bad. We make major mistakes, such as skipping or rearranging steps. Thus it would be useful to have animation sequences portraying the behaviour of programs constructed automatically as a by-product of their execution, and therefore guaranteed to portray this execution faithfully.

Animation is a compelling medium for the display of program behaviour. Since programs are inherently temporal, executing through time, they can be vividly represented by an animated display which portrays how they carry out their processing and how their essential state changes over time. Furthermore, many algorithms employ repetitive computations, whether expressed iteratively or recursively. These can be viewed efficiently when displayed as a motion picture. In so doing, we can perceive structure and relationships of causality, and ultimately infer what the program is doing.

Software visualization can therefore be a powerful tool for presenting computer science concepts and assisting students as they struggle to comprehend them. This chapter traces the author's early investigations of this concept, presents a detailed description of the contents and development of a successful 30-minute teaching film *Sorting Out Sorting*, and outlines other work in pedagogical uses of program animation since *Sorting Out Sorting*.

Animating programs for pedagogical purposes is not a trivial endeavor. There are numerous intricate details in most computer programs. To be effective, algorithm animation must abstract or highlight only the essential aspects of an algorithm. We must decide which program text and which data to represent, how they are to be visualized, and when to update their representations during the execution of a program, Most importantly, we must try to enhance relevant features and suppress extraneous detail, to devise clear, uncluttered, and attractive graphic designs, and to choose appropriate timing and pacing.

Early Work

In 1971, having completed GENESYS [Baecker 69a] [Baecker 69b] [Baecker 70], a pioneering interactive computer animation system for artists, I turned my attention to the role of computer animation for computer science [Baecker 73]. I was surprised that computer scientists had not reacted more enthusiastically to Ken Knowlton's dramatic early computer animation explaining the instruction set of a low-level list processing language [Knowlton 66a] [Knowlton 66b]. Two notable exceptions were Bob Hopgood [Hopgood 74] and Kellogg Booth [Booth 75], whose early films are reviewed in Chapter 2.

We carried out a number of program animation experiments in the next seven years. Students in computer graphics classes developed animations of specific algorithms, such as bubble sort, recursive merge sort, hash coding, and hidden line elimination. Ed Yarwood explored the concept of *program illustration*, focusing specifically on the integration of program source text with diagrams of program state [Yarwood 74]. Several students built extensions to language processors to aid the animation of programs in specific languages such as Logo and PL/I [Baecker 75]. Finally, in 1978, we decided to use this experience to produce a teaching film on the subject of *sorting algorithms*.

From 1978 to 1981 we produced a 30-minute colour sound film, entitled *Sorting Out Sorting*, which uses animation of program data coupled with an explanatory narrative to teach nine different internal sorting methods. The film, now primarily distributed as a videotape [Baecker 81], was generated with a 16mm computer-output film recorder.

Sorting Out Sorting

Sorting Out Sorting explains the nine sorting algorithms sufficiently well so that a student who has watched the animation carefully could program some of them herself. It also illustrates the differences in efficiency of the various algorithms.

The movie has been used successfully with computer science students at various levels. As a motivational aid, and to introduce the concept of the efficiency of different solutions to the same problem, it is shown in introductory computer science courses at the university, community college, and high school level. As an explanation of solution methods, it is shown in first or second courses on programming. It can also be used in introductory courses on data processing, algorithms, or complexity.

Internal Sorting Methods

Internal sorting methods are algorithms for rearranging items within a data structure into some predefined order. Typically this order is that of increasing numerical value, decreasing numerical value, or alphabetical order of a field within the data structure.

There are over one hundred internal sorting algorithms [Knuth 73] [Lorin 75] [Wirth 76]. All have both advantages and disadvantages. Typical tradeoffs are between the algorithm's *difficulty of programming* and *complexity,* or *speed of execution*, and between its *time* and *space* requirements.

Internal sorting methods compare items with other items to determine if they are in the correct order or if items need to be moved. Items are then moved zero or more times until they reach their final and correct positions. Once all items have reached their final positions, the data is sorted and the algorithm is finished.

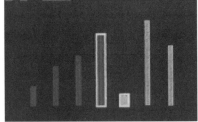

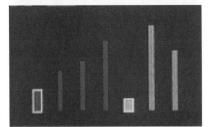

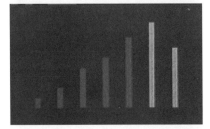

Figure 1a-d. (a is at the top.) Linear Insertion: a) first comparison of the 4th pass, with the first 4 items already correctly ordered; b) final comparison of the 4th pass; c) end of the 4th pass, after the 5th item has been moved to the front; d) data is sorted. Colours (shown here as gray scale) denote "unsorted" and "sorted," i.e., in the correct position thus far. Borders indicate that two items are being compared. *See Plate 8*

Execution time is therefore primarily determined by the times required for *data comparisons* and for *data movements*. The execution time of internal sorting algorithms over n items of data is, in most cases, proportional to either n^2 or n log n. As n becomes large, differences between the times required become very significant. However, the simplest algorithms to design, program, and understand are those whose execution time is a function of n^2.

The film deals with three distinct groups of algorithms — the *insertion sorts*, the *exchange sorts*, and the *selection sorts*. Other techniques, such as the *merge sorts* and the *distribution sorts*, are not covered. Our treatment is closest in content and spirit to that found in Section 2.2 of [Wirth 76].

Structure and Content of the Film

A program may be viewed as a mechanism for transforming one set of data into a new set of data. If we consider a program's state to be determined by its data, then one way of animating and portraying the program is to show how the data is transformed over time. By viewing these sequences of transformations, or possibly several such sequences resulting from different initial sets of data, one can induce the algorithm upon which the program is based.

For example, assume that we wish to order a single array of numerical data into increasing order. We can portray each data item as a vertical bar (Fig. 1), whose height is proportional to the value of the item. Initially, the heights of successive items will vary upwards and downwards. Successive steps of a sorting method will produce rearrangements of the data, until ultimately we should have the elements arrayed in order of increasing height with the smallest one on the left and the largest one on the right.

The movie begins with the *insertion sorts*, in which successive items of data are inserted into their correct position relative to items previously considered. The process is analogous to picking up cards of a bridge hand and inserting them into their correct positions relative to the cards already in one's hand.

The Linear Insertion Sort (Fig. 1) is the simplest of the insertion sorts. For each new item, we scan through the array sorted thus far, looking for the correct position; having found it, we move all the larger items one slot to the right and insert the new item. The Binary Insertion Sort speeds up this technique by using a binary search to find the item's correct position.

In the Shellsort (Fig. 2), we first perform insertion sorts on subsequences of the data spaced widely apart, thus moving items closer to their ultimate destination more quickly. We then perform insertion sorts on subsequences of the data spaced more closely together. We continue in this way until we do as the final pass a regular insertion sort. Because items have already been moved close to where they belong, this pass is extremely efficient.

In the *exchange sorts*, we interchange pairs of items until the data is sorted.

In the Bubblesort (Fig. 3), we pass through the data from one end to the other, interchanging adjacent pairs of items which are ordered incorrectly relative to each other. Each such pass "bubbles" one more item into its correct position, as for example the smallest items shown at the top in Figure 3. The Shakersort improves on this technique by alternating passes in both directions, and by keeping track of when and where no exchanges were made in order to reduce the number of comparisons on future passes.

The Quicksort (Fig. 4) selects an item at the beginning of the data (the "pivot"), and proceeds by exchanging items from that end that are larger than the pivot with items from the other end that are smaller than the pivot. The pivot is then moved between the two sets of data, so that it is in its correct final position, correctly dividing the set of smaller items from the set of larger items. The Quicksort is then applied recursively to each set. The Quicksort is one of the most efficient of those presented in the film.

The *selection sorts* are those which the algorithm selects, one by one, the data items and positions them in the correct order.

In the Straight Selection Sort, the data is scanned for the smallest item, which is then inserted, with a single data movement, into its final position in the array. Each pass selects the next smallest item from the remaining data. Tree Selection significantly reduces the number of comparisons by organizing the data into a tree, at the cost of requiring more storage.

Heapsort (Fig. 5) preserves most of Tree Selection's efficiency gains without using extra storage. It does this by repeatedly organizing the data into a special kind of binary tree called a *heap*, in which each parent is greater than its children, and then moving the top of the tree into its correct final position.

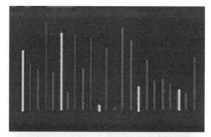

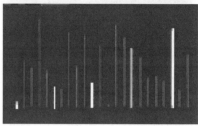

Figure 2a-b. Shellsort. The two frames show the beginning and end states of the 1st pass, which performs an insertion sort on a subsequence of the data consisting of every 5th item.

Figure 3. Bubblesort. The two highlighted items are about to be swapped. The top three items have reached their correct positions.

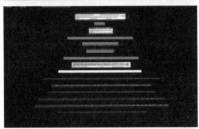

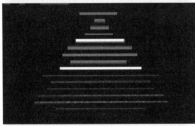

Figure 4a-d. Quicksort: a) The 9th topmost item is in its correct position. The top item is the new pivot. We have found an item larger than it (the 3rd), and one smaller (the 8th), and interchange them to achieve b). Soon, we reach c) in which this pivot has been moved into its correct final position (#5). In d), the top 9 elements have been sorted; we will begin again recursively on the bottom 6.

Problems

A problem in early drafts of the film was a lack of consistent visual conventions. The student who is presented with the animation of several algorithms at once should be able to forget about the *technique* of presentation and concentrate instead on what is being taught. Without an appropriate set of visual conventions, such as one colour to denote "sorted" items and another for "items still to be considered," the viewer may spend more energy trying to figure out what the picture means than she will expend in trying to follow the algorithm.

A central problem is that of *timing*. The steps of the algorithms must first be presented slowly, to give time both for the narrator to explain what is happening and for the student to absorb it. However, once the algorithm is understood, later steps may be boring. This is particularly true in the case of the insertion sorts, which appear to slow down as they go along, whereas the exchange and selection sorts begin slowly and appear to speed up towards the end.

We needed a visually interesting and convincing way to convey the message that some simple algorithms which are easy to code are nonetheless not appropriate for sorting large data sets. One way to do this is by means of animated performance statistics. Yet if we also wish to do this by showing the algorithms operating upon large amounts of data, then we have new representation problems. To fit the desired information legibly onto the screen and to compress the animation into a reasonable span of time requires the design of different methods of portraying the data and different conventions for illustrating the progress of the algorithms.

To summarize, we are faced, throughout the film, with the problem that totally literal and consistent presentations can be boring. Consistency is required so that changes made for visual purposes not be interpreted falsely as clues relevant to understanding the algorithm. Being literal and explaining things step-by-step is required to aid initial understanding, but we must go beyond this to add visual and dramatic interest as we present more advanced material.

Solutions

The presentation of nine algorithms, grouped into three groups of three, lends itself to a pleasing symmetry. We present each group as a separate act of the film. In each case, we present the algorithms within each group in increasing order of efficiency, and hence increasing order of complexity of explanation.

With each group, we adopt a different set of visual cues, while retaining the same underlying conventions. Thus, in each group, one colour is used to indicate items "yet to be considered"; a second colour denotes those items which are "already sorted"; and a third is used to form borders around items which are currently being compared. Whenever items are dimmed and faded into the background, they are "not currently being considered" within the context of the algorithm.

The items themselves are represented by vertical bars in the first group; by horizontal, centered bars in the second group; and by single-digit numbers in the third. In each case the final increasing order attained by the algorithm is from left to right or from top to bottom.

Only the data appears on the screen. There are no pointers, no labels, no gimmicks of any kind. Attributes of the data and processes affecting them are conveyed entirely by the visual clues described in the last two paragraphs, by the motion of the data, by the accompanying narrative, and to a lesser extent by the music track, which is not directly driven by the data but conveys the feeling of what is going on.

Each of the nine parts begins with an animation sequence of the title of the algorithm. The letters of the title appear initially in a scrambled order, and are then rearranged by the algorithm about to be taught until they spell the title correctly. The same colour conventions apply to "sorted items" and "yet to be sorted items" as will apply later. The whole process takes from ten to twenty seconds. It is not intended that the first-time viewer be able to understand from this sequence how the algorithm operates. Yet it does provide a feel for the flow of the sorting method, and for the order in which the items become sorted.

There follows a presentation of the algorithm itself, on a sufficiently small and well-chosen set of data to illustrate at a slow pace how the method works. Where necessary, the pace of the sort is decreased to allow time for complex narration and for the viewers to digest what it is going on. The pace is sometimes increased after a few initial passes have provided a clear explanation and the scene starts to become boring.

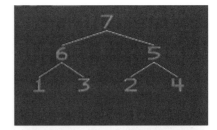

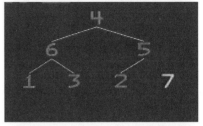

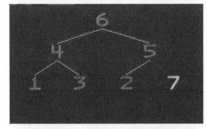

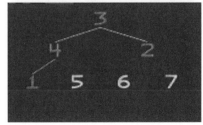

Figure 5a-d. Heapsort: a) The data is organized into a heap, in which every parent item is greater than its children. We then move the top, largest item into its correct position at the end of the array, shown in b). We then need to fix up the tree so it once again is a heap, shown in c). A somewhat later stage is shown in d).

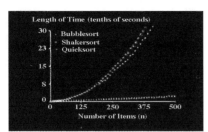

Figure 6. Total execution time of the three Exchange Sorts. Each curve plots growth in execution time as the size of the data set grows. The difference between the two n^2 sorts, Bubblesort and Shakersort, and the $n \log n$ Quicksort, represented by the single low curve on the graph, is evident.

After all three algorithms of each class have been presented, we illustrate their efficiency with three line graphs, comparing their efficiency on sorts of n items, where n ranges from 10 to 500. The three graphs, presented in succession, show number of data comparisons, number of data movements, and actual execution time of a DEC PDP-11/45. Rather than being static, each graph begins with just the labeled axes and "grow" three coloured lines, one for each algorithm (Fig. 6). This technique permits the narrator to focus on each algorithm in turn, and comment on why its line in the graph is shaped as it is. It also depicts clearly the difference between the $n \log n$ and n^2 algorithms.

To illustrate the difference in efficiency even more dramatically, we then run a "race" of all three technique simultaneously on the screen, sorting 250 items of data. Each algorithm is accompanied by a digital clock measuring film time, which stops as soon as the data is sorted (Fig. 7). A title for each algorithm appears as soon as the data is sorted. The slowest algorithms take over two minutes to run, while the $n \log n$ sorts are finished in five to fifteen seconds.

After all three groups of sorts have been presented, we close with a "grand race" of all nine algorithms, sorting 2500 items of data each (Fig. 8). Each item of data is represented by a coloured dot. The value of the item is represented by its vertical position, and its position in the array by its horizontal position. Thus unsorted data appears a cloud, and sorted data appears as a diagonal line.

The fastest algorithm, Tree Selection and Quicksort, finishes in 20 seconds each; the other $n \log n$ algorithms within another 20. Their sorted data then fades out, leaving room for the final credits, while the n^2 sorts plod along, until they, too, fade out. This happens long before they are finished, for, as the narrator notes, it would take another 54 minutes for Bubblesort to complete.

The grand race not only illustrates performance, but illuminates the algorithms. We see how Shellsort moves all the data close to its final position, then finishes the job on the final pass. We see the recursive behaviour of Quicksort as it picks up rectangular regions of the array and squashes them into a line. We see the peculiar way in which Heapsort organizes and shapes the data into a funnel as it picks off successive largest remaining elements.

As an Epilogue to the film, we replay the entire film at 12 times normal speed. This provides an opportunity for review, and shows visual patterns unique to each method that are not obvious at normal speed.

The Success of Sorting Out Sorting

Sorting Out Sorting has been both successful and influential. It is a significant contribution to the pedagogical tools available for teaching sorting methods to computer science students. It encapsulates in 30 minutes of usually vivid and occasionally compelling imagery the essence of what written treatments require 30 or more detailed pages to convey. Interviews with students and an informal, unpublished experiment make it clear that the film communicates effectively both the substance of the algorithms and the concept of their relative efficiency.

More than 600 copies have been sold over the past 15 years, mostly by word-of-mouth and with no effective marketing. I still routinely encounter individuals whom I have never met before who are effusive in their praise of the film. Two letters written to me are particular interesting:

> "I was impressed by the amount of careful thought that was evident in all aspects of the production; the different presentations were always dramatically well-timed, and the visual logic of each section flowed well... the film said visually exactly what needed to be said..." (Scott Kim, 20 July 1981)

and

> "I am profoundly deaf... I was not able to understand ANY of the voice-over commentary on the film. I could hear someone talking; I could hear music, and beeps; but I could not understand WHAT was being said. Interestingly enough, this was not any particular disadvantage. I felt that I could understand most of the film... without hearing any of the commentary." (Bev Biderman, 12 March 1982)

The film was also instrumental in stimulating further work in algorithm animation, most notably that of Marc Brown [Brown 88a] (also see Chapters 7 and 12), which together with SOS in turn inspired much of the work in the field.

The film also goes beyond a step-by-step presentation of the algorithms, communicating an understanding of them as *dynamic processes*. We can see the programs in process, running, and we therefore see the algorithms in new and unexpected ways. We see sorting waves ripple through the data. We see data reorganize itself as if it had a life of its own. These views produce new understandings which are difficult to express in words.

The film does have weaknesses. The typography is atrocious. Colour is mediocre. Timing is not always optimal, for it is hard to find the right speed for a diverse audience. The film stresses average efficiency too strongly, ignoring best cases and worst case analysis, and also the subtleties that enter into a real-

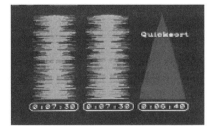

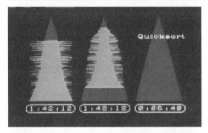

Figure 7a-d. The race of the three Exchange Sorts. a) The Quicksort completes after roughly 7 seconds. b) It then takes over 1 minute 40 seconds for the Shakersort to approach completion. c) At 2 minute 21 seconds, it completes. d) The Bubblesort finally completes at just over 2 minutes 45 seconds. Notice that Bubblesort works from the top down, and Shakersort works from both the top and the bottom.

world choice of technique for a particular problem. Pedagogically, it is regrettable that it omits merge sorts and distribution sorts. Yet it works, and works very well, even today, 15 years later.

Work on the film has taught us a number of lessons about algorithm animation:

• Effective symbolism depends upon the size of the subject and its scale within the total composition, and the context within which the image is displayed.
• Significant insights into algorithm behaviour can be gained while only viewing the data, if the illustrations and the timing are designed carefully, and are accompanied by appropriate narration.
• Control over motion dynamics must be powerful and flexible to produce effective animated communications.
• Timing is the key to effective motion dynamics and algorithm animation — fancy rendering and smooth motion are not necessarily required.

Recent Developments

After completing SOS, I took a long hiatus from this research, turning my attention to typographic enhancements of the appearance of source code, and to issues of computer program publishing (see [Baecker 90a]; also the Chapter 4 by Baecker and Marcus).

More recently, we developed two generations of a Logo environment for novice programmers that incorporates tools for software visualization and auralization. The work on LogoMotion is documented in [Buchanan 88] and Baecker and Buchanan [Baecker 90b]. The work on the successor system, LogoMedia, is documented in [DiGiano 92a] and [DiGiano 92b].

In addition to the tight integration of capabilities for program visualization and auralization, two aspects of this work are particularly exciting. The LogoMedia system introduce a novel *probe* metaphor, which students can attach unobtrusively to locations in the program or to data items used by the program. This allows one to specify and tailor visualizations of an algorithm without modifying the program. DiGiano also carried out a ethnographic study of three programmers using LogoMedia on a variety of debugging tasks. The very encouraging results from this study are reported in [DiGiano 92a].

In the last three years, we have also been engaged in developing a novel computer literacy course [Baecker 95b] and in applying software visualization tools in this course. The course makes use of the Logo Microworlds

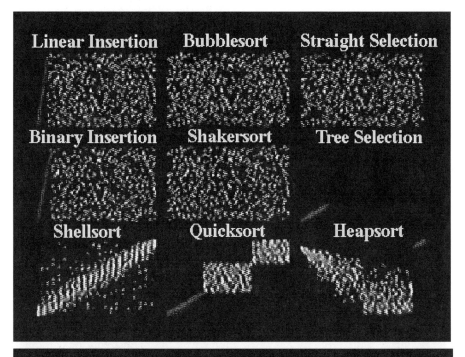

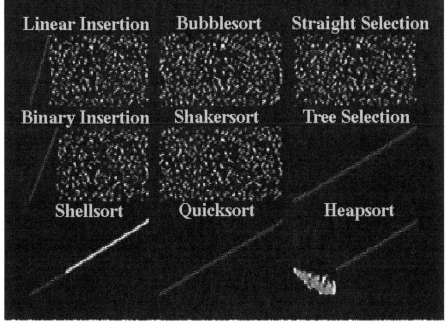

Figure 8.a-b The "grand race."
Unsorted data appears as a cloud;
sorted data becomes a diagonal line.
The difference between the n log n sorts
(Shellsort, Quicksort, Treesort, and
Heapsort) and the n² sorts are clearly
visible. Notice Shellsort's pushing of
the data towards the line, Quicksort's
recursive subdivisions, and Heapsort's
strange data funnel.

environment [LCSI 93]. We have developed a number of experimental animated program execution machines which illustrate and bring to life the underlying syntax and semantics of the execution of Logo programs (Fig. 9). The top image in Fig. 9 shows the Logo Plumber, a Microworlds program that displays the execution of Logo expressions in terms of a plumbing metaphor developed in [Harvey 97]. The bottom image in Fig. 9 shows the Logo Visualizer, a Microworlds program that displays the execution of Logo statements and procedures in a subset of the Logo language. Just as *Sorting Out Sorting* brings to life and makes visible how nine sorting algorithms work, these machines bring to life and make visible how the Logo language works.

Conclusions

We have described the development and principles governing the success of the computer animated teaching film *Sorting Out Sorting,* and have also mentioned two recent projects in the educational uses of software visualization. Although this work is very promising, it is distressing to see how difficult it still is to describe and control algorithm animations, how hard it is to get these techniques to scale (see Chapter 15 by Eisenstadt and Brayshaw, Chapter 21 by Eick, and Chapter 20 by Kimelman, Rosenberg, and Roth), and how little the work represented in this volume has been adopted by the mainstream of computer science education and practice.

Acknowledgments

Sorting Out Sorting was designed by Ronald Baecker, with assistance from David Sherman, and programmed by David Sherman, with assistance from Anthony Ayiomamatitis, David Gotlib, Thomas O'Dell, and Richard Outerbridge. Martin Tuori at the Defense and Civil Institute of Environmental Medicine graciously contributed the use of a film plotter. Initial versions of the animated program execution machines are due to Diba Bot and Isabel Jevans. The versions shown here are the work of Abba Lustgarten and Alexandra Mazalek. Jason Chang helped with the figures for this paper. The Natural Sciences and Engineering Research Council of Canada provided financial support. *Sorting Out Sorting* may be obtained in Canada from the Information Commons, University of Toronto, 130 St. George St., Toronto Ontario M5S 3H1 Canada, (416)978-6049, fax (416)978-0440, and elsewhere in the world from Morgan Kaufmann Publishers, 340 Pine Street, Sixth Floor, San Francisco CA. 94104 USA, (415)392-2665, mkp@mkp.com.

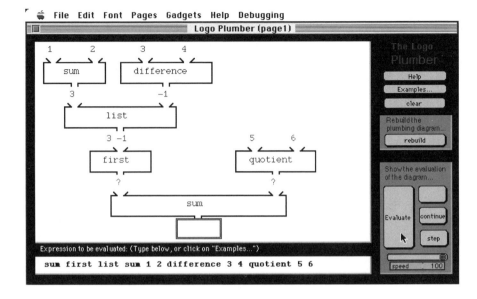

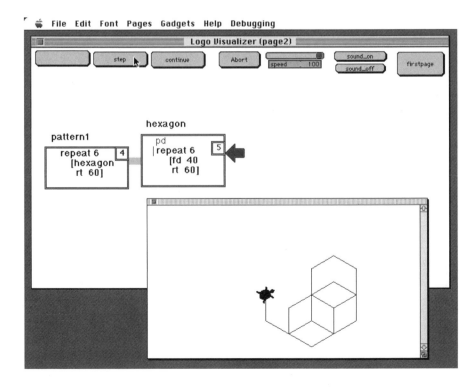

Figure 9a-b. Two animated program execution machines.

The top image displays the execution of Logo expressions in terms of a plumbing metaphor. The sum, difference, *and* list *procedures have been evaluated; the* first *procedure will be done next. Data flows through an interconnected set of procedures like water flows through a set of pipes.*

The bottom image displays the execution of Logo statements and procedures in a subset of the Logo language. We are in the 4th iteration of calls to a hexagon *procedure within the* pattern1 *procedure. The image drawn by the turtle geometry commands within the procedures is shown in the enclosed window. The execution of successive statements and their effects in the drawing are displayed in synchrony, helping to convey how the Microworlds Logo interpreter executes a program.*

In both cases, we provide single step, pause and continue, and speed controls to aid usability. The graphics is augmented with sound effects to engage the user.

Software Visualization in Teaching at Brown University

Chapter 25

John Bazik,
Roberto Tamassia,
Steven P. Reiss
and
Andries van Dam

Introduction

In the summer of 1983, students in Brown University's introductory algorithms and data structures course first saw the concepts they were learning brought to life through software visualization. What they saw that summer was the first algorithm animation from the BALSA system: intuitive graphical illustrations of the inner workings of sorting, searching and other basic algorithms [Brown 88a]. That summer marked the beginning of a long and sometimes difficult experiment in integrating teaching and technology that continues today.

To our knowledge, no conclusive study has ever established the educational value of software visualization techniques. But the evidence of their value is overwhelming. Year after year students report, directly and on anonymous questionnaires, that algorithm animation and program visualization tools help them understand the concepts they are learning. This is also confirmed by experiments conducted at Georgia Tech, which show that an algorithm animation system can improve the performance of students in an algorithms course [Lawrence 94].

But our experience is far from an unqualified success. The bright promise of these techniques is dimmed by the cost of their design, manufacture, integration and maintenance. A considerable machinery of software and human effort underlies our achievements, and when we have been unable to sustain this machinery, the educational environment has suffered.

Still, the techniques pioneered almost fifteen years ago remain an essential part of computer science education at Brown. A number of other tools have joined BALSA, enhancing its features or introducing software visualization to students in new ways. The use of these tools in hundreds of hours of instruction has taught the instructors as much as the students. These experiences are the subject of this paper.

Software visualization is used at Brown in three components of the educational process: the lecture, the programming lab and the assignment. We discuss these components in turn below.

Tools for Lecturing

The first and still the most visible role of software visualization in education is the lecture demonstration. Live, in-class software demonstrations have been a fixture of Brown's introductory computer science courses since the first BALSA demos, and this technology has become as routine as whiteboards and overhead projectors.

The Classroom

The world's first workstation-equipped lecture hall was constructed at Brown in 1982. This banked auditorium contained a network of 55 of the earliest Apollo workstations, one for the instructor and the rest arrayed in rows throughout the room. Such a room is predicated on a central role for technology in teaching, and BALSA was designed with this in mind. Using the network, BALSA painted its animation simultaneously on the displays of all machines. The instructor interacted with the BALSA program while students enjoyed an intimate view of the proceedings – on the same machines they would later use to do their assignments.

Today, 64 Sun workstations with 3D graphics acceleration populate Brown's second electronic lecture hall (see Fig. 1). This room is the primary resource for undergraduates in the Computer Science Department; it is here that all introductory course lectures are given and that students come to work on their assignments. The palette of tools for teaching has expanded well beyond BALSA, and to support their use in this classroom of networked, X-based UNIX workstations, the display-sharing tool XMX was developed [Bazik]. Unlike BALSA's built-in display-sharing capabilities, which supported BALSA only, XMX supports the multi-screen display of any X-based application. With XMX, the instructor's session, composed of a window manager, shells, desktop utilities and other programs, is shown in real time on all the workstation displays in the room. Any tools available in the department's computing environment can be used in the classroom. Systems designed to aid in teaching can be developed as single-user applications, and common single-user applications can be used to teach. With the advent of PC and MacIntosh emulators under UNIX, there are few limitations on what software can be used.

Figure 1. Brown's electronic classroom.

The value of a live, in-class software demonstration lies in the interaction of the instructor and students with the software. Without interaction (or with only minimal interaction – start, pause, stop), a demonstration differs little, pedagogically, from a film or videotape. The opportunity to exploit this technology begins when the instructor interacts with the software during class, controlling execution, choosing data sets, replaying, annotating. The demonstration is responsive, through the instructor, to the needs of the class, and students see an exploration rather than an illustration.

Visualizations Suitable for Lecture

What makes a software visualization work in a lecture? Chief among these is a short cognitive distance between concept and visualization. How closely the graphics on the screen correspond to the mental model is the best measure of a visualization's usefulness in class. When the mapping is direct and obvious, the representation is transparent and students "get it" right away. They can then concentrate on the ideas being illustrated, rather than the illustration itself.

The earliest BALSA demos show some obvious semantic mappings. In the sorting demos, an array of integers is represented as a row of sticks, the heights of which correspond to their values (see Fig. 2). It is immediately apparent that these represent things of differing value and the visual result of sorting them is easy to predict and understand. Two-dimensional graph algorithms also have an obvious representation on a two-dimensional computer screen. Exploring breadth-first and depth-first search on a map of the Paris Metro, where stations are interconnected nodes, is an intuitive exercise (see Fig. 3). As paths are traversed, they are redrawn in a different pattern or color: as nodes are visited, they change from circles to squares. In this way, progress through the data set, and the nature of the algorithm, are plain.

Figure 2. Vertical sticks data view of BALSA. The array is partially sorted.

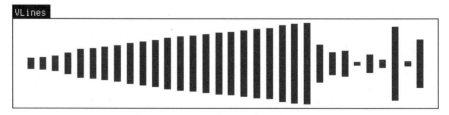

Control over the visual complexity of the demonstration is another key feature of software visualization teaching tools. This complexity is manifest in the size of the data set displayed, the number of views, the number of meters – visual elements tied to processes or data – in each view and the speed at which the demonstration progresses. For a first encounter with a concept, a simple intuitive view is needed with few distractions, a small data set and a pace appropriate to the view. When the high-level nature of the process becomes apparent to most students, additional views, meters, and data and repeated runs at varying speeds reveal more and lead to deeper and better understanding.

Single-view algorithm animation provides the first step in this process. Deeper exploration requires that more information be presented: synchronized views of code or pseudocode, additional animation views, data and variable views, data histories. The original BALSA system is a comprehensive environment in this sense and supports the gradual increase of screen information as a concept is explored. Some later systems [Stasko 89] focus on doing one type of view better or more easily, but lack the completeness we enjoy with BALSA.

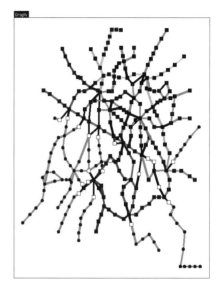

Figure 3. A depth-first search of the Paris Metro.

Obstacles to Teaching with Visualization Tools

Much of the success of the BALSA system at Brown is due to the tight integration of its development with the development of a textbook and curriculum for a particular course. BALSA was more than a resource for that course -- the course was rendered in software in the BALSA system and the two remained intertwined for many years. Without that kind of effort to motivate its use, a visualization tool that finds its primary application in the classroom must be very relevant and easy to use in order to convince teachers to invest the time to learn its features and interface and adapt their courses to it.

As our BALSA visualizations have not kept up with curricular changes over the years, the appeal of using other, familiar tools for teaching is strong. As an example, Framemaker, a desktop publishing tool used at Brown, has been pressed into service as a software visualization tool on occasion. With its keyboard macro facility, a convex hull algorithm can be animated in much the same way as animation produced by more specialized systems. To the student, the effect is very similar; to the instructor, the ability to develop a classroom demonstration using a familiar tool is very attractive.

A programming environment that students already know and use is a familiar and convenient vehicle for classroom demonstrations. At Brown, students in introductory programming classes use the MEADOW programming environment to do all their assignments. Because MEADOW offers automatic visualization of programs – graphical views of code and execution – it is also used for lecture demonstrations. Because the tool has a life outside of the lecture, it gives students a familiar context for the material presented, reducing the amount of explanation needed, and offers the instructor, who is already familiar with its workings, an easy base from which to develop new demonstrations.

For a specialized algorithm animation system to win a place in the classroom, the illustrations it presents must closely reflect the course curriculum. Demonstrations that stray from the material being presented, even in subtle ways, lose their appeal. An animation that illustrates a sorting algorithm and emphasizes its nested loop structure has less relevance when the algorithm is taught using object-oriented techniques. To the extent that there are concepts commonly taught and standard ways of presenting them, there are opportunities for particular demonstrations to fit neatly into courses taught at schools everywhere. But more often than not, illustrations need to be developed for, or adjusted to, specific courses and instructors.

Maintenance

A fundamental problem faces instructors who adopt these technologies for teaching: they make themselves dependent on systems and techniques that cannot simply be set up and ignored. Year after year, as hardware and software are upgraded, as the curriculum changes, as new concepts find their way into syllabi, the software systems that support teaching must keep pace. None of the visualization tools used at Brown are commercial products (we do not consider Framemaker a visualization tool although it is sometimes used as such). Most were developed in-house and a few come from other universities or research labs that offer little or no support. In Brown's Computer Science Department, one staff member and a handful of hired students struggle to perform this essential maintenance.

Tools for Programming

Our experience with programming environments for students has mirrored our experience with lecture demonstration tools: their value to students and to the educational process is obvious and their cost in development and maintenance is high. By building our own tools, we can innovate, provide advanced systems for education and adapt those systems to our changing needs. But we live with ever-changing, never-finished software that we struggle to transform into the production environment students and instructors expect.

Two programming environments have served undergraduate computer science education at Brown. Passé and MEADOW each offer a complete environment for editing, compiling and debugging programs. They also assume the role of primary user interface by providing access to news, mail, printing and some simple UNIX functions. Passé was designed specifically for teaching introductory programming, MEADOW is a research project adapted for educational use. Both systems have achieved some success, and both have suffered from similar maladies.

The software visualization technologies that these systems offer are two types of program view: program structure and data. The program structure view is drawn statically from the code. For a procedural programming language, it is a call graph in which nodes represent procedures and directed arcs represent procedure invocation. For an object-oriented language, a class browser better represents the structure; the program-structure view is both a help in understanding a large system and, in integrated environments like those described here, a navigational aid for moving through the code.

The data view graphically renders data structures created and values assigned while a program is running. It lets students see, at a glance, what their program is doing – how nodes are created and linked into a list or the state of an array at any point in the computation. Sophisticated environments provide data hiding, allowing a high-level view of a large data structure that, at the click of the mouse, can zoom in on a particular component to reveal more information about its type and current values.

Passé

Passé (see Fig. 4) was designed as a self-contained Pascal development environment. The heart of the system is a Pascal interpreter that provides standard debugging features, such as breakpoints, and also drives multiple synchronous views of a program's execution. Its built-in program editor and other tools are accessible from a menu bar at the top of the screen. Because

Passé was written for the X Window System at the Xlib level and because it interprets code rather than compiling it, it has a very responsive feel.

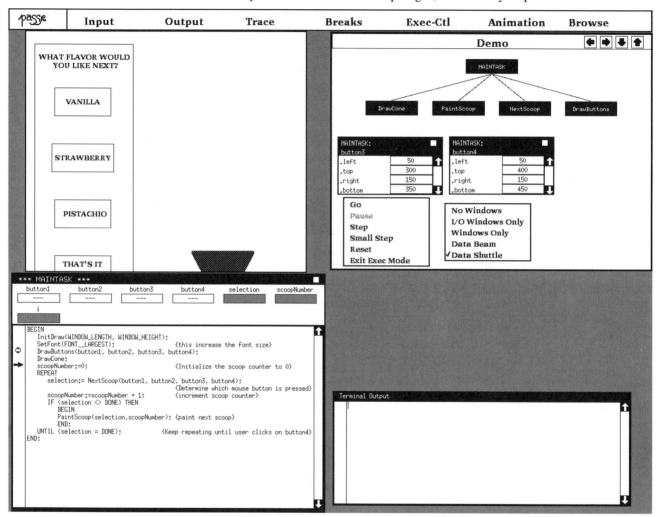

Figure 4. Screen shot of the Passé student programming environment. Note the call-graph and data view in the Demo *window.*

Passé was popular with both students and instructors. The call-graph visualization (called the task tree in Passé) helped students navigate their code, and the data display helped them understand what it was doing. Passé's limitations were designed-in: created with a specific course in mind, Passé did not implement important language features needed by other classes. When the authors left Brown and the staff was faced with supporting two programming environments, Passé was superseded by the already existing MEADOW.

MEADOW

MEADOW (see Fig. 5) is a student version of FIELD, an extensible collection of integrated programming tools based upon standard UNIX utilities like dbx and make [Reiss 94a]. FIELD and MEADOW add to these utilities a graphical user interface and additional tools for visualizing both the static structure of a software project and its run-time behavior.

FIELD was designed for use by programmers at all skill levels. It offers features rich enough for sophisticated users but is sufficiently configurable that a student environment can be fashioned from it. MEADOW strips away some of the complexity of the FIELD user interface, leaving only the tools and options useful to novice programmers. The MEADOW environment includes a program editor, program text and graphical output windows, a static visualization of program structure and a dynamic data display view. MEADOW has been the standard environment for introductory programming students at Brown since 1989.

In 1993 the Computer Science Department revised its undergraduate curriculum to make a wholesale shift from teaching procedural programming to teaching object-oriented methodologies. Students no longer learn procedural programming in Pascal, they learn object-oriented programming in OOPAS (Object-Oriented Pascal), a locally developed variant of Turbo Pascal. When the department moved to object-oriented programming techniques, MEADOW moved too: it was given a native understanding of OOPAS and outfitted with a class browser to replace the procedure-oriented flow view. Retaining our software infrastructure while making this dramatic change was a considerable advantage. Since our tools are developed here, we are able to adapt them to our changing needs. The control we have is a benefit, but with it comes the responsibility for ensuring that the software continues to work well.

When MEADOW, which had always strained our computing resources, was updated for the new curriculum, the data display view became less responsive, since MEADOW had to perform expensive searches of the class hierarchy to produce the same visualization. The updated view was much slower than its predecessor and students found it frustrating to use. The advantage it offered was lost because its performance was not maintained.

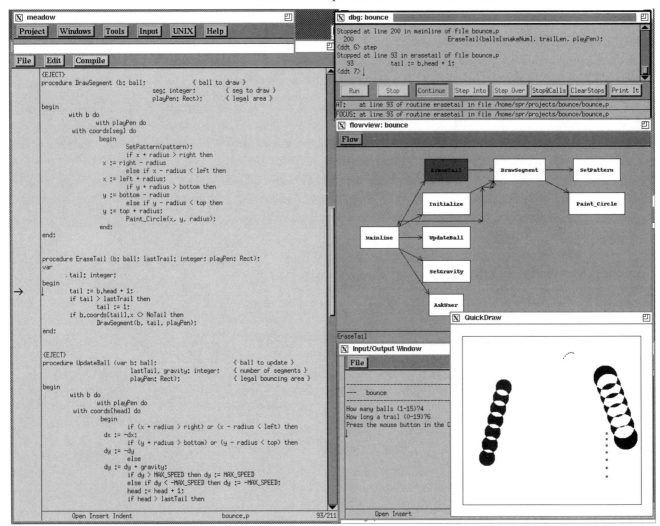

Figure 5. The MEADOW student programming environment with editor, control, call-graph and output windows visible.

Part of the original dream of software visualization tools in education was that students, introduced to these tools in lecture and immediately grasping their importance as a learning tool, would seek them out on their own time and use them to study and explore concepts out of class. Though Brown students are mature and intellectually motivated, the reality does not resemble that dream. In fact, as machines have become faster and environments more powerful and accessible, students find it easier to invest less in learning up front and to let trial and error and the sure verdict of the compiler lead their efforts. Though visualization eases understanding, understanding is still more work than guessing, and guessing is an increasingly effective approach if not to learning, then at least to accomplishing assigned tasks.

Can software visualization be made a necessary part of a student's learning experience? In 1991, students in our introductory algorithms and data structures course were asked to run an algorithm animation, on their own time, and write an explanation of what it was showing. The effect of this on students was so positive that it encouraged a different approach to the use of this technology in education – the visualization as assignment. Since then, we have used visualization at Brown as a part of student project work and also as the project itself.

Piper

Over the years, a technique evolved for filling the gap between automatic program visualization available through systems like MEADOW and algorithm animation like that produced by BALSA. Our goal was automatic algorithm animation: providing students with high-level views of their program while they are developing and debugging it. The system that resulted, Piper, is a framework for the creation of visualizations that are custom-made for each assignment. Students implementing an algorithm call Piper to produce a graphical display of the execution of their code. Piper handles all input and output, including graphical user interaction such as collecting graph data from mouse inputs.

Because Piper visualizations are tailored to each task, they can provide a visualization that is more intuitive than could be generated from their source code. A student coding a red-black tree uses the Piper visualization for a red-

Tools as Homework

black tree: Piper does not need to infer the structure of the data from the code and knows beforehand the best way to draw the tree in a window (see Fig. 6).

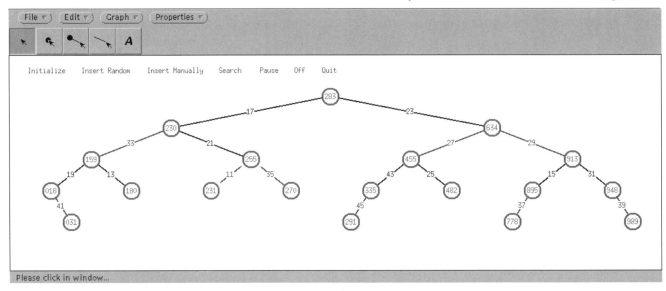

Figure 6. Piper visualization of a red-black tree (original display is in color).

That Piper makes assumptions like this is both its strength and its weakness. Without them, it could not offer the high-level visualization that is its primary feature. But assumptions can get students into trouble. Piper's designers sought to minimize the programming overhead imposed on students. The idea was that they should be able to concentrate on implementing the algorithm they were assigned, and get the visualization almost for free by inserting only a few discrete library calls into their code. But a visualization of a non-working program requires a finer granularity of interesting events. If, for instance, a library call triggers a complex action, like a right-rotation of a node in a red-black tree, it fails to disclose the many possible programming errors in the actual code for that task. If the visualization is the only feedback the student has, it can hide errors rather than reveal them and thus complicate the student's job.

An uneasy balance was struck by having complex atomic actions in Piper actually walk the student's data structure to ensure its consistency before performing a visualization event. The programming overhead is kept to a minimum and, though Piper does not give the kind of detailed feedback one would wish for, neither does it cover up mistakes.

Student-Designed Visualizations

The simple interface offered by Piper is appropriate for introductory students whose time would not be well spent struggling with complex visualization software. But in more advanced classes, other ways of using software visualization tools can provide instructive learning experiences.

One approach makes the creation of a new visualization the assignment. Students in Brown's computational geometry course study complex algorithms that are often as challenging to understand as they are to implement. As a final exercise, students have the option of creating a visualization of one of the algorithms presented in the course. No such system as Piper is available to provide encapsulated routines with preprogrammed graphical views: students in the seminar must take on the role of algorithm animation designer and implementer.

Several years of projects from this course offer insights into both student psychology and the process of creating animation. Perhaps most surprising is that students rarely choose to create their visualizations using systems designed to support that endeavor. Instead, they most often use the low-level tools or more general-purpose systems with which they are already familiar. Having labored to understand arcane and elaborate algorithms and being about to devote significant time and effort to illustrating them, students seem unwilling to stray from their own skill set or to be constrained in their design by an algorithm-animation system. Instead they produce hand-crafted visualizations that are often more ambitious and more innovative than anything these systems could produce.

Some recent student projects from this course rely on direct manipulation to drive the visualization. Sweep-line graph algorithms lend themselves to direct manipulation in an obvious way. Because their progress, literally or conceptually, is along one dimension of a two- or three-dimensional space, it is easy to tie a visualization of such an algorithm to a scroll bar and give direct control of it to the user.

One student project illustrates Fortune's algorithm or the "cone method," which constructs a Voronoi diagram from a field of points. A visualization of this three-dimensional sweep-plane algorithm depicts a projection of the space onto a plane (see Fig. 7). A vertical line representing the progress of the algorithm through the data set is manipulated directly by the user. The algorithm, as implemented, is reversible, so the visualization can be moved forward or backward, and the portion of the data set not yet encountered by the algorithm (to the right of the line) can be altered at any time.

Figure 7. Student visualization of cone method algorithm for drawing Voronoi diagrams.

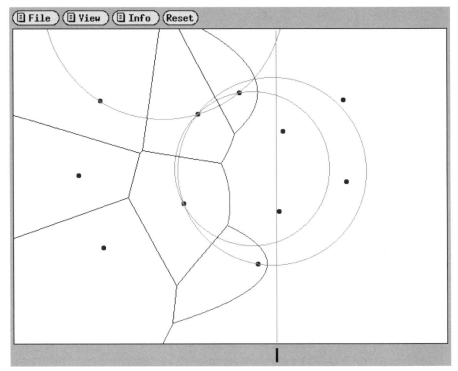

This spare, easy-to-use demonstration is a powerful tool for exploring the behavior of the algorithm. Because it offers only direct manipulation for controlling the progress of the algorithm, it forces the user to choose the speed of execution and to use that to focus on the most interesting intervals. The operations play, pause, stop, rerun, etc., are all implicit in the user's movement of the slider. And that, coupled with the ease with which the data set can be changed, encourages the user to explore the algorithm by varying the speed and data set through many runs and partial runs.

The very best student-written visualizations are introduced into the curriculum as lecture demonstrations. Using student projects to teach is an excellent way to motivate new projects, and students are both a creative and economical source of new visualizations.

Brown's computer science curriculum feels the influence of industry trends and local research. Courses increasingly use the World Wide Web to reach students and Java will soon be the language in which introductory programming concepts are taught. We continue to experiment with more interactive uses of visualizations and other software in our electronic classroom. And two current research efforts promise new visualization technologies for education.

A new programming environment research prototype named Desert updates the integrated and open framework developed in FIELD. Among its new features is a flexible 3D visualization tool that allows the programmer to specify from a variety of sources what information about the program is to be displayed and how it should be presented [Reiss 96].

Current research on algorithm animation at Brown includes the development of Mocha, a new model for providing algorithm animation over the World Wide Web. Mocha is a distributed model with a client-server architecture that optimally partitions the software components of a typical algorithm animation system and leverages the power of the Java language [Baker 95b].

Current Work

The Computer Science Department of Brown University has a long history of teaching with software visualization. Beginning with BALSA and the inauguration of our first electronic classroom in the early 1980s, instructors at Brown have used software visualization as illustrations in lectures, as part of the student programming environment and as assigned tasks for students to complete. We have built and sampled a number of different systems and many individual demonstrations.

Summary

Our experience has shown that effective visualizations for teaching must be easy to understand and easy to use, provide multiple views and allow the complexity of the display to be gradually increased. Visualization tools that are used for more than lecture demonstrations, like the automatic visualization tools of a programming environment, gain easier acceptance because they are used outside the classroom. Integrating software visualization tools into the educational process is difficult for many reasons, the most crippling in the academic environment being the need for ongoing software maintenance to keep the tools working and up to date.

Perhaps the greatest testament to the value of algorithm animation specifically and software visualization generally in the educational process is that we are still doing it after all these years, despite considerable difficulties in creating, integrating and maintaining these tools. Though research in algorithm animation is less active at Brown now than it has been, its promise and real results have compelled its continued use here. Even so, we search for better, and better-supported, tools.

Acknowledgments

Some of the work described here is supported in part by the National Science Foundation under grants CCR-9423847, ASC-8920219 and CCR-9422625, and by ARPA order 8225, ONR grant N00014-91-J-4052.

Using Software to Teach Computer Programming: Past, Present and Future

Chapter **26**

Paul Mulholland
and
Marc Eisenstadt

Introduction

Over the past twenty years, we have undergone a change of perspective in the way we teach programming. Having begun by worrying in detail about the needs of novices, and trying to understand their problems and misconceptions, we developed a range of environments and automated debugging assistants to help them (this work is described in detail in [Eisenstadt 92a]). Our empirical studies [Eisenstadt 84a] [Eisenstadt 92a] suggested that algorithm design and planning were not nearly as big an obstacle to our students as the lack of a clear execution model. For example, in tackling the averaging problem used by PROUST [Johnson 85], our subjects had no trouble computing averages, but their algorithms were based on an intuitive approach of applying nested functions to aggregate data objects (i.e. first add up all the items, then tally them separately). The stumbling block was the mismatch between the subjects' intuitive approach and the rather artificial constraints imposed by the behaviour of a Pascal WHILE loop, and a critical issue for us was how to impart a clear model of this constrained behaviour. We therefore decided to move our emphasis to the "software maintenance" side of programming, as opposed to the "design" and "planning" sides. We realised eventually that the debugging/maintenance needs of experts were fundamentally the same as the pedagogical needs of our novices: both needed to see in a perspicuous fashion what was happening during program execution, though at different levels of granularity. This resulted in a shift in our emphasis from automated debugging assistants to software visualization. To justify this shift, let's consider the evolution of our view in detail.

Learning by debugging

In 1976, we faced the challenge of teaching programming in very adverse circumstances: we wanted to teach AI programming to Psychology students at the UK's Open University. Our students were (a) computer-illiterate or computer-phobic, (b) working at home with no computer hardware, and therefore having to attend a local study centre to use a dial-up teletype link to a DEC system-20, (c) studying Psychology with no intention of learning programming, (d) only allocated a period of two weeks to get through the computing component embedded within a larger Cognitive Psychology course. Our approach, described in [Eisenstadt 83], was to design a programming language called SOLO (essentially a semantic-network variant of LOGO) which enabled students to do powerful things on the first day, embed this language in a software environment which corrected "obvious" errors (such as silly spelling mistakes) automatically, make the workings of the underlying virtual machine both highly explicit and very visible, and develop a curriculum sequence which from start to finish tried to motivate the student by highlighting the relevance of each programming task to the student's main academic interest—cognitive psychology. Visibility of the underlying virtual machine was achieved by printing out changes to the semantic network as they were made by the user, although the innards of control flow were not particularly visible in the sense that we describe below.

Our students wrote plenty of buggy SOLO programs, and we were highly motivated to understand the nature of our students' problems, and also to develop automatic bug detectors and intelligent tutoring systems which capitalised on this understanding. We studied and modelled our student's misconceptions in some detail [Kahney 82] [Kahney 83] [Kahney 92], finding that deep-seated problems such as understanding recursion were often due to a student's failure to map analogically from the detailed curriculum examples to the programming task at hand. Indeed, Conway [Conway 87] found that explicit instruction about how to perform the analogical mapping was of direct benefit to the students. We extended our studies to other languages including Pascal [Eisenstadt 84a], and found that although the fundamentals of iteration were not problematic to novices, the contorted mapping to specific language constructs was problematic: novices seemed to prefer to apply nested functions to aggregate data objects rather than cycling through individually-indexed objects. All of these studies confirmed our view that novices employed quite sensible models of the world, but that programming language instructors in general (including ourselves) consistently failed in helping novices to map their pre-existing models onto the specific ones required to deal with programming. Some of our studies e.g. [Kahney 82] directly led to a revision of our SOLO curriculum.

We built a variety of automatic debuggers for SOLO [Laubsch 81] [Hasemer 84] and other languages, including Lisp [Domingue 87] (see figure 1) and Pascal [Lutz 92]. The approaches varied, but all involved some sort of cliché detection and near-miss analysis, and were strongly influenced by the MIT Programmer's Apprentice project [Rich 79] [Rich 90]. As AI researchers, we were very pleased when our programs could automatically detect a bug and make sense of the student's problem. As programming language instructors, however, we faced an awkward dilemma. Explaining the root cause of the bug to the student seemed inordinately difficult, because it involved concepts that the student didn't really understand (if the student had understood, he or she wouldn't have been caught by that particular bug in the first place). This is a standard pedagogical problem, namely how to help the student leap across "islands of understanding", and was regrettably outside the scope of our work on automatic debugging. When we tried out our systems on our residential summer school students, we observed that what appeared to help them the most was *showing* them (on a blackboard) what their program was doing and why. Indeed, they didn't particularly need the automatic bug detectors once they could see what was really happening.

At the same time, our students were feeling frustrated about reaching the limit of SOLO's powers very quickly, and not being able to extend their programs to handle more complex tasks. Rather than continue with SOLO development, we decided to teach Prolog, which exhibited many of the same pattern-matching capabilities of relevance to our students, but was much more powerful, and quite widely used in the AI community. We were working on a project at the time to develop a graphical debugger for professional Prolog users, and decided it would be useful to "dovetail" our teaching and research activities. This meant trying to develop a cradle-to-grave environment that would be useful for our novices, but which extended all the way to the capabilities of professional Prolog

The ITS years

```
                 ITSY Editor Window
(defun buggy-first (1)
  (car(1)))

(defun wrong1 (a b)
  (+ a (wrong2)))

(defun wrong2 ()
  (* b 2))

(defun rotate-r (1)
  (list (cadr 1) (caddr 1) (car 1)))

*_
Your function ROTATE-R seems to be wrong
it gives (2 3 1) with the argument (1 2 3 4 5)
when it should give (5 1 2 3 4)
```

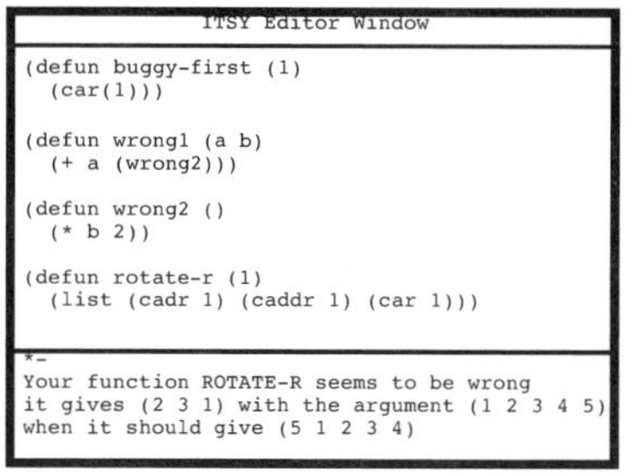

Figure 1. ITSY adapted from [Domingue 87].

programmers. "Seeing what was happening" was a very useful way to overcome some (though not all) of the bottlenecks we had witnessed among the novices who were having trouble mapping their real world models onto a programming framework. At the same time, our experts needed to "see the wood for the trees," i.e. to have a way of homing in quickly on trouble spots. The difference between the viewpoints required by the two audiences was not simply one of physical scale size, such as might be provided for free on a graphics workstation, but rather one of *abstraction level*, which required careful attention. The end result of this line of work was TPM, The Transparent Prolog Machine [Eisenstadt 88a] [Brayshaw 91] [Kwakkel 91] and its accompanying textbook and video curriculum material [Eisenstadt 88b] [Eisenstadt 90a].

The SV story

Figure 2. Example of a TPM coarse-grained view of program execution.

Our work with TPM (see figure 2) suggested that it might be possible to cater for quite a wide audience and a wide range of problems by focusing on the common thread which ran through the entire learning experience: visualization. We were developing video-based teaching material for novice Prolog programmers at the same time as we were implementing graphics facilities for helping experts observe a 2- or 3-thousand node search space. Only by forcing these two paths to converge could we cater for the "upwardly mobile student" who learned about Prolog in the early phases and then went on to become a serious Prolog user. By stepping back to think about the end-point of the learning trajectory, we were able to provide a useful spin-off for those at the beginning of the trajectory.

At the same time as our work on program visualization was developing, some of our colleagues at the Open University had come up with an approach to constructing Intelligent Tutoring Systems that they called Guided Discovery Tutoring [Elsom-Cook 90]. This approach excited us, because it combined ITS work with a strong emphasis on software environments in which students were free to explore and develop in their own way, but under the benign watchful eye of a tutorial assistant. This was in contrast to the earlier ITS work on programming which embodied a different "instruction-based" paradigm. In that earlier paradigm, students were led through a structured curriculum, embarking on well-defined tasks, and even designing and implementing their programs according to a model of "good practice" which had been painstakingly captured by the ITS designers (indeed this very model was critical because it facilitated automated diagnosis when students go wrong). The "instruction-based" paradigm appears to embody clean, top-down, robust and reliable software-engineering practice (i.e. it aims to get the design and specification right from the beginning), but in reality it can act as a straight-jacket for many students. Although it is hard to argue against such a noble-sounding path, we stress that it is not the *only* path, and moreover it is simply not appropriate for all students. Nor is it the path followed by most professional programmers. (This could be why we have a "software crisis" at the moment, but we doubt it. There are many other issues involved, which are beyond the scope of this chapter to address.)

We said at the beginning of this section that our overall emphasis shifted from the "design" and "planning" aspect of programming towards the "software maintenance" side. This would appear to be encouraging students to engage in brute force "hacking" (in the old sense) rather than in good software engineering practice. However, the tenets of Guided Discovery Tutoring, like the seminal work of [Papert 80], suggested to us that we could indeed trust students to do some unstructured exploration, and gently nudge them in a different direction if they were ready for it. This "gentle nudge" could take the form of a whole curriculum sequence, or it could be a matter of just showing the students a particular way of thinking about program execution. To explore this assumption we carried out a number of empirical studies aimed at ascertaining the extent to which students were able to benefit from a range of SV environments. The next two sections will outline the empirical findings and their ramifications for the educational role of SV.

Our recent work provides support for the argument that no SV will ever be universally superior across all kinds of users and tasks [Mulholland 95]. Two important factors influencing performance are (a) the programmers' expertise with the programming language in question, and (b) their level of familiarity with the SV itself. It does seem possible, however, that a particular SV could be most suitable for a novice population. This is for two reasons. Firstly, a crucial factor in how well a novice is able to use an SV is the extent to which the notation helps to combat misunderstandings. A notation successful in this venture will undoubtedly prove to be a reasonable tool. Another important factor is how well the SV facilitates the utilisation of strategies the novice is able to employ. Strategies relying on explicit information such as mapping between the trace and the code, and control flow and data flow strategies are of particular importance.

The truth about SV

It seems far less likely that an SV will be most appropriate for all experts irrespective of the kinds of task they wish to perform. This is for two reasons. Firstly, experts have a sound knowledge of the execution model and therefore do not suffer from the associated misunderstandings. As a result, the ability of the SV to present information in a way that deals with potential misunderstandings is far less important. Secondly, experts are able to develop a much more elaborate collection of strategies, many utilising implicit information. With experience of an SV the experts are able to tune their strategies to fit the features of the SV. For experts the relative efficacy of SVs will to some extent always be a matter of taste.

The important distinction between novices and experts suggested by the results is how increased familiarity with the SV may affect the nature of the strategies used. Once novices have become reasonably familiar with the notation it seems that any further exposure to the SV without a corresponding shift in expertise will not alter the way in which the SV is utilised. Their use of the SV is restricted by the kinds of strategies they are able to employ. Their level of expertise confines them to using strategies which rely on the information explicit within the trace. The effect of notational familiarity on novices using explicit and implicit information is summarised in figure 3. Novices also seemed not only affected but confined by the kinds of misunderstandings they have of the language. Protocol evidence revealed many instances where when confronted with a disparity between the SV and their incorrect assumptions the subjects would reinterpret the display in such a way as to be consistent with their expectations rather than the disparity leading them to challenge their expectations and the misunderstanding from which they originated.

Familiarity does, however, affect the way in which experts make use of the SV. Initially the expert will rely on strategies drawing on explicit information, as they fully develop an understanding of how the notation of the SV corresponds to the execution model. With greater experience the expert is able to draw on implicit information within the trace as Gestalts or visual clichés become noticeable. The effect of notational familiarity on experts using explicit and implicit information is summarised in figure 4. When using an SV to provide an explanation, experts experienced with the SV are able to draw attention to function related information at an earlier stage as they are already aware how the higher level abstractions of the program map onto the patterns found within the display. Experts unfamiliar with the SV are required to initially work with explicit information and tie the declarative account to the SV at a later stage.

These results allow us to comment on whether text or graphics is the most appropriate medium for displaying such information. As we have seen, experts given sufficient familiarity are able to incorporate implicit information into their strategies. Novices, it seems, are not. This suggests that a notation which necessitates access to implicit information is not suitable for programmers of low expertise or those intending to use the technology for a short period of time. As a graphical notation will probably rely more heavily on implicit information, evidence suggests that these should be reserved until the student has acquired a level of expertise which permits them to appreciate abstractions. Exposing the novice to such an SV would be to encourage them to perform like mini-experts rather than learning through the application of strategies appropriate to their skill level, though whether this is necessarily worse would require further study.

These results are consistent with the literature on novice expert differences and the development of expertise. For example, Chi *et al.* [Chi 81] found that novices tend to focus on the surface features of the language whereas experts tend to use higher level structural representations. Similarly, Davies [Davies 94a] found that experts tend to externalise higher level structures during program comprehension but novices tend to externalise code-level information. There is a wealth of evidence from a number of domains to suggest that these performance differences are due to the knowledge structures of experts and novices differing qualitatively rather than quantitatively and that knowledge has to be restructured during an intermediate stage before progressing to full expertise. For example, Lesgold *et al.* [Lesgold 88] found that during some phase in the development of expertise in radiological diagnosis the number of errors made temporarily increases. They suggested this kink in the learning curve could be a consequence of a restructuring of the knowledge underlying performance. Similarly, Davies [Davies 94b] in his investigation of recall for focal and nonfocal lines in Pascal programs found expertise to develop in a non-linear fashion

Acceptance that there is no software panacea suggests new ways in which the proper role for SV within an educational setting could be established. This covers two related questions:

1) How should SV be incorporated into computer programming education?

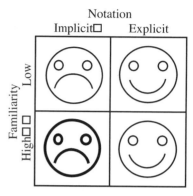

Figure 3. The effect of notational familiarity on novices using explicit and implicit information.

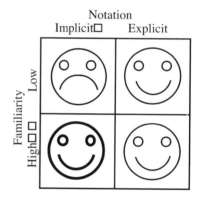

Figure 4. The effect of notational familiarity on experts using explicit and implicit information.

Finding the role of SV within education

As considered above, an important design aim in the development of SVs has been to find a single representation of a programming language suitable for all levels of expertise. Not only do the presented findings suggest none of the SVs studied can confidently claim universal superiority but that because of the qualitative differences between programmers of different levels of expertise such an aspiration will inevitably fail.

This could be empirically studied by comparing two approaches to incorporating SV into programming education. One approach could use a single SV throughout the course. We have used (though not evaluated) this approach in the development of a Prolog course which uses the TPM notation throughout all materials [Eisenstadt 87]. The work presented above suggests that TPM may not be a very suitable SV for the early novice, though it could be argued that the difficulties confronting the early novice are possibly outweighed by the extra cost of having to transfer between different notations during the course, should TPM be presented at a later stage. An alternative view would be that novices will learn more effectively through a notation suited to their characteristics and strategic capabilities than through a notation which requires them to aspire to expert strategies from an early stage. For example, Prolog could be taught by initially using an SV such as Theseus [Mulholland 95] (see figure 5) and transferring to TPM when the students are reaching the stage of being able to externalise their knowledge and use abstractions. It could be argued that the change in notation will not adversely effect the students as their knowledge is undergoing restructuring which will parallel the notational transition.

2) Could SV be used specifically to support the transition between novice and expert?

The dual SV approach to programming education discussed above would aim to mirror the transition from novice to expert in the learning materials. A more specific issue is how SV could support the knowledge restructuring stage as students move from novice to expert. Karmiloff-Smith [Karmiloff-Smith 79] [Karmiloff-Smith 94] provides some evidence that representational diversity is a crucial component in the attainment of expertise. Her theory of human development has highlighted the importance of what she termed Representational Redescription (RR). RR is the process of learning by iteratively rerepresenting knowledge in different formats. Karmiloff-Smith's observations of children have

```
·  ?  fun(What)
  «1 fun({What=X})
    ?  car(What)
   +1 car({What=mini})
    ?  gold(mini)
   -d gold(mini)
      ^^^^^^^^^^^^^^^^^
·  >2 fun({What=X})
·    ?  bike(What)
·   +1 bike({What=honda})
·    ?  silver(honda)
·   +1 silver(honda)
·   +2 fun({What=honda})
```

Figure 5. Example of a Theseus trace.

found that the child will initially develop competence at some skill. The focus of this stage is what she terms "behavioural mastery" rather than the development of a deeper level of understanding. The child will then "unpack" the structures underlying that competence in order to make them more explicit to the individual. This occurs by initially making the new internal (rather than the external) representation the main driving force. During this phase new kinds of errors previously absent appear as a result of the incompleteness of the internal representation. Later the external and internal representations become reconciled leading to a new competence underpinned by a deeper understanding. This process of unpacking knowledge to refine the internal representation is facilitated by iteratively redescribing the knowledge in different internal representational formats.

A similar process may also apply to the development of computer programming expertise. We found that novices will often use strategies such as mapping between the SV and the code without having a high level understanding of the constructs being compared [Mulholland 95]. This process sometimes led to errors but also often led to the subject making the correct response for incomplete reasons. For these subjects, their next goal would not be an increase in competency, but rather an examination of the strategies being used and an understanding of the limits of their applicability.

Unpacking competent behaviour to foster a deeper understanding is a process SV may be able to support. SVs can be used to provide abstract and diverse representations of the same execution. For example, a diverse range of representations of Parlog execution are found in the Multiple Representation Environment [Brayshaw 94]. These differ both in terms of the notational formalisms used and the levels of abstraction on which they work. Similarly, Algorithm Animation environments such as BALSA [Brown 88a], TANGO [Stasko 90b] and VIZ [Domingue 91] provide a range of diverse perspectives on program execution. These could provide external support and prompting for the necessary internal redescription processes. The diverse range of abstractions available could be used to suggest ways in which the students could redescribe their knowledge. A similar role could be found for bug location agents which can be used to delegate certain kinds of search and inference processes to the software environment [Brayshaw 93a]. This could facilitate the externalisation and examination of internal representations and processes.

Conclusion

An important consequence of this work would be to identify the level and kind of support necessary for each stage of the learning process. Many references have been made to the role free-exploratory learning could play in computer programming education, particularly when supported by a rich environment e.g. [Ramhadan 92]. The kind of research outlined above would aim to identify the stages during the learning process where exploration was most appropriate. This would most likely parallel the stages of expertise where the students are able to externalise and evaluate their own knowledge in light of what is being shown to them, rather than when the students merely reinterpret incoming information in order to preserve some consistency with their own expectations.

Such an issue will become more important as new technology such as the internet becomes applied to distance education, where multimedia course materials can be used to fuller effect and the opportunity exists for the student to take a more independent role within the learning process. However, the introduction of rich interactive environments will not guarantee a fruitful learning experience. Rather, the nature of the environment and the level of free exploration must be appropriate to the characteristics of the learner.

Animated Algorithms

Peter A. Gloor

Introduction

This chapter introduces *Animated Algorithms*, a multimedia system for computer science education that illustrates a new class of educational multimedia applications characterized by a seamless integration of different multimedia data types. The combination of hypertext, computer animation, and digital video results in an interactive hypermedia learning environment impossible to realize before the advent of multimedia technology. *Animated Algorithms* is an integrated hypermedia learning environment for teaching and studying computer science algorithms. It tries to aid in the understanding of core algorithmic concepts that are especially difficult to comprehend by students. Algorithms are a complex subject to teach and understand. One of the difficulties in understanding an algorithm is the development of a sophisticated conceptualization of the algorithm from written explanations and pseudocode. Our system applies the concepts of algorithm animation, hypertext, and digital video to facilitate this task.

System Overview

Animated Algorithms [Gloor 93] is intended to be used to complement a conventional textbook for the "Introduction to Algorithms" course. It assists in the understanding of core concepts, like the O- and Ω- Notation, and the comprehension of advanced subjects, like Fibonacci-Heaps. The algorithm animations can be used either for classroom teaching, or for the individual to study new algorithms and deepen the understanding of known ones. The hypertext part provides individual access to a vast reference book covering the whole field of algorithms.

The system has been implemented on the Macintosh. As multimedia authoring system we used HyperCard [Winkler 90]. Apple's digital video architecture QuickTime™ [Apple 91] allowed to integrate digital video segments into our multimedia documents without needing additional hardware.

The goal of Animated Algorithms is to offer an integrated hypermedia learning environment for computer science algorithms. It contains three complementary components: A full hypertext version of the book "Introduction to Algorithms" by Thomas H. Cormen, Charles E. Leiserson, and Ronald L. Rivest [Cormen 90], interactive animations of the most important algorithms, and movies explaining the use of the hypertext interface and the animations.

Figure 1. Screen dump of "Animated Algorithms"

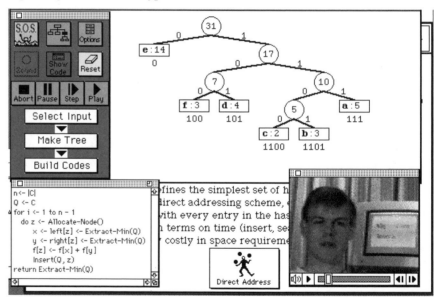

The screen dump in figure 1 displays the main components of Animated Algorithms: the window in the lower right corner shows a "talking head" digital movie explaining the features of the algorithm, the top half of the screen depicts an animation of the "Huffman Tree" algorithm, and in the background there is some hypertext visible which explains the fundamentals of "Huffman Trees".

The hypertext, including the figures, is stored in HyperCard stacks. It contains tools for instructors and students to facilitate navigation, text annotation, tracking of preexisting links, full-text search, and the adding of links and paths through the document. The algorithm animations which are implemented in HyperCard are linked with the hypertext and can be controlled interactively by the user. They also include extensive on-line help to make them self-contained. Some animations include scripting facilities allowing users to program animations of specific data structures. The movies, ("talking heads" and demonstrations) provide a way to view non-interactive versions of the algorithm animations.

The hypertext, consisting of 1850 text nodes and figures, is implemented in HyperCard stacks. It contains tools for navigation, text annotation, tracking of pre-existing links, full-text search, and the adding of links and "paths" through the document. Innovative hypertext concepts first explored in Animated Algorithms are described in [Gloor 96].

The animations, which are implemented in HyperCard, are linked with the hypertext and can be controlled interactively by the user. This interactivity not only includes the ability to single-step through the pseudocode, but also (in certain animations) the ability to choose initial conditions and the specification of assumptions which the algorithm makes, enabling the user to affect the action of the algorithm. Some animations include scripting facilities allowing users to program animations of specific data structures. The animations also include extensive on-line help, making them self-contained.

Project Goals

Most of the animations for the Animated Algorithms system have initially been developed by students either as homework assignments for algorithm animation classes or as thesis work. The students had taken algorithm classes before and thus had already a profound knowledge of the subject. It was our goal to make them productive in developing animations as fast as possible. Therefore the development environment needed to fulfill stringent boundary conditions:

- *Rapid development:*
  The development environment should allow for early student integration into the development process. That means that the students should become productive developing animations very quickly. In particular, the system should be easy to learn for computer science majors (and not for graphics

designers). We therefore favored an approach based on a programming language over a strictly mouse or menu based animation development system. Basic programming languages, such as C or Pascal, had to be excluded because of productivity limitations. We also excluded the option of developing a dedicated animation shell from scratch. Instead we looked for an appropriate off the shelf scripting language animations package.

- *Portable:*
  We wanted to create a system that we could distribute easily without having to pay tremendous royalties. The software should also run on a broad hardware base.
- *Homogeneous:*
  We not only wanted to have a collection of algorithm animations, but also a usable and homogeneous system at the end of the course. In particular, the user interface should be uniform and easy to use on different algorithms.
- *Color and Sound:*
  It would be nice to have not only black and white silent animations, but also color and sound. But on the other hand algorithm animations need not be high quality Gouraud shaded ray traced[1] computer animations. We therefore decided to have as much graphic quality as possible, but that all other aspects mentioned here should have preference. In particular we gave interactivity preferential treatment over sophistication in output quality.
- *Speed:*
  The animations should run at a comfortable speed. Ideally they should be independent from hardware and degrade gracefully if the system ran on slower hardware. This requirement contrasts to the demand for high quality color animations.
- *Hypertext:*
  It was our goal to get not only algorithm animations, but also a hypermedia environment explaining them. We needed an extendible application development system exceeding bare animation capabilities. Ideally the system should offer built in hypertext linking capabilities.

---

[1]Gouraud shading is a computer graphics procedure to get smoothly shaded surfaces of three-dimensional objects. Ray tracing is another process that allows for more than one light source with mirroring of the light sources.

We soon decided to use the Macintosh as hardware base because of its wide availability and acceptance among schools and universities. We investigated HyperCard [Winkler 90], MacroMedia Director[2] [Vaughn 94] and AddMotion[3] [AddMotion 90] for development environment. To our surprise we finally ended up using HyperCard almost exclusively, adding some simple color animations with AddMotion. The frame-based structure and clumsy scripting language made MacroMedia Director a bad choice for computer scientists developing algorithm animations.

We defined a simple uniform framework for all animations with each algorithm animation having an animation window and an algorithm window (figure 2).

The Animation System

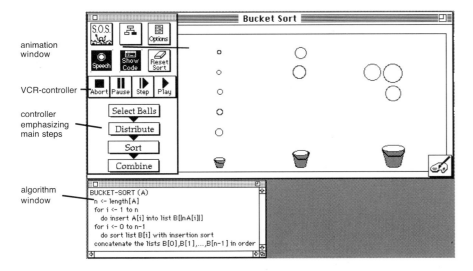

Figure 2. Basic animation screen layout

The algorithm window shows the code for whatever algorithm is currently in progress. The current line of the code (that is, the line being animated) is

---

[2]MacroMedia Director is a powerful standalone animations package with a built in scripting language, Lingo. It is based upon the cast, score, and stage movie maker metaphors.

[3]AddMotion is an animation package embedded within HyperCard, that extends HyperCard's built in animation capabilities.

highlighted to emphasize which part of the algorithm is currently running. We employ a VCR type controller (see figure 2) as the basic user interface metaphor for all of the algorithms. Frequently, this controller is augmented by buttons emphasizing the main steps of an algorithm. This interface allows for a better in-depth understanding of the algorithm. Obviously, these extra commands are sometimes difficult to define or even inappropriate, and can only be applied if the algorithm lends itself well to substructuring.

Figure 3. Overview map for hashing chapter

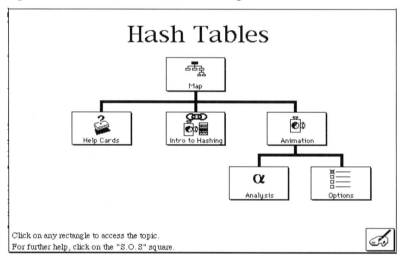

Figure 4. Help card for options menu

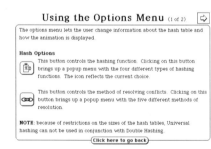

Our goal is not to produce a monolithic collection of algorithm animations, but to implement an integrated learning environment. Because each topic should be self contained, it has its own, hierarchically structured overview map. Figure 3 shows the overview map for the hashing animations.

The overview map presents all options currently available. In figure 3 the student has the following possibilities:

- getting help for using the stack,
- reading an introduction to hashing,
- interactively executing the hashing algorithms,
- going to an analysis card for comparison of the different hashing algorithms,
- reviewing animation options,
- returning to the global animation overview map card.

Figure 4 shows the help card for the options menu. It illustrates our efforts to offer extensive on-line help making animations as self explaining and easily usable as possible.

Algorithm animations support the student in various learning situations:

Educational Benefits of Algorithm Animation

- *Motivation enhancement:*
  Through appealing presentation of the complex material, students are better motivated to study complicated subjects. In addition, the ease of access to cross-references by hypertext removes barriers to an in-depth understanding of the topic being studied.
- *Skill mastery through additional practice opportunities:*
  Students get a new way to experience algorithms. In addition to doing paper exercises and writing programs, they can see algorithms visually and study their features by watching and interacting with animations [Lawrence 94].
- *Development of analytic skills:*
  Algorithm animations assist in the development of analytic skills, as students are asked to collect their own data for algorithm analysis and subsequent design of improved algorithms.
- *Provision of additional context knowledge:*
  The hypertext reference provides easy access to the whole field of algorithms. By offering linking and path mechanisms, it encourages the student to browse in related topics, and to explore additional subjects.

Algorithm animations offers distinct advantages compared to traditional teaching aids, such as textbook and blackboard:

- *Presentation aid in the classroom :*
  Animations support the teacher in explaining the dynamic behavior of an algorithm during the lecture. If computer screen projection is available in the classroom, the teacher can run algorithm animations interactively to compare, for example, the relative search times of red-black trees and binary search trees using the same data sets.
- *Individual improvement of student's understanding:*
  Using the algorithm animations interactively, the student can playfully and without stress explore the peculiarities of an algorithm. By allowing students to manipulate the algorithm and its input, and then study the resulting

actions of the algorithm, they are able to form a conceptual model of the algorithm in addition to learning the code. They also can modify parameters and analyze algorithms empirically. As has been verified by Lawrence, Badre and Stasko in an experiment [Lawrence 94], this interactivity adds a new level of effectiveness to a hypermedia learning environment, making it an even more effective tool in teaching concepts, as it forces learners to take part in the lesson, as opposed to simply watching a movie.

• *Reference library for the student:*
  Using the exhaustive search and navigation capabilities of an integrated hypermedia learning environment, a student can easily access the vast information contained in systems like "Animated Algorithms".

Animated Algorithms version 1.0 was finished in January 1993. It has been thoroughly tested in the development lab and has been used repeatedly in the MIT "Introduction to Algorithms" course on a voluntary basis, with students asked to voluntarily complete questionnaires concerning their reactions to the learning environment. The main benefit reported has been improved student motivation, as students used particular animations to get a better understanding of the algorithm.

The hypertext part has been tested by volunteers (students and computer science professors), which were particularly impressed with the "path" feature, and the capability to traverse the document on various levels of complexity. Also the reference capabilities of the hypertext, as, e.g., full-text search, were appreciated.

While even the most sophisticated hypermedia learning environment never will be able to replace human teachers, it hopefully will assist them in teaching complex subjects. There are numerous situations where a human instructor is not readily available, be it for classwork assignments or for the self-tutoring student. We are convinced that our Animated Algorithms system provides a useful tool that aids both the teacher in explaining and the student in understanding complex algorithms.

Evaluation

Section
VII

The previous sections all involved the technology of software visualization, application domains for these systems, and potential uses of the technology. This section steps back from that work and looks at critically evaluating the systems and visualizations that have been built. This area is one of the emerging foci of current software visualization research.

The first two chapters involve empirical studies of different software visualization technologies. Chapter 28 ("Empirically Assessing Algorithm Animations as Learning Aids") describes the evaluation of algorithm animations as pedagogical aids. It focuses on two studies of algorithm animations used to teach students new algorithms. Study results were mixed, and the chapter explores reasons why software visualizations may or may not assist student learning. Chapter 29 ("A Principled Approach to the Evaluation of SV: A Case-Study in Prolog") describes a study of different visualizations used to portray Prolog program executions. The research uses protocol analysis to determine the efficacy of SV tools and to prescribe how they could be improved to facilitate better understanding.

Finally, Chapter 30 ("Cognitive Questions in Software Visualization") provides a fitting close to this book. It takes a critical look at some of the premises and claims made by software visualization system developers, and it provides knowledge gained from prior experiments, cognitive science and psychology to assess those claims. The chapter presents a framework under which software visualization researchers and developers can evaluate their work and plan new contributions to the discipline.

Empirically Assessing Algorithm Animations as Learning Aids

Chapter 28

John Stasko
and
Andrea Lawrence

Learning about computer algorithms is difficult. This is because algorithms are by nature abstract, and understanding how the myriad of variables in an algorithm are used and how control flows in the algorithm can be quite challenging. Algorithm animation systems were developed because researchers harbored a fundamental belief that computer visualizations could assist students to learn about and to understand algorithms better. By giving concrete depictions to the abstractions and operations of algorithms, algorithm animations should make algorithms more meaningful. The dynamics of animation, in particular, should help to convey the temporal evolution of a computer algorithm; Animation seems ideally suited to portraying a process.

Although all algorithm animations fundamentally have the same purpose, how an algorithm animation is used can vary quite a bit. Three applications do appear to be most common, however:

- An algorithm animation is used in a class to accompany a lecture and help the instructor explain key concepts.

- An algorithm animation is used in a formal laboratory setting where students interact with computers.

Introduction

- An algorithm animation is used informally by students out of class at their leisure to help learn more about an algorithm.

For over 10 years now algorithm animations have been used in these ways with the hopes of aiding the instructional process. Many unsupported claims have been made about the naturalness and power of animations. One fundamental question remains unanswered, however. Do algorithm animations truly assist teaching and learning, and if so, how can they be best utilized?

This chapter reviews recent research that is beginning to answer that question, and it describes one of the few attempts made to investigate some of these claims. It describes empirical studies that assess the value of algorithm animations as learning aids. As we shall see, determining in some easily quantifiable way how much algorithm animation can help is a difficult, if not impossible, task. Furthermore, simply characterizing what it means to learn about an algorithm is difficult. Does it mean that a student is able to carry out the procedural steps of the algorithm? Or does it mean something else, perhaps that the student is able to easily code the algorithm, that the student can evaluate and compare the algorithm to other similar ones, or even that the student can transfer this understanding to other similar problems?

In reviewing the research literature on related topics, one encounters a number of studies of the general effect of animation on learning (not necessarily on algorithms). All these studies examined animation in a multimedia context with some learning or training goal. They can help provide us with some intuition about how algorithm animations can assist learning.

Rieber conducted studies with both adults and children to evaluate animation's influence on learning science concepts [Rieber 90a]. With adults, animation had no significant effect, but practice did have a positive effect. With children, animation had a positive effect but only when used in close congruence with the learning task. Rieber also has summarized earlier animation research in computer based instruction [Rieber 89].

Mayer and Anderson have conducted a number of studies of the use of animation to help understand a mechanical process [Mayer 91] [Mayer 92]. Animation had little effect on retention, but it did provide positive results when paired concurrently with explanations.

Palmiter and Elkerton studied the use of animation as an aid to authoring tasks on a computer [Palmiter 91]. Initially, participants who were aided by animation performed faster and more accurately than participants assisted by text-only. After one week elapsed, however, the animation participants had regressed to be equal with the text-only participants. Palmiter speculates that animation may evoke a form of mimicry somewhat short of true understanding [Palmiter 93].

In the remainder of this chapter, we focus on algorithm animation and discuss empirical studies conducted to help learn about the use of algorithm animations in educational settings. While the studies described here do not answer the fundamental question posed earlier, the data they provide, and even more so the processes of the studies themselves, can help us to characterize the positive learning effects of algorithm animations and determine how they can be used for maximum benefit. In particular, these studies have helped us develop a number of opinions and beliefs about the animations, which are described in the final section of the chapter.

This section describes an initial experiment we conducted that examined the efficacy of algorithm animations as learning aids [Stasko 93a]. The participants in the study learned about a data structure called a pairing heap [Fredman 86] that is sometimes used to implement a priority queue. The experiment was conducted in a traditional experimental psychology manner: One set of participants learned about pairing heaps with only textual aids and another group had access to an algorithm animation. A post-test was administered after these learning sessions to evaluate the students' knowledge of pairing heaps. The animation of pairing heaps used in this study was built with the XTango algorithm animation system [Stasko 92a]. A frame from this animation is shown in Figure 1. XTango is available via anonymous ftp from the site `ftp.cc.gatech.edu` as file `pub/people/stasko/xtango.tar.Z`, and the animation used in this experiment is included in the distribution [Stasko 92b].

Experiment 1 - Graduate Students and the Pairing Heap

Figure 1. View of a pairing heap in the XTango animation.

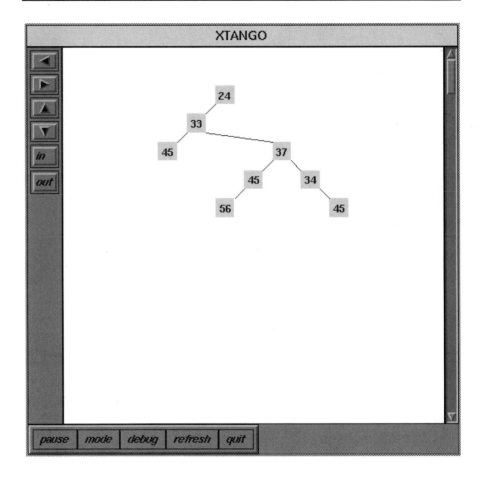

Procedure

The participants of the study, all volunteers, were computer science graduate students who had taken or were taking advanced computer algorithms courses. None of the students had ever studied pairing heaps. The students participated in the study through individual sessions. Each participant was randomly assigned to be in one of two groups, with ten persons total per group. The first group received textual descriptions of the pairing heap algorithm, and the other group received the same textual descriptions supplemented by the opportunity to interact with the pairing heap animation. The textual descriptions consisted of the first few pages of two journal articles about pairing heaps. These pages described the data structure, how it is implemented, and how operations on it work. By providing excerpts from articles, we sought to mimic how students often learn about algorithms and data structures in their day-to-day academic environment.

In the study, students in the text-only group were given 45 minutes to read and study the pairing heap descriptions. Students in the text-animation group were given an initial maximum of 30 minutes to read the articles, and the remaining time (to a total of 45 minutes) to interact with the animation. These students received written instructions about how to operate the animation, but they were not forced to view any particular set of operations. Rather, they were allowed to interact with the animation in any manner they desired. We chose not to present a prepared animation demonstration, in fear of unfairly favoring the animation group by presenting certain important facts about the algorithm.

When the participants had completed the 45 minute learning session, we gave them a set of questions to test their understanding of the pairing heap algorithm. Neither group was allowed to use the textual description during the post-test, nor was the animation available. The participants were given a maximum of 45 minutes to work on the post-test. Three different orderings of questions were used to remove any question sequencing effects. All the questions were designed to have one correct answer, and not be open to interpretation. Unfortunately, this precluded essay-style questions that often can identify a deeper understanding of an algorithm, but this was sacrificed in this study in order to seek quantifiable data.

The post-test included many different styles of questions, broadly organized around six major sections. They are grouped below:

- Eight true-false questions about manipulations on the pairing heaps. **Example**: If we run the delete operation on the heap root, this is equivalent to running the delete min operation.

- Four questions involving numerical complexity issues about how the pairing heap operations function. **Example**: What is the maximum number of comparison-link actions performed during a decrease key operation on a pairing heap which had n nodes prior to the decrease-key operation?

- Two questions involving analysis of how certain valued nodes in the heap are manipulated. **Example**: Suppose we have an existing pairing heap with root having key value x. If we insert a node with key=5, then we insert a node with key=10, and finally we perform a delete min, can the former root with key=x be the root again? If it can, for what values of x can it happen?

- Two questions about the mapping from a binary representation of a pairing heap to a multiway tree representation. **Example**: Given the following binary tree pairing heap (figure was shown), draw the corresponding multiway tree representation.

- Two questions examining the student's understanding of how pairing heaps are built up from insert operations. **Example**: Given the following sequence of operations (list was given), draw how the resulting heap would look using the multiway representation.

- Six questions presenting a picture of a pairing heap and asking the students how the heap would change if a particular operation were to occur. Three of these questions (b, c, f) used the multiway tree representation and three (a, d, e) used the binary representation. **Example**: If we run the delete operation on the node with key=13 in the binary pairing heap representation pictured below (figure was shown), how will the resulting heap appear?

These questions tested many facets of the pairing heap algorithm. Virtually every question in some way required knowledge of a) the invariant properties of the heap, such as the key value relationship between a parent and child node and b) the methodologies of the different operations on the heap.

Certain questions in particular focused on different types of knowledge, however. For instance, the true-false questions tested more declarative or factual understanding. The computational complexity questions required analytical thinking. The six questions about performing operations on the heap tested strictly procedural knowledge.

Our hypothesis prior to the study was that the animation would assist students learn about the algorithm, and in particular, would be more beneficial to procedural understanding than to declarative. Animations primarily depict how an algorithm functions, but they do not explain the reasoning for particular actions.

Results

Table 1 presents the results of the study. It lists the number of correct replies from the 10 participants in each group. The results are listed in the same order as the description of the question categories described above.

		Text Only	Text & Animation
True-False	a	6	6
	b	7	10
	c	8	10
	d	7	7
	e	7	8
	f	7	8
	g	7	7
	h	9	10
Complexity	a	2	5
	b	1	2
	c	6	8
	d	2	4
Analytical	a	8	9
	b	7	7
Tree rep.	a	6	6
	b	6	6
Inserts	a	2	4
	b	3	5
Operations	a	2	3
	b	4	2
	c	2	3
	d	1	4
	e	0	1
	f	2	1

Table 1. Results of the posttests. Each value lists the number of correct replies out of a total of 10 participants.

The animation group averaged 13.6 correct replies and the text-only group averaged 11.2 correct replies out of the 24 questions. A box-plot summary of the participants' individual scores is presented in Figure 2. We performed a two

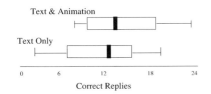

Text & Animation

Text Only

0   6   12   18   24

Correct Replies

Figure 2. Summary of the participants' total scores on the posttest.

sample t-test on these scores and found a nonsignificant trend favoring the animation group (t=1.111, df=18, p<0.13).

Note that the animation group did as well as or better than the text-only group on all but two questions. Those two questions were procedural questions asking about the results of a delete min and delete operation on a multiway representation of a pairing heap. The XTango animation only displayed the binary tree representation of the pairing heap, so the animation group's deficiency here is somewhat understandable.

The animation group completed their posttests slightly faster than did the text-only group. The animation group finished in an average of 37.6 of the maximum 45 minutes and the text-only group averaged 41.0 minutes. Three animation participants and four text-only participants required the full 45 minutes. Perhaps animation facilitates faster learning. This is certainly an issue deserving further study.

Discussion

In general, the performance of all the participants was poorer than we expected, and the animation's benefits over the text-only presentation was not as strong as we had expected. In particular, the animation group did not seem to benefit greatly in the procedural questions. Their performance seemed to be aided more in the declarative style questions, such as the true-false ones, and on the analytical questions.

A number of factors may have contributed to this result. In an analysis of the experimental materials using an informal version of the programming walkthrough procedure [Bell 91], it appeared that neither the text nor the animation could be expected to produce high performance. Most of the test items require the ability to accurately carry out the main procedures of the algorithm, and neither presentation seemed likely to give participants that ability. It appeared that actual experience in carrying out the procedures, or a presentation of the motivation for the steps in the procedures, which might allow participants to reconstruct the procedures at test time, would be required.

Other factors may have contributed to the disappointing results as well. The participants in this study, both the text-animation and text-only groups, may have benefited by knowing what types of examination questions to expect. We simply told the participants that they would be tested after the initial learning period. By providing sample questions, we would have allowed the participants to tailor their learning process in a more focused manner. The animation group, in particular, could have directed their interactions with the animation in ways to clarify the most important topics and features of the pairing heap algorithm.

In order to learn more about the animation, we also included a post-experiment questionnaire for the participants in the animation group. It included three questions: whether the participant felt that the animation aided understanding the pairing heap algorithm, what the participant liked about the animation, and what the participant didn't like about the animation.

All ten animation participants reported that they felt the animation assisted them in understanding the algorithm. Often recognized was that the animation grabbed their interest. This fact appears to be one of the primary advantages of algorithm animation. A few students qualified their replies to the first question, however. One said, "The algorithm animation is good, but explanations of what is happening would help." This thought was echoed by others as well. Another student noted a loss of the animation's effectiveness as time went along, stating, "When viewing the animation it was clear what was happening, but I found it difficult to remember after finishing the animation." This comment reinforces the findings of Palmiter and Elkerton cited earlier [Palmiter 91].

In describing what they liked about the animation, the participants most often cited its interactivity, that is, the capability for them to try out their own examples. Also noted was the relative speed control capability and the visual effect of highlighting (flashing in a different color) nodes being compared. Finally, a number of the participants recognized the smooth movements of the heap during operations as assisting their understanding. One participant stated, "I liked how the computer slowly changed the diagram, letting me see how the change was made rather than an instantaneous change."

In citing their dislikes in the animation, the participants noted the absence of a multiway tree view of the pairing heap and the absence of a way to step through the animation a frame at a time (XTango only includes a *pause/unpause* button). The most often cited negative comment was the inability to rewind or replay the animation. The participants said that after an operation occurred, they often wanted to look at the heap as it appeared before the operation. This is an important point, and should be considered by the developers of future algorithm animation systems. Finally, a number of participants felt that the animation should have been accompanied by textual explanations of what was occurring at that moment in the animation. One participant even asked for the addition of audio voice-over explanations.

Experiment 2 - Undergraduate Students and Kruskal's Algorithm

In the previous study, graduate students learned about a complex data structure and algorithm with the assistance of animations. The next study differs significantly in that the participants were students from an introductory undergraduate computer science course and the algorithm they learned is not as complex as the pairing heap. The experiment also involved students interacting with animations in ways the prior experiment did not. The study described here [Lawrence 94] is actually just one experiment from a series of experiments conducted to understand how algorithm animations can assist undergraduate computer science education [Lawrence 93].

Procedure

The algorithm examined in this experiment was Kruskal's Minimum Spanning Tree Algorithm. Kruskal's MST Algorithm finds a set of edges of a graph that form a connected, acyclic path to all vertices of the graph and that are also of minimum cost or weight. The participants of the study were students at the Georgia Institute of Technology enrolled in CS 1410, the first programming course for Computer Science majors at the Institute at that time. The students were volunteers who received class credit for their participation. Sixty-two students participated in the experiment. The experiment was a 2 x 2 (nested 2) design as represented in Table 2. One variable was how the examples in a lecture about Kruskal's algorithm were presented, either using prepared slides (transparencies) or using an algorithm animation. The second variable was whether the lecture was followed by a laboratory session or not. This design also encompassed a nested 2 level factor under laboratory session; students either passively viewed animations in the lab or they actively interacted with the animations.

		Polka Animation	Prepared Slides
Lecture Only		15	15
Lecture plus Lab	Passive Lab	7	9
	Active Lab	7	9

Table 2. Number of participants in each of the conditions of the experiment.

All groups in the study listened to a lecture about Kruskal's algorithm. The lecture was written in advance and given by the same person to ensure that each group would receive the same information. Students in the Lecture/Animation groups had individual workstations to view an animated example of the Kruskal's Minimum Spanning Tree Algorithm. The animation was built using the Polka algorithm animation system [Stasko 93b]. Figure 3 shows a frame from a Polka animation of Kruskal's MST algorithm. Students in the Lecture/Slides group were shown the same example graph by means of a series of prepared transparencies. These transparencies were created from window-dumps of the Polka example. The key difference in these two conditions was that the animation illustrated more states of the algorithm as well as the transitions between states.

Students in the laboratory groups additionally viewed an animation of Kruskal's algorithm created with the XTango algorithm animation system [Stasko 92a]. All students were given a sheet of instructions on how to use the XTango animations. Students in the Passive group were given a list of prepared graphs (stored in files) and they ran the animation using those files as input. The students were told to observe the workings of the Kruskal MST Algorithm on those prepared graphs. Students in the Active group were told how to interactively create example graphs using the mouse. They were instructed to do this for a number of different graphs and then observe the workings of the MST algorithm on those graphs. All students were allowed twelve minutes for the laboratory session. The time limit was derived from a previous experiment where it was determined that the average time a student spent experimenting with the graphs was twelve minutes [Lawrence 93]. The version of the animation used in this experiment was based on previous experiments which indicated that a monochrome version of the algorithm with algorithmic steps appearing as text was best, as measured by performance on a post-test [Lawrence 93]. This type of animation was used for both the lecture example and for the animation laboratory.

Figure 3. Polka animation of Kruskal's MST algorithm.

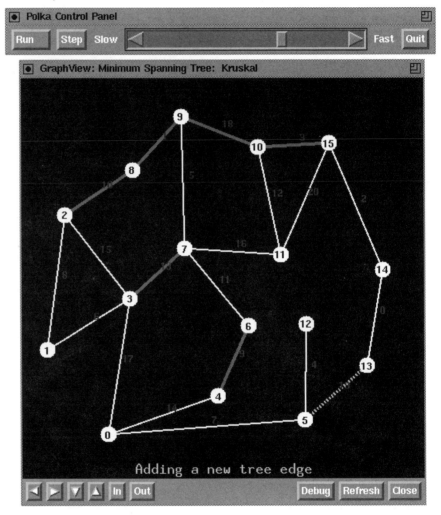

Following the sessions, all students completed a multiple-choice/true-false online test requiring application or understanding of the algorithm. The students also completed a free response written test that was designed to require the students to articulate concepts relating to understanding the algorithm. The fixed choice test was designed to concentrate on questions of procedure and the small steps of the algorithm. The free response test was designed to concentrate on conceptual issues including motivation as well as the overall algorithm. Questions on this test required an explanation, an example, or a conclusion about a concept.

Two sample questions from the on-line test appear below.

1. In Kruskal Algorithm, the first step in finding the Minimum Spanning Tree is:

   ____ Sort the edges by weight

   ____ Select the two shortest edges

   ____ Select the shortest edge from node 1

   ____ None of the above

2. In the given graph, if edges HG, IC, GF, CF, and AB are already in the path, which edge will be added next?

   ____ IG

   ____ CD

   ____ HI

   ____ None of the above

Two example questions from the free-response test appear below.

1. Under what conditions would the next shortest edge not be added to the Minimum Spanning Tree?

2. What, in your opinion, is the key part of the algorithm which guarantees the Spanning Tree obtained will be minimal?

We hypothesized that the participants who received the lecture accompanied by the animated example would perform better than those participants who received the slides example. We also hypothesized that the addition of a laboratory session would lead to improved performance.

Results

The results of the experiment indicated that an advantage was shown for students who interacted with the algorithm animation in the laboratory session. (Cell means for the experiment appear in Table 3.) The advantage was more marked for those questions that required knowledge at a deeper level, that is, the free-response test. Questions on this test required drawing conclusions from the questions asked, as well as demonstrating a holistic version of the algorithm.

Students who received the laboratory session also performed better on the on-line true/false or multiple choice questions, but not at significant levels. This finding indicates that the animation session was more crucial for those conceptual questions than for the more basic operational level of question.

Study of the results for the two laboratory conditions indicated that students who were in the active condition and created their own data sets for the algorithm achieved higher scores than those who observed prepared data sets. The result suggests that active engagement with an algorithm animation can be important. Below we discuss the results of the two respective tests in more detail, and we describe statistical analyses undertaken to determine which of these differences were significant.

Table 3. Cell Means for results on the two post-tests of understanding.

Fixed Response Test (Total = 19)			
LABORATORY CONDITION		Polka Animation	Prepared Slides
Lecture Only		11.87	11.80
Lecture plus Lab	Passive Lab	13.71	13.22
	Active Lab	13.83	13.89

Free Response Test (Total = 21)			
LABORATORY CONDITION		Polka Animation	Prepared Slides
Lecture Only		14.47	16.13
Lecture plus Lab	Passive Lab	16.43	16.67
	Active Lab	18.14	17.89

On-line test The on-line test was scored from a maximum possible of nineteen points, one point for each correct question. The questions on the on-line test were either true/false or multiple-choice. The two factors in the first analysis of variance on test scores were Lecture Only versus Lecture Plus Lab and Animation versus Prepared Slides.

There was no significant difference between the two lecture groups in the study (slides versus animation). This may be explained by the fact that both groups were able to use visual techniques to supplement the algorithm and that either of these methods was adequate for the purpose.

In a comparison of groups that received the laboratory session, results indicated that students completing a laboratory session performed marginally, but not significantly, better than those who had no laboratory session ($F=2.80$, d.f.1,59, $p< 0.1$) as measured by the on-line test. Cell means were 13.5 (of 19) for the laboratory session, compared to 11.83 for the no-laboratory condition.

Free response test The free response post-test requiring statement or application of concepts had seven questions, each counted as three points, for a maximum high score possible of twenty-one points. The three points were necessary because each correct answer consisted of a number of components, and the three point scale allowed each component to be graded. The questions were designed to address the basic concepts necessary for understanding of the algorithm, in addition to requiring a complete demonstration of the working of the algorithm on a provided graph.

Parallel analysis of variance was performed on the free-response test results. Results of this analysis indicated that students who completed a laboratory session performed significantly better on the free-response post-test ($F=4.36$, d.f. 1,58, $p< 0.05$) than those who did not. The amount of difference in this result indicates that student laboratory participation is more effective for questions which require more conceptual knowledge than questions which require recognition of the individual steps of the algorithm. No significant difference was discovered between the lecture groups viewing demonstrations as slides versus animations. This result also seemed to indicate that the type of visual presentation is not as strong a differentiating factor as the type of reinforcing experience.

The results described above led to further study of the differences among the conditions based upon the type of laboratory session -- active, passive, or none. Using this as the factor in a second analysis, we discovered cell means indicating that those students in the active condition had the highest scores on the free-response test. These results appear in Table 4. Analysis of Variance for the three possible lab conditions indicated that laboratory condition was notable, but was just outside significance ($F = 2.83$, d.f. 2,59, $p< 0.07$). Pairwise t-tests were performed to determine where the difference in condition actually lay. The

Cell Means	
No Laboratory	15.3
Passive	16.6
Active	18.0

Table 4. Cell means for the three lab conditions, number correct of twenty-one, on the free-response test.

significant difference (p=0.05) was discovered between the active and the no laboratory condition.

Discussion

This experiment was interesting in several different aspects. First, it appeared that the lecture material used (animation versus slides) did not make a significant difference in teaching the algorithm. In fact, the animation in lecture group did slightly worse on the free response test when no lab was involved. Even though it is valuable to have a visual aid to concept formation, the animation, while enjoyable to the student, did not provide added clarity over the transparencies in our study. Certainly, this result could be a factor of the particular algorithm we utilized. Other algorithms may benefit more from animation.

A second aspect of interest was that the advantage of the interactive laboratory session was confirmed. We found that these students excelled when compared to the students who did not participate in a laboratory session as well as to the students who were in the passive laboratory condition. Of special interest is the fact that the intuitive advantage of the laboratory group was not statistically supported. Simply having a laboratory session was not enough to improve performance; the issue of control and interaction also was necessary. A possible implication of this result is that one valuable use of algorithm animations will be to make them available to the students outside the classroom setting to reinforce concepts learned in class. Such availability may be provided in either a closed laboratory or open laboratory setting where students would create sample data sets and observe the workings of the algorithms on these sample data sets. Our result suggests that active student participation is a key issue in this design process.

A third item of interest was that while those in the active laboratory performed at a slightly higher level for both portions of the test, the difference was larger for the free response test than for the on-line test. The nature of the two tests is important in understanding this result. In general, the questions on the on-line test required recognition of the correct response rather than generation of a response. These questions might be described as being more on a procedural and operational level than on a conceptual level. This speaks to the issue of what types of learning are most affected by the use of the animations. A previous hypothesis was that these animations may aid in concept formation. The results support that hypothesis.

Other empirical studies of algorithm animation have been conducted recently and they help provide us with even more information about the value of animations as learning aids. Whitney and Urquhart utilized algorithm animations as instructional aids for a course on analysis of algorithms [Whitney 90]. The authors observed that stronger students in the class appeared to benefit more from the animations than the poorer students.

Byrne, Catrambone and Stasko examined the relation of viewing an animation to making predictions about an algorithm's performance [Byrne 96]. They hypothesized that animation would evoke prediction, and that this would assist students to learn an algorithm. Both prediction and animation were beneficial to psychology students learning about depth-first search as measured on a post-test. Neither was significantly effective in assisting computer science students learn about binomial heaps, however.

Yet other studies utilized an ethnographic approach, as opposed to a traditional experimental psychology approach, in studying algorithm animations. In an ethnographic approach, the experimenters make detailed observations of a relatively small number of participants. The experimenters use techniques such as talk-aloud sessions and videotape analysis to better understand the process of learning from algorithm animations. Wilson and colleagues studied how students learned about artificial intelligence search algorithms from animations [Wilson 95]. They found that it is critical for an animation to convey *why* changes in the display (algorithm) occur. That is, animations must be keyed to learning objectives. Douglas, Hundhausen and McKeown studied how students visualized different sorting algorithms [Douglas 94] [Douglas 95]. They found that student conceptualizations did not always match well with the depictions supported easily by and often shown in algorithm animation systems.

Other research is examining how students use algorithm animations in instructional settings. Kehoe and Stasko found that students do explicitly utilize animations, when available, to help learn about algorithms [Kehoe 96]. They found that students used animations in markedly different manners, however, suggesting flexibility be a key component in animation design. Gurka and

Other Studies

Citrin examined different empirical studies on algorithm animation and extracted a list of variables and experimental concerns for future work [Gurka 96].

Evaluation

As is evident by the summaries of the studies presented earlier, we find a mixed set of results if we examine the numbers solely. Particular experiments suggest that algorithm animations may not be that helpful for learning about algorithms. Others suggest that their value as a learning aid is quantifiable. It is important to remember that each experiment uses a particular set of animations that may be problematic themselves. The data from any particular experiment should not be overemphasized.

On the other hand, the data from these recent experiments when taken as a whole can help our intuition about how algorithm animations function as learning aids. If we look at the general patterns of the data, certain consistent results seem to emerge. But perhaps even more importantly, the actual process of conducting the experiments has strongly influenced our beliefs about the pedagogical value of algorithm animations. Simply observing session after session, watching participants interact and learn both with and without animations, has helped us to better understand algorithm animations in educational settings. Below we discuss some of the observations and beliefs gained from these empirical studies of the past few years.

First, we harbor the fundamental view that algorithm animations have pedagogical value even if their utility as learning aids is minimal. This is because the animations evoke enthusiasm and interest in students. In study after study, qualitative data gathered from post-experiment surveys indicated that the participants liked the animations and felt they were interesting [Badre 92] [Kehoe 96]. Good teachers know that engaging students' interest and instilling enthusiasm about a subject is an invaluable aid to instruction. If algorithm animations function in no role other than this, they still should earn use and interest.

Our second belief, perhaps the most controversial, is that algorithm animations used as passive videos of an algorithm's operations will have minimal impact on learning. This view slowly grew after observing innumerable participants watch animations and seemingly gain little from them. We have developed the following hypothesis to explain this view.

An algorithm animation is fundamentally a visual mapping of the data objects and operations of an algorithm. To understand and benefit from an algorithm animation, the student must first understand this visual mapping. But if a student is initially attempting to learn the algorithm, the student does not understand its data and objects, and hence does not have the basis to comprehend the visual mapping. Except in cases where the mapping is very straightforward (many sorting visualizations come to mind as examples) a student cannot "get" what the picture is, so he or she cannot translate the graphical actions to the represented algorithm. Time after time we witnessed students view algorithm animations in a puzzled manner, unable to decipher the visual mapping. One way to address this problem is to make sure the visualization itself is thoroughly explained and described initially.

Our skepticism of algorithm animations used in this traditional sense is furthered by the shear difficulty of incorporating them into a classroom setting. Few schools have "electronic classrooms" with large groups of PCs or workstations available. In the absence of such facilities, projection devices linked to computers can display one machine's output onto a screen for all students to view. Even this capability is still fairly rare today, and even if the technology exists, preparing and incorporating algorithm animations into lectures usually is laborious and time-consuming.

Our third belief is that the pessimism expressed above should not deter instructors completely---Algorithm animations can serve as valuable learning aids when used in the proper ways. Fundamentally, it is critical that students actively interact with the animations. For instance, students can enter data for an algorithm to use as input, then they can watch its animation. Alternatively, students can watch an animation and then predict what happens next. It is simply critical to engage the student with the animation, as opposed to passively viewing its operations. Certainly, laboratory sessions or even time away from the classroom can be used and animations provided for students to "try out." Even in class, students can be queried to describe what will happen in an animation. If a proper description of the visual mapping is provided and students are actively engaged this way, we are confident that algorithm animations can become valuable instructional aids.

Our final view takes this last argument one step further. If one can somehow enable students to design and develop algorithm animations themselves, tremendous educational benefits will result. This is an idea developed in ongoing work with an undergraduate algorithms class at the Georgia Institute of Technology. In this class we have used the *animator* front-end to the XTango and the *Samba* front-end to the Polka animation system [Stasko96a] [Stasko 97]. Each takes a series of simple ASCII commands with parameters, one command per line, and uses them as animation directives. For example, commands for drawing objects (line, circle, text, etc.) and commands for generating actions (move, color, jump, etc.) exist. By incorporating output statements into a program in any computer language, a descriptive trace stream of operations in the program is produced when the program is run. The animation tools simply read this stream and generate the corresponding animation. We have had excellent results using this type of assignment in class, both from student interest and student learning perspectives, and we hope to study its application more.

Conclusion

Empirical studies and research into the educational values of algorithm animations continue. We feel that this an important and relatively unexplored corner of software visualization, ripe for future inquiry and analysis. The relative scarcity of empirical study in the area is accompanied by virtually no work on effective design and display of algorithm animations---what makes one animation more effective than another. We hope that both these areas gain further attention, and that future research is able to tell us even more about the utility of algorithm animations as learning aids.

Acknowledgments

The two studies reported here were the results of team efforts. Albert Badre and Clayton Lewis collaborated with the authors on the first study and Albert Badre collaborated with the authors on the second study. Portions of this chapter are reprinted, with permission, from [Stasko 93a] Copyright 1993 ACM and [Lawrence 94] Copyright 1994 IEEE.

A Principled Approach to the Evaluation of SV: a Case Study in Prolog

Paul Mulholland

A large amount of Software Visualization (SV) technology has been developed. This is particularly the case for the Prolog programming language whose execution model causes particular difficulties for the learner (e.g. [Taylor 88] [Fung 90] [Schertz 90]. As a result, a wide range of Prolog SVs (or tracers) exist and though many claims are made regarding their usefulness and suitability for various potential user populations there is little empirical evidence. This chapter reports an empirical investigation into the suitability of four tracers for an early novice population.

The methodology aims to learn from the lessons of SV and Computer Based Training (CBT) evaluation which has provided many conflicting results that cannot be clearly interpreted. The empirical approach uses protocol analysis [Ericsson 84] to develop a fine-grained account of the user, identifying information access, the use of strategies, and misunderstandings of the SV and execution. This approach allows differences in performance to be more confidently explained.

The results show overall performance differences across subjects using the SVs which can be interpreted using the protocols. The interpretation permits prescriptions to be made as to the suitability of the four tracers for novices and suggestions as to how each could be improved.

Background

A number of studies have been undertaken to investigate the relative advantages of various types of display for computer-based instruction (CBI) or computer-aided learning (CAL). Most of these have focused on determining the efficacy of particular display features such as graphics, animation or colour. These studies have produced a number findings which appear to be contradictory.

Rigney and Lutz [Rigney 76] and Alesandrini and Rigney [Alesandrini 81] investigated the usefulness of graphical representations for the presentation of chemistry concepts. Both studies found animation to be an advantageous feature. Other studies have failed to find any benefit for animation in educational technology. For example, in a study by Reed [Reed 85] subjects were given rules enabling them to estimate how long it would take the computer to perform algebra word problems. Those receiving a dynamic simulation of the behaviour of the computer performed no better than those viewing a static representation. In a study of the effects of graphics and animation on learning outcomes Baek and Layne [Layne 88] found an advantage for graphics and animation over text for teaching a mathematical concept, whereas Peters and Daiker [Peters 82] found no advantage for graphics or animation in a CAL environment.

This kind of problem has also pervaded evaluation studies into the efficacy of textual and graphical programming notations. Cunniff and Taylor [Cunniff 87] investigated the effect of textual and graphical presentation on novice code comprehension. The study investigated the comprehension of equivalent code written in one graphical (FPL) and one textual (Pascal) language. Subjects had to perform three tasks thought to be central to computer program comprehension: the recognition and counting of types of program constructs, determining the values assigned to specific variables, and determining the number of times particular program segments will be executed. They found faster response times with FPL than Pascal. The accuracy of responses was also superior in FPL. This was particularly so with questions requiring the comprehension of program conditionals. There were also far more errors using Pascal than FPL on questions relating to the values of variables.

A rather different result was gained by Badre and Allen [Badre 89] in their comparison of a graphical and a diagrammatic programming notation. Overall they found no difference in bug location time between the two notations. They then separately analysed the performance of the novice and expert programmers within the subject sample. They found no effect of notation for experts but did find a superior performance for the textual notation among the novice subjects.

Within the evaluation of SV global classifications have been applied to the test materials rather than the features of the SV itself, though once again the findings have been less than straightforward. Patel et al [Patel 91] performed a direct comparison between three Prolog trace formats. They investigated the relative speed with which subjects could access information from static displays of three Prolog SVs. Five programs were used: three focused on backtracking (i.e. the retrying of earlier goals) and two on recursion. One SV performed best overall, though the pattern of results could not be explained by the distinction between recursion and backtracking.

From the review it can be seen that much of the empirical work in the fields of ITS, SV and program notations suffers from the problem of trying to find global generalisations that are not there. Many of the studies derive performance results without deriving the information necessary to explain them. Observations are usually not made of for example how the subjects approached the task and what features they found confusing. Evaluation studies therefore seem to be providing a set of isolated findings which can often on the surface appear contradictory. As only global measures of performance have been used in many of the studies, it is necessary to rely on anecdotal explanations of any apparent contradictions. A research methodology that sought to focus more on providing a qualitative account of why a particular result occurred would hopefully be able to move away from isolated observations toward building an overall picture of what is occurring.

The next two sections shall outline a software environment and psychologically motivated empirical framework which provide a foundation for the evaluation study.

The Prolog Program Visualization Laboratory (PPVL)

```
car(mini).
car(jaguar).
gold(ring).
bike(bone_shaker).
bike(honda).
silver(honda).
fun(Object) :-
        car(Object),
        gold(Object).
fun(Object) :-
        bike(Object),
        silver(Object).
```
Figure 1. The **fun** *program.*

```
call  fun(_1)
UNIFY 1    []
  call  car(_1)
  UNIFY 1    [_1 = mini]
  exit  car(mini)
  call  gold(mini)
  fail  gold(mini)
  redo  car(mini)
  fail  car(_1)
UNIFY 2    []
  call  bike(_1)
  UNIFY 1    [_1 = honda]
  exit  bike(honda)
  call  silver(honda)
  UNIFY 1    []
  exit  silver(honda)
exit  fun(honda)
```
Figure 2. Spy trace of the query
fun(What)*.*

PPVL provides an experimental laboratory on which to base a systematic comparison of tracers. PPVL incorporates four Prolog SVs (Spy, PTP, TPM and TTT) providing the first opportunity to study a number of fully implemented tracers within the same environment. PPVL is implemented in MacProlog[TM] version 4.5 running on Macintosh[TM] system 7.1. PPVL provides common interface and navigation for all tracers so differences in performance due to the ease of use of different interface technologies are minimised. PPVL also internally records all user activity at the terminal.

The empirical work considered here will focus on the visualization of Prolog. Prolog is a logical programming language. It allows programs to be written and read in a declarative way consistent with the predicate logic assertions it represents. There are two main kinds of construct used in Prolog. These are *facts* and *rules*. Facts are unconditionally true. Rules specify something that is true given that one or more conditions are satisfied. The **fun** program (figure 1) contains six facts (**car**, **gold**, **bike** and **silver**) and two (**fun**) rules. Each separate rule or fact constitutes a *clause*. The real world or declarative meaning of the first rule can be expressed as *"something is fun if it is a car and is gold"* and the second can be expressed as *"something is fun if it is a bike and is silver"*. The first part of the rule, constituting the goal (in this case **fun(Object)**) is known as the *head* of the rule. The subgoals which have to be satisfied (in this case **car** and **gold** or **bike** and **silver**) in order for the goal in the head of the rule to be true form the *body* of the rule.

The Spy tracer (see figure 2) is a stepwise, linear, textual SV system which adopts the Byrd Box model of Prolog execution [Byrd 80]. The model uses a procedural interpretation of Horn clause logic. The head of a rule is classed as a procedure and the body treated as one or more sub procedures. Byrd's aim in the development of Spy was to provide a basic but complete account of Prolog underpinned by a consistent execution model.

PTP (Prolog Trace Package) (see figure 3) was developed by Eisenstadt [Eisenstadt 84b [Eisenstadt 85b] to provide a more detailed and readable account of Prolog execution than is found in Spy. PTP aimed to make the account of execution as explicit as possible, thereby reducing the amount of interpretation required by the user. Particular areas where PTP aimed to improve on Spy were the presentation of more specific status information and a more explicit presentation of unification.

TPM (Transparent Prolog Machine) (see figure 4) aimed to provide the very detailed account provided by PTP in a much more accessible form. TPM uses an AND/OR Tree model of Prolog execution [Eisenstadt 90] [Brayshaw 91]. Execution is shown as a depth first search of the execution tree. Unlike the other SVs, TPM incorporates two levels of granularity. The Coarse Grained View (CGV) uses an AND/OR tree to provide an overview of how clauses are interrelated during execution. Fine grained views (FGVs) giving the unification details for a particular node are obtained by selecting the node in question. The fine grained view uses a lozenge notation to show variable binding.

The Textual Tree Tracer (TTT) (see figure 5) has an underlying model similar to TPM but uses a sideways textual tree notation to provide a single view of execution which more closely resembles the source code [Taylor 91]. Unlike linear textual tracers such as Spy and PTP, current information relating to a previously encountered goal is displayed with or over the previous information. This keeps all information relating to a particular goal in the same location. For example, all information pertaining to the **car** subgoal is contained in lines 2 and 3 of the trace, though in PTP is spread over lines 3, 4, 7, 8, and 9. Seven symbols relating to clause status are employed, five of these distinguishing types of failure. The variable binding history is shown directly below the goal to which it relates. The aim behind TTT was to provide the richness of information found in the TPM trace in a form more closely resembling the underlying source code. This approach illuminates an important trade-off in the design of the SV notation. TPM aims to show the structure and nature of the execution in an maximally clear form. For TTT, constructing a SV notation near to the underlying source code was a primary aim. The designers of TTT felt that the "tracer should be designed so as to enhance the ease with which the trace output can be correlated with the source code of the program being traced" (p. 4) [Taylor 91].

The review of previous studies suggests a number of requirements of future empirical work. A first important characteristic is that the results should provide some integrated understanding of the subjects' performance in relation to the task and their individual characteristics. For example, in terms of understanding

```
 1: ?  fun(_1)
 2: >  fun(_1) [1]
 3:    ?  car(_1)
 4:    +*car(mini) [1]
 5:    ?  gold(mini)
 6:    -0gold(mini)
 7:    ^  car(mini)
 8:    <  car(mini) [1]
 9:    --~car(_1)
10: <  fun(_1) [1]
11: >  fun(_1) [2]
12:    ?  bike(_1)
13:    +*bike(honda) [1]
14:    ?  silver(honda)
15:    +*silver(honda) [1]
16: +  fun(honda) [2]
```

Figure 3. PTP trace of the query **fun(What)**.

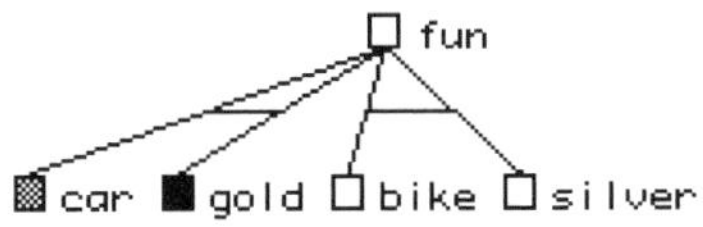

Figure 4. TPM CGV of the query **fun(What)**.

```
>>>1: fun(What)     1F/2S
|2      What = honda
***2: car(What)       1SF
|1      What ≠ mini
***3: gold(mini)      Fu
***4: bike(What)      1S
|1      What = honda
***5: silver(honda)   1S
```

Figure 5. TTT trace of the query **fun(What)**.

Methodological requirements

performance within the context of the task, Patel et al [Patel 91] raised the issue as to whether performance differences between subjects using different SVs were due to information access or task modification. By this they meant on one hand, whether the nature of the SV had affected the rate in which necessary information can be accessed from the display, without altering the strategic approach taken to the task, or alternatively whether the nature of the SV could affect the approach taken by the subject in performing the task. A desirable quality of the methodology would be that it could produce results that could shed light on this kind of issue.

In order to provide an integrated understanding of performance it will be necessary to derive a far more fine-grained account of the subject rather than relying solely on gross performance measures. An accepted method of gaining a fine-grained account of the cognitive activities occurring when performing some task is protocol analysis [Ericsson 84]. This study employs the technique of getting subjects to work in pairs and talk between themselves during the task to allow the recording of a protocol without placing artificial demands on the subject. The effectiveness of using subject pairs to evaluate human computer interfaces has already been expounded by Suchman [Suchman 87].

The methodology should also have a theoretical basis in what is already known from previous evaluation studies and general research within the psychology of programming. Research in the psychology of programming can be used to motivate what kinds of things could be looked for or expected within the protocols. Previous research can be used to show what kinds of experimental hypotheses are likely or unlikely to yield meaningful results. One aspect of previous studies to which this particularly applies is classification according to features of the display or source code. Global classifications of display features such as the use of colour or animation tend to miss the key issue, and produce confusing or contradictory results. The important point is what certain features are used to represent rather than whether they are used at all. Additionally, this form of display classification could not hope to distinguish between many Prolog SVs such as Spy, PTP and TTT though there may be large performance differences between them. Patel et al [Patel 91] found EPTB [Ditchev 87] to be significantly better than Spy though both are textual tracers with very similar dynamics. The focus of the methodology will therefore be more concerned with providing a framework for understanding what occurs rather than for testing global hypotheses.

Another desirable criteria is generalizability. This applies both to the empirical findings and the methodology itself. The more fine-grained account of how the subjects perform should provide a picture not only of how well subjects did in some particular situation but also why they performed as they did. This information will allow justifiable assertions as to what range of situations or subjects the findings will likely apply. This may permit some basic prescriptions to be made as to how suitable particular SVs are likely to be for certain situations. The results of a fine-grained account could also be used to motivate improvements to existing SV systems. Ideally the methodology should also be applicable to new or different programming languages or types of SV.

Outline of the study

The study was carried out involving 64 Open University summer school cognitive psychology students taking an Artificial Intelligence project. Students taking the project are required to model a simple cognitive theory in Prolog. Each summer school project lasts approximately 2.5 days. Each tracer was used as the main teaching focus and sole debugging aid for one week (i.e. two AI project groups). Prior to the summer school the students had completed assessed work using Prolog to model a simple AI problem.

A four way between subjects design was used with 16 subjects per cell working in pairs. Each pair of subjects were given five minutes to familiarise themselves with a program presented on a printed sheet. They each retained a copy of this program throughout the experiment. The program was an isomorphic variant of the one used by Coombs and Stell [Coombs 85] to investigate backtracking misconceptions. They were then asked to work through the traces of four versions of the program which had been modified in some way. Their task was to identify the difference between the program on the sheet and the one they were tracing. They had no access to the source code of the modified versions. After five minutes the subjects were given the option to move onto the next problem. This was used as an upper bound for timing data. Verbal protocols were taken throughout.

Program modifications were selected which required the novice to focus on different types of information in order to correctly identify the change. The four problems given were a change in a relation name, a changed atom name, a data flow change and a control flow change. The data flow change was either passing the wrong variable from a rule or changing a variable within a rule to an atom. The control flow change was either a swap in the subgoal order of a rule or the fact order within the database.

Results

Performance on the task

The mean number of problems solved by each subject pair in total are shown in figure 6. There was a significant main effect for tracer, $F(3, 28) = 3.260$, $p < 0.05$. A planned comparison revealed a significant difference between the graphical and textual tracers, $F(1, 28) = 8.174$, $p < 0.01$.

Figure 6. Mean number of problems completed within five minutes.

Tracer	Spy	PTP	TPM	TTT
Solutions	2.250	2.750	1.500	2.375

Information content

A preliminary analysis of the protocols revealed eight kinds of information discussed within protocol utterances (see figure 7). Some such as CFI, DFI and SOURCE would be expected from the work of Bergantz and Hassell [Bergantz 91] and Pennington [Pennington 87]. Others such as ETO and TRACE reflect the role of the SV within information access and use.

Figure 7. Protocol coding scheme for information types.

Information	Description
CFI	Derive control flow information from the trace
DFI	Derive data flow information from the trace
ETO	Compare to an earlier trace output
GOAL	Comment on the goal of all or part of the program
PRED	Predict future behaviour of the trace
READ	Read the trace output
SOURCE	Refer to or reconstruct source code
TRACE	Comment on navigation or notation of the trace

As control flow and data flow are the more central information types to program comprehension, a two way mixed ANOVA was performed on this data. This revealed significant main effects for SV, $F(3, 26) = 5.155$, $p < 0.01$ and information type, $F(1, 26) = 15.262$, $p < 0.01$. A Tukey (HSD) post-hoc comparison revealed significant differences between PTP and TPM ($p < 0.05$) and TTT and TPM ($p < 0.05$). A one way analysis of variance revealed a significant main effect for trace related utterances (TRACE), F(3, 26) = 5.536, p < 0.01. A Tukey (HSD) post-hoc comparison revealed significant differences between PTP and TPM (p < 0.01) and TTT and TPM (p < 0.05). The frequencies of CFI, DFI and TRACE utterances are shown in figure 8.

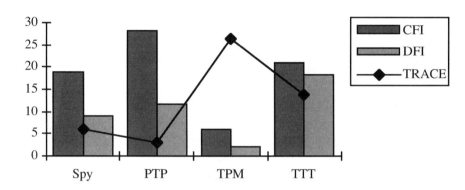

Figure 8. Mean number of CFI, DFI and TRACE utterances.

Strategies

A preliminary analysis of the protocols revealed seven comprehension strategies (see figure 9). The presence of REVIEW and TEST strategies would be expected from the work of among others Green [Green 77] and Katz and Anderson [Katz 88]. The other strategies relate to the way the SV was used within the comprehension process. A strategy was defined as a set of temporally close utterances performing some function relating to the comprehension of either the program, the SV, the execution or the interrelations between them. The strategy may be carried out by one subject or jointly between the pair.

Strategy	Description
REVIEW CF	Review previous execution steps
REVIEW DF	Review previous data flow
TEST CF	Predict and test future steps of the trace
TEST DF	Predict and test future bindings of variables
EXPERIENCE	Compare against previous experience of the tracer
SOURCEMAP	Map successive steps of the trace against the code
OVERVIEW	Comment on the overall trace output at some point

Figure 9. Strategies identified in the protocols.

A two factor ANOVA comparing the four SVs across the two review strategies revealed a main effect for tracer, F(3, 26) = 3.495, p < 0.05 and a significant interaction between SV and strategy, $F(3, 26) = 4.304$, $p < 0.05$. Simple effects were found for the strategy RDF, $F(3, 43) = 5.528$, $p < 0.01$ and the tracer TTT, $F(1, 26) = 9.333$, $p < 0.01$. A Tukey (HSD) post-hoc comparison revealed a significant difference between PTP and TPM ($p < 0.05$). The review strategies are shown graphically in figure 10.

Figure 10. Mean number of REVIEW CF and REVIEW DF strategies for each SV.

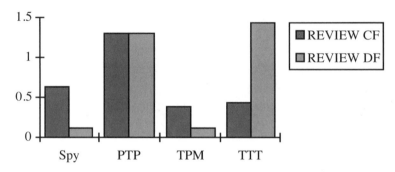

A two factor ANOVA comparing the four SVs across the two test strategies revealed a main effect for tracer, $F(3, 26) = 3.253$, $p < 0.0378$. A Tukey (HSD) post-hoc comparison revealed a significant difference between PTP and TPM ($p < 0.05$). The test strategies are shown graphically in figure 11.

Figure 11. Mean number of TEST CF and TEST DF strategies for each SV.

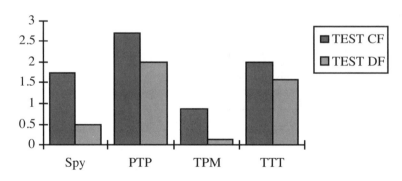

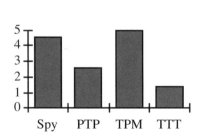

Figure 12. Mean number of SOURCEMAP strategies for each SV.

A one way analysis of variance of the distribution of the SOURCEMAP strategy revealed a main effect for SV, $F(3, 26) = 5.656$, $p < 0.01$ (figure 12). A Tukey (HSD) post-hoc comparison revealed a significant difference between TTT and TPM ($p < 0.01$) and TTT and Spy ($p < 0.05$).

Misunderstandings

A preliminary analysis of the protocols revealed four main misunderstandings of the trace: clause-goal, control flow, data flow and timing.

Clause-goal misunderstanding refers to when the clause in the program is compared in an inappropriate way to the goal as currently shown in the trace. Control flow misunderstandings tended to result from an incorrect model of control flow being used by the subject which the SV has failed to counteract. Two different kinds of data flow misunderstanding were identified. Some examples appeared to result from a disparity between the binding observed in the trace and the binding (wrongly) expected by the subjects. Other instances of data flow misunderstanding resulted from subjects using an incorrect or incomplete model of how data flow occurs in Prolog. Time misunderstandings are those resulting from a failure to appreciate the position in the execution being shown at any particular point.

Misunderstanding	Spy	PTP	TPM	TTT
Clause-goal	1.63	0.57	1.00	1.43
Control flow	0.75	0.00	0.00	0.00
Data flow	1.13	0.43	0.13	0.29
Time	0.00	0.00	2.75	0.43
Total	2.08	1.00	3.88	2.16

Figure 13. Mean number of misunderstandings of the trace per subject pair.

The mean number of misunderstandings of the trace are shown in figure 13. A one way ANOVA of the total number of misunderstandings for each subject pair revealed a main effect for trace, $F(3, 26) = 3.669$, $p < 0.05$. A Tukey (HSD) post-hoc comparison revealed a significant difference between PTP and TPM ($p < 0.05$).

In terms of completion rates, TTT and PTP both significantly outperformed TPM. Spy faired less well than the other two textual tracers and TPM performed worst overall. The results therefore show that the features of the SV have a significant effect on its usability for Prolog beginners.

Discussion

Though the performance rates of TTT and PTP subjects were similar, the protocols suggest there were important differences in how the subjects used and adapted to the two tracers. The information content shows that PTP subjects derived more control flow information whereas TTT subjects focused more on data flow. The linear indented display of PTP showing clause entering and exiting provides a very clear model of control flow. The more compact TTT display showing higher level variable names permeating through the trace provides a good model of data flow.

Similarly far more control flow strategies were identified in the PTP protocols. Subjects had more misunderstandings of TTT than PTP. TTT subjects were more likely to confuse the clause and goal as displayed in the trace. This is understandable because unlike PTP, TTT does not distinguish directly between clause and goal. TTT subjects also showed a number of time misunderstandings. This is no doubt due to the difficulties adapting to using a textual display that develops in a non-linear fashion.

The protocols can also shed some light on why Spy performed less well than the other textual tracers. Spy subjects obtained less control flow and data flow information from the tracer than TTT and PTP subjects. This is largely due to the **UNIFY** lines in the trace being harder to understand (and easier to ignore) than the clause and goal pairings of PTP. This combined with the length of the display made it far more difficult for subjects to derive a control flow or data flow account of the execution. As a result the subjects used far fewer control flow and data flow related strategies to aid comprehension, relying far more on mapping between lines of the trace and the source code. Source-mapping can be thought of as a default strategy the subjects defer to when their understanding is insufficient to permit a higher level strategy. Spy subjects were also far more likely to misunderstand control flow, data flow and confuse the clause and goal as presented in the trace. This again is probably due to the **UNIFY** line failing to clearly show the entering and exiting of clauses, unification or describe the relation between the clause and goal in a way the novice users could understand.

The protocols can also help explain why TPM subjects accomplished far less than those using a textual trace. TPM subjects made fewer control flow and data flow statements though did comment far more on the goals of the program. This suggests that although the subjects could gain a vague understanding of the program on a higher level of abstraction they had difficulty using the trace to extract more fine grained information. TPM subjects also relied heavily on source-mapping and discussing the overall trace to gain an understanding of the execution. This supports the view that when the subjects looked at the trace in more detail they had to rely on a simple strategy requiring little understanding. TPM subjects were the only ones to use an OVERVIEW strategy. This was used to gain a more global account of the execution. Subjects could use the SV to spot basic changes such as incorrect relation names or an incorrect ordering of subgoals but were unable to derive more complex information. TPM subjects also frequently lost their position in the execution. It could therefore be that preserving the entire AND/OR tree shape throughout the execution could be a false blessing when novices are using the trace unaided.

Conclusions

The methodology appeared to serve its purpose of providing a fine-grained account of the performance of subjects, succeeding in identifying information access, strategies, and misunderstandings in the protocols. The protocol-based approach offers explanation as to the reasons why subjects performed the way they did. The approach identified important problems subjects have when using particular SVs, which can be used to motivate design modifications. The methodology was also able to identify interesting differences in how the task was carried out. Using subject pairs was found to be a successful empirical technique, facilitating detailed verbal reports in a naturalistic way.

Acknowledgements

This work was supported by an EPSRC postgraduate research studentship.

Cognitive Questions in Software Visualization

Marian Petre,
Alan Blackwell
and
Thomas Green

Chapter 30

Software visualisation is nifty stuff; but is it the powerful cognitive tool it is often assumed to be? This chapter attempts to moderate the understandable enthusiasm for software visualisation and to raise some of the questions for which the discipline doesn't yet have answers. The chapter is structured as a list of questions with discussion. The questions are not a comprehensive analysis of cognitive challenges in software visualisation. Rather, the chapter attempts to provide a list sufficiently provocative to give designers pause, in order:

a) to establish that good software visualisation isn't simply a matter of mimicking paper-based tasks or doing what is technically easy — and certainly isn't 'solved' yet; but also

b) even simple tools can improve software comprehension, if they're the right ones.

Introduction

Are all aspects of software amenable to visualisation? Software visualisation is trying to find simplicity in a complex artefact (e. g. , thousand-line code), to produce a selective representation of a complex abstraction. What makes it difficult is that it is presenting information artefacts, not physical objects (or even the pseudo-physical objects which superficial interface analogies suggest). It is presenting a logical construction, rather than a physical one. In contrast to the visualisation of a mathematical function, most software visualisation has no

What is visualization suitable for?

simple generating function. The complexity lies not just in the information to be visualised, but in the information's context of use; software visualisation is used to show different sorts of information (relating to source code, to data, to data structures, to execution) for different uses and with different aims, among them:

i) presenting large data sets:

Like the data visualisation in domains such as radiography and meteorology, some software visualisation involves the presentation of large, mainly homogeneous data, e. g. , program performance data. This form of visualisation attempts to make data available for interpretation by presenting a data picture and so capitalising on perceptual effects, such as foreground/background effects, pop-out, detection of discontinuities. And yet, although these are basic mechanisms of perception, experience in other domains makes clear that 'reading' the perceptual qualities of data visualisations is a matter of considerable skill.

ii) demonstrating the virtual machine:

Some software visualisation attempts to create a visible, dynamic, machine model, often relying on kinematic or mechanical metaphors. This form of visualisation is intended to make the behaviour of the interpreted program visible, often for pedagogic purposes.

iii) changing the perspective:

Some visualisation tries to bring large software engineering problems within the scope of a single view, so that a user can grasp particular tasks or functions in relation to the software as a whole. They aim for the sort of perspective change one might characterise as "the helicopter over the landscape": putting one's locale in perspective as part of a much larger landscape by providing a viewpoint high above ground level, and giving an opportunity to locate other features and functions in the landscape. This is an attempt at complexity control, helping to keep a large problem "in a single head" by visualising the overall structure and providing some assistance for navigating or traversing that structure.

iv) display-based reasoning:

Some software visualisation provides an alternative formalism, not a data picture or a machine model, but a regular, symbolic re-presentation of software with a new emphasis, in order to support an otherwise ill-supported style of reasoning. The notion is that an effective display can ease the user's reasoning; the likelihood is that having an effective display changes the user's tactics, if not the nature of the user's reasoning. The display becomes a focus for reasoning, for example by replacing some internal representations with external ones, and hence allowing the user to use different tactics in finding, recalling, examining, or comparing information [Davies 93] [Davies 96].

This may be a continuum of uses, but what is required by a presentation of a large homogeneous data set may be very different from what is required by a formalism for depicting machine behaviour. We don't yet know if the differences amount to different judgements on a consistent set of criteria, or if different criteria apply. We must beware assuming that the space is adequately defined by a simple model of perception and perceptual inference. We must know more about uses, about tasks within uses, and about representations for tasks.

Simply restated, the question of suitability is multi-faceted:

- What sort of visualisation — depiction, description, presentation, abstraction —
- is suitable for which information
- and which uses
- by which users?

Does Visualisation Mean Pictures?

How do we distinguish software visualisation systems from other ways of viewing software? The obvious definition is that visualisation systems present software in graphical form. This position is expressed by Myers as follows:

"In Program Visualization, the program is specified in a conventional, textual manner, and the graphics is used to illustrate some aspect of the program or its run-time execution". [Myers 90]

There are cases, of course, where this definition might not be literally true. What if the program has been specified diagramatically, using a visual programming language? Most software visualisations do depict the behaviour of textual programs, but they would be equally valid if used to depict the same algorithm implemented in a visual language. There are a number of such situations where the relationship between text and graphics in visualisation is not obvious. Consider some of the following cases:

- A textual program is re-expressed in a graphical form – representing identifiers by icons, and syntactic constructs by connections or containment.
- In an even more likely situation, the identifiers are still represented by their textual names, but are connected by graphical elements to indicate syntax, as in a flow chart.

- In some kinds of flowchart, lines or other graphical annotations are superimposed on a program listing in order to clarify the program structure.
- Advanced "pretty printers" clarify program structure by automatically indenting lines, or by changing the type styles of program elements.

The first of these cases obviously meets the criteria of Myers' definition (and would be recognised by most of us as a software visualisation system), but we feel increasingly uncomfortable in referring to the other cases as software visualisation. In an extreme example, imagine a system that takes a complicated spaghetti-like visual program, and makes it easy to understand by formatting it as nicely structured text, introducing meaningful words to refer to the arbitrary icons, and describing the relationships between the parts using a constrained and well-defined vocabulary of keywords. This seems to be a useful visualisation, but is actually the reverse of the commonly accepted use of the term.

There is no longer a clear dividing line between graphics and typography in the print media. It is also increasingly hard to distinguish between graphical and textual programming systems (to an extent that puzzles Visual Basic users when they are excluded from a visual programming forum). Is there a dividing line after which we can confidently say that something is not a visualisation system? Rather than defining the amount of graphics that constitutes a visualisation, it is better to encourage a "broad church" based on characteristics that are independent of the difficult divide between text and graphics. This allows us to recognise the importance of facilities such as the 'code view' that was included in the Balsa system. The code view simply presented pretty-printed program text, dynamically displayed and highlighted as the program executed. In an environment concentrating on animated graphics, these textual views were still found to be helpful to a wide range of users [Brown 85a].

The essence of visualisation from this point of view is the provision of an alternative representation or alternative emphasis within a representation. Alternative representations include changes in structure as well as changes in modality, while alternative emphases include the explicit presentation of temporal behaviour through facilities such as instantaneous animation or historical integration. In a mechanical domain, Mayer and Gallini [Mayer 90] found evidence for improved understanding of devices when explanatory text and illustrations were integrated by the inclusion of simple information about causal state changes.

As an interesting exercise in visualisation design, try asking how many of the following objectives could be achieved without using graphics:

• Emphasise data structure rather than algorithm or vice-versa.
• Illustrate causal relationships.
• Create a profile of resource utilisation.
• Search through an execution trace.
• Contrast two space-packing heuristics.

All of these classic "visualisations" can be communicated in textual terms, although this becomes more difficult in the case of spatial application domains. Multiple representations and emphases are characteristic of text as much as they are of pictures. The nature of visualisation should therefore reside in the structure of these transformations in multi-modal presentation far more than from the presentation mode itself. This could be seen as an appeal for would-be visualisers to respect Knuth's ideal of literacy in programming as much as the novelty of new pictorial conventions [Knuth 92]. In either case literacy, whether verbal or visual [Dondis 73] relies far more on understanding of structure and dynamics than it does on presentation mode.

What is visualisation for? What is the relationship of software visualisation to mental representation? In order to consider these questions, we shall discuss a 'space of intentions' for software visualisations. This is simply a device for discussion; the distinctions are only valued briefly as a means of examining the relationship between internal and external representations. The distinctions are in any case not clear; they overlap in this discussion, and visualisations produced to serve one intention might well serve many categories of intention. The section is in two halves, one concerned with experts, the other with non-experts.

Is SV a way into 'the expert mind' or a way out of our usual world view?

Consider what software visualisation for use by experts might be intended to do.

1. To externalise images of thought, to "get things out of the head". This intention is to produce visualisations closely related to the expert's mental images, whether externalisation's of actual mental images, or illustrations of mental images, closely related but not actually what the expert sees in his 'mind's eye'.
   These could be thought of as external memory extensions, to 'download' and 'set aside' information whose importance is no longer immediate.

'Setting aside' concepts or portions of a problem that have been thought about is one of the techniques that experts use to keep problems tractable.

2. To provide a focus for communication between experts. This intention is to produce visualisations close enough to the expert's thinking to facilitate discussion of problems and solutions with peers. These could be the externalisations intended by (1), they could derive from local representational idiom, from standard representations in the domain or in familiar tools, or they could simply be recognisably useful representations of focal information (e. g. , concepts or phenomena). This is the least distinct intention, because nearly any representation can assist communication, particularly among experts.

3. To provide tools for thinking. This intention is to produce visualisations that complement and supplement experts' thinking, rather than mimic their internal representations.
a) These 'supplementary representations' can display information that needs to be taken into account but which the expert would prefer not to hold internally. These might be a sort of 'external memory', allowing experts to free their working memory by using display-based reasoning strategies.
b) The 'supplementary representations' might provide alternative views of the problem, perhaps casting the information in terms of another programming paradigm. Experts are observed to shift deliberately among paradigms, styles of reasoning, and representations in order to consider different aspects of a design. But shifting paradigm—particularly to an unfamiliar paradigm—may not be easy; the visualisation may provide a route to thinking outside the expert's usual world view.
c) The 'supplementary representations' can provide a direct visual mapping to the problem, so that graphically sensible things in the representation map to semantically sensible things in the algorithm or problem. Occasionally the algorithm can be mapped onto a physical arrangement (e. g. , binary chop into a sorted list), but this sort of physical analogy is a special case only. This intention is to make it possible to manipulate or reason about graphical transformations and infer semantic transformations from that information (e. g. , a geometric relationship that relates to a complex equation relationship in an algorithm, such as an informative plot of coefficients in a complex equation, when coefficients that fall inside a depicted circle have special importance—an example from visualisations useful in filter design). For example, Bauer and Johnson-Laird [Bauer 93] found that use of an appropriate graphical representation could improve performance in logical deduction.
d) The 'supplementary representations' can provide navigational assistance, helping the expert to keep track of the relationship of a sub-

problem to the whole and to other parts. It can also remove the need to add new labels to keep track of relationships [Larkin 87]

4. To harness the computer as a collaborator in problem solving. For problems without an apparent solution, experts often explore solutions in tandem with the machine, by programming it to enact a simplification, to analyse a sub-problem, or to process a partial solution (e. g. , finding repetitive patterns in a signal). This intention is to make visible the activity of the computer in these tasks, so that the expert can relate what it does to the larger problem, in order to determine whether it contributes to a final solution. This can encompass a partial automation of the interpretation of a visualisation, alerting the programmer to events or emerging phenomena in the visualisation domain, not just in the problem domain. As a visualisation of machine activity, these need have little to do with the expert's internal imagery, although the expert must be able to relate the computer's activity to his understanding of the problem.

The discussion so far assumes that visualizations for experts reflect or augment a rich and largely appropriate mental imagery. For the sake of this discussion, we assume that non-experts have a less developed or less appropriate internal imagery, and that therefore visualisations for non-experts often have an instructive role. What might the intentions for software visualisation for use by non-experts include?

5. To provide a glimpse of an expert's imagery. To 'look inside' the expert mind and possibly make expert insight visible to the non-expert. (cf. (1)) This intention is to help non-experts 'see' information more expertly and hence inform them.

6. To provide a visualisation of an expert's reasoning process. This intention is to make explicit thinking that experts do invisibly or 'effortlessly', and hence to provide a sort of 'scaffolding' for non-experts when their own 'vision' is immature. Of course a visualisation tool won't turn a novice into an expert, but it can teach by making portions of expert reasoning explicit and accessible. Although based on how experts behave, this intention is to support non-experts in developing their own reasoning, for example by providing additional ways of 'seeing', implying different ways of reasoning, indicating which information is of importance in which contexts (cf. (3b)).
The modest version of this intention provides tools for novices that are consistent with expert behaviour, so that as novices become more experienced they also grow into effective, professional behaviour. The more directive version biases the tools to a particular, rationalised style of reasoning, providing a visualisation of a chosen paradigm, in order to influence users' thinking.

7. To provide a glimpse of how programs or computers work, a visualisation of execution. (See Section 1, ii). This is an important role in environments designed for novices. Du Boulay, O'Shea and Monk [du Boulay 81] show the importance of simplicity and visibility of function (the 'glass box') in environments designed for novices, while Jones [Jones 93] extends their work, showing with reference to several types of visualisation that novices also need to have views of state, procedure and function.

8. To provide additional ways of seeing, depicting behaviour, or apprehending relationships non-experts find difficult to envision. In doing so, the visualization provides a sort of 'imagery' training, showing what information is useful and offering ways of 'seeing' it. Like (6), this intention is a sort of scaffolding, supporting acquisition of skills by providing structure in the visualisation, although this intention need not refer to expert behaviour, but rather focuses on the needs of less experienced users. This too is an important role in environments for novices [Cañas 94].

This discussion, although one hopes instructive, is uncomfortable, because the distinctions among intentions are not crisp, and because distinctions among intentions need not imply distinctions among resultant visualisations. A visualisation that allows an expert to extend his own thinking is likely to be a suitable basis for communication with his peers (of whom he is his closest example), and may well promote insight by making something visible to a non-expert. Nevertheless, although some visualisations may be generic, many are not, and it is not appropriate to assume that what comes out of an expert's mind will somehow magically launch a non-expert into expert reasoning. Visualisations are not useful without insight about their use, about their significance and limitations. Further, one needs insight about one visualisation's relationship to other visualisations, understanding about how they do and do not map to each other.

Why are experts often resistant to other people's visualisations?

One of the recurrent themes in the psychology of programming is comparison of novice and expert behaviour, and often detection of differences between them. So it is unsurprising that one of the questions in software visualisation is whether visualisations designed for experts will be suitable for novices, and vice versa.

One way to slice into this question is to consider why experts create tools for themselves, and to study those visualisations.

Many of the most familiar visualisation tools made by 'other people' than the programmer, such as debuggers or execution models, visualise aspects of a single paradigm. These can be particularly useful to novices in developing a reasoning model of the virtual machine, say, or to experts searching for particular phenomena. But the things that one can visualise 'clearly' within one domain tend not to be what experts build their own tools for. Experts working close to the edge of what's possible have a greater tendency to break both their applications and their development systems than novices, and hence they are likely to have explored the paradigm, to have found its boundaries and problems.

Most errors that consume expert time are not within-paradigm, but looking below the paradigm at internal operation in order to debug abnormal behaviour of entities that are correct within the paradigm, i. e. , unknown side-effects, rather than syntactic errors. So visualisations within-paradigm are uninformative.

As a result, experts have a tendency to create a visualisation for a particular problem (e. g. , specific data structure)—even if it will never be useful for another problem. One of us (MP) has observed that experts have a capacious willingness to grow a new, specific tool or to modify an old, specific one.

What puts experts sufficiently in need of visualisation tools to invest in them, even to the extent of creating them?
- taking over someone else's ('half-baked') program
- really big problems
- mixed-technology problems or problems that cross domains (i. e. , different computers, different operating systems, different programs — hence often different representations)

Many of the most difficult problems—and those most difficult to reason about— involve the concatenation of tools or programs, e. g. , outputting probe results into files (or pipes) to another tool, rather than just displaying results on screen. Hence, experts spend time modelling the behaviour of partially known objects, e. g. , this computer must talk to that remote peripheral, which we don't know much about. So software visualisation is a way of coping with unknowns, with the unseen: visualisation of partially visible, often heterogeneous, systems. This needn't mean that the visualisations are necessarily complex or elaborate. Software comprehension, although itself complex, may still be ameliorated by simple tools, if they're the right ones. The advantage of simple tools is that they are less likely to carry the 'baggage' of a particular paradigm-and so they might assist the expert in finding things outside the paradigm.

Why don't they use other people's visualisations more often? In part because of the specificity of the problems they most need to visualise. But in part because visualisation tools are not very useful without insight about their use and significance. Experts know that they need to understand what tools are for, what their limitations are, when not to use them-and they can judge the cost of acquiring this meta-knowledge as too prohibitive.

What do experts demand from visualisation tools? MP's observations indicate that experts want:

- control: Experts want to control their focus, and hence the focus of the visualisation. They want to be able to 'set-aside' concepts or portions of a problem that they know about or that are otherwise outside their focus.
- scale: Visualisations must cope with 'real-sized' problems. This emphasises the importance of navigation tools and search tools.
- speed: Visualisations must be sufficiently responsive. Experts' visualisations tend to be functional rather than pretty; experts will not buy beauty at the expense of efficiency.
- truth: Visualisations must maintain accuracy, and experts resist 'someone else's simplification'. Experts express frustration with novice environments which do not preserve accuracy or which misleadingly simplify and so fail to reflect the 'real world'.

In short, what experts want from visualisation tools is pretty much what they want from conventional programming languages [Petre 91].

Are visualizations trying to provide a representation that is more abstract, or more concrete?

Is visualisation a magic window into the invisible world of abstractions? Many people feel intuitively that software is hard to understand because it is so mathematical – it deals with symbols rather than things. If it is abstraction that makes software (and mathematics) difficult, perhaps we can make it easier to understand by presenting it in concrete pictorial form, as when an arithmetic exercise asks us to subtract two apples from five apples.

On the other hand, the creation and interpretation of pictures is itself an exercise in abstraction [Arnheim 70]. The first pictures we create as children (or even as adults) are not copies of images from our visual fields, but constructions made from the standard symbolic elements in the childhood pictorial vocabulary – heads, arms, houses and smiling suns. Many adults still find it difficult to create realistic drawings because they maintain the habit of using cartoon-like symbols [Edwards 79].

These two views of the relationship between vision and abstraction are difficult to reconcile, and we must ask whether we can form any coherent view of the nature of abstraction in visualisation. It is tempting to believe that we can, if only because we have established the convention of direct manipulation interfaces in which we treat images on a computer screen as if they were physical objects. At the same time it is undeniable that the pictures we see when viewing a software visualisation have little actual resemblance to concrete objects in the physical world.

Perhaps we must explicitly acknowledge the dual nature of visualisation. Any visualisation relies on a pictorial language, and language is fundamentally about abstraction; like icons and Greek letters, words are arbitrary symbols that have a conventional correspondence to classes of objects in the world and relations between those classes. The main function of language is to provide us with a means of manipulating these abstractions. At the same time as providing a language, visualisations also provide a model – a depiction of a device whose behaviour we can envisage in terms of the constraints and causality of the physical world.

Is it possible for a visualisation environment to satisfy both of these requirements equally well? The pictorial language function provides a way of moving away from conventional software representations in order to express more general principles – it takes the concrete elements of a specific software situation, and expresses them in general, abstract, terms so that they are easier to assimilate. The device model function provides a way of visualising behaviour with the help of localised influence, attention and causation – by making the abstract more concrete, it is easier to apprehend.

The possible functions of abstraction in working with visualisations are difficult to ascertain. The relative priorities of these functions are also difficult to establish. It is hard to say in general what level of abstraction is suitable for software workers. Abstractions come at different granularities, and the probability that a given abstraction is relevant to a problem often seems inverse to its complexity. Should we therefore aim to create a vocabulary of abstraction, or a mechanism for hiding it? Should we facilitate (or even require) the creation of new abstractions, or is visualisation primarily a communicative device for conveying one person's abstract view of a particular situation?

What model are we representing?

Myers [Myers 90] makes a necessary distinction between visualisations that represent the code, the data, or the algorithm. But that is not enough. We should also distinguish between representations of external structure versus representations of cognitive structure, and representations of structure versus representations of purpose or expectation.

Early experiments such as that by Soloway and Ehrlich [Soloway 84], now well-known, showed that Pascal novices learn to think in terms of 'plan' structures, which are groupings of statements that together achieve a stated goal or purpose. The classic example is the 'Running Total' plan. Although this research has been around for over a decade, very few attempts at software visualisation have attempted to display representations of cognitive structures. Exceptions are Bonar and Liffick's [Bonar 90] Bridge system and more recently Ebrahimi [Ebrahimi 92]; Bowles et al. [Bowles 94] describe a Prolog system for novices that represents the code as 'techniques', which are very similar to the plan concept. This last has received some degree of empirical evaluation by Ormerod and Ball [Ormerod 96], indicating that the idea is good but that the problems of interacting with such high-level representations (especially, editing them) are not yet fully resolved.

Although the systems mentioned above were all program construction environments, rather than tools for visualising existing software, they point a direction. And indeed, recent work by Rist and Bevemyr [Rist 90]; see also [Rist 96] has shown that static analysis can extract these 'plan' structures from Pascal programs algorithmically, which leads to the possibility of plan visualisation tools.

If the 'plan' structure is indeed how programmers conceptualise programs, then visualising code in those terms would be a great improvement over visualising it in lower-level structures of individual statements or control structures. The difference would be comparable to working with a drawing package instead of a paint package – the drawing package groups pixels into lines, circles, etc. , and allows those structures to be picked out and if necessary manipulated individually.

But, are these structures cognitive? Certainly, the original claim was that 'programming plans' were a 'natural' cognitive construct; but another view is that 'plans' are built only because Pascal is a procedural language, in which the programmer's purposes are diluted and dispersed here and there. The structures extracted by Rist's analysis are, at bottom, based on dataflow. Perhaps all that the Pascal environments are doing is helping users understand dataflow, providing a re-representation. Maybe, then, a dataflow language would not need to be conceptualised in any different terms than the ones it already exists in.

The contrary viewpoint is that programmers only build 'plan' representations of software for certain particular tasks [Bellamy 90]. If they are doing other tasks, then they will use a different representation, such as control-flow representation. If that analysis is correct, then a dataflow language would need to be parsed for control flow and for sequential information. That would correspond to the Prolog techniques editor, which categorises simple Prolog functions in terms of types of recursion etc.

Whichever of those views may turn out to be nearer the truth, the fact is that at present there is a shortage of software visualisations explicitly built around cognitive representations. And outside the domain of code, there is not even much idea what a cognitive representation would look like.

It is a truism of HCI that systems should be designed to support the tasks the user needs/wants to do. But descriptions of visualisation systems rarely specify any particular task that they are intended to support.

What kind of tasks are we supporting?

What would be required to support the task of algorithm comprehension? To understand an algorithm means building a mapping between the user's conception of events and entities in the program, and the user's conception of events and entities in the work domain. Both of those domains will be represented in cognitive terms, not in external terms (for example, the program domain might be represented in terms of the plan structures described in the previous section). Thus Robertson et al. [Robertson 90] showed that programmers understand code by searching through it in various complex ways, focusing on small functionally coherent groupings, presumably plan-like. Even more telling, Pennington [Pennington 87] took a sample of professional programmers and showed that of those programmers, the ones who achieved highest comprehension scores "tended to think about both the program world and the domain world to which the program applies while studying the program". This 'cross-referencing' strategy was sharply revealed in the high scorers, much less apparent in the low scores - a clear indication of the process of building a mapping between the two worlds.

Thus supporting users in understanding an algorithm requires more than illustrating the primitive code: it requires illustrating the algorithm is a useful form. Two axioms about information representation are:

> (1) Finding and using information is easier when the form of the information sought has a 'cognitive fit' with the form of the information presented.

Vessey [Vessey 90] shows that the mental representation formed in problem solving depends on the (external) representations of both the problem and the problem-solving task. When these two external representations are different in form, the problem-solver has to do extra work to translate between them; whereas "matching representation to task leads to the use of similar, and therefore consistent, problem-solving processes, and hence to the formation of a consistent mental representation. There will be no need to transform the mental representation to accommodate the use of different processes to extract information from the problem representation and to solve the problem. " (p. 221)

> (2) If the presentation is designed to highlight some kinds of information, then it is likely to obscure other kinds.

For example, a programming language using a procedural model highlights the sequential information but makes the declarative structure harder to extract. This point was made a long time ago, e. g. [Green 81]. By axiom (1), the kinds that are not highlighted will be harder to obtain.

Perhaps these axioms explain why animation systems using code steppers, such as the derivatives of Balsa [Brown 85a], have not yet proved stunningly successful methods to support the comprehension of algorithms [Fix 96]. For an animation constrains their users to view the code in the order of execution, whereas which has a poor cognitive fit with the plan-and-goal structures that users are trying to extract from the code. The animation highlights sequence, which is the wrong information for algorithm comprehension, and obscures the plan structures.

If we are going to make use of these two axioms effectively, we need to ask ourselves:

- What tasks do programmers actually do? (Pennington and Grabowski [Pennington 90] have made a helpful start on this one.)
- How do we provide support for those tasks?
- How will those tasks change when visualisation systems are available? For change they will: Caroll et al. [Caroll 91] give numerous and persuasive illustrations of the 'task-artifact' cycle in which improving the artifact, to support existing tasks, necessarily creates new tasks and new possibilities for the user.

What if there aren't enough dimensions?

What is the difference between the textual source code for a piece of software and a pictorial visualisation of the software? Many computer scientists point to a fundamental difference in information content between the two [Blackwell 96]. Text is essentially linear and one-dimensional, while pictures are two dimensional. Moving pictures, in the case of an animated visualisation, add a time dimension to the two dimensions of the pictorial plane. Virtual reality systems add a further dimension by persuading our binocular perceptual apparatus that it is seeing a three dimensional world.

Computer scientists have regularly assumed that information content increases exponentially with dimensionality. This is certainly true of on-line storage requirements; the pixels of digitised images are slowly clogging the Internet, and on-line digitised video is only seen regularly by those with luxurious access to bandwidth and storage. To a computer scientist, then, the real-time video channel of the human eye supplies a kind of super network connection from computer to brain. An ACM report on visualisation to the NSF was explicitly criticised for making this argument, on the grounds that the information contained within a real-world situation is very different from the information required to make any kind of image of that situation [Lewis 91].

So how much information can really be presented in a multi-dimensional software visualisation? The first point to note is that even text is not really one dimensional. A language compiler may read source code in a linear fashion, but programmers certainly do not write it in that way – they write a bit, go back and see what they have done, and modify it until it looks right [Green 87]. After it is complete, human readers of source code take note of secondary notation [Green in press] such as indentation, vertical and horizontal patterns, distribution of white space, and the many creative uses of ASCII text that can be seen within comment delimiters.

According to Bertin [Bertin 81], the art of presenting graphical information lies largely in assigning the available dimensions of the plane to the independent scales and categories of information that are to be presented. Physical dimensions are a scarce commodity in our universe, however, and Bertin identifies only eight variables that can be utilised in a printed graphic image. Apart from the X and Y dimensions, there are two more ordered variables: the density of ink used to make marks, and the size of the marks. There are also four categorical dimensions: texture, colour, orientation and shape of marks. Source code is just one way of making this assignment in a software visualisation. In source code, groups of shapes (ASCII characters) are given specific meanings and organised according to standard conventions – typically sequence of execution along the Y dimension, and control nesting in the X dimension. Some program editors also assign colour or density values to differentiate between information that is relevant to the compiler or relevant to the programmer.

Control nesting and execution sequence are reasonably sensible variables to assign to two of our scarce physical dimensions. They must both be represented by ordered values, so colour or shape could not easily be substituted for them. Execution sequence is related to flow of time, which is a continuous variable that is by convention assigned to either X or Y – so users expect it. Finally, both control nesting and execution sequence are fundamental properties of computing machines, so this conventional depiction of software is sufficiently general to visualise a program written in any language equivalent to a Turing machine. As with most properties of Turing machines, however, this generality is also at a sufficiently low level to make it uninteresting – but it has already allocated the two most versatile variables of the graphical plane.

Visualisation technologies can incorporate more information by presenting third or fourth continuous dimensions, but each comes at sufficient cost that we must be quite careful about how we allocate variables to dimensions. That cost is both computational, and perceptual – the third dimension of perception is limited in that we can only see one side of solid objects, and the time dimension even more so because perception of temporal events is necessarily transient. How irritating that software is one of the most complex intellectual domains, and that there are hundreds of independent variables that we must juggle in our heads and would prefer to assign to one of those four dimensions to be visualised.

Visualisation design means trying to fit many variables into a few dimensions. There are far more variables than dimensions, so we should encourage an attitude of dimensional restraint in software visualisation. Rather than rushing to the latest technology in order to use up all the dimensions of human perception, a more economical line of research might be to discover how much can be achieved by the subtle application of two.

Some popular software visualisations are particularly unsubtle, in that they use the most valuable plane dimensions to portray topographic domain information such as the map used by a travelling salesman, or the floor of a bin-packing warehouse. The allocation of the plane should be the most careful decision taken in designing a new visualisation, but simply using it to portray the problem domain is a 'no-brainer'. Such a visualisation tells you little about the algorithm, and may even be deceptive – ordinary students find it so easy to solve the travelling salesman problem when given a visual presentation of the problem that they may not realise why the choice of algorithm is significant [MacGregor 96].

The information that is available in a situation is ultimately dependent on how that situation is decoded by the observer [Lewis 91]. Dimensional restraint will be best discovered by avoiding unsubtle algorithms with built-in continuous variables, and devising new coding strategies for informational challenges. This means breaking out of the shallow (but entertaining) concerns of building sexy virtual reality systems and thinking a lot harder about what to do with the two dimensional display devices that are already in front of our eyes.

Are representations good for everyone? What is the importance of individual skill and variation?

The unifying aim of software visualisation is to make information apparent — ideally to make selected, elusive information 'visible', even obvious. By doing so, one hopes that users will more readily be able to find, recognise and interpret the information they need. The hope is that software visualisation can capitalise on native human perception to make relevant information salient. But we must interpret what we perceive, and what we perceive is influenced by what we've learned about interpretation.

Readership skills:

Does visibility lead to effective interpretation? There is increasing evidence, from sources ranging from data interpretation to visual programming, that visibility doesn't guarantee effective interpretation, particularly for novices. Interpreting representations is an acquired skill [Petre 95] [Petre 93]. Arnheim [Arnheim 69] makes this argument in the context of interpreting paintings; the issue is more critical in the precise interpretation of software visualisations. Novice 'readers' tend to lack search and inspection strategies, and tend to be distracted by surface features. Worse, 'visibility' is confused with significance, and confused with relevance to the immediate task, so that novices can be misled by mis-cueing. Expert 'readers' are better attuned to the ways in which underlying structures are cued in the surface layout, and they are better able to recognise what is relevant and to disregard what is irrelevant.

Sweepingly stated, visibility is not solely a characteristic of a representation; visibility is (in part) in the eye of the beholder. Experts are distinguished by their acquired ability to 'see': to perceive as salient the information relevant to a task, and to choose what not to see — to ignore inessentials.

Graphical cultures:

Those cues to inspection and navigation through visualisations that do exist rely on what Petre and Green [Petre 92] have called 'secondary notation' — layout and presentation conventions that are not formally defined, and often not explicit. Readers are informed by their knowledge of context and culture. Relying on cues governed by conventions implicit in a culture, means making use of information 'invisible' to the uninitiated. This may make visualisations difficult to access. Little of graphical culture is codified, and some conventions vary among subcultures.

Presentation skills:

The hope in visualisation is that expertise in presentation can compensate for inexpertness in readership. It may be that disciplined and insightful use of conventions and 'secondary notation' can direct attention to relevant information, assuming that readers can somehow be made to 'see' the cues. This entails identifying and capturing what is most important, and guiding the reader by associating perceptual cues with this carefully selected information. This also means providing support in the environment for the acquisition of readership skills and of the culture, through explicit conventions and tools.

'Cognitive style':

It has become an axiom in the psychology of programming that "individuals differ". Results will differ among individual users as well as individual visualisations. Whether or not one accepts the notion that there are recognisable 'cognitive styles' that influence an individual's reading and reasoning (e. g. , making graphical representations appear more or less congenial than textual ones), one must recognise that individual readership is profoundly influenced by experience. Knowing what to expect, where to look, and what to look for—the cognitive components of an inspection—affects individual strategies, and increasing expertise is evidently reflected in changes of perceptual strategy. Hence, visualisation is acutely vulnerable to weaknesses in individual expressive, perceptive, and interpretive skill.

Software visualisation systems usually present two or more representations of the same information – e. g. an algorithm presented as program text and in a visual form. Presenting two representations is not automatically better than one. In fact, all else being equal, one representation is likely to be better than two. A single representation uses less screen space, avoids problems of switching from one representation to the other and of finding the right place in each one, avoids problems of working which bit of one is equivalent to which bit of the other, and so on. And since many problems can be solved with minimal resources, using a single representation is bound to remain a popular option for some conditions.

When are two representations better than one?

Programmers would rely on a single representation if it were sufficient, but when one is not, then users must learn how to do "inter-representational reasoning", working between the two representations, comprehending the correspondence between them, and keeping track of both at the same time. There is not much research on the cognitive difficulties involved; most research on how diagrams help reasoning is about how diagrams can be used in isolation – i. e. how one representation can be used, not about how two or more can be used together, and what effects result.

So why use two or more? And why should either of them be graphical? We shall consider how programmers might use multiple representations.

(i) The simple case

In the simple case, the representations will be used separately. For some of the user's tasks, or (more likely in expert practice) some part of a task, a single representation may be sufficient, and so one will be all that is used. Different sub-tasks may be suited by different representations, and so the user may switch representations with tasks. Different problems are solved with different representations. Experts often behave in this way, switching among representations (and among programming paradigms) in order to focus on particular aspects or sub-tasks of a problem [Petre 96].

(ii) Multiple identical representations

Multiple representations can be useful to the reader just by providing different views on a conceptual space, even where the representation format of each view is identical. Engineers and architects give detailed information about three dimensional objects by the use of multiple views or elevations. The same principle has been shown to be applicable to more abstract spaces by Shah and Carpenter [Shah 95], who found that even experienced readers of graphs find it difficult to appreciate the interaction of three variables when they are presented by several lines on a single, conventional line graph.

(iii) Bridging representations

One representation may be more suitable for expressing the problem, but less congenial to the user (see Section 10), and so a second representation helps the user to reason about the first. For example, many people have difficulty interpreting contour maps, but are assisted by a 3-D rendering, which helps them to relate the terrain they see to the contour line depiction. The bridging representation may assist the user to extend search and reasoning strategies appropriately. For example, if the user has a search strategy that works for one representation, a different representation may either facilitate indexing, or force exploration.

(iv) Heterogeneous inference

A more interesting case is what has been called 'heterogeneous inference' [Stenning 95a], where two forms of representation need to be used simultaneously for best results. The user needs the alternation between representations in order to encompass the whole of the problem.

Stenning, Cox and Oberlander [Stenning 95b] have further developed these ideas in the context of a pedagogic environment for learning first-order predicate calculus called Hyperproof [Barwise 94]. In Hyperproof, a simple domain of geometric solids is displayed, and users learn how to construct proofs about that world. Proofs can be constructed using standard logic calculus or the users can take advantage of the graphical display. The argument put forward by Stenning and Oberlander is that the two forms of representation (logical and graphical, in their system) are complementary as regards two of the most important cognitive processes required in reasoning. These processes are abstraction, the construction of expressions that apply to more than a single instance, and mental modelling, the hypothesized process by which people reason. Abstraction is easy in the logical calculus, which makes it easy to say "All blue cubes are bigger than all red spheres", but less easy to say "That blue cube there is an exception"; abstraction is harder in the graphical representation, which makes it easy to refer to particular instances, such as a big red sphere, but difficult – even with special graphical notations used in Hyperproof - to handle facts about all solids of a certain type.

And it is exactly that limited power to represent abstractions that is, they claim, the advantage of graphical representations for constructing mental models. A mental model, in the sense they use it (derived from the work of Byrne and Johnson-Laird, [Byrne 90]) is an internal representation of the states of the world, actual and possible. Reasoning about a process in the world requires setting up a mental model of each of the possible starting states. The more states that have to be represented, the harder the reasoning will be. When the external representation is graphical, its limited power of expressing abstractions will make it easier to construct the required set of mental models, for the simple reason that the external 'sentences' will unpack into fewer different possibilities and hence fewer mental models will need to be constructed.

(v) Useful awkwardness

Finally, there is the possibility that a second form of representation can supply not just different information, but also a 'useful awkwardness'. Having to make the mental transference between representations (and possibly between paradigms) forces reflection beyond the boundaries and details of the first representation and an anticipation of correspondences in the second. The deeper level of cognitive processing can reveal glitches that might otherwise have been missed. Far too little is known about this process. The translation can sometimes be provocative, sometimes obstructive, but we cannot at present predict which.

How can we reconcile warring conventions? And how do conventions arise?

When the user of a software visualisation interprets what he or she sees, that interpretation is structured and informed by a broad general knowledge of graphical conventions, many of which do not need to be made explicit in order to be understood. Some graphical conventions are so firmly established that it does not occur to us to question that for example larger areas represent higher numbers or that time flows from left to right. The conventions established by illustrators for printed visualisations of quantitative information been collected and systematised in classic texts such as Tufte, [Tufte 83] and Bertin [Bertin 81].

Despite the guidance of such sytematisers, only some of the knowledge that allows us to interpret graphical information displays is independent of cultural context [Tversky 91]. This cultural dependency is certainly not recognised by context-free mathematical analyses which treat different linear dimensions as fundamentally undistinguished, and able to be assigned arbitrarily.

An example of conflict between mathematical and metaphorical conventions lies in the case where altitude is an independent variable in a data set, as often occurs in meteorological data. The independent variable is normally placed on the X axis, but meteorologists quite reasonably preserve the vertical metaphor by placing altitude on the Y axis. This results in a visual presentation that can only be readily interpreted by a specialist audience [Gattis 96].

Such conflicts easily arise in a domain such as meteorology, where a notation has evolved over time through a number of media, but metaphorical conflicts are already apparent between older software visualisations. Consider the case of a push-down stack, which is often expressed in terms of the plate-stacker analogy, where another plate is added to the top of the pile, pushing down the older items below it. This is in contrast to the normal illustration of a machine stack, which is conventionally illustrated in a memory space with higher addresses (where the stack starts) at the top of the page. The older items in the stack therefore appear above the new items at the "top".

The two conventions for visualising stacks naturally arise from requirements to emphasise different aspects of the situation. There are many sources of such alternative conventions that will be encountered by the users of larger scale visualisations. These include textbook illustrations which are often designed to elucidate by analogy, design notations which are increasingly promoted by CASE tool vendors, and the metaphors of technical jargon, which have evolved from regular usage in order to provide efficient communication between experts. Users may also come to a visualisation with their own images adapted from unrelated domains [Ford 94]. Where such an original image is useful, it can eventually be absorbed as a new convention. These intuitive choices of new representations are unfortunately the only way in which conventions appear to arise, despite the fact that we know enough to apply principles of notational design [Scaife in press].

There could be a useful harvest of originality to be reaped from this diversity, but different conventions are often incompatible. It is more likely that once they become widespread the habits of their use will result in complete entrenchment, as has become the case with the QWERTY keyboard. Where such a convention is owned by a commercial entity, the advantages of such entrenchment are those of a captive user base, meaning that CASE tool vendors, for example, are tempted to promote notational elements that can be drawn only using their own products (at one time, there were suspicions that the 'clouds' of the Booch object-oriented design method were prescribed with such a purpose in mind).

In the rest of this chapter we have discussed the ways in which the conventions used for visualisation have an influence on the way we approach cognitive tasks when using them. This influence has already been noted in more general problem solving, where there is evidence that students produce incorrect solutions to certain kinds of problem if they do not follow established notational conventions, or are unclear about the correspondence between the convention they choose and their problem domain [Cox in press].

This discussion of the ways in which conventions arise and then compete does not hold much hope for an improved situation in future. The combination of cultural dependency, conflicting metaphors, commercial interests and unsupported intuitions mean that software visualisation can apparently look forward to further battle between conventions, with wider popularisation of specific visualisations simply widening the battlefield. The people with most influence on the future are those designing new visualisations today, who should be conscious of the conflict between their desire for unfettered originality and the value of widely accepted conventions.

Why do people like graphical widgets, anyhow?

Given the growing evidence that graphical representations can be harder work and produce poorer performance than textual ones, why are they so appealing? It may be simply that graphical representations provide an alternative to text. Myers [Myers 90] offers a typical description of the attraction: ". . . graphics tends to be a higher-level description of the desired actions (often de-emphasising issues of syntax and providing a higher level of abstraction) and may therefore make the programming task easier even for professional programmers." (p. 100)

In a recent survey, programmers of all levels were interviewed about their preferences among graphical and textual representations. Graphical representations were described as:

- richer; providing more information with less clutter and in less space
- providing the 'gestalt' effect: providing an overview; making structure more visible; clearer
- having a higher level of abstraction, a closer mapping to the problem domain
- more accessible; easier to understand; faster to grasp
- more comprehensible

- more memorable
- more fun
- 'non-symbolic'; less formal

Richness: Graphical representations appear potentially richer than textual ones. The experts observed by Petre and Green [Petre 96] believed that the graphical properties and the secondary notation made electronics schematics and comparable programming notations richer than any textual equivalent and argued that our experimental tasks did not exploit this richness.

'Gestalt' overview: Graphics may benefit from a 'gestalt' response, an informative impression of the whole which provides insight into the structure. Because people need help in grasping complex structures quickly, this purported 'gestalt' attribute makes graphics appealing. Yet in the reading comprehension experiments, programmers did not recognise structural similarities among the graphical representations and often found it difficult to compare two graphical programs. In contrast, those programmers who did notice structural similarities among the programs presented were all looking at the textual representations.

Mapping to the domain: Graphical representations appear to offer potential for 'externalising the objects of thought'—for providing a more direct mapping between internal and external representations by providing representations close to the domain level that make structures and relationships accessible. Kosslyn [Kosslyn 78] and Rohr [Rohr 86] suggest that if relations among objects are visually or spatially grasped, it is easier to derive a mental model of a system structure from a graphical representation than from a textual one. But meeting that potential is a challenge. Experience in digital electronics warns that a typical novice error when learning to draw 'schematics') logical representations of the circuit) is too 'literal' a transcription of the domain, a failure to abstract; novices often reflect the eventual physical layout rather than the logical layout. In effect, they draw a picture of the artefact, rather than depict the structure of the solution.

Accessibility and comprehensibility: It may be that an analog representation appears more accessible than a descriptive one—a notation incorporating pictures may seem less daunting than one comprising abstract symbols. A representation that exploits perceptual cueing takes advantage of the abilities of the human visual system. The analog quality appeals to mundane experience, making the notation appear less esoteric. Cynically, this is a variation of the 'Cobol effect' familiar in the history of programming languages: because the vocabulary (in this case the component shapes) looks familiar and ordinary, novices believe they can understand the program. Yet graphical representations can take longer to read and understand, and they are often misunderstood by novices, who cannot 'see' the available cues.

Fun: Graphical representations may just seem more fun or gratifying; the fact that secondary notation is 'outside the rules' allows the programmer more freedom to 'play around' with layout. The overheads of planning layouts may not matter if there is satisfaction simply in the tinkering required.

The importance of sheer likeability should not be underestimated; it can be a compelling motivator. In general, affect may be as important as effectiveness. The illusion of accessibility may be more important than the reality.

Can I take a version to bed?

The first generation of packaged software application included on-line help systems which raised windows on the screen that were not only written in a minute font, but gave users no chance to compare information in one section with information in another. The help files couldn't be printed out and perused off-line, so working the application in anger was a frustrating experience in which the user's immediate plan of action was continually interrupted by forays into an impoverished information retrieval system.

This illustrates the problems of information that cannot be printed out and taken away to be used, when, and how, it is convenient. Users may want to know that information in order to prepare a teaching course, for instance; or they may want to be just lie in bed and peruse it until it has soaked into their heads.

There is a moral to these examples: do not presume upon your user's contexts. They know when, why and how they want to use the information; you will never guess in advance. What does this tell us about software visualisation? At present we only know how to design for one context. Many existing environments are tied to one particular task, such as code inspection, exploratory programming or teaching.

To see how important context can be, consider some other examples of information appliances that can be used in bed. Mobile phone manufacturers, desperate for new sales, invented pagers to create a different context of use for their technology. This was also a benefit to users, because pagers made telephone interchange asynchronous. Sony invented the Walkman to change the context of use of sound reproduction. Software visualisation builders are in danger of designing a tool that is not available in the context in which it is most needed, since we know from observation that people reason about programs in non-standard environments. There is a whole culture of professional programmers that solve their problems over pizza, in bed, or in the shower, and we ignore this fact at out peril.

Many programmers still prefer to use physical printout during code program comprehension and debugging, not just dynamic screens. Possibly this trend will be changing, with the rise of object-oriented programming (which is non-linear in a way that makes hard copy difficult to follow) and component assembly programming, but we believe that as soon as adequate tools are available for presenting useful linearised views of OO programs, they will once again be taken home to brood over, make notes on, and spill coffee on.

Conclusion

Each of the authors has contributed three gnomic pearls:

It's not all sewn up;

> don't assume too much;

> there is no panacea.

You can't highlight everything;

> think what each feature is for;

> the mental representation matter.

Neuropsychologists have still not located the programming centre of the brain;

> real programs are bigger (and deeper and messier) than you think;

> language generates 90% of the pain, but only does 10% of the work.

And finally, a question for the reader: Why has there been no sequel to 'Sorting out sorting'?

Acknowledgement

The section 'Why do people like graphical widgets, anyhow?' appeared previously in 'Why looking isn't always seeing: readership skills and graphical programming' [Petre 95] and is reproduced here by permission of the Association for Computing Machinery. This chapter was written while the third author was employed at the MRC applied Psychology Unit, Cambridge, UK.

Bibliography

[Abrams 68] Abrams M., "A Comparative Sampling of the Systems for Producing Computer-drawn Flowcharts," *Proceedings of the ACM National Conference*, 1968, pp. 743-750.

[AddMotion 90] AddMotion User Guide, Motion Works Inc., Suite 300-1334 West 6th Avenue, Vancouver BC, Canada, 1990.

[Agrawal 91] Agrawal H., deMillo R. and Spafford E., "An Execution-Backtracking Approach to Debugging," *IEEE Software*, May 1991.

[Appelbe 89] Appelbe B., Smith K., and McDowell C., "Start/Pat: a parallel-programming toolkit," *IEEE Software* , Vol. 6, No. 4, July 1989, pp. 29-38.

[Apple 91] Apple Computer, *The QuickTime Architecture*, Apple Computer, Cupertino CA, 1991.

[Arnheim 69] Arnheim R., *Visual Thinking*, 1st ed., University of California Press, 2nd ed., London, Faber and Faber, 1969.

[AT&T 85] AT&T Bell Laboratories, *The C Programmer's Handbook*, Prentice-Hall, 1985.

[Avrahami 89] Avrahami G., Brooks K. and Brown M., "A Two-View Approach to Constructing User Interfaces," *Computer Graphics*, Vol. 23, No. 3, July 1989, pp. 137-146.

[Badre 89] Badre A., and Allen J., "Graphic language representation and programming behaviour," *Designing and using human-computer interfaces and knowledge based systems*, Slavendy G. and Smith M. eds., Elsevier, Amsterdam, 1989, pp. 59-65.

[Badre 92] Badre A., Beranek M., Morris J. and Stasko J., "Assessing program visualization systems as instructional aids," Tomek I., editor, *Computer Assisted Learning, ICCAL '92*, volume 602 of *Lecture Notes in Computer Science*, Springer-Verlag, Wolfville, Nova Scotia, Canada, June 1992, pp. 87-99.

[Baecker 68] Baecker R., "Experiments in On-Line Graphical Debugging: The Interrogation of Complex Data Structures," *Proceedings of the First Hawaii International Conference on the System Sciences*, January 1968, pp. 128-129.

[Baecker 69a] Baecker R., *Interactive Computer-Mediated Animation*, Ph.D. Thesis, M.I.T. Department of Electrical Engineering, April 1969. Reprinted as M.I.T.

Project MAC TR-61. Also available as AD 690 887 from the Clearinghouse for Federal Scientific and Technical Information.

[Baecker 69b] Baecker R., "Picture-driven animation," *Spring Joint Computer Conference*, volume 34, AFIPS Press, 1969, pp. 273-288.

[Baecker 70] Baecker R., Smith L. and Martin E., *GENESYS -- An Interactive Computer-Mediated Animation System*, 17 minute color sound film, M.I.T. Lincoln Laboratory, 1970.

[Baecker 73] Baecker R., "Towards Animating Computer Programs: A First Progress Report," *Proceedings of the Third NRC Man-Computer Communications Conference*, May 1973, 4.1-4.10.

[Baecker 74] Baecker R., "Interactive computer GENESYS mediated animation," John Halas, editor, *Computer Animation,* Hastings House, New York, NY, 1974, pp. 97-115.

[Baecker 75] Baecker R., "Two Systems which Produce Animated Representations of the Execution of Computer Programs," *SIGCSE Bulletin*, Vol. 7, No. 1, February 1975, pp. 158-167.

[Baecker 81] Baecker R., With the assistance of Dave Sherman, *Sorting out Sorting*, 30 minute color sound film, Dynamic Graphics Project, University of Toronto, 1981. (Excerpted and "reprinted" in *SIGGRAPH Video Review 7*, 1983.) (Distributed by Morgan Kaufmann, Publishers.)

[Baecker 83] Baecker R. and Marcus A., "On Enhancing the Interface to the Source Code of Computer Programs," *Proceedings of the Computer-Human Interface*, December 1983, pp. 251-255.

[Baecker 86] Baecker R., "An Application Overview of Program Visualization," *Computer Graphics*, Vol. 20, No. 4, July 1986, pp. 325.

[Baecker 90a] Baecker R. and Marcus A., *Human Factors and Typography for More Readable Programs*, Addison-Wesley, Reading, Massachusetts, 1990.

[Baecker 90b] Baecker R. and Buchanan J., "A Programmer's Interface: A Visually Enhanced and Animated Programming Environment," *Proceedings 23rd Hawaii International Conference on System Sciences*, January 1990, pp. 531-540.

[Baecker 90c] Baecker R. and Small I., "Animation at the Interface," *The Art of Human-Computer Interface Design*, Laurel B. ed., Addison-Wesley, Reading, MA, 1990, pp. 251-267.

[Baecker 91] Baecker R., Small I. and Mander R., "Bringing Icons to Life," *Proceedings of the ACM SIGCHI '91 Conference on Human Factors in Computing Systems*, ACM Press, New Orleans, LA, May 1991, pp. 1-6.

[Baecker 95a] Baecker R., Grudin J., Buxton W. and Greenberg S. *Readings in Human Computer Interaction: Toward the Year 2000,* Morgan Kaufmann, 1995.

[Baecker 95b] Baecker R., "A New Approach to a University `Computer Literacy' Course," *Proceedings 12th International Conference on Technology and Education,* March 1995, pp. 247-249.

[Baek 88] Baek Y. and Layne B., "Color, graphics and animation in a computer-assisted learning tutorial lesson," *Journal of Computer-based Instruction,* Vol.15, No. 4, 1988, pp. 131-135.

[Baker 72] Baker F., "Chief Programmer Team Management of Production Programming," *IBM Systems Journal,* Vol. 11, No. 1, 1972, pp.56-73.

[Baker 95a] Baker M. and Eick S., "Space-Filling Software Displays," *Journal of Visual Languages and Computing,* Vol. 6, No. 2, June 1995, pp. 119-133.

[Baker 95b] Baker J., Cruz I., Liotta G. and Tamassia R., "A New Model for Algorithm Animation Over the WWW," *ACM Computing Surveys,* Symposium on Multimedia Systems, Vol. 27, No. 4, 1995, pp. 568-572.

[Ball 96] Ball T. and Eick S., "Software Visualization In the Large,'' *Computer,* Vol. 29, No. 4, April 1996, pp. 33-43.

[Balzer 69] Balzer R., "EXDAMS, EXtensible Debugging and Monitoring System," *Proceedings of the Spring Joint Computer Conference,* 1969.

[Balzer 83] Balzer R., Cheatham T. and Green C., "Software Technology in the 1990's: Using a New Paradigm," *Computer,* Vol. 16, No. 11, 1983, pp. 39-45.

[Barghouti 95] Barghouti N., Koutsofios E. and Cohen E., "Improvise: An Interactive, Multimedia Process Visualization Environment," *Proceedings of Fifth European Software Engineering Conference,* Springer-Verlag, September 1995.

[Barstow 87] Barstow D., "Artificial Intelligence and Software Engineering. *Proceedings of the 9th International Conference on Software Engineering,* 1987, pp. 200-211.

[Barwise 94] Barwise J. and Etchemendy J., *Hyperproof.,* CSLI Lecture Notes, Chicago, University of Chicago Press, 1994.

[Baskerville 85] Baskerville D., "Graphic presentation of data structures in the DBX debugger," Technical Report UCB/CSD 86/260, University of California at Berkeley, Berkeley, CA ,1985.

[Bates 89] Bates P., "Debugging heterogeneous distributed systems using event-based models of behavior," *SIGPLAN Notices,* Vol. 24, No. 1, January 1989, pp. 11-22.

(Proceedings of the Workshop on Parallel and Distributed Debugging, Madison, WI, May 1988).

[Batini 84] Batini C., Talamo M. and Tamassia R., "Computer Aided Layout of Entity-Relationship Diagrams," *The Journal of Systems and Software*, Vol. 4, 1984, pp. 163-173.

[Bauer 93] Bauer M. and Johnson-Laird P., "How diagrams can improve reasoning," *Psychological Science,* Vol. 4, No. 6, 1993, pp. 372-378.

[Bazik] Bazik J., "XMX – An X Protocol Multiplexor," http://www.cs.brown.edu/software/xmx/.

[Becker 87] Becker R. and Cleveland W., "Brushing scatterplots," *Technometrics*, Vol. 29, 1987, pp. 127-142.

[Begeulin 91] Begeulin A., Dongarra J., Geist A., Manchek R. and Sunderam V., "Graphical development tools for network-based concurrent supercomputing," *Proceedings of Supercomputing '91,* Albuquerque, NM, November 1991, pp. 435-444.

[Begeulin 93] Begeulin A. and Seligman E., "Causality-preserving timestamps in distributed programs," Technical Report CMU-CS-93-167, Carnegie Mellon University, Pittsburgh, PA, June 1993.

[Belady 76] Belady L. and Lehman M., "A Model of Large Program Development," *IBM Systems Journal* Vol. 15, No. 3, 1976.

[Bell 91] Bell B., Rieman J. and Lewis C., "Usability testing of a graphical programming system: Things we missed in a programming walkthrough," *Proceedings of the ACM SIGCHI '91 Conference on Human Factors in Computing Systems*, New Orleans, LA, May 1991, pp. 7-12.

[Bellamy 90] Bellamy R. and Gilmore D., "Programming plans: internal or external structures," *Lines of Thinking: Reflections on the Psychology of Thought*t, Gilhooly K., Keane M., Logie R. and Erdos G. eds., Vol. 2 , Wiley, 1990.

[Bentley 91a] Bentley J. and Kernighan B., "A System for Algorithm Animation: Tutorial and User Manual," *Computing Systems*, Vol. 4, No. 1, 1991, pp. 5-30.

[Bentley 91b] Bentley J. and Kernighan B., "A System for Algorithm Animation (Tutorial and User Manual)," AT&T Bell Laboratories, Murray Hill, New Jersey 07974, Computing Science Technical Report 132, August 1991.

[Bentley 92] Bentley J. and Kernighan B., "ANIM," software available via anonymous ftp, AT&T Bell Laboratories, Murray Hill, NJ, 1992.

[Bergantz 91] Bergantz D. and Hassell J., "Information Relationships in PROLOG programs: how do programmers comprehend functionality?" *International Journal of Man-Machine Studies*, Vol. 35, 1991, pp. 313-328.

[Bertin 81] Bertin J., *Graphics and Graphic Information Processing*. (Tr. W. J. Berg & P. Scott) Berlin: Walter de Gruyter, 1981.

[Bertin 83] Bertin J., *Semiology of Graphics*, University of Wisconsin Press, Madison, WI, 1983.

[Blackwell 96] Blackwell A., "Metacognitive theories of visual programming: what do we think we are doing?" *Proceedings of the 1996 IEEE Symposium on Visual Languages,* Boulder, CO, September 1996, pp. 240-246.

[Böcker 90] Böcker H. and Herczeg J.,"Browsing through program execution," *INTERACT '90*, Elsevier Science Publishers B.V., North Holland, 1990, pp. 991-996.

[Boecker 86] Boecker H., Fischer G. and Nieper H., "The Enhancement of Understanding through Visual Representations," *Proceedings of the ACM SIGCHI '86 Conference on Human Factors in Computing Systems*, April 1986, pp. 44-50.

[Boehm 81] Boehm B., *Software Engineering Economics*, Prentice-Hall, 1981.

[Bonar 90] Bonar J. and Liffick B., "A visual programming language for novices," *Principles of Visual Programming Systems*, Chang S.-K. ed., Prentice-Hall, Englewood Cliffs, NJ, 1994, pp. 326-366.

[Booch 94] Booch G., *Object Oriented Design with Applications*, Benjamin/Cummings, 1994.

[Booth 75] Booth K., *PQ Trees*, 12-minute color silent film, 1975.

[Bowles 94] Bowles A., Robertson D., Vasconcelos W., Vargas-Vera M. and Bental D., "Applying Prolog programming techniques," *International Journal of Human-Computer Studies*, Vol. 41, No. 3, 1994, pp. 329-350.

[Brayshaw 88] Brayshaw M. and Eisenstadt M., "Adding Data and Procedural Abstraction to the Transparent Prolog Machine," *Logic Programming,* Kowalski R. and Bowen K. eds., Cambridge, MA, MIT Press, 1988.

[Brayshaw 91] Brayshaw M. and Eisenstadt M., "A Practical Tracer for Prolog," *International Journal of Man-Machine Studies*, Vol. 35, No. 5, 1991, pp. 597-631.

[Brayshaw 93a] Brayshaw M., "Intelligent Inference for debugging concurrent programs," *Proceedings of the Conference on Expert Systems and Database Applications (DEXA-93),* Berlin, Springer-Verlag, 1993.

[Brayshaw 93b] Brayshaw M., "MRE: A Flexible and Customisable Program Visualisation Architecture," *People and Computers VIII.*, Alty J., Diaper D. and Guest S. eds., Cambridge University Press, 1993.

[Brayshaw 94] Brayshaw M., *Information Management and Visualization for Debugging Logic Programs.* PhD Thesis, Human Cognition Research Laboratory, The Open University, Walton Hall, Milton Keynes, UK, 1994.

[Brayshaw 96] Brayshaw M., "Visual Models of Parallel Logic Programs," *Journal of Visual Languages and Computing*, in press.

[Broder 90] Broder A. and Karlin, A., "Multilevel Adaptive Hashing," *Proceedings of the First Annual ACM-SIAM Symposium on Discrete Algorithms*, Philadelphia, PA, 1990, pp. 43-53.

[Brown 83] Brown M., Meyrowitz N. and van Dam A., "Personal Computer Networks and Graphical Animation: Rationale and Practice for Education," *ACM SIGCSE Bulletin*, Vol. 15, No. 1, Feb. 1983, pp. 296-307.

[Brown 84a] Brown M. and Sedgewick R., "Progress Report: Brown University Instructional Computing Laboratory," *ACM SICCSE Bulletin*, Vol. 16, No. 1, Feb. 1984, pp. 91-101.

[Brown 84b] Brown M. and Sedgewick R., "A system for algorithm animation," *Proceedings of ACM SIGGRAPH '84*, Minneapolis, MN, July 1984, pp. 177–186.

[Brown 85a] Brown M. and Sedgewick R., "Techniques for Algorithm Animation," *IEEE Software,* Vol. 2, No. 1, January 1985, pp. 28-39.

[Brown 85b] Brown G., Carling R., Herot C., Kramlich D. and Souza P., "Program visualization: graphical support for software development," *Computer,* Vol. 18, No. 8, August 1985, pp. 27-35.

[Brown 88a] Brown M., *Algorithm Animation*, MIT Press, Cambridge MA, 1988.

[Brown 88b] Brown M., "Exploring Algorithms Using Balsa-II," *Computer*, Vol. 21, No. 5, May 1988, pp. 14-36.

[Brown 88c] Brown M., "Perspectives on Algorithm Animation," *Proceedings of the ACM SIGCHI '88 Conference on Human Factors in Computing Systems*, ACM, May 1988, Washington D. C., pp. 33-38.

[Brown 91] Brown M., "ZEUS: A system for algorithm animation and multi-view editing," *Proceedings of the 1991 IEEE Workshop on Visual Languages*, Kobe, Japan, October 1991, pp. 4-9.

[Brown 92] Brown M. and Hershberger J., "Color and Sound in Algorithm Animation," *Computer*, Vol. 25, No. 12, December 1992, pp. 52-63.

[Brown 93] Brown M. and Najork M., "Algorithm Animation using 3D Interactive Graphics," *Proceedings of the 1993 ACM Symposium on User Interface Software and Technology* , Atlanta, GA, November 1993, pp. 93–100.

[Brown 96a] Brown M. and Najork M., "Collaborative Active Textbooks: A Web-Based Algorithm Animation System for an Electronic Classroom," *Proceedings of the 1996 IEEE International Symposium on Visual Languages*, Boulder, CO, September 1996, pp. 266-275.

[Brown 96b] Brown M. and Raisamo, R., "JCAT: Collaborative Active Textbooks in Java," submitted for publication.

[Buchanan 88] Buchanan J., *LOGOmotion: A Visually Enhanced Programming Environment*, M.Sc. Thesis, Dept. of Computer Science, University of Toronto, 1988.

[Buxton 90] Buxton W., Gaver W. and Bly S., "The Use of Non-Speech Audio at the Interface," *SIGCHI'90 Tutorial Notes*, ACM, New York, 1990.

[Byrd 80] Byrd L., "Understanding the control flow of Prolog programs," *Proceedings of the Logic Programming Workshop,* Debrecen, Hungary, 1980.

[Byrne 90] Byrne R. and Johnson-Laird P., "Models and deductive reasoning," *Lines of Thinkingg: Reflections on the Psychology of Thought.*, Gilhooly K., Keane M., Logie R. and Erdos G. eds., Wiley, New York, 1990.

[Byrne 96] Byrne M., Catrambone R. and Stasko J., "Do Algorithm Animations Aid Learning?", Technical Report GIT-GVU-96-18, GVU Center, Georgia Institute of Technology, Atlanta, GA, August 1996.

[Cañas 94] Cañas J., Bajo M. and Gonzalvo P., "Mental models and computer programming," *International Journal of Human Computer Studies,* Vol. 40, No. 5, 1994, pp. 795-811.

[Carroll 91] Carroll J., Kellogg W. and Rosson, M., "The task-artifact cycle," *Designing Interaction: Psychology at the Human-Computer Interface,* Carroll J. ed., Cambridge, Cambridge University Press, 1991, pp. 74-102.

[Chandy 88] Chandy K. and Misra J., *Parallel Program Design: A Foundation*, Addison-Wesley, New York, NY, 1988.

[Chang 87] Chang S., "Visual languages: A tutorial and survey," *IEEE Software*, Vol. 4, No. 1, January 1987, pp. 29-39.

[Chang 90] Chang S.-K., *Principles of Visual Programming Systems*, Prentice-Hall, Englewood Cliffs, NJ, 1990.

[Chaparos 81] Chaparos A., *Notes for a Federal Design Manual*, Chaparos Productions, Washington, D.C., 1981.

[Chen 89] Chen, Y., "The C Program Database and Its Applications'', *Proceedings of the Summer 1989 USENIX Conference,* 1989.

[Chen 95] Chen Y., Fowler G., Koutsofios E. and Wallach R., "Ciao: A Graphical Navigator for Software and Document Repositories," *Proceedings of the International Conference on Software Maintenance*, 1995.

[Chi 81] Chi M., Feltovich P. and Glaser R., "Categorisation and representation of physics problems by experts and novices," *Cognitive Science*, Vol. 5, 1981, pp. 121-152.

[Chifosky 88] Chikofsky E. and Rubenstein B., "CASE: Reliability Engineering for Information Systems," *IEEE Software*, Vol. 5, No. 2, March 1988, pp. 11-16.

[Clancey 84] Clancey W. and Letsinger R., "NEOMYCIN: Reconfiguring a Rule-based Expert System for Application to Teaching," *Readings in Medical Artificial Intelligence: The First Decade*, Clancey, W. and Shortliffe, E. eds., Addison-Wesley, Reading, MA, 1984, pp. 361-381.

[Conroy 70] Conroy K. and Smith R., "NEATER2: A PL/I Source Statement Reformatter," *Communications of the ACM*, Vol. 13, 1970, pp. 669-675.

[Conway 87] Conway M. and Kahney H., "Transfer of Learning in Inference Problems: Learning to Program Recursive Functions," *Advances in Artificial Intelligence*, Hallam J. and Mellish C. eds., 1987, pp. 239-250.

[Coombs 85] Coombs M. and Stell J., "A model for debugging Prolog by symbolic execution: the separation of specification and procedure," Research Report MMIGR137. Department of Computer Science, University of Strathclyde, 1985.

[Cormen 90] Cormen T., Leiserson C. and Rivest R., *Introduction to Algorithms*, MIT Press, Cambridge MA, 1990.

[Couch 88] Couch A., *Graphical Representations of Program Performance on Hypercube Message-Passing Multiprocessors*, Ph. D. Thesis, Dept. of Computer Science, Tufts University, TR 88-4, 1988.

[Couch 93] Couch A., "Categories and Context in Scalable Execution Visualization," *Journal of Parallel and Distributed Comput.ing,* Vol. 18, No. 2, June 1993, pp. 195-204.

[Cox 92] Cox K. and Roman G.-C., "Abstraction in Algorithm Animation," *Proceedings of the 1992 IEEE Workshop on Visual Languages,* Seattle, WA, September 1992, pp. 18–24.

[Cox 94] Cox K. and Roman G.-C., "A Characterization of the Computational Power of Rule-Based Visualization," *Journal of Visual Languages and Computing,* Vol. 5, No. 1, January 1994, pp. 5-27.

[Cox 95] Cox R. and Brna P., "Supporting the use of external representations in problem solving: the need for flexible learning environments," *Journal of Artificial Intelligence in Education,* Vol. 6, No. 2, 1995, pp. 239-302.

[Cunniff 87] Cunniff N. and Taylor R., "Graphical vs. textual representation: an empirical study of novices' program comprehension," *Proceedings of the Empirical studies of programmers: second workshop,* Norwood, NJ, Ablex, 1987, pp. 114-131.

[Cypher 93] Cypher A., editor. *Watch What I Do: Programming by Demonstration,* MIT Press, Cambridge, MA, 1993.

[Dahl 72] Conroy K. and Smith R., "NEATER2: A PL/I Source Statement Reformatter," *Communications of the ACM,* Vol. 13, 1972, pp. 669-675.

[Dart 87] Dart S., Ellison R., Feiler P. and Habermann A., "Software Development Environments," *Computer,* Vol. 20, No. 11, November 1987, pp. 18-28.

[Davies 94a] Davies S., "Externalising information during coding activities: effects of expertise, environment and task," *Proceedings of the Empirical Studies of Programmers: Fifth Workshop,* Cook C., Scholtz J. and Spohrer J. eds., Norwood, NJ, Ablex, 1994, pp. 42-61.

[Davies 94b] Davies S., "Knowledge restructuring and the acquisition of programming expertise," *International Journal of Human Computer Studies,* Vol. 40, 1994, pp. 703-726.

[Davies 96] Davies S., "Display-based problem-solving strategies in computer programming," *Proceedings of the Empirical Studies of Programmers: Sixth workshop,* Gray W. and Boehm-Davis D. eds., Norwood, NJ, Ablex, 1996.

[Davis 93] Davis J. and Morgan T., "Object-oriented development at Brooklyn Union Gas," *IEEE Software,* Vol. 10, No. 1, January 1993, pp. 67–74.

[Delisle 84] Delisle N., Menicosy D. and Schwartz M., "Viewing a programming environment as a single tool," *SIGPLAN Notices,* Vol. 19, No. 5, May 1984, pp. 49-56.

[De Pauw 93] De Pauw W., Helm R., Kimelman D. and Vlissides J., "Visualizing the behavior of object-oriented systems," *Proceedings of the 1993 European Conference on Object-Oriented Programming,* 1993, pp. 326–337.

[De Pauw 94] De Pauw W., Kimelman D. and Vlissides J., "Modeling object-oriented program execution," *Proceedings of OOPSLA 1994*, 1994, pp. 163–182.

[DeTreville 93] DeTreville J., "The GraphVBT interface for programming algorithm animations," *Proceedings of the 1993 IEEE Symposium on Visual Languages*, Bergen, Norway, August 1993, pp. 26-31.

[Dewar 86] Dewar A. and Cleary J., "Graphical display of complex information within a Prolog debugger," *International Journal of Man Machine Studies*, Vol. 25, 1986, pp. 503-521.

[DiBattista 94] Di Battista G., Eades P., Tamassia R. and Tollis I., "Algorithms for drawing graphs: an annotated bibliography," *Computational Geometry Theory Applications*, Vol. 4, 1994, pp. 235--282, subsumed by http://www.cs.brown.edu/people/rt/gd-biblio.html.

[DiGiano 92a] DiGiano C., "Visualizing Program Behaviour Using Non-speech Audio," M.Sc. Thesis, Dept. of Computer Science, University of Toronto, 1992.

[DiGiano 92b] DiGiano C. and Baecker R. "Program Auralization: Sound Enhancements to the Programming Environment," *Proceedings Graphics Interface '92*, Vancouver, B.C., May 1992, pp. 44-52.

[Ding 90] Ding C. and Prabhaker M., "A framework for the automated drawing of data structure diagrams," *IEEE Transactions on Software Engineering*, Vol. 16, No. 5, May 1990, pp. 543-557.

[Ditchey 87] Ditchev C. and du Boulay J., "An enhanced trace tool for Prolog," *Proceedings of the Third International Conference, Children in the Information Age*, Sofia, Bulgaria, 1987.

[Dobkin 88] Dobkin D., Guibas L., Hershberger J. and Snoeyink J., "An Efficient Algorithm for Finding the CSG Representation of a Simple Polygon," *Computer Graphics*, Vol. 22, No. 4, August 1986, pp. 31-40.

[Domingue 87] Domingue J., "ITSY: An Automated Programming Advisor," HCRL Tech Report No. 22, Open University, Milton Keynes, UK, 1987.

[Domingue 88] Domingue J., "TRI: The Transparent Rule Interpreter," Proceedings of Expert Systems'88, Shadbolt, N. ed., *Research and Development in Expert Systems VII*, Cambridge University Press, December 1988, pp. 126-138.

[Domingue 89] Domingue J. and Eisenstadt M., "A New Metaphor for the Graphical Explanation of Forward Chaining Rule Execution," *Proceedings of The Twelfth International Joint Conference on Artificial Intelligence*, Detroit, MI, 1989, pp. 129-134.

[Domingue 91] Domingue J., Price B. and Eisenstadt M., "Viz: A Framework for Describing and Implementing Software Visualization Systems," *Proceedings of NATO Advanced Research Workshop: User-centred requirements for Software Engineering Environments*, September 1991.

[Domingue 95] Domingue J., "Using Software Visualization Technology in the Validation of Knowledge Based Systems," *Proceedings of the 9th Knowledge Acquisition for Knowledge-Based Systems Workshop*, Banff, Alberta, February 1995.

[Dondis 73] Dondis D., *A Primer of Visual Literacy*, MIT Press, Cambridge, MA, 1973.

[Dongarra 87] Dongarra J. and Sorenson D., "SCHEDULE: Tools for Developing and Analyzing Parallel Fortran Programs," *The Characteristics of Parallel Algorithms*, Jamieson L., Gannon D., and Douglas R. eds., MIT Press, Cambridge, MA, 1987, pp. 363-394.

[Dongarra 90] Dongarra J., Brewer O., Kohl J. and Fineberg S., "A tool to aid in the design, implementation, and understanding of matrix algorithms for parallel processors, *Journal of Parallel and Distributed Computing,* Vol. 9, No. 2, June 1990, pp. 185-202.

[Donzeau-Gouge 84] Donzeau-Gouge V., Heut G., Kahn G., and Lang B., "Programming environments based on structured editors: the MENTOR Experience," . D. Barstow, H. Shrobe and E. Sandewall editors, *Interactive Programming Environments*, McGraw-Hill, New York, 1984.

[Douglas 94] Douglas S., McKeown D. and Hundhausen C., "Exploring human visualization of algorithms," Technical Report CIS-TR-94-27, University of Oregon, Eugene, OR, 1994.

[Douglas 95] Douglas S., Hundhausen C. and McKeown D., "Toward empirically-based software visualization languages," *Proceedings of the 1995 IEEE Symposium on Visual Languages*, Darmstadt, Germany, September 1995, pp. 342-349.

[du Boulay 81] du Boulay J., O'Shea T., and Monk J., "The black box inside the glass box: presenting computing concepts to novices," *International Journal of Man Machine Studies*, Vol. 16, No. 3, 1981, pp. 237-249.

[Duisberg 86a] Duisberg R., "Animated graphical interfaces using temporal constraints," *Proceedings of the ACM SIGCHI '86 Conference on Human Factors in Computing Systems*, Boston, MA, April 1986, pp. 131-136.

[Duisberg 86b] Duisberg R., *Constraint-Based Animation: Temporal Constraints in the Animus System.*, PhD thesis, Dept. of Computer Science, University of Washington, Seattle, WA, 1986.

[Duisberg 87] Duisberg R., "Visual programming of program visualizations," A gestural interface for animating algorithms," *Proceedings of the 1987 IEEE Workshop on Visual Languages*, Linkoping, Sweden, August 1987, pp. 55-66.

[Ebrahami 92] Ebrahimi A., "VCPL: a visual language for teaching and learning programming," *Journal of Visual Languages and Computing*, Vol. 3, No. 3, pp. 299-317.

[Edelsbrunner 86] Edelsbrunner H. and Guibas L., "Topologically Sweeping an Arrangement," *Proceedings of the 18th ACM Symposium on the Theory of Computing*, ACM Press, New York, 1986, pp. 389 -403

[Edwards 79] Edwards B., *Drawing on the Right Side of the Brain.*, J. P. Tarcher,Los Angeles, CA, 1979.

[Eick 92a] Eick S., "Visualizing Large Software Systems," *ASA '92 Conference Proceedings* , Boston, Massachusetts, 1992, pp. 1-11.

[Eick 92b] Eick S. and Steffen J., "Visualizing Code Profiling Line Oriented Statistics," *Proceedings of the Visualization '92 Conference* , October 1992, pp. 210-217.

[Eick 92c] Eick S., Steffen J. and Sumner E. Jr., "SeeSoft—A Tool For Visualizing Line Oriented Software Statistics", *IEEE Transactions on Software Engineering*, Vol. 18, No. 11, November 1992, pp. 957-968.

[Eick 94a] Eick S., "Graphically Displaying Text," *Journal of Computational and Graphical Statistics*, Vol. 3, No. 2, 1994, pp.59-67.

[Eick 94b] Eick S., Nelson M. and Schmidt J., "Graphical Analysis of Computer Log Files," *Communications of the ACM*, Vol. 37, No. 12, December 1994, pp. 50-56.

[Eisenstadt 83] Eisenstadt M., "A User Friendly Software Environment for the Novice Programmer," *Communications of the ACM*, Vol. 27, No. 12, December 1983, pp. 1056-1064.

[Eisenstadt 84a] Eisenstadt M., Breuker J. and Evertsz R., "A cognitive account of "natural" looping constructs," *Proceedings of the First IFIP Conference on Human-Computer Interaction, INTERACT '84*, London, 1984, pp. 173-177.

[Eisenstadt 84b] Eisenstadt M., "A Powerful Prolog Trace Package," *Proceedings of the 6th European Conference on Artificial Intelligence,* Pisa, Italy, 1984.

[Eisenstadt 85a] Eisenstadt M., "Retrospective Zooming: a knowledge based tracing and debugging methodology for logic programming," *Proceedings of the Ninth International Conference on Artificial Intelligence (IJCAI-85)*, Los Angeles, CA, Morgan Kaufmann, 1985.

[Eisenstadt 85b] Eisenstadt M., "Tracing and debugging Prolog programs by retrospective zooming," *Artificial Intelligence Programming Environments*, Hawley R. ed., Ellis Horwood, Chichester, UK, 1985.

[Eisenstadt 87] Eisenstadt M. and Brayshaw M., "An integrated textbook, video and software environment for novice and expert Prolog programmers," *Understanding the novice programmer*, Soloway E. and Spohrer J. eds., Erlbaum, Hillsdale, NJ, 1987.

[Eisenstadt 88a] Eisenstadt M. and Brayshaw M., "The Transparent Prolog Machine (TPM): an execution model and graphical debugger for logic programming," *Journal of Logic Programming*, Vol. 5, No. 4, 1988, pp. 277-342.

[Eisenstadt 88b] Eisenstadt M., *Intensive Prolog*. Associate Student Central Office (Course PD622), The Open University, Milton Keynes, UK: Open University Press, 1988.

[Eisenstadt 90a] Eisenstadt M. and Brayshaw M., "A fine grained account of Prolog execution for teaching and debugging," *Instructional Science*, Vol. 19, No. 4/5, 1990, pp. 407-436.

[Eisenstadt 90b] Eisenstadt M., Domingue J., Rajan T. and Motta E., "Visual Knowledge Engineering," *IEEE Transactions on Software Engineering* Special Issue on Visual Programming, Vol. 16, No. 10, October 1990, pp. 1164-1177.

[Eisenstadt 92a] Eisenstadt M., Price B. and Domingue J., "Software Visualization: Redressing ITS Fallacies," *Proceedings of NATO Advanced Research Workshop on Cognitive Models and Intelligent Environments for Learning Programming*, Genova, Italy, 1992.

[Eisenstadt 92b] Eisenstadt M. and Breuker J., "Naive iteration: an account of the conceptualizations underlying buggy looping programs," *Novice Programming Environments: Explorations in Human-Computer Interaction and Artificial Intelligence,* Eisenstadt M., Keane M. and Rajan T. eds., LEA, Hove, UK, 1992.

[Eisenstadt 93a] Eisenstadt M., "Tales of debugging from the front lines," *Empirical Studies of Programmers: Fifth Workshop*, Cook C., Scholtz J. and Spohrer J. eds., Norwood, NJ: Ablex, 1993.

[Eisenstadt 93b] Eisenstadt M., Price B. and Domingue J., "Software visualization as a pedagogical tool," *Instructional Science*, Vol. 21, 1993, pp. 335-364.

[Elsom-Cook 90] Elsom-Cook M. ed., *Guided discovery tutoring : a framework for ICAI research.*, Chapman, London , 1990.

[Engstrom 87] Engstrom B. and Capello P., "The SDEF systolic programming system," *Proceedings of the International Conference on Parallel Processing,* St. Charles, IL, August 1987, pp. 645-652.

[Ericsson 84] Ericsson K. and Simon H., A. *Protocol analysis: Verbal reports as data,* MIT Press, Cambridge, MA, 1984.

[Evans 66] Evans T. and Darley D., "On-line Debugging Techniques: A Survey," *Proceedings of the Fall Joint Computer Conference,* Vol. 29, 1966, pp. 37-50.

[Feiner 82] Feiner S., Nagy S. and van Dam A., "An Experimental System for Creating and Presenting Interactive Graphical Documents," *ACM Transactions on Graphics,* Vol. 1, No. 1, 1982, pp. 59-111.

[Fischer 81] Fischer C., Johnson G. and Mauney J., "An Introduction to Editor Allen Poe," Technical Report TR 451, University of Wisconsin-Madison, Madison, WI, October 1981.

[Fisk 67] Fisk C., Caskey D. and West L., "ACCEL: Automated Circuit Card Etching Layout," *Proceedings of the IEEE,* Vol. 55, No. 11, November 1967, pp. 1971-1982.

[Fix 96] Fix V. and Sriram P., "Empirical studies of algorithm animation for the selection sort," *Empirical Studies of Programmers: Sixth Workshop,* Gray W. and Boehm-Davis D. eds., Ablex, Norwood, NJ, 1996, pp. 271-282.

[Flinn 90] Flinn S. and Cowan W., "Visualizing the Execution of Multi-processor Real-Time Programs," *Proceedings of Graphics Interface '90,* Halifax, Nova Scotia, 1990, pp. 293-300.

[Foley 86] Foley J. and McMath C., "Dynamic Process Visualization," *IEEE Computer Graphics and Applications,* Vol. 6, No. 2, March 1986, pp. 16-25.

[Foley 90] Foley J., van Dam A., Feiner S. and Hughes J., *Computer Graphics Principles And Practice,* Second Edition, Addison-Wesley, Reading MA, 1990.

[Ford 93] Ford L., "How programmers visualise programs," Technical Report R271, Department of Computer Science, University of Exeter, UK, 1993.

[Forgy 82] Forgy C., "Rete: A Fast Algorithm for the Many Pattern/ Many Object pattern Matching Problem," *Artificial Intelligence,* Vol. 19, 1982, pp. 17-37.

[Francioni 91] Francioni J., Albright L. and Jackson J., "Debugging parallel programs using sound," *SIGPLAN Notices,* Vol. 26, No. 12, December 1991, pp. 68-75.

[Fredman 86] Fredman M., Sedgewick R., Sleator D. and Tarjan R., "The Pairing Heap: A new form of self-adjusting heap," *Algorithmica,* Vol. 1, March 1986, pp. 111-129.

[Frick 95] Frick A., Ludwig A. and Mehldau H., "A Fast Adaptive Layout Algorithm for Undirected Graphics," *Proceedings of Graph Drawing 94,"* Lecture Notes in Computer Science 894, Springer-Verlag, 1995, pp. 388-403.

[Friedman 89] Friedman J., Hershberger J. and Snoeyink J., "Compliant Motion in a Simple Polygon," *Proceedings of the 5th ACM Symposium on Computational Geometry*, ACM, New York, 1989, pp. 115-186.

[Fruchterman 91] Fruchterman T. and Reingold E., "Graph Drawing by Force-Directed Placement," *Software -- Practice and Experience*, Vol. 21, No. 11, 1991, pp. 1129-1164.

[Fung 90] Fung P., Brayshaw M., Du Boulay B. and Elsom-Cook M., "Towards a taxonomy of novices' misconceptions of the Prolog interpreter," *Instructional Science*, Vol. 19, No. 4/5, 1990, pp. 311-336.

[Furnas 86] Furnas G., "Generalized Fisheye Views," *Proceedings of the ACM SIGCHI '86 Conference on Human Factors in Computing Systems*, Boston, MA, April 1986, pp. 16-23.

[Gamma 95] Evans T. and Darley D., "On-line Debugging Techniques: A Survey, *Proceedings of the Fall Joint Computer Conference,* Vol. 29, pp. 37-50.

[Gansner 93] Gansner E., Koutsofios E., North S. and Vo K.-P., "A technique for drawing directed graphs," *IEEE Transactions on Software Engineering*, Vol. 19, No. 3, 1993, pp. 214--230.

[Gantt 19] Gantt H., "Organizing for Work," *Industrial Management,* Vol. 58, August 1919, pp. 89-93.

[Gattis 96] Gattis M. and Holyoak K., "Mapping conceptual to spatial relations in visual processing," *Journal of Experimental Psychology, Learning, Memory and Cognition*, Vol. 22, No. 1, 1996, pp. 231-239.

[Gaver 89] Gaver W., "The SonicFinder: An Interface That Uses Auditory Icons," *Human-Computer Interaction*, Vol. 4, No. 1, 1989, pp. 67-94.

[Gaver 91] Gaver W., O'Shea T. and Smith R., "Effective Sounds in Complex Systems: The ARKola Simulation," *Proceedings of the ACM SIGCHI '91 Conference on Human Factors in Computing Systems,* ACM Press, New Orleans, LA, May 1991, pp. 85-90.

[Gerstner 78] Gerstner K., *Compendium for Literates*. MIT Press, Cambridge, MA, 1978.

[Gibbs 94] Gibbs W., "Software's Chronic Crisis," *Scientific American*, September 1994.

[Glassman 93] Glassman S., "A turbo environment for producing algorithm animations," *Proceedings of the 1993 IEEE Symposium on Visual Languages*, Bergen, Norway, August 1993, pp. 32-36.

[Glinert 90a] Glinert E. ed., *Visual Programming Environments: Applications and Issues,* IEEE Computer Society Press, New York, 1990.

[Glinert 90b] Glinert E. ed., *Visual Programming Environments: Paradigms and Systems,* IEEE Computer Society Press, New York, 1990.

[Gloor 92] Gloor P., "AACE - Algorithm Animation for Computer Science Education," *Proceedings of the 1992 IEEE Workshop on Visual Languages,* Seattle, WA, September 1992, pp. 25-31.

[Gloor 93] Gloor P., Dynes S. and Lee I., *Animated Algorithms.* MIT Press, Cambridge, MA. 1993. (CD-ROM)

[Gloor 96] Gloor P., *Elements of Hypermedia Design: Techniques for Navigation and Visualization in Cyberspace,* Birkhauser Publishers, Cambridge MA, 1996.

[Goldberg 83] Goldberg A. and Robson D., *Smalltalk-80: the language and its implementation,* Addison-Wesley, Reading, MA, 1983.

[Goldstein 47] Goldstein H. and von Neumann J., "Planning and Coding Problems of an Electronic Computing Instrument," *von Neumann, J., Collected Works,* Taub A. ed., Macmillan, 1947, pp. 80-151.

[Graham 82] Graham S., Kessler P. and McKusick M., K., "gprof: A Call Graph Execution Profiler," *Proceedings of the s-1 SIGPLAN '82 Symposium on Compiler Construction, SIGPLAN Notices,* Vol. 17, No. 6, 1982, pp. 120-126.

[Graham 92] Graham S., Harrison M. and Munson E., "The proteus presentation system," *Software Engineering Notes* Vol. 17, No. 5, December 1992, pp. 130-138.

[Gray 87] Gray W. and Anderson J., "Change-episodes in coding: when and how do programmers change their code?" *Empirical Studies of Programmers: Second Workshop,* Olson G., Sheppard S. and Soloway E. eds., Ablex, Norwood, NJ, 1987, pp. 185-197.

[Green 77] Green T., "Conditional program statements and their comprehensibility to professional programmers," *Journal of Occupational Psychology,* Vol. 50, 1977, pp. 93-109.

[Green 81] Green T., Sime M. and Fitter M., "The art of notation," *Computing Skills and the User Interface,* Coombs M. and Alty J. eds., Academic Press, London, 1981.

[Green 87] Green T., Bellamy R. and Parker J., "Parsing and Gnisrap: a model of device use," *Empirical Studies of Programmers: Second Workshop,* Ablex, Norwood, NJ, 1987, pp. 132-146.

[Green 96] Green T. and Petre M., "Usability analysis of visual programming environments," *Journal of Visual Languages and Computing,* Vol. 7, No. 2, 1996, pp. 131-174.

[Griswold 94] Griswold R. and Jeffery C., "Nova: Low-Cost Data Animation Using a Radar-Sweep Metaphor," *Proceedings of UIST '94,* Monterey, CA, November 1994, pp. 131-132.

[Griswold 96] Griswold R. and Griswold M., *The Icon Programming Language,* 3rd ed., Peer-to-Peer Communications, San Jose, CA, 1996.

[Gu 95] Gu W., Eisenhauer G., Kraemer E., Schwan K., Stasko J., Vetter J. and Mallavarupu N., "Falcon: On-line Monitoring and Steering of Large-Scale Parallel Programs," *Proceedings of the Fifth Symmposium on the Frontiers of Massively Parallel Computation,* McClean, VA, February, 1995, pp. 422-429.

[Guarna 89] Guarna V. Jr., Gannon D., Jablonowski D., Malony A. and Gaur Y., "Faust: an integrated environment for parallel programming," *IEEE Software,* Vol. 6, No. 4, July 1989, pp. 20-27.

[Guibas 78] Guibas L. and Sedgewick R., "A Dichromatic Framework for Balanced Trees," *Proceedings of the 19th Annual Symposium on the Foundations Computer Science,* October 1978, pp. 8-21.

[Gurka 96] Gurka J. and Citrin W., "Testing Effectiveness of Algorithm Animation," *Proceedings of the 1996 IEEE International Symposium on Visual Languages,* Boulder, CO, September 1996, pp. 182-189.

[Hackstadt 94] Hackstadt S. and Malony A., "Next-Generation Parallel Performance Visualization: A Prototyping Environment for Visualization Development," *Proceedings of the 1994 Conference on Parallel Architectures and Languages Europe (PARLE '94),* Athens, Greece, July 1994, pp. 192-201.

[Haibt 59] Haibt L, "A Program to Draw Multi-level Flowcharts," *Proceedings of the Western Joint Computer Conference,* San Francisco, CA, March 1959, pp. 131-137.

[Harbison 84] Harbison S. and Steele G. Jr., *C: A Reference Manual,* Prentice-Hall, 1984.

[Harel 88] Harel D., "On Visual Formalisms," *Communications of the ACM,* Vol. 31, No. 5, May 1988, pp. 514-530.

[Harter 85] Harter P., Heimbigner D. and King R., "IDD: An interactive distributed debugger," *Proceedings of the Fifth International Conference on Distributed Computing Systems,* Denver, CO, May 1985, pp. 498-506.

[Harvey 97] Harvey B., *Computer Science Logo Style. Volume 1: Symbolic Computing.* Second Edition, MIT Press, Cambridge, MA. 1997 to appear.

[Hasemer 84] Hasemer T., "MACSOLO/AURAC: A programming environment for novices," *Proceedings of the 6th European Conference on Artificial Intelligence,* Pisa, Italy, 1984.

[Hasemer 92] Hasemer T., "Syntactic debugging of procedural programs," *Novice Programming Environments: Explorations in Human-Computer Interaction and Artificial Intelligence,* Eisenstadt M., Keane M. and Rajan T. eds., Lawrence earlbaum Assoc., Hove, UK, 1992.

[Heath 89] Heath M., "Visual animation of parallel algorithms for matrix computations," *Proceedings of the Hypercube Conference,* Monterey, CA, 1989, pp. 735-738.

[Heath 91] Heath M. and Etheridge J., "Visualizing the performance of parallel programs," *IEEE Software*, Vol. 8, No. 5, 1991, pp. 23–39.

[Heath 95a] Heath M., Malony A. and Rover D., "The Visual Display of Parallel Performance Data," *Computer*, Vol. 28, No. 11, November 1995, pp. 21-28.

[Heath 95b] Heath M., Malony A. and Rover D., "Parallel Performance Visualization: From Practice to Theory," *IEEE Parallel and Distributed Technology*, Vol. 3, No. 4, November 1995, pp. 44-60.

[Helm 92] Helm R., Huynh T., Marriott K. and Vlissides J., "An object-oriented architecture for constraint-based graphical editing," *Proceedings of the Third Eurographics Workshop on Object-Oriented Graphics*, Champéry, Switzerland, October 1992, pp. 1-22. Also available as IBM Research Division Technical Report RC 18524 (79392).

[Helmbold 90] Helmbold D., McDowell C. and Wang J., "Traceviewer: A graphical browser for trace analysis," Technical Report UCSC-CRL-90-59, Univ. of California at Santa Cruz, Santa Cruz, CA, October 1990.

[Helmbold 91] Helmbold D. and McDowell C., "Computing reachable states of parallel programs," *SIGPLAN Notices,* Vol. 26, No. 12, December 1991, pp. 69-78. (Proceedings of the SIGPLAN/SIGOPS Workshop on Parallel and Distributed Debugging, Santa Cruz, CA, May 1991).

[Helttula 89] Helttula E., Hyrskykari A.,and Raiha K.-J., "Graphical Specification of Algorithm Animations with ALADDIN," *Proceedings of the 22nd Annual Hawaii International Conference on System Sciences*, Kailua-Kona, Hawaii, January 1989, pp. 892-901.

[Heltulla 90] Heltulla E., Hyrskykari A. and Räihä K.-J., "Principles of ALADDIN and Other Algorithm Animation Systems," *Visual Languages and Applications*, Ichikawa T., Jungert E., and Korfhage R. eds., Plenum, London, 1990, pp. 175-187.

[Henry 90] Henry R., Whaley K. and Forstall B., "The University of Washington Illustrating Compiler," *The ACM SIGPLAN'90 Conference on Programming Language Design and Implementation*, ACM, New York, June 1990, pp. 223-233.

[Herot 82] Herot C., Brown G., Carling R., Friedell M., Kramlich D. and Baecker R., "An Integrated Environment for Program Visualization," *Automated Tools for Information Systems Design*, Schneider H.-J. and Wasserman A. eds., North-Holland Publishing Company, 1982, pp. 237-259.

[HPF] High Performance Fortran Forum. *High Performance Fortran Language Specification, Version 1.0.* Rice University, Houston, TX, May 1993.

[Himsolt 89] Himsolt M., "GraphEd: An Interactive Graph Editor," *Proceedings of STACS 89*, Lecture Notes in Computer Science 349, Springer-Verlag, 1989, pp. 532-533.

[Hollingsworth 91] Hollingsworth J., Irvin R., and Miller B., "The Integration of Application and System Based Metrics in a Parallel Program Performance Tool," *SIGPLAN Notices*, Vol. 26, No. 7, July 1991, pp. 189-200, (Proceedings of the Third Symposium on Principles and Practice of Parallel Programming, Williamsburg, VA.)

[Hollingsworth 93] Hollingsworth J., Irvin R. and Miller B., "Dynamic Control of Performance Monitoring on Large Scale Parallel Systems," *Proceedings of the 7th ACM International Conference on Supercomputing*, Tokyo, July 1993, pp. 185-194.

[Holt 89] Holt R. and Cordy J., "The Turing Programming Language," *Communications of the ACM*, Vol. 31, No. 12, 1989, pp. 1410-1423.

[Hopgood 74] Hopgood F., "Computer Animation Used as a Tool in Teaching Computer Science," *Proceedings IFIP Congress*, 1974, pp. 889-892.

[Hough 87] Hough A. and Cuny J., "Belvedere: Prototype of a pattern-oriented debugger for highly parallel computation," *Proceedings of the 1987 International Conference on Parallel Processing*, University Park, PA, August 1987, pp. 735-738.

[Hudson 93] Hudson S. and Stasko J., "Animation support in a user interface toolkit: Flexible, robust and reusable abstractions," *Proceedings of the 1993 ACM Symposium on User Interface Software and Technology*, Atlanta, GA, November 1993, pp. 57-67.

[Hueras 77] Hueras J. and Ledgard H., "An Automatic Formatting Program for Pascal," *SIGPLAN Notices*, Vol. 12, No. 7, 1977, pp. 82-84.

[Hume 90] Hume A. and McIlroy M., *UNIX Research System Programmer's Manual*, Tenth Edition, Holt Dryden Saunders, 1990.

[IBM AIX Performance] IBM Corporation. *AIX Version 3.1 for RISC System/6000 Performance Monitoring and Tuning Guide*, IBM Corporation, order number SC23-2365-00.

[Isoda 87] Isoda S., Shimomura T., and Ono Y., "VIPS: A visual debugger," *IEEE Software*, Vol. 4, No. 3, May 1987, pp. 8-19.

[Iversen 92] Iversen W., "The Sound of Silence," *Computer Graphics World*, January 1992, pp. 54-62.

[Jeffery 94] Jeffery C. and Griswold R., "A Framework for Monitoring Program Execution in Icon," *Software: Practice & Experience*, Vol. 11, No. 4, November 1994, pp. 1025-1049.

[Jerding 95] Jerding D. and Stasko J., "The Information Mural: A Technique for Displaying and Navigating Large Information Spaces," *Proceedings of the IEEE Information Visualization Conference*, Atlanta, GA, October 1995, pp. 43-50.

[Johnson 85] Johnson W. and Soloway E., "PROUST: An automatic debugger for Pascal programs," *Byte*, Vol. 10, No. 4, 1985, pp. 170-190.

[Johnson 91] Johnson B. and Shneiderman B., "Tree-Maps: A Space-Filling Approach to the Visualization of Hierarchical Information Structures," *Proceedings of the 2nd International IEEE Visualization Conference*, San Diego, CA, October 1991, pp 284-291.

[Jones 93] Jones A., "Conceptual models of programming environments: How learners use the glass box," *Instructional Science*, Vol. 21, No. 6, 1993, pp. 473-500.

[JPDC 93] *Journal of Parallel and Distributed Computing*, Special Issue on Tools and Methods for Visualization of Parallel Systems and Computations, Vol. 18, No. 2, June 1993.

[Kahn 90] Kahn K. and Saraswat V., "Complete Visualizations of Concurrent Programs and Their Execution," *Proceedings of the 1990 IEEE Workshop on Visual Languages*, Skokie, IL, September 1990, pp. 7-15.

[Kahney 82] Kahney J. and Eisenstadt M., "Programmers' mental models of their programming tasks: The interaction of real-world knowledge and programming knowledge," *Proceedings of the Fourth Annual Cognitive Science Society Conference*, Ann Arbor, MI, 1982, pp. 143-145.

[Kahney 83] Kahney J., "Problem solving by novice programmers," *The psychology of computer use*, Green T., Payne S. and van der Veer G. eds., Academic Press, London, 1983.

[Kahney 92] Kahney H., "Some pitfalls in learning about recursion," *Novice Programming Environments: Explorations in Human-Computer Interaction and*

Artificial Intelligence, Eisenstadt M., Keane M. and Rajan T. eds., Lawrence Earlbaum, Hove, UK, 1992.

[Kaiser 88] Kaiser G., Feiler P. and Popovich S., "Intelligent assistance for software development and maintenance," *IEEE Software,* Vol. 5, No. 3, May 1988, pp. 40-45.

[Karlin 91] Karlin A., Li K., Manasse M. and Owicki S., "Empirical Studies of Competitive Spinning for a Shared Memory Processor," *Proceedings of the 13th Annual ACM Symposium on Operating Systems Principles*, ACM, New York, 1991, pp. 41-55.

[Karmiloff-Smith 79] Karmiloff-Smith A., "Micro- and macrodevelopmental changes in language acquisition and other representational systems," *Cognitive Science*, Vol. 3, 1979, pp. 91-118.

[Karmiloff-Smith 94] Karmiloff-Smith A., "Precis of Beyond Modularity: A developmental perspective on cognitive science," *Behavioural and Brain Sciences,* Vol. 17, No. 4, 1994, pp. 693-745.

[Katz 88] Katz I. and Anderson J., "Debugging: an analysis of bug location strategies," *Human-Computer Interaction*, Vol. 3, 1988, pp. 351-399.

[Kehoe 96] Kehoe C. and Stasko J., "Using Animation to Learn about Algorithms: An Ethnographic Case Study", Technical Report GIT-GVU-96-20, GVU Center, Georgia Institute of Technology, Atlanta, GA, September 1996.

[Keller 93] Keller P. and Keller M., *Visual Cues: Practical Data Visualization.*, IEEE Press, Piscataway, NJ, 1993.

[Kernighan 76] Kernighan B. and Plauger P., *Software Tools*, Addison-Wesley, Reading, MA, 1976.

[Kernighan 78] Kernighan B. and Ritchie M., *The C programming language,* Second Edition, Prentice-Hall, Englewood Cliffs, NJ, 1978.

[Kimelman 91] Kimelman D. and Ngo T., "The RP3 Program Visualization Environment", *The IBM Journal of Research and Development*, Vol. 35, No. 6, November 1991, pp. 635-651.

[Kimelman 94] Kimelman D., Rosenburg B. and Roth T., "Strata-Various :-) Multi-Layer Visualization of Dynamics in Software System Behavior," *Proceedings of IEEE Visualization '94*, Washington D. C., October. 1994, pp. 172-178.

[Kimelman 95] Kimelman D., Mittal P., Schonberg E., Sweeney P., Wang K. and Zernik D., "Visualizing the Execution of High Performance Fortran (HPF) Programs," *Proceedings of the 1995 International Parallel Processing Symposium,* San Jose, CA, April 1995, pp. 750-757.

[Kleyn 88] Kleyn M. and Gingrich P., "Graphtrace—understanding object-oriented systems using concurrently animated views," *Proceedings of Object-Oriented Programming Systems, Languages, and Applications Conference*, 1988, pp. 191–205.

[Knowlton 66a] Knowlton K., *L6: Bell Telephone Laboratories Low-Level Linked List Language,* 16-minute black-and-white film, Murray Hill, N.J., 1966.

[Knowlton 66b] Knowlton K., *L6: Part II. An Example of L6 Programming*, 30-minute black-and-white film, Murray Hill, N.J., 1966

[Knuth 63] Knuth D., "Computer-drawn Flowcharts," *Communications of the ACM ,* Vol. 6, 1963, pp. 555-563.

[Knuth 73] Knuth D., *The Art of Computer Programming, Volume 3: Searching and Sorting*, Addison-Wesley, Reading, MA, 1973.

[Knuth 84] Knuth D., "Literate Programming," *The Computer Journal,* Vol. 27, No. 2, 1984, pp. 97-111.

[Knuth 92] Knuth D., *Literate Programming*, CSLI Publications, Stanford University, 1992.

[Kohl 92] Kohl J. and Casavant T., "A software engineering, visualization methodology for parallel processing systems," *Proceedings of the Sixteenth Annual International Computer Software and Applications Conference (COMPSAC '92),* Chicago, IL, September 1992, pp. 51-56.

[Kohn 93] Kohn J. and Williams W., "ATExpert, *Journal of Parallel and Distributed Computing,* Vol. 18, No. 2, June 1993, pp. 205-222.

[Koike 92] Koike H., "An Application of Three-Dimensional Visualization to Object-Oriented Programming," *Proceedings of Advanced Visual Interface '92,* Rome, Italy, May 1992, pp. 180–192.

[Kolence 73] Kolence K. and Kiviat P., "Software Unit Profiles and Kiviat Figures," *Perf.ormance Evaluation Review,* Vol. 2, No. 3, September 1973, pp. 2-12.

[Kosslyn 78] Kosslyn S., "Imagery and internal representation," *Cognition and Categorization.*, Rosch E. and Lloyd B. eds., Lawrence Erlbaum, 1978, pp. 227-286.

[Koutsofios 91] Koutsofios E. and Dobkin D., "Lefty: A two-view editor for technical pictures," *Proceedings of Graphics Interface '91*, Calgary, Alberta, 1991, pp. 68-76, 1991.

[Kraemer 93] Kraemer E. and Stasko J., "The Visualization of Parallel Systems: An Overview," *Journal of Parallel and Distributed Computing*, Vol. 18, No. 2, June 1993, pp. 105-117.

[Kraemer 94] Kraemer E. and Stasko J., "Toward flexible control of the temporal mapping from concurrent program events to animations, *Proceedings of the Eighth International Parallel Processing Symposium*, Cancun, Mexico, April 1994, pp. 902-908.

[Kwakkel 91] Kwakkel F., *TPM for Macintosh*, Human Cognition Research Laboratory, Open University, Walton Hall, Milton Keynes, UK, 1991.

[LCSI 93] LCSI, MicroWorlds Reference. Logo Computer Systems Inc., Montreal PQ. Canada, 1993.

[Lamping 94] Lamping J. and Rao R., "Laying out and Visualizing Large Trees Using a Hyperbolic Space," *Proceedings of UIST '94*, Monterey, CA, November 1994, pp. 13-14.

[Lamport 78] Lamport L., "Time, clocks, and the ordering of events in a distributed system," *Communications of the ACM*, Vol. 21, No. 7, July 1978, pp. 558-565.

[Larkin 87] Larkin J. and Simon H., "Why a diagram is (sometimes) worth 10,000 words," *Cognitive Science*, Vol. 11, No. 1, 1987, pp. 65-99.

[Laubsch 81] Laubsch J. and Eisenstadt M., "Domain specific debugging aids for novice programmers," *Proceedings of the Seventh International Joint Conference on Artificial Intelligence (IJCAI-81)*, San Mateo, CA, Morgan Kaufmann, 1981, pp. 964-969.

[Laubsch 92] Laubsch J. and Eisenstadt M., "The automatic debugging of recursive side-effecting programs," *Novice Programming Environments: Explorations in Human-Computer Interaction and Artificial Intelligence,* Eisenstadt M., Keane M. and Rajan T. eds., Lawrence Erlbaum, Hove, UK, 1992.

[Lawrence 93] Lawrence A., "Empirical Studies of the Value of Algorithm Animation in Algorithm Understanding," PhD thesis, Georgia Institute of Technology, Atlanta, GA, 1993.

[Lawrence 94] Lawrence A., Badre A. and Stasko J., "Empirically evaluating the use of animations to teach algorithms," *Proceedings of the 1994 IEEE Symposium on Visual Languages*, St. Louis, MO, October 1994, pp. 48-54.

[LeBlanc 85] LeBlanc R. and Robbins A., "Event-driven Monitoring of Distributed Programs," *Proceedings of the Fifth International Conference on Distributed Computing Systems*, Denver, CO, May 1985, pp. 515-522.

[LeBlanc 87] LeBlanc T. and Mellor-Crummey J., "Debugging parallel programs with Instant Replay," *IEEE Transactions on Computers*, Vol. C-36, No. 4, April 1987, pp. 471-482.

[LeBlanc· 90] LeBlanc T., Mellor-Crummey J. and Fowler R., "Analyzing parallel program execution using multiple views," *Journal of Parallel and Distributed Computing*, Vol. 9, No. 2, June 1990, pp. 203-217.

[Lehr 89] Lehr T., Segall Z., Vrsalovic D., Caplan E., Chung A. and Fineman C., "Visualizing Performance Debugging", *Computer*, Vol. 22, No. 10, October 1989, pp. 38-51.

[Lejter 92] Lejter M., Meyers S., and Reiss S., "Support for maintaining object-oriented programs," *IEEE Trans. on Software Engineering* Vol. 18, No. 12, December 1992, pp. 1045-1052.

[Lesgold 88] Lesgold A., Rubinson H., Feltovich P., Glaser R., Klopfer D. and Wang Y., "Expertise in a complex skill: Diagnosing X-ray pictures," *The nature of expertise.*, Chi M., Glaser R. and Farr M. eds., Erlbaum, Hillsdale, NJ, 1988, pp. 311-342.

[Lewis 83] Lewis J., An Effective Graphics User Interface for Rules and Inference Mechanisms. *Proceedings of the ACM Conference on Computer and Human Interaction*, December 1983, pp. 139-143.

[Lewis 91] Lewis C., "Visualization and Situations," *Situation Theory and Its Applications,* Barwise J., Gawron J., Plotkin G. and Tutiya S. eds., CSLI Publications, Stanford, CA, 1991.

[Lieberman 84a] Lieberman H., "Steps Toward Better Debugging Tools for Lisp," *ACM Symposium on Lisp and Functional Programming,* ACM Press, Austin, Texas, August 1984, pp. 247-255.

[Lieberman 84b] Lieberman H., "Seeing What Your Programs Are Doing," *International Journal of Man-Machine Studies* , Vol. 21, No. 4, October 1984, pp. 311-331.

[Lieberman 87] Lieberman H., "Reversible Object-Oriented Interpreters," *First European Conference on Object-Oriented Programming,* Springer-Verlag, Paris, France, 1987.

[Lieberman 89] Lieberman H., "A Three-Dimensional Representation for Program Execution," *Proceedings of the 1989 IEEE Workshop on Visual Languages,* Rome, Italy, October 1989, pp. 111–116.

[Lieberman 91] Lieberman H., "A Three-Dimensional Representation for Program Execution," *Visual Programming Environments: Applications and Issues*, Glinert E. ed., IEEE Press, 1991.

[Lipton 85] Lipton R., North S. and Sandberg J., "A Method for Drawing Graphs," *Proceedings of the Symposium on Computational Geometry*, June 1985, pp. 153-160.

[London 85] London R. and Duisberg R., "Animating Programs Using Smalltalk," *Computer*, Vol. 18, No. 8, August 1985, pp. 61-71.

[Lorin 75] Lorin H., *Sorting and Sort Systems,* Addison-Wesley, Reading, MA, 1975.

[Lutz 92] Lutz R., "Plan Diagrams as the Basis for Understanding and Debugging Pascal Programs," *Novice Programming Environments: Explorations in Human-Computer Interaction and Artificial Intelligence*, Eisenstadt M., Keane M. and Rajan T. eds., Lawrence Erlbaum Associates, Hove, UK, 1992, pp. 243-285.

[Lyons 92] Lyons K., "Cluster Busting in Anchored Graph Drawing," *Proceedings of the CAS Conference,* IBM Centre for Advanced Studies, Toronto, Canada, 1992, pp. 327-338.

[MacGregor 96] MacGregor J. and Ormerod T., "Human performance on the travelling salesman problem," *Perception and Psychophysics*, Vol. 58, No. 4, 1996, pp. 527-539.

[Mackinlay 86] Mackinlay J., "Automating the Design of Graphical Presentations of Relational Information," *ACM TOGS*, vol. 5, No. 2, April 1986, pp. 110-141.

[Malony 89] Malony A., Reed D., Arendt J., Aydt R., Grabas D. and Totty B., "An Integrated Performance Data Collection, Analysis, and Visualization System," *Proceedings of the Fourth Conference on Hypercube Concurrent Computer Applications,* Monterey, CA, March 1989, pp. 229-236.

[Malony 90] Malony A. and Reed D., "Visualizing Parallel Computer System Performance," *Parallel Computer Systems: Performance Instrumentation and Visualization.*, Simmons M., Koskela R. and Bucher I. eds., ACM, New York, 1990.

[Malony 94] Malony A., Mohr B., Beckman P., Gannon D., Yang S. and Bodin F., "Performance Analysis of pC++: a Portable Data-Parallel Programming System for Scalable Parallel Computers," *Proceedings of the International Parallel Processing Symposium*, Cancun, Mexico, April 1994, pp. 75-84.

[Marcus 92] Marcus A., *Graphic Design for Electronic Documents and User Interfaces*, ACM Press, 1992.

[Marcus 95] Marcus A., "Principles of Effective Visual Communication for Graphical User Interface Design," *Readings in Human Computer Interaction: Toward the Year 2000,* Baecker R., Grudin J., Buxton W. and Greenberg S. eds., Morgan Kaufmann, 1995, pp. 425-441.

[Martin 85] Martin J. and McClure C., *Diagramming Techniques for Analysts and Programmers*, Prentice-Hall, 1985.

[Mayer 90] Mayer R. and Gallini J., "When is an Illustration Worth Ten Thousand Words?," *Journal of Educational Psychology*, Vol. 82, No. 4, 1990, pp. 715-726.

[Mayer 91] Mayer R. and Anderson R., "Animations Need Narrations: An Experimental Test of a Dual-Coding Hypothesis," *Journal of Educational Psychology*, Vol. 83, No. 4, 1991, pp. 484-490.

[Mayer 92] Mayer R. and Anderson R., "The Instructive Animation: Helping Students Build Connections between Words and Pictures in Mulitmedia Learning," *Journal of Educational Psychology*, Vol. 84, No. 4, 1992, pp. 444-452.

[Messina 93] Messina P. and Sterling T. eds., *System Software and Tools for High Performance Computing Environments*, Society of Industrial Appled Mathematics, April, 1993.

[Miller 90] Miller B., Clark M., Hollingsworth J., Kierstead S., Lim S. and Torzewski T., "IPS-2: The Second Generation of a Parallel Program Measurement System," *IEEE Transactions on Parallel and Distributed Systems*, Vol. 1, No. 2, April 1990, pp. 206-217.

[Miller 93] Miller B., "What to draw? When to draw? An Essay on Parallel Program Visualization," *Journal of Parallel Distributed Computing*, Vol. 18, No. 2, June 1993, pp. 265-204.

[Moen 90] Moen S., "Drawing Dynamic Trees," *IEEE Software*, Vol. 7, No. 7, July 1990, pp. 21-28.

[Moher 88] Moher T., "PROVIDE: A Process Visualization and Debugging Environment," *IEEE Transactions on Software Engineering*, Vol. 14, No. 6, June 1988, pp. 849-857.

[Moher 93] Moher T., Mak D., Blumenthal B. and Leventhal L., "Comparing the Comprehensibility of Textual and Graphical Programs: the Case of Petri Nets," *Empirical Studies of Programmers: Fifth Workshop*, Cook C., Scholtz J. and Spohrer J. eds., Norwood, NJ: Ablex, 1993, pp. 137-161.

[Mott 87] Mott P. and Brooke S., "A Graphical Inference Mechanism," *Expert Systems*, Vol. 4, No. 2, May 1987, pp. 106-117.

[Motta 91] Motta E., Rajan T., Domingue J., and Eisenstadt M., "Methodological Foundations of KEATS, The Knowledge Engineers' Assistant," *Knowledge Acquisition,* Vol. 3, No. 1, 1991, pp. 21-47.

[Mountford 90] Mountford S. and Gaver W., "Talking and Listening to Computers," *The Art of Human-Computer Interface Design*, Laurel B. ed., Addison-Wesley, Reading, MA, 1990, pp. 319-334.

[Mukherjea 93] Mukherjea S. and Stasko J., "Applying Algorithm Animation Techniques for Program Tracing, Debugging, and Understanding," *Proceedings of the 15th International Conference on Software Engineering*, Baltimore, MD, May 1993, pp. 456-465.

[Mukherjea 94] Mukherjea S. and Stasko J., "Toward Visual Debugging: Integrating Algorithm Animation Capabilities within a Source Level Debugger," *ACM Transactions on Computer-Human Interaction*, Vol. 1, No. 3, September 1994, pp. 215-244.

[Mulholland 95] Mulholland, P. "A Framework for Describing and Evaluating Software Visualization Systems: A Case-Study in Prolog," Ph.D. Thesis, The Knowledge Media Institute, The Open University, 1995.

[Muller 92] Muller H., Tilley S., Orgun M., Corrie B. and Madhavji N., "A Reverse Engineering Environment Based on Spatial and Visual Software Interconnection Models," *Software Engineering Notices*, Vol. 17, No. 5, December 1992, pp. 88-98.

[Myers 83] Myers B., "Incense: A System for Displaying Data Structures," *Proceedings of ACM SIGGRAPH '83*, July 1983, pp. 115-125.

[Myers 86] Myers B., "Visual Programming, Programming by Example, and Program Visualization: A Taxonomy," *Proceedings of the ACM SIGCHI '86 Conference on Human Factors in Computing Systems*, Boston, MA, April 1986, pp. 59-66.

[Myers 88] Myers B., "The State of the Art in Visual Programming and Program Visualization," Computer Science Dept., Carnegie-Mellon University, Pittsburgh, PA, Technical Report CMU-CS-88-114, 1988.

[Myers 90] Myers B., Taxonomies of Visual Programming and Program Visualization. *Journal of Visual Languages and Computing*, Vol. 1, No. 1, March 1990, pp. 97-123.

[Myers 92] Myers B., "Demonstrational Interfaces: A Step Beyond Direct Manipulation," *Computer*, Vol. 25, No. 8, August 1992, pp. 61-73.

[Nassi 73] Nassi I. and Shneiderman B., "Flowcharting Techniques for Structured Programming" *SIGPLAN Notices*, Vol. 8, No. 8, 1973, pp. 12-26.

[Naur 63] Naur P. ed., "Revised Report on the Algorithmic Language ALGOL 60," *Communications of the ACM*, Vol. 6, No. 1, 1963, pp. 1-17.

[Nelson 84] Nelson D. and Leach P., "The Evolution of the Apollo DOMAIN," *Proceedings of the 17th Hawaii International Conference on System Sciences,* January 1984, pp.470-479.

[Netzer 95] Netzer R. and Miller B., "Optimal Tracing and Replay for Debugging Message-Passing Parallel Programs," *Journal of Supercomputing,* Vol. 8, No.4, 1995, pp. 371-88.

[Nielson 90] Nielson G., Shriver B. and Rosenblum J., *Visualization in Scientific Computing,* IEEE Computer Society Press, Washington, 1990.

[Norman 86] Norman D., "Cognitive Engineering," *User Centered System Design,* Norman D. and Draper S. eds., Lawrence Erlbaum Associates, 1986.

[North 91] North S., "Drawing Graphs with DOT," Technical Report, AT&T Bell Laboratories, 1991.

[North 92] North S., "Drawing Graphs with Neato," Technical Report, AT&T Bell Laboratories, 1992.

[North 93] North S., "Drawing Ranked Digraphs with Recursive Clusters," *Proceedings of ALCOM Workshop on Graph Drawing '93,* September, 1993. Revised version at http://www.research.att.com/~north/papers/clust93.ps.gz.

[North 94] North S. and Koutsofios E., "Applications of Graph Visualization," *Proceedings of Graphics Interface '94,* 1994, pp. 235--245.

[Notkin 85] Notkin D., Ellison R., Kaiser G., Kant E., Habermann A., Ambriola V. and Montanegero C., "Special Issue on the GANDALF Project," *Journal of Systems and Software,* Vol. 5, No. 2, May 1985.

[Oman 90a] Oman P. and Cook C., "The Book Paradigm for Improved Maintenance," *IEEE Software,* January 1990, Vol. 7, No. 1, pp. 39-45.

[Oman 90b] Oman P. and Cook C., "Typographic Style is More than Cosmetic," *Communications of the ACM,* Vol. 33, No. 5, May 1990, pp. 506-520.

[Oman 97] Oman P., *Programming Style Analysis,* Ablex, 1997 to appear.

[Ormerod 96] Ormerod T. and Ball L., "An Empirical Evaluation of TEd, a Techniques Editor for Prolog Programming," *Empirical Studies of Programmers: Sixth Workshop.,* Gray W. and Boehm-Davis D. eds., Norwood, NJ: Ablex, 1996, pp. 147-161.

[Pain 87] Pain H. and Bundy A., "What Stories Should We Tell Novice Prolog Programmers," *Artificial Intelligence Programming Environments,* Hawley R. ed., New York: Wiley, 1987.

[Palmiter 91] Palmiter S. and Elkerton J., "An Evaluation of Animated Demonstrations for Learning Computer-Based Tasks," *Proceedings of the ACM SIGCHI '91 Conference on Human Factors in Computing Systems*, New Orleans, LA, May 1991, pp. 257-263.

[Papert 80] Papert S., *Mindstorms: Children, Computers and Powerful Ideas,* Harvester, Brighton, UK, 1980.

[Parnas 72] Parnas D., "On the Criteria to be Used in Decomposing Systems into Modules," *Communications of the ACM*, Vol. 15, 1972, pp. 1053-1058.

[Parnas 85] Parnas D. and Weiss D., "Active Design Reviews: Principles and Practices," *Proceedings of the 8th International Conference on Software Engineering,* August 1985, pp. 132-136.

[Patel 91] Patel M., du Boulay B. and Taylor C., "Effect of Format on Information and Problem Solving," *Proceedings of the 13th Annual Conference of the Cognitive Science Society*, Chicago, 1991, pp. 852-856.

[Paulisch 90] Newbery Paulish F. and Tichy W., "Edge: An Extendible Graph Editor," *Software -- Practice and Experience,* Vol. 20, No. S1, 1990, pp. S1/63--S1/88. Also available as Technical Report 8/88, Fakultat fur Informatik, University of Karlsruhe, 1988.

[Pennington 87a] Pennington N., "Stimulus Structures and Mental Representations in Expert Comprehension of Computer Programs," *Cognitive Psychology*, Vol. 19, 1987, pp. 295-341.

[Pennington 87b] Pennington N., "Comprehension Strategies in Programming," *Empirical Studies of Programmers: Second Workshop,* Olson G., Sheppard S. and Soloway E. eds., Norwood, NJ: Ablex, 1987, pp. 100-113.

[Pennington 90] Pennington N. and Grabowski B. "The Tasks of Programming," *The Psychology of Programming,* Hoc J.-M., Green T., Gilmore D. and Samurçay R. eds., Academic Press, London, 1990, pp. 45-62.

[Pereira 86] Pereira L., "Rational Debugging in Logic Programming," *Third International Conference on Logic Programming*, Springer-Verlag, 1986, pp. 203-210.

[Peters 82] Peters H. and Daiker K., "Graphics and Animation as Instructional Tools: A Case Study," *Pipline*, Vol. 7, No. 1, 1982, pp. 11-13.

[Petre 91] Petre M., "What Experts Want From Programming Languages," *Ergonomics* (Special Issue on Cognitive Ergonomics), Vol. 34, No. 8, 1991, pp. 1113-1127.

[Petre 92] Petre M. and Green T., "Requirements of Graphical Notations for Professional Users: Electronics CAD Systems as a Case Study," *Le Travail Humain* , Vol. 55, No. 1, 1992, pp. 47-70.

[Petre 93] Petre M. and Green T., "Learning to Read Graphics: Some Evidence That "seeing" an Information Display is an Acquired Skill," *Journal of Visual Languages and Computing*, Vol. 4, No. 1, 1993, pp. 55-70.

[Petre 95] Petre M., "Why Looking Isn't Always Seeing: Readership Skills and Graphical Programming," *Communications of the ACM*, Vol. 38, No. 6, June 1995, pp. 33-44.

[Petre 96] Petre M., "Programming Paradigms and Culture: Implications of Expert Practice," *Programming Language Choice: Practice and Experience.*, Woodman M. ed., International Thomson Computer Press, London, 1996, pp. 29-44.

[Plummer 88] Plummer D., "Coda: an Extended Debugger for Prolog," *Logic Programming,Volume 1,* Kowalski R. A. and Bowen K.A. eds., MIT Press, 1988, pp. 496-511.

[Poltreck 86] Poltreck S., Steiner D. and Tarlton P., "Graphic Interfaces for Knowledge-Based System Development," *Proceedings of the ACM Conference on Computer Human Interaction,* 1986.

[Price 90] Price B., "A Framework for the Automatic Animation of Concurrent Programs," M.Sc. Thesis, Dept. of Computer Science, University of Toronto, Canada, 1990.

[Price 91] Price B. and Baecker R., "The Automatic Animation of Concurrent Programs," *The First International Workshop on Computer-Human Interfaces*, ICSTI, Moscow, USSR, August 1991, pp. 128-137.

[Price 92] Price B., Small I. and Baecker R., "A Taxonomy of Software Visualization," *The 25th Hawaii International Conference on System Sciences*, Kauai, HI, January 1992, pp. 597-606.

[Price 93] Price B., Baecker R. and Small I., "A Principled Taxonomy of Software Visualization," *Journal of Visual Languages and Computing*, Vol. 4, No. 3, 1993, pp. 211-266.

[Ramadhan 92] Ramadhan H., "Intelligent Systems for Discovery Programming," CSRP 254, Department of Cognitive and Computing Science, University of Sussex, 1992.

[Raman 94] Raman T., "Audio System for Technical Reading", PhD Thesis, Cornell University, 1994.

[Raman 95] Raman T., "Emacspeak–A Speech Interface", *Proceedings of the ACM SIGCHI '96 Conference on Human Factors in Computing Systems*, Vancouver, Canada, May 1996, pp. 66-71.

[Ramsey 94] Ramsey N., "Literate Programming Simplified," *IEEE Software*, Vol. 11, No. 5, September 1994, pp. 97-105.

[Reed 85] Reed S., "Effect of Computer Graphics on Improving Estimates to Algebra Word Problems," *Journal of Educational Psychology*, Vol. 77, No. 3, 1985, pp. 285-298.

[Reed 91] Reed D., Olson R., Aydt R., Madhyastha T., Birkett T., Jensen D., Nazief B. and Totty B., "Scalable Performance Environments for Parallel Systems," *Proceedings of the Sixth Distributed Memory Computing Conference*, Munich, Germany, April 1991, pp. 562-569.

[Reingold 81] Reingold E. and Tilford J., "Tidier Drawings of Trees," *IEEE Transactions on Software Engineering*, Vol. SE-7, No. 2, March 1981, pp. 223-228.

[Reiss 84] Reiss S., "Graphical Program Development with PECAN Program Development Systems," *Proceedings of the ACM SIGSOFT/SIGPLAN Symposium on Practical Software Development Environments*, April 1984.

[Reiss 85] Reiss S., "PECAN: Program Development Systems that Support Multiple Views," *IEEE Transactions on Software Engingeering*, Vol. SE-11, March 1985, pp. 276-284.

[Reiss 87] Reiss S., "Working in the Garden Environment for Conceptual Programming," *IEEE Software*, Vol. 4, No. 6, November 1987, pp. 16-27.

[Reiss 89] Reiss S., Meyers S. and Duby C., "Using GELO to Visualize Software Systems," *Proceedings of UIST '89*, Williamsburg, VA, November 1989, pp. 149-157.

[Reiss 90a] Reiss S., "Interacting with the FIELD Environment," *Software Practice and Experience*, Vol. 20, No. S1, June 1990, pp. 89-115.

[Reiss 90b] Reiss S., "Connecting Tools Using Message Passing in the FIELD Environment," *IEEE Software*, Vol. 7, No. 4, July 1990, pp. 57-67.

[Reiss 90c] Reiss S. and Stasko J., "The Brown Workstation Environment: a User-Interface Toolkit", *Engineering for Human-Computer Interaction*, Cockton G. ed., North-Holland, Napa CA, August 1990, pp. 215-232, .

[Reiss 93] Reiss S., "A Framework for Abstract 3-D Visualization," *Proceedings of the 1993 IEEE Symposium on Visual Languages*, Bergen, Norway, August 1993, pp. 108–115.

[Reiss 94a] Reiss S., *FIELD: A Friendly Integrated Environment for Learning and Development*, Kluwer, Norwell, MA, 1994.

[Reiss 94b] Reiss S., "3-D Visualization of Program Information," *SIGCHI '94 Software Visualization Workshop*, Boston, Massachusetts, 1994.

[Reiss 95] Reiss S., "An Engine for the 3D Visualization of Program Information," *Journal of Visual Languages*, Vol. 6, No. 3, September 1995, pp. 299-323.

[Reiss 96] Reiss S., "Simplifying Data Integration: The Design of the Desert Software Development Environment," *Proceedings of the 18th International Conference on Software Engineering*, March 1996, pp. 398-407.

[Rich 79] Rich C., Schrobe H. and Waters R., "Overview of the Programmer's Apprentice," *Proceedings of the Sixth International Joint Conference on Artificial Intelligence*, 1979, pp. 827-8.

[Rich 88] Rich C. and Waters R., "The Programmer's Apprentice: a Research Overview," *Computer*, Vol. 21, No. 11, 1988.

[Rich 90] Rich C. and Waters R., *The Programmer's Apprentice*, Addison-Wesley, London, 1990.

[Richer 85] Richer M. and Clancey W. "Guidon-Watch: A Graphic Interface for Viewing a Knowledge-Based System," *IEEE Computer Graphics and Applications*, Vol. 5, No. 11, 1985.

[Rieber 89] Rieber L., "A Review of Animation Research in Computer-Based Instruction," *Proceedings of the 1989 Annual Convention of the Association for Educational Communications and Technology*, No. 11, 1989, pp. 369-390.

[Rieber 90a] Rieber L., Boyce M. and Assad C., "The Effects of Computer Animation on Adult Learning and Retrieval Tasks," *Journal of Computer-Based Instruction*, Vol. 17, No. 2, Spring 1990, pp. 46-52.

[Rieber 90b] Rieber L., "Effects of Animated Graphics on Student Learning," *Journal of Educational Psychology*, Vol. 1, 1990, pp. 123-321.

[Rigney 76] Rigney J. and Lutz K., "Effect of Graphic Analogies of Concepts in Chemistry on Learning and Attitude," *Journal of Educational Psychology*, Vol. 68, No. 3, 1976, pp. 305-311.

[Rist 91] Rist R. and Bevemyr J., "PARE: a Cognitively-Based Program Analyzer," Unpublished MS, Department of Computer Science, University of Technology, Sydney, Australia, 1991.

[Rist 96] Rist R., "System Structure and Design," *Empirical Studies of Programmers: Sixth Workshop*, Gray W. and Boehm-Davis D. eds., Ablex, Newark, N. J., 1996, pp. 163-194.

[Robertson 90] Robertson S., Davis E., Okabe K. and Fitz-Randolf D., "Program Comprehension Beyond the Line," *Human-Computer Interaction – INTERACT '90*, Diaper D., Gilmore D., Cockton G. and B. Shackel eds., North Holland, Amsterdam, 1990, pp. 959-963.

[Robertson 93] Robertson G., Card S. and Mackinlay J., "Information Visualization Using 3D Interactive Animation," *Communications of the ACM*, Vol. 36, No. 4, April 1993, pp. 56–71.

[Rochkind 75] Rochkind M., "The Source Code Control System," *IEEE Transactions on Software Engineering,* Vol. SE-1, No. 4, 1975, pp. 364-370.

[Rohr 86] Rohr G., "Using Visual Concepts," *Visual Languages*, Chang S.-K., Ichikawa T. and Ligomenides P. eds., Plenum Press, New York, 1986, pp. 1-34.

[Roman 89] Roman G.-C. and Cox K., "A Declarative Approach to Visualizing Concurrent Computations," *Computer*, Vol. 22, No. 10, October 1989, pp. 25-36.

[Roman 90] Roman G.-C. and Cunningham H., "Mixed Programming Metaphors in a Shared Dataspace Model of Concurrency," *IEEE Transactions on Software Engineering*, Vol. 16, No. 12, December 1990, pp. 1361-1373.

[Roman 92] Roman G.-C., Cox K., Wilcox C. and Plun J., "Pavane: A System for Declarative Visualization of Concurrent Computations," *Journal of Visual Languages and Computing*, Vol. 3, No. 1, January 1992, pp. 161-193.

[Roman 93] Roman G.-C. and Cox K., "A Taxonomy of Program Visualization Systems," *Computer*, Vol. 26, No. 12, December 1993, pp. 11-24.

[Rover 93] Rover D. and Wright C., "Visualizing the Performance of SPMD and Data-Parallel Programs," *Journal of Parallel Distributed Computing,* Vol. 18, No. 2, June 1993, pp. 129-146.

[Rowe 87] Rowe L., Davis M., Messinger E., Meyer C., Spirakis C. and Tuan A., "A Browser for Directed Graphs," *Software -- Practice and Experience, Vol.* 17, No. 1, 1987, pp. 61-76.

[Ruder 77] Ruder E., *Typographie*, Third Edition, Verlag Arthur Niggli Teufen AR, Switzerland, 1977.

[Sandewall 90] Sandewall E., "Lisp as a Very High Level Implementation Language", *Proceedings of EUROPAL'90 the First European Conference on the Practical Applications of Lisp,* Domingue J., Rajan T. and Roth A., 1990, pp. 29-34.

[Sanger 87] Sanger D., "The Computer Contribution to the Rise and Fall of Stocks," *New York Times*, December 15, 1987, pp. 1.

[Sarukkai 92] Sarukkai S. and Gannon D., "Performance Visualization of Parallel Programs using SIEVE.1," *Proceedings of the 1992 International Conference on Supercomputing*, Washington, D.C., July 1992, pp. 157-166.

[Scaife 96] Scaife M. and Rogers Y. "External Cognition: how do Graphical Representations Work?" *International Journal of Human Computer Studies*, Vol. 45, No. 2, August 1996, pp. 185-213.

[Scanlan 89] Scanlan D., "Structured Flowcharts Outperform Pseudocode: An Experimental Comparison," *IEEE Software*, Vol. 6, No. 5, 1989, pp. 28-36.

[Schertz 90] Schertz Z., Goldberg D. and Fund Z., "Cognitive Implications of Learning Prolog - Mistakes and Misconceptions," *Journal of Educational Computing Research*, Vol. 6, No. 1, 1990, pp. 89-110.

[Sedgewick 83] Sedgewick R., *Algorithms*, Addison-Wesley, Reading, MA, 1983.

[Sedgewick 84] Sedgewick R. and Vitter J., "Shortest Paths in Euclidean Graphs," *Proceedings of the 25th Annual Symposium on the Foundations of Computer Science*, November 1984.

[Shadbolt 93] Shadbolt N., Motta E. and Rouge A., "Constructing Knowledge-Based Systems," *IEEE Software,* Vol. 10, No. 6, November 1993, pp. 34-38.

[Shah 95] Shah P. and Carpenter P., "Conceptual Limitations in Comprehending Line Graphs," *Journal of Experimental Psychology: General*, Vol. 124, No. 1, 1995, pp. 43-61.

[Shapiro 82] Shapiro E., *Algorithmic Program Debugging* , MIT Press, 1982.

[Shneiderman 80] Shneiderman B., *Software Psychology Human Factors in Computer and Information Systems*, Little, Brown, and Company, 1980.

[Shilling 94] Shilling J. and Stasko J., "Using Animation to Design Object-Oriented Systems," *Object Oriented Systems*, Vol. 1, No. 1, September 1994, pp. 5-19.

[Shimomura 91] Shimomura T. and Isoda S., "Linked-list Visualization for Debugging," *IEEE Software*, Vol. 8, No. 3, May 1991, pp. 44-51.

[Shu 88] Shu N., *Visual Programming*, Van Nostrand Reinhold, New York, NY, 1988.

[Simpson 89] Simpson J. and Weiner C. eds., *The Oxford English Dictionary, XIX,* Oxford University Press, 1989, pp. 699-700.

[Small 89] Small I., "Program Visualization: Static Typographic Visualization in an Interactive Environment," M.Sc. Thesis, Department of Computer Science, University of Toronto, February 1989.

[Snyder 84] Snyder L., "Parallel Programming and the Poker Programming Environment," *Computer*, Vol. 17, No. 7, July 1984, pp. 27-36.

[Socha 89] Socha D., Bailey M. and Notkin D., "Voyeur: Graphical Views of Parallel Programs," *SIGPLAN Notices*, Vol. 24, No. 1, January 1989, pp. 206-215 (Proceedings of the Workshop on Parallel and Distributed Debugging, Madison, WI, May 1988).

[Soloway 84] Soloway E. and Ehrlich K., "Empirical Studies of Programming Knowledge," *IEEE Transactions on Software Engineering*, Vol. SE-10, 1984, pp. 595-609.

[Soloway 85] Soloway E., "From Problems to Programs Via Plans: the Content and Structure of Knowledge for Introductory Lisp Programming," *Journal of Educational Computing Research*, Vol. 1, No. 2, 1985, pp. 157-172.

[Stasko 89] Stasko J., "TANGO: A Framework and System for Algorithm Animation," PhD thesis, Brown University, Providence, RI, May 1989. Available as Technical Report No. CS-89-30.

[Stasko 90a] Stasko J., "The Path-Transition Paradigm: A Practical Methodology for Adding Animation To Program Interfaces," *Journal of Visual Languages and Computing*, Vol. 1, No. 3, September 1990, pp. 213-236.

[Stasko 90b] Stasko J., "TANGO: A Framework and System for Algorithm Animation," *Computer*, Vol. 23, No. 9, September 1990, pp. 27-39.

[Stasko 91a] Stasko J., "Using Direct Manipulation to Build Algorithm Animations by Demonstration," *Proceedings of the ACM SIGCHI '91 Conference on Human Factors in Computing Systems*, New Orleans, LA, May 1991, pp. 307-314.

[Stasko 91b] Stasko J., Appelbe W. and Kraemer E., "Applying Program Visualization Techniques to Aid Parallel and Distributed Program Development," Technical Report GIT-GVU-91/08, Graphics, Visualization, and Usability Center, Georgia Institute of Technology, Atlanta, GA, June 1991.

[Stasko 92a] Stasko J., "Animating Algorithms with XTANGO," *SIGACT News*, Vol. 23, No. 2, Spring 1992, pp. 67-71.

[Stasko 92b] Stasko J. and Turner C., "Tidy Animations of Tree Algorithms," *Proceedings of the 1992 IEEE Workshop on Visual Languages*, Seattle, WA, September 1992, pp. 216-218.

[Stasko 92c] Stasko J. and Patterson C., "Understanding and Characterizing Software Visualization Systems," *Proceedings of the 1992 IEEE Workshop on Visual Languages*, Seattle, WA, September 1992, pp. 3-10.

[Stasko 93a] Stasko J., Badre A. and Lewis C., "Do Algorithm Animations Assist Learning? an Empirical Study and Analysis," *Proceedings of the INTERCHI '93 Conference on Human Factors in Computing Systems*, Amsterdam, Netherlands, April 1993, pp. 61-66.

[Stasko 93b] Stasko J. and Kraemer E., "A Methodology for Building Application-Specific Visualizations of Parallel Programs," *Journal of Parallel and Distributed Computing*, Vol. 18, No. 2, June 1993, pp. 258-264.

[Stasko 93c] Stasko J. and Wehrli J., "Three-dimensional Computation Visualization," *Proceedings of the 1993 IEEE Symposium on Visual Languages*, Bergen, Norway, August 1993, pp. 100-107.

[Stasko 95a] Stasko J. and McCrickard D., "Real Clock Time Animation Support for Developing Software Visualizations," Technical Report GIT-GVU-95/21, Graphics, Visualization, and Usability Center, Georgia Institute of Technology, Atlanta, GA, July 1995.

[Stasko 95b] Stasko J. and McCrickard D., "Real Clock Time Animation Support for Developing Software Visualizations," *Australian Computer Journal*, Vol. 27, No. 3, pp. 118-128.

[Stasko 96a] Stasko J., "Using Student-Built Algorithm Animations as Learning Aids," Technical Report GIT-GVU-96-19, GVU Center, Georgia Institute of Technology, Atlanta, GA, August 1996.

[Stasko 97] Stasko J., "Using Student-Built Algorithm Animations as Learning Aids," *Proceedings of the 1997 ACM SIGCSE Conference*, San Jose, CA, February 1997.

[Steffen 85] Steffen J., "Interactive Examination of a C Program with Cscope," *USENIX Dallas 1985 Winter Conference Proceedings,* USENIX Association, El Cerrito, California, 1985, pp. 170-175.

[Stenning 95a] Stenning K. and Oberlander J. "A Cognitive Theory of Graphical and Linguistic Reasoning: Logic and Implementation," *Cognitive Science*, Vol. 19, No. 1, 1995, pp. 97-140.

[Stenning 95b] Stenning K., Cox R. and Oberlander J., "Contrasting the Cognitive Effects of Graphical and Sentential Logic Teaching: Reasoning, Representation and Individual Differences,"*Language and Cognitive Processes*, Vol. 10, No. 3/4, 1995, pp. 333-344.

[Stockham 65] Stockham T. Jr., "Some Methods of Graphical Debugging," *Proceedings of the IBM Scientific Computing Symposium on Man-Machine Communications*, May 3-5, 1965, pp. 57-71.

[Stone 89] Stone J., "A Graphical Representation of Concurrent Processes," *SIGPLAN Notices*, Vol. 24, No. 1, January 1989, pp. 226-235. (Proceedings of the Workshop on Parallel and Distributed Debugging, Madison, WI, May 1988).

[Suchman 87] Suchman L., *Plans and Situated Actions: The Problem of Human Machine Communication,* Redwood, Trowbridge, UK, 1987.

[Sugiyama 81] Sugiyama K., Tagawa S. and Toda M., "Methods for Visual Understanding of Hierarchical Systems," *IEEE TSMC*, Vol. 11, No. 2, 1981, pp. 109-125.

[Sugiyama 91] Sugiyama K. and Misue K., "Visualization of Structural Information: Automatic Drawing of Compund Digraphs," *IEEE TSMC*, Vol. 21, No. 4, 1991, pp. 876-892.

[Sunderam 90] Sunderam V., "PVM: A Framework for Parallel Distributed Computing," *Concurrency: Practice & Experience*, Vol. 2, No. 4, December 1990, pp. 315-339.

[Takahashi 94] Takahashi S., Miyashita K., Matsuoka S. and Yonezawa A., "A Framework for Constructing Animations via Declarative Mapping Rules," *Proceedings of the 1994 IEEE Symposium on Visual Languages*, St. Louis, MO, October 1994, pp. 314-322.

[Tal 95] Tal A. and Dobkin D., "Visualization of Geometric Algorithms," *IEEE Transactions on Visualization and Computer Graphics,* Vol. 1, No. 2, June 1995, pp. 194–204.

[Tamassia 90] Tamassia R., "Planar Orthogonal Drawings of Graphs," *Proceedings of the IEEE International Symposium on Circuits and Systems*, 1990.

[Taylor 88] Taylor J., "Programming In Prolog: An In-Depth Study of the Problems for Beginners Learning to Program in Prolog," PhD Thesis, Department of Cognitive and Computing Sciences, University of Sussex, 1988.

[Taylor 89] Taylor R. et. al., "Foundations for the Arcadia Environment Architecture," *SIGPLAN Notices* , Vol. 24, No. 2, February 1989, pp. 1-13.

[Taylor 91] Taylor C., du Boulay B. and Patel M., "Outline Proposal for a Prolog 'Textual Tree Tracer' (TTT)," CSRP No. 177, Department of Cognitive and Computing Sciences, University of Sussex, 1991.

[Teitelman 85] Teitelman W., "A Tour Through Cedar," *IEEE Transactions on Software Engineering* Vol. SE-11, No. 3, March 1985, 1985, pp. 285-302.

[Teitlebaum 81] Teitelbaum T. and Reps T., "The Cornell Program Synthesizer: a Syntax-Directed Programming Environment," *Communications of the ACM* Vol. 24, No. 9, September 1981, pp. 563-573.

[Tesler 81] Tesler L., "The Smalltalk Environment," *BYTE*, Vol. 6, No. 8, August 1981, pp. 90-147.

[Tichy 85] Tichy W., "RCS -- System for Version Control," *Software--Practice and Experience*, Vol. 15, No. 7, 1985, pp. 637-654.

[Tick 91] Tick E. and Park D.-Y., "Kaleidoscope Visualization of Fine-Grain Parallel Programs," CIS-TR-91-18, Department of Computer and Information Science, University of Oregon, October 1991.

[Topol 95a] Topol B., Stasko J. and Sunderam V., "Integrating Visualization Support into Distributed Computing Systems," *Proceedings of the 15th International Conference on Distributed Computing Systems*, Vancouver, B.C., May 1995, pp. 19-26.

[Topol 95b] Topol B., Stasko J. and Sunderam V., "The Dual Timestamping Methodology for Visualizing Distributed Applications," Technical Report GIT-CC-95/21, College of Computing, Georgia Institute of Technology, Atlanta, GA, July 1995.

[Topol 96] Topol B., Stasko J. and Sunderam V., "Monitoring and Visualization in Cluster Environments," Technical Report GIT-CC-96-10, College of Computing, Georgia Institute of Technology, Atlanta, GA, March 1996.

[Tufte 83] Tufte E., *The Visual Display of Quantitative Information*, Graphics Press, Cheshire, CT, 1983.

[Tufte 90] Tufte E., *Envisioning Information*, Graphics Press, Cheshire CT, 1990.

[Tversky 91] Tversky B. , Kugelmass S. and Winter A., "Cross-Cultural and Developmental Trends in Graphic Productions," *Cognitive Psychology*, Vol. 23, No. 4, 1991, pp. 515-557.

[Upson 89] Upson C., Faulhaber T., Kamins D., Laidlaw D., Schlegel D., Vroom J., Gurwitz R. and van Dam A., "The Application Visualization System: A Computational Environment for Scientific Visualization," *IEEE Computer Graphics and Applications*, Vol. 9, No. 4, July 1989, pp. 30–42.

[van Tassel 74] van Tassel D., *Program Style, Design, Efficiency, Debugging and Testing*, Prentice-Hall, 1974.

[Vaughn 94] Vaughn T., *Multimedia Making It Work*, Osborne McGraw-Hill, Berkeley CA, 1994.

[Vessey 90] Vessey I., "Cognitive Fit: a Theory-Based Analysis of the Graphs Versus Tables Literature," *Decision Sciences,* Vol. 22, No. 2, 1990, pp. 219-240.

[Vitter 84] Vitter J., "US&R: A New Framework for Redoing," *IEEE Software*, Vol. 1, No. 4, October 1984, pp. 39-52.

[Wasserman 81] Wasserman A., *Tutorial: Software Development Environments,* IEEE Computer Society Press, 1981.

[Watt 94] Watt S., "Froglet: A Source-Level Stepper for Lisp," KMI-TR-10 Knowledge Media Institute, The Open University, Milton Keynes, England, April 1994.

[Weinberger 84] Weinberger P., "Cheap Dynamic Instruction Counting,'' *AT&T Bell Laboratories Technical Journal*, Vol. 63, No. 8, 1984, pp. 1815-26.

[Weizenbaum 69] Weizenbaum J., "Eliza — A Computer Program for the Study of Natural Language Communication between Man and Machine," *Communications of the ACM* , Vol. 9, No. 1, January 1969, pp. 36-45.

[Weizenbaum 86] Weizenbaum J., *Computer Power and Human Reason,* W.H. Freeman, 1986.

[West 93] West A., "Animating C++ Programs," Technical Report, Objective Software Technology, Livingston, Scotland, 1993. (Also available on the World-Wide Web from http://www.scotnet.co.uk/ost/ost.html.)

[Whitney 90] Whitney R. and Urquhart N., "Microcomputers in the Mathematical Sciences: Effects of Courses, Students, and Instructors," *Academic Computing*, Vol. 4, No. 6, March 1990, pp. 14-18, 49-53.

[Wielinga 92] Wielinga B., Schreiber A. and Breuker J., "KADS: A Modelling Approach to Knowledge Engineering," *Knowledge Acquisition Journal,* Vol. 4, No. 1, 1992.

[Wilson 95] Wilson J., et al. "Students' Use of Animations for Algorithm Understanding," (short paper), *Proceedings of the ACM SIGCHI '95 Conference on Human Factors in Computing Systems* (Conference Companion), Denver, CO, May 1995, pp. 238-239.

[Wilde 92] Wilde N. and Huitt R., "Maintenance Support for Object-Oriented Programs," *IEEE Transactions on Software Engineering*, Vol. 18, No. 12, December 1992, pp. 1038–1044.

[Winkler 90] Winkler D. and Kamins S., *Hypertalk 2.0: The Book,* Bantam Books, 1990.

[Wirfs-Brock 90] Wirfs-Brock R., Wilkerson B. and Wiener L., *Designing Object-Oriented Software*, Prentice Hall, Englewood Cliffs, NJ, 1990.

[Wirth 71] Wirth N., "Program Development by Stepwise Refinement," *Communications of the ACM,* Vol. 14, No. 4, April 1971, pp. 221-227.

[Wirth 76] Wirth N., *Algorithms + Data Structures = Programs*, Prentice-Hall, 1976.

[Wirth 77] Wirth N., "Modula: A Language for Modular Multiprogramming," *Software — Practice and Experience*, Vol. 7, No. 1, January 1977, pp. 3-35.

[Wittie 89] Wittie L., "Debugging Distributed C Programs by Real Time Replay," *SIGPLAN Notices*, Vol. 24, No. 1, January 1989, pp. 57-67. (Proceedings of the Workshop on Parallel and Distributed Debugging, Madison, WI, May 1988).

[Worley 92] Worley P. and Drake J., "Parallelizing the Spectral Transform Method," *Concurrency: Practice and Experience*, Vol. 4, No. 4, June 1992, pp. 269-291.

[Yan 93] Yan J., et al., "The Automated Instrumentation and Monitoring System," AIMS Reference Manual. Report 108795, NASA Ames Research Center, Moffett Field, CA, November 1993.

[Yan 95] Yan J., Sarukkai S. and Mehra P., "Performance Measurement, Visualization, and Modeling of Parallel and Distributed Programs Using the AIMS Toolkit," *Software Practice and Experience*, Vol. 25, No. 4, 1995, pp. 429-461.

[Yarwood 74] Yarwood E., "Toward Program Illustration," M.Sc. Thesis, Department of Computer Science, University of Toronto, 1974.

[Yourdon 79] Yourdon E., *Structured Walkthroughs*, Prentice-Hall, 1979.

[Zaremba 95] Zaremba D., "Adding Data Visualization to DEC FUSE," *Digital Technical Journal*, Vol. 7, No. 2, 1995, pp. 20-33.

[Zelkowitz 73] Zelkowitz M., "Reversible Execution," *Communications of the ACM,* September 1973.

[Zernik 91] Zernik D. and Rudolph L., "Animating Work and Time for Debugging Parallel Programs - Foundations and Experience," *SIGPLAN Notices*, Vol. 26, No. 12, December 1991, pp. 46-56. (In Proceedings of the SIGPLAN/SIGOPS Workshop on Parallel and Distributed Debugging, Santa Cruz, CA, May 1991.)

[Zhao 95] Zhao Q. and Stasko J., "Visualizing the Execution of Threads-Based Parallel Programs," Technical Report GIT-GVU-95/01, Graphics, Visualization, and Usability Center, Georgia Institute of Technology, Atlanta, GA, January 1995.

[Zimmermann 88] Zimmermann M., Perrenoud F. and Schiper A., "Understanding Concurrent Programming through Program Animation," *The Nineteenth ACM SIGCSE Technical Symposium on Computer Science Education*, 1988, pp. 27-35.

[Zimmerman 89] Zimmerman M., Perrenoud F. and Schiper A., "Graphical Animation of Concurrent Programs," *SIGPLAN Notices,* Vol. 24, No. 1, January 1989, pp. 342-344, (Proceedings of the Workshop on Parallel and Distributed Debugging, Madison, WI, May 1988).

Contributors

Ronald Baecker
Knowledge Media Design Institute
Department of Computer Science
University of Toronto
10 King's College Road, Room 4306
Toronto, Ontario M5S 3G4 Canada
rmb@dgp.toronto.edu

John Bazik
Department of Computer Science
Brown University
Providence, RI 02912
jsb@cs.brown.edu

Alan Blackwell
MRC Applied Psychology Unit
(and Hitachi Europe Advanced Software Centre)
15 Chaucer Road
Cambridge CB2 2EF, U.K.
alan.blackwell@mrc-applied-psychology.cambridge.ac.uk

Mike Brayshaw

Department of Information Systems
School of Management
Lincoln University campus
University of Lincolnshire and Humberside
Lincoln, LN6 7TS, UK
mbrayshaw@lincoln.ac.uk

Marc H. Brown

Systems Research Center
Digital Equipment Corporation
Palo Alto, CA 94301
mhb@pa.dec.com

Wim De Pauw

IBM TJ Watson Research Center
P.O.Box 704
Yorktown Heights NY 10598
wim@watson.ibm.com

John Domingue

Knowledge Media Institute
The Open University
Milton Keynes MK7 6AA, UK

Stephen G. Eick

Bell Laboratories/Lucent Technologies
Room 1G-351
1000 E. Warrenville Road
Naperville, IL 60566
eick@research.bell-labs.com

Marc Eisenstadt
Knowledge Media Institute
The Open University
Milton Keynes MK7 6AA, UK
M.Eisenstadt@open.ac.uk

Christopher Fry
Chief Technical Officer
PowerScout Corporation
49 Melcher Street
Boston, MA 02210
cfry@powerscout.com

Peter A. Gloor
Dept. Head Workgroup/Workflow
STG Coopers & Lybrand, Zurich
Switzerland
Peter_Gloor@ch.coopers.com
gloor@acm.org

Thomas Green
Computer Based Learning Unit
University of Leeds
Leeds LS2 9JT, U.K.
thomas.green@ndirect.co.uk

Michael T. Heath
Department of Computer Science
University of Illinois at Urbana-Champaign
Urbana, IL 61801-2987
Email: heath@cs.uiuc.edu

John Hershberger
Mentor Graphics Corp.
1001 Ridder Park Drive
San Jose, CA 95131
john_hershberger@mentorg.com

Clinton L. Jeffery
Division of Computer Science
University of Texas at San Antonio
San Antonio, TX 78249
jeffery@cs.utsa.edu

Doug Kimelman
IBM Thomas J. Watson Research Center
P.O. Box 704
Yorktown Heights, NY 10598
dnk@watson.ibm.com

Eileen Kraemer
Computer Science Department
School of Engineering and Applied Science
Washington University in St. Louis
St. Louis, MO 63130
eileen@cs.wustl.edu

Andrea Lawrence
Department of Computer Science
Spelman College
Atlanta, GA 30314
lawrence@spelman.edu

Henry Lieberman

Media Laboratory

Massachusetts Institute of Technology

20 Ames St. 305 A

Cambridge, Mass. 02139 USA

lieber@media.mit.edu

Allen D. Malony

Department of Computer and Information Science

University of Oregon

Eugene, Oregon 97403

malony@cs.uoregon.edu

Aaron Marcus

Aaron Marcus and Associates, Inc.

1144 65th St., Suite F

Emeryville, CA 94608-1053

Aaron@AMandA.com

Paul Mulholland

Knowledge Media Institute

The Open University

Walton Hall

Milton Keynes, MK7 6AA UK

P.Mulholland@open.ac.uk

Marc A. Najork

Systems Research Center

Digital Equipment Corporation

Palo Alto, CA 94301

najork@pa.dec.com

Stephen North
AT&T Laboratories
180 Park Ave.
Florham Park, NJ 07932
north@research.att.com

Marian Petre
Centre for Informatics Education Research
Faculty of Mathematics and Computing
Open University
Milton Keynes MK7 6AA, U.K.
m.petre@open.ac.uk

Blaine Price
The Open University
Milton Keynes MK7 6AA, UK
B.A.Price@open.ac.uk

Steven P. Reiss
Department of Computer Science
Brown University
Providence, RI 02912
spr@cs.brown.edu

Gruia-Catalin Roman
Department of Computer Science
Washington University
Saint Louis, Missouri 63130
roman@cs.wustl.edu

Bryan Rosenburg
IBM T.J. Watson Research Center
P.O. Box 218
Yorktown Heights, NY 10598
rosnbrg@watson.ibm.com

Tova Roth
IBM T.J. Watson Research Center
30 Saw Mill River Road
Hawthorne, NY 10532
tova@waton.ibm.com

Diane T. Rover
Department of Electrical Engineering
260 Engineering Building
Michigan State University
East Lansing, MI 48824
rover@ee.msu.edu

Robert Sedgewick
Department of Computer Science
Princeton University
Princeton, NJ 08544
rs@cs.princeton.edu

Ian Small
CKS Group
10260 Bandley Drive
Cupertino, CA 95014
ian@cks.com

John Stasko
Graphics, Visualization and Usability Center
College of Computing
Georgia Institute of Technology
Atlanta, GA 30332-0280
stasko@cc.gatech.edu

Roberto Tamassia
Department of Computer Science
Brown University
Providence, RI 02912
rt@cs.brown.edu

Andries van Dam
Department of Computer Science
Brown University
Providence, RI 02912
avd@cs.brown.edu

John Vlissides
IBM T.J. Watson Research Center
P.O. Box 704
Yorktown Heights, NY 10598
vlis@watson.ibm.com

Index